GW00541791

WHITTINGHAM VALE

Northumberland
Its History, Traditions and Folk Lore

by

David Dippie Dixon

FRANK GRAHAM
6 Queen's Terrace, Newcastle-upon-Tyne, 2

First published 1895
This Edition 1979

ISBN 0 85983 122 1

Printed and Bound in Great Britain by
The Scolar Press
59/61 East Parade Ilkley West Yorkshire

WHITTINGHAM VALE,

NORTHUMBERLAND:

ITS HISTORY, TRADITIONS, AND FOLK LORE.

BY DAVID DIPPIE DIXON.

WITH ILLUSTRATIONS BY JOHN TURNBULL DIXON.

"*Northumberlonde, hasty and hot;*
Westmerlonde, to prod the Scot."

NEWCASTLE-UPON-TYNE:
PRINTED AND PUBLISHED BY ROBERT REDPATH.
1895.

THE
VALE OF
WHITTINGHAM
BY
D. D. DIXON
1895
J. Turnbull Dixon 1893

PREFACE.

> "Breathes there a man, with soul so dead,
> Who never to himself hath said,
> This is my own, my native land?"

IT was this love for the happy scenes of his boyhood that first prompted the Author to attempt the sixteen chapters contained in this volume, descriptive of the history, traditions, and folk lore of the Vale of Whittingham. This Vale of Whittingham forms the upper portion of Alndale — a lovely Northumbrian valley, which, stretching inland about twenty miles from the east coast of Northumberland, terminates at the foot of the southern outliers of the Cheviot range of hills—the "duns" and "laws" of Alnham. There, within bowshot of Alnham Church, the river Aln first trickles forth, and winding its meandering course through the rich tillage and pasture lands of the fertile Vale of Whittingham, passes on its way Eslington, the ancestral home of the famous Collingwoods; the village of Whittingham, with its interesting church and pele tower; and Bolton, the halting place of the English Army on its way to Flodden under the Earl of Surrey, in 1513. Until entering the woods of Alnwick Park, under the shadow of Brizlee Tower, the river glides along through woody glades in sight of the charming ruins of Hulne Abbey. Further on, its waters washing the walls of Alnwick Abbey—another relic of the monastic age—and leaving on its right the old Border town of Alnwick, with its historic castle, the feudal stronghold of the Percies, it enters the North Sea, amid lofty sandbanks, at the ancient port of Alnmouth. As a sixteenth century writer briefly describes it :—"The Alne is a pretie riueret, the head whereof riseth in the hills west of Alnham towne, and is called by Ptolomie Celnius. Between Ailmouth and Wooden it sweepeth into the ocean."

The compiling of this volume, the result of many leisure hours, has been a labour of love, and whilst the greatest care has been exercised to render the historical portion as accurate as possible, yet the Author is aware that the astute minds of his more learned patrons will probably find within its pages numerous errors: to these he would be thankful for any amendments they might offer. The traditions and folk lore have been collected mostly by himself, and, in dealing with this very interesting branch of local history, the Author trusts he has not—inadvertently—hurt the feelings of any of the surviving relatives of those persons of whom he speaks. Although the work may in some degree answer the purpose of a guide for the use of visitors, it will be found that the writer has dwelt more on the ancient history of the Vale and its early owners than on its modern aspect and its present day inhabitants.

The "Annals of the Vale" was an afterthought, and therefore appears as an Appendix, and although the "Annals" may not be of much value to the general reader, the Author feels assured that the events recorded therein will be read with very great interest by those living in the locality.

The Author would here beg to acknowledge his indebtedness to a number of kind friends for valuable help generously accorded him during his researches. To Lord Ravensworth his especial thanks are due for several interesting communications in connection with Eslington, as well as for the kindly interest his lordship has taken in the work; to Major Browne for his courtesy in granting free access to the Museum and other parts of Callaly Castle and its policies; to Mr. Henry Wallace (of Trench Hall), for much useful information relating to the Eslington estate, besides many other kindnesses; to Canon Greenwell (of Durham), who graciously took the trouble to translate several medieval documents of great interest, the writer feels extremely grateful. To the Rev. Wm. Nall (vicar of Alnham), Rev. Wm. Sheild (vicar of Whittingham), Rev. R. H. Davidson (minister of the Presbyterian Church at Glanton), and the Rev. Father Taylor (of St. Mary's, Whittingham), he is much indebted for details respecting their several churches and for the liberty kindly granted to make extracts from their Church Registers. To Mr. Horatio A. Adamson (of North Shields), for a copy of an interesting document relating to Lorbottle; Mr. Cuthbert Carr (of Hedgeley), for notes about Prendwick, and Mr. Frank Chrisp for the use of his map of Prendwick farm, he is very much indebted, as well as to Mr. Lionel Crawford (of Cross-hill), Mr. William Cowley (of Mile farm), Mr. W. J.

Errington (of Greenville), Mr. P. Dodds (of Biddlestone), and Mr. T. Tomlinson (estates office, Alnwick Castle), for lists of field names. To Mr. Christopher Thompson (of Whittingham), for a description of the old tower at Whittingham previous to the restoration of 1845; to Mr. James Thomson (of Shawdon Lodge), for notes on Shawdon; to Mr. William Brown (of Alnham), for information with reference to the parish and village of Alnham; to Mr. C. F. Graham (of Rothbury), for population statistics; to Mr. John Johnson (electrician at Callaly Castle), for a description of the electric light apparatus there; and to Mr. Joseph Oliver (of Eslington Park), Mr. William Dixon (of Whittingham), Mr. Joseph Suthren (of Whittingham), Mr. John Mills (of Whittingham), Mr. James Nichol (Inland Revenue Office, Taunton), and Mr. James Laidler (of South Cartington)—to each and all of these the Author begs to express his gratitude for many interesting details imparted to him relating to the Vale.

D. D. D.

Rothbury, February 18th, 1895.

CONTENTS.

CONTENTS.

ILLUSTRATIONS.

ERRATA.

At page 12, line 26, instead of *Flamavill*, read "Flammavill."

At page 29, line 26, instead of *tovres*, read "toures."

At page 84, line 34, instead of *Northumherland*, read "Northumberland."

At page 93, line 5, instead of *ar*, read "at."

At page 94, line 2, instead of *Wednerday*, read "Wednesday."

At page 114, line 14, instead of *aud*, read "and."

At page 118, line 23, instead of *cboice*, read "choice."

At page 144, line 5, instead of *Roll*, read "Rolls."

At page 242, line 16, instead of *hedgerows*, read "hedgerow."

At page 249, line 11, instead of *Royal Cheviot Legion*, read "Cheviot Legion."

"WHITTINGHAM VALE."

SUBSCRIBERS TO THE TWO HUNDRED DEMY QUARTO COPIES.

Lord Armstrong, C.B., Cragside, Rothbury (3 copies).
Mrs. Ainger, Southdene, Mowbray Road, Upper Norwood, London, S.E.
Mr. Joseph Archer, Coquet House, Rothbury.
Mr. J. O. Archer, Percy Place, Alnwick.
Mrs. Atkinson, Scarborough.

Mr. G. B. Bainbridge, Espley Hall, Morpeth.
Mr. J. Balmbra, Alnwick.
Dr. F. Barrow, Rothbury.
Mr. Joseph Barlow, Newcastle (4 copies).
Lady Bedingfield, Oxburgh, Norfolk.
Mr. Wm. Beech, Great Ryle, Whittingham.
Mr. Thomas Bell, Tynemouth.
Miss Beveridge, Rothbury.
Mrs. Bewick, Warwick Villa, Rothbury.
Mrs. Blair, Alnwick.
Mr. Hippolyte J. Blanc, 73, George Street, Edinbro.
Mr. J. Bolam, Bilton House, Lesbury.
Mr. Robert G. Bolam, J.P., Berwick.
Mr. T. Bowden, 42, Mosley Street, Newcastle.
Mr. W. Brewis, 17, Regent Terrace, Edinbro'.
Mrs. Browell, Snitter, Rothbury.
Mr. Fred. Brown, Bridge of Aln.
Mr. W. Brown, Titlington Mount, Alnwick.
Major Browne, Callaly Castle, Whittingham.
Mr. T. Bulman, 45, Leazes Terrace, Newcastle.

Dr. Burman, Alnwick.
Mr. A. Burgess, 30, Grosvenor Place, Newcastle.
Mrs. Buston, Esplanade, Whitby.

Mr. Alex. Cameron, 81, Heaton Park Road, Newcastle.
Mrs. C. Carr, Mount Pleasant, Wooler.
Mr. J. R. Carr-Ellison, Hedgeley, Alnwick.
Mr. J. Y. Carse, Amble, Acklington.
Mr. W. L. Charlton, Reenes, Bellingham.
Mr. Frank Chrisp, Prendwick.
Rev. Thomas Clavering, St. Joseph's, Cockermouth (2 copies).
Mr. T. Clavering, 14, Woodside Terrace, Glasgow.
Mr. N. G. Clayton, The Chesters, Humshaugh.
Mr. W. Collie, Thirlestane Road, Edinbro'.
Mr. E. J. Collingwood, Lilburn Tower, Alnwick.
Mr. F. J. W. Collingwood, Glanton Pyke.
Mr. Joseph Cowen, Stella Hall, Blaydon.
Miss Crawford, Cross Hill, Whittingham.
Mr. W. J. Crawhall, Clifton, Bristol.
Mr. J. Crawhall, Ealing, Middlesex.
Mrs. Crozier, North Lodge, Cragside, Rothbury.
Mr. W. D. Cruddas, Haughton Castle, Humshaugh.
Mr. E. Cunnington, Castle Inn, Whittingham.

Mr. M. H. Dand, Hauxley Cottage, Acklington.
Miss Dawson, Well Close House, Rothbury.
Miss Mary Dawson, St. Mary's, Whittingham.
Mr. B. Densham, 19, Chichester Road, Croydon, Surrey.
Miss Dixon, Rothbury.
Mrs. Dixon, Dunbritton, Pollockshields, Glasgow.
Mr. David D. Dixon, Rothbury.
Mr. G. A. Dixon, Adelaide, Australia.
Mr. Henry Dixon, Whittingham.
Mr. John T. Dixon, Rothbury.

Mr. T. C. Dixon, Whittingham.
Mr. William Dixon, Whittingham.
Mr. R. Donkin, Haw Hill House, Rothbury.
Mr. R. Donkin, jun., Whitton Terrace, Rothbury.
Mr. George Dryden (Contractor), Glanton.
Mr. John Dryden (Draper), Glanton.
Mr. J. Dryden, Crawley, Eglingham, Alnwick.
Mr. G. Drysdale, Great Ryle, Whittingham.

Dr. Embleton, 19, Claremont Place, Newcastle.
Mr. W. J. Errington, Greenville, Glanton.

Mr. T. Milnes Favell, Seabridge Hall, Newcastle-under-Lyne.
Mr. J. G. Fenwick, Moorlands, Gosforth.
Mr. W. Fenwick, Glen Allen, Alnwick.
Mr. Edward Fisher, Newton Abbot, Devon.
Mr. C. D. Forster, 89, Jesmond Road, Newcastle.

Dr. Gibb, Sandyford Park, Newcastle.
Mr. Wm. Glendenning, 4, Lovaine Place, Newcastle.
Mr. Goldstone, Sunderland.
Mr. J. Graham, Bondgate, Alnwick.
Canon Greenwell, 27, North Bailey, Durham.

Mr. R. Hood Haggie, Blythewood North, Newcastle.
Mr. James Hardy, LL.D., Old Cambus Townhead, Cockburnspath, N.B.
Mr. J. B. Harris, Osborne Road, Newcastle.
Mr. T. Harvey, Railway Station, Whitley.
Mr. W. Hawthorn, Wreighburn House, Rothbury.
Mrs. Chipchase Henderson, Abbot Meadow, Melrose.
Mr. G. Henderson, 54, Westmorland Road, Newcastle.
Mr. James Henderson, Middlesbro'.
Mr. R. O. Heslop, Corbridge (2 copies).

Lady Florentia Hughes, Kinmel Park, Abergele, North Wales (2 copies).
Mr. C. E. Hunter, Selaby Hall, Darlington.
Mr. E. Hunter, 8, Wentworth Place, Newcastle.
Mr. Thomas Huggan, Callaly, Whittingham.

Rev. R. M. Ilderton, 37, Elsdon Road, Gosforth.

Dr. Jack, Rothbury.
Mr. A. H. Japp, LL.D., National Liberal Club, Whitechall Place, London, S.W.
Messrs. Johnson, Dodds and Co., Bigg Market, Newcastle.
Sir James Joicey, Bart., M.P., Longhirst Hall, Morpeth.
Rev. G. H. Jones, Rothbury.

Mr. Robert Kyle, Syon, Brentford, Middlesex.

Mr. J. Lamb, 5, Kelmscott Road, London, S.W.
Miss Langlands, 4, Strathearn Place, Edinbro'.
Mr. A. Lawson, Queen's Head Hotel, Rothbury.
Mr. Henry Layton, jun., Whittingham.
Hon. Athol Liddell, Winter Villa, Stonehouse, Devon.
Lady Lilian Liddell, 9, Mansfield Street, London, W.
Mrs. Logan, Greenville, Glanton.

Mr. J. S. Mack, Coveyheugh, Reston, Berwickshire.
Mr. M. Mackay, 8, Milton Street, Newcastle.
Dr. Marshall, Chatton Park, Belford.
Mr. J. Marr, Parkside, Roker.
Miss Martin, The Mansion, Glanton, R.S.O.
Mr. T. Matheson, Oldgate Street, Morpeth.
Mr. G. Matthews, 17, Riversdale Terrace, Sunderland.
Mr. W. Maudlen, Gosforth.
Rev. J. A. Collingwood Maughan, Prudhoe-on-Tyne.
Messrs. Mawson, Swan and Morgan, Newcastle.

Mrs. McGreggor, Glasgow.
Mr. J. E. McPherson, Bentinck Villas, Newcastle.
Mr. Cuthbert Medd, The Park, Harrow.
Rev. B. R. Mein, M.A., Thropton Manse, Rothbury.
Mr. J. Stanley Mitcalfe, Percy Park, Tynemouth.
Mr. C. E. Moore, "Gazette" Office, Alnwick.

Newcastle Public Library, Newcastle-upon-Tyne.
Mr. J. T. Nisbet, 8, St. Mary's Terrace, Ryton.
Lady Noble, Jesmond, Newcastle (2 copies).
Lord Northbourne, Bettishanger, Dover.

Mr. C. Ogilvy, 28, Cluny Gardens, Edinbro' (3 copies).
Mr. Oliver, 36, Hotspur Street, Tynemouth.
Mr. J. Oliver, Eslington Park, Whittingham.

Right Hon. Earl Percy, Alnwick Castle.
Mr. Howard Pease, Arcot Hall, Dudley, R.S.O.
Mr. J. W. Pease, Pendower, Newcastle.
Mr. W. R. Plummer, 4, Queen's Square, Newcastle.
Mr. J. E. Potts, 79, Worship Street, London, E.C.
Mr. T. Pringle, 139, Sidney Grove, Newcastle.
Mr. R. Proudlock, Thropton, Rothbury.

Earl of Ravensworth, Ravensworth Castle.
Sir M. W. Ridley, Bart., M.P., Blagdon.
Sir John W. B. Riddell, Hepple, Rothbury.
Mrs. Rayne, Thropton, Rothbury.
Mr. R. Redpath, Linden Terrace, Newcastle.
Mr. J. Miller Richard, 65, Nicholson Street, Edinbro'.
Mr. J. P. Ridley, Bank House, Rothbury.
Rev. E. Robert, St. Mary's, Alnwick.
Mr. Watson-Askew Robertson, Ladykirk, Norham-on-Tweed (2 copies).
Miss Anna Robinson, Sudbrook Holme, Lincoln.

Mr. Jos. Robinson, Snipe House, Alnwick.
Mrs. Robson, Branxton, Cornhill.
Mr. John Rogerson, Whittingham.

Mr. S. Sanderson, The Elms, Berwick.
Mr. J. Scott, Bridge Street, Rothbury.
Rev. W. Sheild, Whittingham.
Mr. William Shotton, 12, Crossley Terrace, Newcastle.
Mr. Thomas Simpson, 12, Haldane Terrace, Newcastle.
Mr. George Skelley, Alnwick.
Rev. Brice Smith, Hameringham Rectory, Horncastle.
Mr. C. J. Spence, South Preston Lodge, North Shields.
Rev. Canon Stark, North Shields.
Mr. R. Stewart, 54, South Clerk Street, Edinbro'.
Mr. J. Stone, Milfield House, Newburn.

Mr. G. M. Tait, Suffolk Villa, Compton Road, London, N.
Mr. John Tate, Oaklands, Alnwick.
Mr. W. J. Taylor, Sandhill, Newcastle.
The Rev. Father Taylor, St. Mary's, Whittingham.
Mr. George Telford, Railway Station, Whittingham.
Mr. H. W. Ternent, Gainford, Darlington.
Mr. W. Ternent, Gainford, Darlington.
Mr. W. W. Tomlinson, 6, Bristol Terrace, Newcastle.
Major Thompson, Walworth Hall, Darlington.
Mr. Andrew Thompson, The Villa, Glanton.
Mr. G. H. Thompson, Bailiffgate, Alnwick.
Miss Turnbull, Harbottle, Rothbury.
Mr. G. Turnbull, Great Tosson, Rothbury.
Mr. R. A. Turnbull, 6, Jesmond Terrace, Newcastle.
Mr. T. C. Turnbull, 96, Kingsley Terrace, Newcastle.

Mr. M. Vint, 6, Newgate Street, Newcastle.

Mr. Henry Wallace, Trench Hall, Gateshead.

Rev. John Walker, Whalton Rectory.
Miss Watson, 65, Eccleston Square, London, S.W.
Dr. R. Spence Watson, Bensham Grove, Gateshead.
Mr. W. A. Watson-Armstrong, Cragside, Rothbury.
Mr. George Weatheritt, Whittingham.
Mr. R. Welford, 25, King Street, Newcastle.
Rev. E. Williams, Church Lodge, Rothbury.
Messrs. Wilson and Todhunter, White Hart Yard, Newcastle.
Mr. John A. Woods, Benton Hall, Newcastle.
Mr. Joseph Woolf, The Grange, Whittingham.
Rev. W. S. Wrenford, Matfen Vicarage.
Mr. Andrew Wright, Deaf and Dumb Institution, Newcastle.

Rev. E. M. Young, Whitton Tower, Rothbury.

WHITTINGHAM VALE.

CHAPTER I.

GENERAL DESCRIPTION OF THE VALE.

Its Extent—Fertility—Early History—Ancient British Remains—Roman Causeways—Anglo-Saxon Settlements—Danish Inroads—Its Norman Owners—Defence of the Borders—Pele Towers—Wardens of the Marches—Border Garrisons—Beacons—The Middle Marches—A Muster of Armed Borderers—Watch and Ward—Village Enclosures—The Union—Our Happy Borderland in the Nineteenth Century.

THE Vale of Whittingham is a district contained in the upper reaches of the river Aln, and may be said to include within its area the parishes of Whittingham and Alnham, as well as portions of Edlingham and Bolton. Titlington Mount and Jenny Lantern Hill, both outshoots of the Kyloe range, with Glanton Pike, and the porphyritic hills of Fawdon and Ryle, are its northern boundary, which also form the watershed between the vales of the Breamish and the Aln; while on the south, the dark-wooded heights of Thrunton and Callaly Crags and the heather-clad uplands of Rimside Moor form an effectual barrier, some six miles in breadth, between Coquetdale and Alndale. The vale extends from Alnham on the extreme west to Bolton on the east, a distance of about nine miles; in width it varies from two to six miles, from north to south, and consists for the most part of rich alluvial soil on a subsoil of strong clay. The large dimensions and luxurious growth attained by the trees in the woodlands and in the hedgerows are indications of the depth and strength of its soil, and add much to the beauty and variety of the landscape. Mackenzie, in his History of Northumberland (1825), thus speaks of its many good qualities:—"The valley of Whittingham has long been famed for the luxuriance of its soil, the excellence of its culture, and the beauty of its aspect. On its rich pastures, cattle and sheep attain to a large size, and every object wears the countenance of opulence. This lovely valley extends about four miles in width, and forms a striking contrast with the adjoining mountains, bogs, rocks, and heath which compose the surface of Rimside Moor."

From the hills of Alnham to the sandbanks of Alnmouth, the whole of the vale of the Aln is rich in ancient remains, historic associations, and legendary lore, which gives to the antiquarian rambler an interest few districts can surpass. Of its earlier inhabitants—the Celts or Britons—there are numerous traces in the circular camps and fortifications yet visible on the hills in the neighbourhood, which show that some two or three thousand years ago the vale must have been the scene of populous British settlements. Earthworks and encampments are found on spots that are in our day mountain, moss, and moor. The higher lands, more than the valleys, appear to have been preferred by our aboriginal ancestors for their habitations. Forests and a dense growth of primeval scrub seem to have then overspread the lower portions of the valley, while the camps and dwellings of the Celts occupied the heights, which became the centres of a population, and system of terrace cultivation, traces of which are still seen on the southern slopes of the hills. Reaveley Hill, in Breamish Water, is a good example of this primeval mode of tillage.[1] It was probably not until after the civilizing effects of the Roman occupation, also the formation of homestead and township by the Anglo-Saxon settler, that those bare and exposed situations were left for the more sheltered ones on the richer soil near the river. Remains of those ancient hill forts are found on Callaly Castle Hill, at Cross Hill, Rabbit Hall,

[1] "Gunnar Peak Camp, North Tynedale." By Rev. G. Rome Hall, F.S.A. Arch. Æliana, New Series, Vol. x., pp. 18-19.

Glanton, Crawley, Beanley, and Rough Castles, while the hills of Fawdon, Ryle, Prendwick, and Alnham are studded with camps and cairns, whose erection is attributed to the Britons; as well as the "Brough" on Ingram Hill, and the strongly-fortified town of Greaves Ash, near Linhope, in the upper valley of the Breamish. Numerous urns, stone axes, and other relics have also been found at various times, in different parts of the vale; and here we shall do well to give the following extracts from an able paper "On Urns and other Antiquities found round the southern skirts of the Cheviot Hills,"[1] by James Hardy, LL.D., in which the learned writer gives the result of several years careful investigation :—

GREENVILLE.

"We must now cross the Breamish to Greenville, the residence and property of the Rev. James Blythe, Presbyterian minister of Branton,[2] which lies between Glanton and Branton. Here a very beautiful small clay urn, like a little teacup in size, is preserved by Mr. Blythe, almost unique for its simple adornment, combined with a neat form. The chevron ornament is in scorings, not in dots. Its dimensions are—diameter at top, 3¾ inches; at bottom, 1½ inch; circumference at broadest part of it, 10 inches; height, 3½ inches. "This with another very similar, only larger, was found imbedded," says Mr. Blythe, "below an immense collection of large stones heaped together in a field on my property, which field is about a quarter-of-a-mile to the north-west of Greenville, and about a mile south-east of Brandon. Many of the undermost stones in the heap had been exposed, apparently, to the action of intense heat; some were quite soft, sandy, and rotten, others seemed to have been in a state of fusion by the heat. I caused the stones that were sound and suitable to be carted away for building purposes. When cleared the ground was ploughed,

[1] History of the Berwickshire Naturalists' Club, Vol. xi., No. 1, p. 269, *et. seq.*

[2] Written in 1885.

and by the plough the urns were turned up. Unfortunately, the larger of the two was broken to pieces by the plough. When found, the little urn was filled with a black, hard substance, which, some say may have been the heart of a distinguished individual. This is very unlikely."

INGRAM, REAVELEY, CHESTERS, GREAVES ASH, ETC.

"The results in barrow-opening are thus summarily enumerated in Mr. Tate's MS. Notes, 1861 :—Ingram Hill, opposite Chesters Camp, three barrows opened, all showing charred wood. Reaveley Hill, a long barrow in a slack, had a row of stones through the middle—charred wood found three feet below the natural surface. Knock Hill, two large barrows opened—only burnt wood; to the north, two opened—only burnt wood. At Hartside and Greaves Ash, several barrows were opened, but nothing was found. Domestic pottery was found at Greaves Ash, Chesters (on Prendwick Estate), and Brough Law, of the coarsest kind, made of common clay, out of which even the pebbles had not been removed. In a hut circle of Chesters Camp, a glass bead, globular, perforated in the centre, translucent, of a light green colour, and three-fourths of an inch in diameter was obtained. A fragment of translucent glass was found in a hut at Greaves Ash. A spear or javelin head of common flint was found in Chesters Camp. It is of simple, broad, lanceolate form, 3 inches long and 1½ inch broad, flat on the one surface, but with a sharp, conical ridge on the other. Two fragments with cutting edges were also picked up within the camp, one of common flint, and the other of 'ribboned jasper.' Part of the antler of a red deer was found in the Western Fort at Greaves Ash, and the root portion of another of large size was dug out of the Chesters Camp; and in the latter the humerus and a few teeth of a horse were also recognisable. Three (five) bottom stones of primitive hand mills or querns were found at Greaves Ash. Three of them composed of a variety of syenite with large crystals, which is abundant enough in large rolled blocks in the channel of the Breamish; and the other two are made of sandstone. The syenitic querns are rude and clumsy, being 15 inches diameter and 5 inches in thickness. The sandstone of one of the querns is such as occurs at Titlington, Eglingham, and other moorlands in Northumberland."

ALNHAM MOOR.

"Some years since, when draining the bogs on Alnham Moor, near Ewartly Shank, which stands on a tributary stream that enters the Breamish at Alnham Moor Shepherd's house, the under portion of a small bronze caldron was dug out, which is in the possession of Mr. Henry H. Scott, at Alnham House, where I saw it, along with other friends, in June, 1885. It is of very thin bronze plate, all of one piece. Several of the large rivet holes, by which the upper portion was attached, remain. The bottom is finely watered, like watered silk. Mr. Scott's measurements of it are—diameter at mouth, 17 inches; depth, 10 inches. Mr. Scott kindly sent the caldron to Mr. John Turnbull Dixon, Rothbury, who has taken great pains to furnish an accurate representation of this ancient culinary vessel. It has no connection with illicit distillation, for which this rarely-visited outlandish region was once notorious."

BLAKEHOPE.

"At Blakehope, above Linhope, which is still further with drawn into the centre of the pass that intervenes between the spurs of Hedgehope and Cheviot, and the round-headed Shillmoor, where ran as early as the time of Henry III. and Edward I., the "Theves Rode," still termed the "Salters Road" from its being one of the routes of those adventurers who smuggled salt across the Borders into England, and probably always adopted as a line of communication between the north and south, a somewhat peculiar bronze spear head was found and presented to Canon Greenwell, in whose collection it is."

SCRENWOOD.

Several years ago, in clearing the "redd" from the bank top of a quarry in a little valley east of Screnwood, the workmen came upon a cist-vaen, or stone-lined grave, containing an urn of the British "food vessel" type. This urn, now in the possession of Mrs. Chisholm, of Netherton, measures 8 inches in height and 4½ inches in diameter at the top. It is made of coarse clay, and ornamented with the characteristic zig-zag markings peculiar to urns of the British period. It is figured by Mr. J. T. Dixon, and described by the writer in the History of the Berwickshire Naturalists' Club, Vol. x., No. iii., p. 544.

CALLALY.

Some thirty years ago a large urn, formed of coarse clay, was found at Dancing Hall, near Callaly, and during the early part of 1892, several interesting British burials were laid bare by Major Browne's workmen when clearing the earth from off the surface of a sandstone quarry on the western slopes of Callaly Castle Hill. These consisted of stone-lined graves of the usual type, some of which did not contain any remains, but in one of them there was found a very fine urn, now carefully preserved in the Museum at Callaly Castle. Major Browne has also caused the stone slabs forming one of the cists to be erected in a secluded corner of the Castle grounds, in exactly the same order in which the workmen found them. The urn is 5½ inches in height, 6 inches in diameter at the top, 3¾ inches diameter at bottom, and 4½ inches deep. The upper part of the urn is ornamented with lines and zig-zag markings.

THRUNTON.

Of the discovery of bronze weapons at Thrunton, we read the following notice in the "Proceedings of Antiquaries," Vol. v., p. 429:—" Meeting of the Society of Antiquaries of London, January 30, 1873. Lord Ravensworth exhibited five weapons, consisting of two swords and three spear heads . . . .

of the discovery of which, the following account has been furnished by the exhibitor . . . . . The bronzes were found by some workmen, when digging drains near Thrunton Farm, in the parish of Whittingham, Northumberland. The spot must formerly have been a quagmire, and is supplied with a copious spring of water. The arms were found sticking in the moss, with the points downwards, in a circle about two feet below the surface, perhaps left there by a party of soldiers who had halted at the spring, and been surprised." This find took place about the year 1847, and these interesting relics of the bronze period in Britain are now in the safe keeping of Lord Ravensworth, at Ravensworth Castle.

THE MILE FARM.

Three years ago, a cist was discovered in a mound on Mile Farm, on the Eslington estate, which, thanks to the care of Mr. Wm. Cowley, has been preserved entire. An account of this burial mound, and the manner in which it was discovered, has been kindy communicated by Mr. Cowley, who informs us that, on the top of an earthen mound, in a field known as the "Reindeer Close,"[1] about half-a-mile to the west of Mile farm house, there had been observed lying for some years a large flat slab of freestone, which had broken many a ploughshare, and thrown the plough out of the "foor"[2] to the no small annoyance of the ploughman. Therefore, in 1890, whilst preparing the field for turnips, it was resolved to make an attempt to remove it. In doing so, the slab was broken, and revealed to the workmen the cist beneath. It lies nearly east and west, and is 3 feet 5 inches long by 2 feet 10 inches in width, formed of four side stones, and the cover

---

[1] In 1786, Sir Henry George Liddell, of Ravensworth Castle, brought two reindeer from Lapland, which were kept for some time in this field; hence "Reindeer Close."

[2] A furrow which a plough makes in going up and down to form a rig. This is not an abbreviation of furrow, but the original word, *foor lang*—a furrow long; hence a furlong. "Northumberland Words," by R. O. Heslop.

broken in removal as already referred to—the natural surface of the ground constituting the bottom of the grave. No trace of a burial was found within it, the body having gone entirely to decay.

Flint arrow points, spindle whorls, querns, incised stones, and other British remains have frequently been found in the fields around both Mountain and Mile Farms.[1] A stone-lined grave or cist, similar to that discovered at Mile, was found several years ago on Mountain farm, in or near to which was a sandstone slab, covered with a fine example of the incised circles, such as are found in the rocks at Routing Lynn, Bewick Hill, Chatton Law, and Lordenshaws Camp.

The Romans have also left in the vale of the Aln very distinct marks of their wonderful occupation of this northern part of Britain, in the line of paved roadway, an eastern branch of the Watling Street, which traverses the county of Northumberland from Bewclay, near Portgate, on the Roman Wall, to Berwick-upon-Tweed. Portions of this causeway are found on the farms of High and Low Learchild, Thrunton, Thrunton Low Field, Low Barton, and Bridge of Aln. Another branch road, extending from High Rochester (*Bremenium*) in Redesdale, leads down through the moors and the fells of Redewater to Holystone,[2] in Coquetdale, thence by the Trewhitts, Lorbottle, and Callaly, passes close to Reynard's Lodge, in the parish of Whittingham, and joins the main road somewhere below Thrunton. A complete survey of these roads was made in the years 1857, 1858, and 1859, by Mr. Henry MacLauchlan, hon. member of the Archælogical Institute of Great Britain and Ireland and of the Society of Antiquaries of Newcastle-upon-Tyne, by the direction of the Duke of Northumberland. It is interesting to observe how much local men contribute to the history of their own neighbourhood. Mr. MacLauchlan, in a

---

[1] I have in my collection a very fine flint arrow head, of the laurel leaf type, which was found at Mile, and given to me by my friend Mr. Cowley.

[2] Between Holystone and Yardhope the road is easily traced, where the paving stones are bare to this day. The road is about 14 feet wide.

memoir written during the survey, mentions the names of a noble peer and four gentlemen well known in the vale at that time, but who are now gone to their rest. "We," says Mr. MacLauchlan, "think it right to remark here that our researches immediately south of the Aln were much facilitated in consequence of the recent investigations instituted by Lord Ravensworth, whose property it is. The tenants, Messrs. John Stephenson (Thrunton), George Bennett (Learchild), and Edward Waugh (Thrunton Low Field), marked out on the ground those places where remains had been found in draining and in ploughing, and the same service was rendered to us on the banks of the Aln by James Pigdon."

During the Roman occupation of Britain that wide district north of the Roman Wall, extending from the Tyne to the Firth of Forth—then little more than a vast wilderness of moorland and woodland, where roamed the wolf, the boar, the red deer, and the wild bull, and whose streams were the *habitat* of the beaver—was the scene of a ceaseless border warfare with the unconquered Britons and the Picts. The line of road to the north was guarded by a chain of forts or military stations, smaller than those south of the wall, which served as a base of operations to the legionaries protecting the settlers, who were slowly spreading over the county now known as Northumberland and the Lowlands of Scotland. One such station is supposed to have been at Crawley. In 1822, John Smart, Esq., of Trewhitt House, wrote an account in Archæologia Æliana, Vol. i., old series, of the discovery of a Roman station near Glanton. "It is situated," he says, "at Crawley Tower, which, with the farm offices, occupies its east angle. It is on a considerable eminence, about 400 yards east of Watling Street, between the village of Glanton and the river Bremish. It is 290 feet long, 160 feet broad, and is surrounded by a foss of 30 feet wide, and an agger of 20 feet thick. It commands a most delightful view of the vale of Whittingham, and nearly the whole length of the Bremish from its source to Horton Castle; and certainly the immediate neighbourhood is the best fortified in 'ancient Britain,' as from the station can be seen no less than seven strong British and Saxon camps, several of which have triple ramparts, namely, Harehill, near Bewick; Brough-law, by Ingram; the gorge of the Bremish above Ingram, through which the Britons must have passed when they quitted their strongly fortified town at the foot of Greenshaw Hill, between Linhope and Hartside, the Clinch Hill, Callaly Castle Hill, and Cross Hill, Black Chester, and the Castle Hill, above Alnham."

It is probable that the tract of country afterwards called Northumbria, but at that period the Valentia of the Romans, was not unknown to the Angles, who in their roving voyages may have made descents on its eastern coast even before the departure of the imperial troops of Rome, but it was not until the chieftain Ida, the "Flame-bearer," had established his fortress on the rock of Bamburgh (547), and after several years hard fighting, that the conquest of Northumbria by the Angles was fairly completed, when, pushing their way inland, following up the dales and the streams which drain the higher moorlands and the hill ranges on the west, they claimed for their own the valleys of Northumberland.

It is evident that a numerous band of these Anglo-Saxons[1] had early found their way and settled in the vale of the Aln, whose little townships would soon become centres of social and industrial life. A better description cannot be given of the vale as it would probably appear soon after the Anglo-Saxon settlement than that charming account of old village life found in Green's "Conquest of England," where he says:—"All the features of English life, in fact, all its characteristic figures, were already there. We see the mills grinding along the burns, the

[1] There are writers of no small authority who hold that there was no real difference between Angles and Saxons. "Early Britain" (Church), p. 102. Therefore, in using the term Saxon or Anglo-Saxon, we refer generally to the Tribes who colonized Britain after the Romans.

hammer rings in the village smithy, the thegn's hall rises out of its demesne, the parish priest is at his mass-book in the little church that forms the centre of every township—reeves are gathering their lord's dues, forester and verderer wake the silent woodland with hound and horn, the moot gathers for order and law beneath the sacred oak or by the grey stone on the moor." Such may we picture the vale of Whittingham to have been some twelve centuries ago. Many of its townships are of Anglo-Saxon foundation, and it is to their enduring sway that we have to attribute the greater part of its place names. Although some may be of Celtic origin, yet those of Anglo-Saxon derivation greatly preponderate, while the Danish element in the nomenclature of the vale is rarely met with. Of the later Saxon period the vale certainly possesses a relic of the greatest interest in the tower of the fine old parish church of Whittingham, which shows in its lower stages the long and short blocks of ashlar work disposed at the angles, characteristic of Anglo-Saxon masonry. In the valley there were at a very early date corn mills at Alnham, Screnwood, Callaly, Eslington, Great Ryle, Shawdon, Bolton, Edlingham, Thrunton, and Whittingham, which with Yetlington, Lorbottle, and Prendwick were probably Anglo-Saxon settlements, as may be inferred from the very early record found of them.

A tradition of the Danes yet lingers in the vale of one of those terrible ravages so frequently committed during the ninth century by the cruel followers of the "Raven," who, having landed on the Northumbrian coast, followed up the Aln, plundering as they went, on which the Saxons encamped on Roberts Law, near Trewhitt, sallied forth to defend their homesteads, and met the Danes four miles east of Whittingham. After a sanguinary conflict the Saxons were routed, when it was said the slaughter was so great on both sides that the little burn near the spot ran red for three days and three nights after the battle.[1]

[1] The hamlet near the spot still retains the name of "Battle Bridge."

The Anglo-Saxon Chronicle (amongst many other records of the descents of the Danes) says:—"This year (875), the army went from Repton and Halfdene with some of the army into North-humbria, and took up winter quarters by the river Tyne, and the army subdued the land."

Quaintly does the old rhyme tell England's history:—

"The Romans in England once did sway,
And the Saxons, soon after them, led the way;
And they tugg'd with the Danes till an overthrow
Was given to both by the Norman bow."

A few years after the Norman Conquest the Saxon gentry and landholders were gradually dispossessed and driven from the soil, to make way for the new Norman families; and the Conqueror easily found Norman favourites, to marry the wives or daughters, and to take into their own hands the lands and privileges of the Saxon nobility, whom on the slightest pretext he caused to be beheaded or driven into banishment. The Saxon slave or villan, who belonged to the soil, then became the property of a Norman master, while the Saxon thegn and churl soon became exterminated. In Northumberland one or two Saxon families survived—the Ogles, of Ogle, and the Roddams, of Roddam—who probably did homage for their lands; but, generally speaking, the Norman owner superseded the Saxon thegn, and such names as the following are found in the earliest Pipe Rolls as holding the old Saxon manors in the vale of Whittingham:—William de Flamavill holds lands in Whittingham, Thrunton, Barton, and Glanton, which before was held by Uctred, the son of Gamel.[1] Robert Fitz-Roger, the great Norman Baron of Warkworth, has possessions in Callaly.[2] Roger Fitz-Ralph, the King's forester for Northumberland, holds Great Ryle,[3] and Fawdon is granted by Robert de Umfreville, the first Norman Baron of Redesdale

[1] Pipe Rolls, Hodgson's Northumberland, Part iii., Vol. iii., p. 73.

[2] Hundred Rolls, Hodgson's Northumberland, Part iii., Vol. i., p. 90.

[3] Testa de Nevill, Hodgson's Northumberland, Part iii., Vol. i., p. 222.

and Harbottle, to a Norman squire named Gilbert Batail,[1] while linked with the ancient manor of Edlingham we find the name of Patrick Earl of Dunbar.[2] Such are the names of some of the early Norman owners of lands in Alndale, but if the Domesday Book of William the Conqueror had only included Northumberland, we should then have had a perfect list of its Saxon owners at the Conquest.

No sooner had Northumberland become the property of William's Norman barons, their squires and sub-feudatories, than strongholds, such as the feudal castles of Newcastle, Warkworth, Alnwick, Bamburgh, and Harbottle, began to be erected, as well for the protection of the manor or barony as for the subjugation of the Saxon population. Besides those larger strongholds, there sprung up during the fourteenth and following centuries another class of buildings, known on the Borders as pele towers, which were erected by the Northumbrian landowners as a defence against the plundering raids of the Scots. The vale of the Aln being in rather dangerous proximity to the Borders and much exposed to the continuous inroads of their neighbours from the other side of the Cheviots, its inhabitants were glad to seek the protection of their peles and bassel houses. In the year 1415, there were pele towers at Alnham, Eslington, Callaly, Whittingham, Shawdon, Crawley, Edlingham New Town, and Edlingham. In 1541, the number had increased to thirteen, besides the ordinary bassel houses, a specimen of which can be seen in the arched roof and small mullioned window of the farmhouse at Little Ryle. The additional towers were Ingram, Great Ryle, Prendwick, and Screnwood, with a second tower which had been built at Alnham and Whittingham for the use of the parsons.

During the reign of Henry VIII. the English borderland was, for the sake of better defence against the Scotch, divided into three districts, viz.:—the East West, and Middle Marches,

---

[1] History Berwickshire Naturalists' Club, Vol. x., p. 551.

[2] Escheat Henry III., Hodgson's Northumberland, Part iii., Vol. i., p. 42.

under the command of a Lord Warden, General of the Marches. From Berwick bounds to the Hanging Stone, on the west end of Cheviot, formed the East March; from the Hanging Stone to Cryssoppe Brigg formed the Middle March, and from Cryssoppe to the Solway the West March.[1] Whittingham Vale, Upper Coquetdale, and the valley of the Breamish, were included within the jurisdiction of the Middle March. Over each of these districts were placed gentlemen of rank as Wardens and Deputy Wardens. Harbottle Castle was generally the residence of the Warden of the Middle March, and under him were several Deputy Wardens, each in command of a band of trained men belonging to the various townships, who wore on the sleeve of their jerkin the badge of the Warden. In 1509, an official return was drawn up of the fortresses in North Northumberland, their distance from Scotland, and the number of horsemen their owners could bring into the field. The computed miles are very different from the measurement of the present day. For the defence of the upper valley of the Aln there were garrisons at the following places, where there also were pele towers:—

Owners inabytaunttes or officers.	Holdis and Towneshippes too lay in Garnysons of horsmen. And how fer they bee from Tevedale & the Mars[2] & who be the owners & the inabytaunttes in the howses. Menne.
Heselryg own' Roberd Colyngwood inab't	Eslyngton xx men & from tevedale ix myle & from the mars xv m.
Wylliam Heron own' inab't nihil	Wittynggam xl & from tevedale x myle & from the mars xv m.
My Lorde of Northumberland inab't nihil	Elnam xl & from tevedale vj myle & from the mars xvj m.
Thomas Horsley own' & inab't	Skyrnwood xx & from tevedale vj myle & from the mars xvj m.
John Selbye own' & inab't	Bedylsden xx & from Tevedale iiij myle & from the mars xvij m.[3]

[1] A Book of the State of the Frontiers and Marches betwixt England and Scotland, by Sir Robert Bowes, Knight. Hodgson's Northumberland, Part iii., Vol. ii., p. 208.

[2] A district in Scotland.

[3] C. J. Bates' Border Holds, Vol. i., p. 24.

While, in 1523, the animosity that existed between the Scotch and English Borderers was so great, and hostile inroads were so frequent, that the English Wardens considerably increased the strength of the garrisons in the northern valleys of the Coquet, the Aln, the Breamish, and the Tweed. "Places on the middle mches hereafter written by John Eure peticapitan in thabsence of sir William Eure knight lieutenant of the said mche by the comandment of Thomas lorde Dacre to him given by his familiar and trusty svant Cuthbert Heton gentilman thought unto the said John most beneficiale for garrysons to be laid in as well as for defence of the said border as to the annoysance of the Scotts, whiche townships and places has promised and ar contented to take soldeors to burde that is to say:—Heppell—John Bilton, Sande Snadon & Thomas Johnson xx[ti] persons—Harbottell—Ann Lighton & Hew Grene xviij—Alwenton—Willm Brown xij—Burrodon—John Wardhaughe xij—Bittlesden — Persevell Selby xx—Scranwood—Sande Layng, John Scroggs, Robert Howey, and George Howy xxxij—Alnem—Robert Howy, Robert Watson, Willm Gair, & Thomas Mantyll xxx, & between the towns of Scranwood & Alnem x psons.—Ingham—George Ogle lx.—Whittingham—Thom. Roull, Thomas Tailyor, Cuthbert Dycheburn, & Thomas Yong xxxvj—Unthank—John Unthank xij. at ij[s] viij[d] per week each persons borde."[1]

During the course of the succeeding five and twenty years this distrust and attitude of watchful defence against their neighbours living on the other side of the Cheviots, had not in the least relaxed amongst the inhabitants of Northumberland, for—

> "On steep and on crag,
> Streamed banner and flag,
> And the pennons and plumage of war."

In 1549, a range of beacons were established throughout the county. "Theis be the naymes of the beakons within the

[1] Extract from Lord Dacre's Ledger Book for 1523. Hodgson's Northumberland, Part ii., Vol. ii., p. 476.

Shereifdom of Northumberlande the whiche wer accustomed to give warning to all the holl country of the invasions of the Scottes in England :—

Fyrst the beakon of Rosse Castell.
The beakon of Tytles howghe.
The beakon of Rymes syde.
The beakon of Redde syde.
The beakon of Symon syde.
The beakon of Hedwen Lawes.
The beakon of Harlley crag.
The beakon of Hemsholte.
The beakon of Snogon.
The beakon of Muet Lawe.

And in the list of beacons in Northumberland and of the gentlemen charged with them, on the 24th of May, 1549—we find :—" Rimside and Tytlesheugh "—in the care of Robert Collingwood of Eslington, Henry Collingwood of Ryle, Thomas Clavering of Callaly. At the same time the following were " the names of the gentylmen balyffes and other officers not being in the King his Majesti's garysons within Glendell, Cuykedayll, Bambroughshier, Eelandshyer, and Noramshyer."

Coquetdale :—John Rodham the elder of Shawdon, Lucas Ogle of Eglingham, William Heron of Crawley, Robert Collingwood of Bewick, John Unthank of Unthank, Henry Collingwood of Ryle, Thomas Horsley of Screnwood, Perceval Selby of Biddleston, Perceval Clennell of Clennell, Awder (Alder) of Prendwick, Thomas Ilderton of Ilderton."[1]

In the October of 1549, detachments of foreign troops were also sent into Northumberland to assist in defending the Borders against an expected invasion from the Scots. The following is a list of those stationed in the vale of Whittingham :—

" THE SCOTTISH FRONTIER."

1549—October.—List of the towns at which the horsemen and footmen lay upon the frontier :—

Strangers and armed horsemen :

Capt. Andrea, at Whittingham and Glanton.
Charles de Guavar, at Mikle Ryle, Little Ryle, and Yetlington.

---

[1] Historical MSS. Commission, 1888. Rutland Papers, Vol. i., pp. 37-39.

Captain Lanciano at Estlington and Screnwood.
Captain Hungarian at Bolton and Lemmington.

English Light horsemen:

Francis Wolstrop, at Biddleston.
John Dudley, at Whittingham.
Sir Oswold Wolstrop, at Carkington (Cartington).[1]

The fact of strangers and foreigners having been sent into Northumberland to assist in its defence did not mean that our ancestors had lost any of their characteristic spirit of bravery, or had grown less valorous than in the past, but it was owing to the extreme hostile feeling at that time existing between England and Scotland that these mercenaries were engaged. We need only refer to a muster of armed Northumbrians which had taken place eleven years before (1538), which shows that the old warlike spirit of the Border men had not departed, but that there were yet good men and true to be found in the vale of the Aln and in Breamish Water ready to "rise and follow the fray."

The following extract, giving the list of the men of Alndale whose names appear on the Muster roll of 1538, will no doubt be of some interest to the inhabitants of the valley who, in the present day, fill their places, and many of whom are not only lineal descendants, but bear the same names.

"The avewe of Musters takyn by Sir Cuthbt. Radclyffe Knight Constable of the Kings Castell of Allnwyke and Robt. Collingwode Esquyere the xvii and xviii day of Apryle the xxxti yere of oure souerayne Lorde Kinge Henry the Eight takyn on Abberwyk More and Robert Lawes for Cocdale ande a part of Bourghe ward by vertewe of the Kings comyschone to theym dyrecte wyth others. Daited at Westmynster the fyrst day of Marche, the yere of the reyne of oure saide souerayne Lorde affore sayde."

[1] Historical MSS. Commission, 1888. Rutland Papers, Vol. i., p. 46.

AYLNAM *belong to* ALLWYK
Thomas Gare.
James Howhe.
John Gare.
Thomas Huntley.
Ed. Mantyll.
Thomas Huntley.
Thomas Brokyt.
Jarret Cooke.
Thomas Huntley.
Robt. Howhe.
Ed. Howhe.
Georg Howhe.
John Howhe.
Mathoo Walker.
John Waller.
Alexsander Watson.
Wallme Watson.
John Dawson.
George Wyllson.
Thomas Hone.
John Huntley.
Rog. Bednell.
*Able with horse and harnes.**

FAWDON.
James Thomson.
David Softhlay.
Robt. Rochester.
Robert Warches.
Thomas Whytingame.
John Rochester.
Robert Rochester.
John Rochester.
Able with horse and harnes.

FAWDON *belonging to* ALLNWK.
John Chesman.
John Thomson.
George Rochester.
Ryc. Rochester.
John Taller.
Able men wantinge both horse and harnes.

SHAWDEN.
John Roddem. thellder.
John Roddom.
Raufe Wytwod.
Willme Thomson.
Willme Reede.
Thomas Myller.
John Boroman.
Hable with horse and harnes.

GLANTON.
Edmond Borell.
Henry Donne.
George Reyd.
Willme Huntrelle.
John Woode.
Hable with horse and harnes.

GLANTON.
John Ley.
Thomas Watson.
Thomas Staward.
Ryc. Hopper.
John Hopper.
Robt. Ley.
James Smythe.
Edmond Gybson.
Roy. Nycollson.
Hable men wanting both horse and harnes

LERCHYLLD.
Thomas Lylborne.
John Recherdson.
John Lilborne.
Rauff Potts.
John Potts.
Willme Softley.
Robt. Atkinson.
Thomas Atkinson.
John Thomson.
Willme Jobson.
Hable wantinge bothe horse and harnes.

ABBERWYK.
John Bellingame.
Robt. Browne.
Henry Huntres.
Willme Johnson.
John Myllur.
James Lawson.
John Lawson.
John Kelwell.
Thomas Brone.
James Rowell.
George Dogerson.
Robt. Hogson.
Thomas Castell.
Ryc. Cupp.
Ed. Ellder.
Edmont Routter.
Hable men wanting bothe horse and harnes.

SKARN-WOODE.
Rolande Horsley.
George Howe.
Robt. Whyt.
Wat. Browne.
John Wighthorne.
Alayne Raster.
Hable with horse and harnes.

PRENDYK.
Thomas Allder.
Robt. Allder.
Daue Gare.
George Allder.
Roger Makeforthe.
Hable with horse and harnes.
Robt. Rede.
Thomas Mackforthe.
Not able.

---

*Arms.

ERLINGTON.[*] Robt. Moffete.
Ed. Wyte.
Thomas Moffet.
Henry Ersden.
Ed. Spenke.
Henry Bylton.
Willme Lawre.
George Tyndell.
John Archer.
Henry Crayk.
Sanders Collinwode.
George Collinwode.
Thams Mylle.
Willme Mores.
Oswolde Moffet.
John Ersdon.
George Wilson.
Hable with horse and harnes.
James Lansayse.
Cuthbt. Fare.
Not hable wanting bothe horse and harnes.

THORNTON.[†] Ed. Errington.
Ed. Bottemand.
Edmund Walker.
Thomas Bonwell.
Hewe Browne.
Willme Bowteman.
John Newton.
George Pegden.
Hable with horse and harnes.
Joh. Dychborn.
Edmonde Hudson.
Rog. Newton.
Ryc. Dychborne.
Wanting horse and harnes.

BARTON. William Spenk.
Thomas Pegden.
Thomas Gybson.
Henry Jackson.
Hable with horse and harnes.
James Huntley.
Not able.

MEKYLL RYLE. Thomas Collingwode.
Henry Collingwod.
Thomas Herd.
Ed. Tyndell.
Ed. Nycollson.
Robt. Matlande.
John Perote.
John Wytingame.
John Buttemonte.
Hable with horse and harnes.
Thomas Nycolson.
Thomas Lame.
Thomas Heslope.
Hable men wanting horse and harnes.

BOLLTON. George Syme.
Rauffe Collingwode.
Robt. Bydmore.
Willme Walker.
Ed. Lainge.
Robt. Lasse.
John Carsley.
Ed. Atkynson.
John Huntres.
Georg Carswell.
Rog. Robynson.
Ed. Partus.
Robt. Robinson.
Ryc. Robynson.
Willme Howden.
John Cupp.
Ed. Herryson.
Robt. Bedmore.
John Mantell.
Hyrry Dychborne.
Robt. Atkinson.
Ryc. Gee.
Gylbt. Ledell.
Robt. Red.
Willme Mayson.

TYTLINGTON. Raufe Collinwod.
Ed. Nycollson.
Willme Dychborne.
Willme Hope.
Rog. Huntres.
Thomas Gawe.
Willme Hopper.
Thomas Thomson.
Willme Care.
Robt. Hopper.
Able with horse and hars.
Willme Gybson.
Pet. Yong.
Nycoll Huntrych.
Not able.

WYTINGHAME. Thomas Collingwode.
Thomas Pegden.
Willme Browne.
John Buteman.
Edward Brystoo.
Henry Newry.
John Nycollson.
Thomas Buteman.
John Swayn.
Bog. Brown.
John Jackson.
Thomas Wod.
Gelbt. Buteman.
Henry Brown.
Rog. Peden.
Willme Dowglas.
Georg. Jackson.
Thomas Yong.

[*] Eslington. [†] Thrunton.

WYTINGHAME. Rynyon Wyllsen
Gelbt. Newton.
Ryc Pegden.
Cuthbt. Dychborn.
Thomas Dobson.
Wyllme Newry.
Henry Clay.
Ryc. Davyson.
Henry Taller.
James Pegden.
Thomas Whyt.
Hable men wanting bothe horse and harnes.

GLANTON. John Reyde.
John Glanton.
Ed. Rede.
John Rotter.
Hable with horse and harnes.
Roger Buteman.
Larance Trollope.
Cuthbt. Dycheborn.
Thomas Atkinson.
Not able wanting horse and harnes.

CALLALE. Thomas Claveryng.
John Atkinson.
Robt. Atkinson.
John Fenc'
John Willson.
Willme Willson.
Willme Craswell.
Henry Whytwham.
Cryst. Whytwham

CALLALE. Thomas Mathere.
Edward Buteman.
Thomas Karn'e.
Robt. Marcher.
Hable with horse and harnes.
John Dychson.
Robt. Hyttell.
John Dychborne.
Not able.

YETLINGTON. John Claveryng.
Ronert Layme.
Ed. Hatherwyk.
George Heslope.
Willme Willson.
Thomas Clarke.
George Layng.
John Layng.
Ed. Carysley.
Georg. Trewhat.
Robt. Fawckus.
Willme Clark.
Robt. Karn'e.
Jarre Yowle.
Willme Karne.
Habylle men with horse and harnes.
George Karn'e.
Thomas Brokyt.
Willme Lane.
John Aryden.
Jessper Jobson.
Not hable.

(Signed) CUTHBERT RADCLYFFE.
ROBT. COLLYNGWOD. [1]

A complete system of watch and ward was also kept up night and day along the whole frontier of the three Marches. Life and property on the borders, in those days, were both held under a very uncertain tenure. A thriving homestead, well stocked with sheep and cattle, might in a few hours become a smoking ruin, and the owner, if alive, herdless. Truly does an old writer say "In what a wretched Condition our *English* Borders were before the Union of the Crowns (nor were the *Scotch* in any better) appears from that amazing List that we have of the many Hundreds that were continually employ'd in Night-watches; the rest of the neighbourhood being oblig'd (at all hours) to rise and follow the fray." [2]

---

[1] Arch. Æliana, Vol. iv., p. 157 (old series.)

[2] (Leges Marchiarum) Border Laws, Preface, p. lv.

During the day a strict look-out was kept by watchmen stationed on many of the hill tops. We learn from "*The order of the Watches upon the Middle Marches, made by the Lord* Wharton, *Lord Deputy-Generall of all the three Marches, under my Lord of* Northumberland's *Grace, Lord Warden Generall of all the said Marches, in the month of October, in the Sixth year of the Reign of our Sovereign Lord King* Edward *the Sixth,*"[1] for the protection of Upper Coquet, the Breamish, and the Aln, that "*The Day-Watch of* Cookdaill, *beginning at* Paspethe.

Allenton to watch to *Paspethe* with two Men every Day: Setters and Searchers of this Watch, *John Wylkinson*, the Laird of *Donesgrene*, *John Wylkinson*, otherwise called *Gordes John*.

The Greyt Kneys to be watched with the Inhabitants of *Clennell*, *Newton*, and the *New-hall*: Setters and Searchers of the same *Percevall Clennell* and *William Gallon*.

The Kaye-Cragge to be watched with two Men of *Bedelsdan*: *Percevall Selbe* and *Thomas Davyson* to be Setters and Searchers of this Watch.

The Hogdon Law to be watched with two Men daily, of the Inhabitants of *Cramwodd* and *Elnane*: Setters and Searchers of this Watch, *Thomas Horsley* and *Cuthbert Horsley*.

SHELMORE to be watched with two Men daily, of the Inhabitants of *Predeke*, *Mutell Rayell*,[2] and *Little Rayell*: Setters and Searchers of this Watch, *Thomas Collenwood* and *William Melborne*.

HARTSAID-CRAGG to be watched with the Inhabitants of *Engram*, *Hartsayd*, *Restle*, with two Men daily: Setters and Searchers of this watch, *Hary Colynwood*, *Davide Hall*.

THE *Bell-Carr* to be watched with two Men daily, of the Inhabitors of *Elderton*, *Roden*, *Roston*, and *Rodam*: Setters

---

[1] Border Laws, p. 235.

[2] Great Ryle.

and Searchers of this Watch, *Edward Elderton* and *Anthony Elderton.*

Overseers of this Watch, Ser *George Ratcliff*, and Ser *John Horsley*, Knights; *Robert Colleynwood, Cuthbert Musgrave*, Captain of *Harbottill, Percevall Selbe, Persevall Clenell.*"[1] While each night at sunset men were appointed to watch at all the fords and passes by which it was likely a marauding band might come, warders were stationed every night, as follows :—

"THE Passages from *Allenton* to *Clenell*, to be kept with four Men of the Inhabitors of *Allenton*, the *Parkheyd, Newton, Foxton*, and *Newhall.*

THE Passages from *Clenell* to *Byttelsden* to be kept with four Men nightly of the Inhabitors of *Clenell* and *Burroden*; Setters and Searchers of the Watches, betwixt *Allenton* and *Clenell, Percevall Unthank* and *George Browne.*

THE Passages from *Byttylsden* to *Skarnwood* to be watched with four Men nightly, of the Inhabitors of *Byttelsden, Cotwalles, Netherton* and *Ellebaye.*

THE Passages from *Skarnwood* to *Alnen* to be watched with two Men nightly of the Inhabitors of *Skarnwood* and *Kareslaye-house*: Setters and Searchers of these two Passages, *Persevall Horsley* and *John Shanks.*

THE Passages from *Alnen* to *Clenell-Prendeke*, to be watched with two Men nightly, of the Inhabitors of *Alnen.*

The Passages from *Prendeke* to *Engram* to be watched nightly with six Men of the Inhabitors of *Prendeke, Mikle Ryell, Lyttil Ryell, Unthank, Eslington, Clenche*, and *Fadden*; *Thomas Adden, Harry Colingwodd* and *Rowland Taylour* to be Setters and Searchers of these Watches."[2]

"FROM *Overtrewet* to *Yetlington* to be watched nightly with three Watches of the Inhabitors of *Trewett, Trowett*, and *Lurbottell*; Setters and Searchers, *Spraggae* of *Trewete* and *John Swane.*

---

[1] Border Laws, pp. 268-269. [2] Ibid, p. 271.

FROM *Yetlington* to *Glanton* to be watched with eight Men nightly of the Inhabitors of *Yetlington*, *Callelye*, *Weltinggem* and *Bartone*; Setters and Searchers, *John Claveringe* and *John Buttymane*.

FROM *Glanton* to *Old Bowycke* to be watched with eight Men nightly of the Inhabitors of *Crawlaye*, *Glanton*, *Shaddon*, *Benley*, *New Bowycke* and *Harrop*; Setters and Searchers, *Anthony Rostone* and the *Bayliff* of *Beneleye*.

Overseers of this Watch, *Robert Collingwood* of *Bowyke*, *John Rodam* the Younger, and *William Heron* of *Crawleye*."[1]

"FROM the *Newtown* to *Liersheld*, to be watched with two Men nightly, and thereto is appointed the Town of *Edlingtone* and the *Newtone*.

FROM *Liersheld* to *Bawtonne*, to be watched with two Men nightly, and thereto is appointed the Town of *Lemedon*, and the *Brome-Parke*; Setters and Searchers of these two Watches, *Robert Manners*, and *Robert Killingworthe*.

Overseers of this Watch, *Robert Lysle*, and *Thomas Swinburne*.

FROM *Bowton* to *Lethington*, to be watched with two Men nightly, and thereto is appointed *Bowton*, *Aberwyke*, and the *Woddhall*.

FROM *Tetlington* to *Harroppeswyer*, by North the Hill to be watched with eight Men nightly, of the Inhabitors of *Tetlingtone*, *Basden*, *Sheplay*, *Est Dichburne*, *West Dichburne*, *Eglingham*, and *Harrop*; Setters and Searchers of these two Watches, *Cuthbert Mowe*, *John Wethered*, and the Greeve of *Totlingtone*.

Overseers, *Edward Bednell*, *John Bellingham*, *Luke Ogle*, and *Rauf Collingwood*."[2]

In 1541, a list was drawn up containing the names of the "Gentlemen Inhabitants within the Middle Marchies," from which we extract those of local interest—

---

[1] Border Laws, p. 279. [2] Ibid, p. 285.

"Robert Collingwood of Eslington Esqr.
Robert Clavering of Callillie, Esquier.
Thomas Swynborne of Edlingham Esqr.
Persivall Selby of Bittlesden Esqr.
Persivall Clenalle.
Edward Calland of Trewhett.
Thomas Hersley of Skrenwood.
William Horsley of Netherton.
Raphe Collingwood of Titlington.
John Roddam of Shawden Esquier.
William Heron of Crawley.
John Bradwell of Lamaton.
Edward Bradwell his sonne.
Henry Collingwood of Ryill."[1]

Lord Wharton, Lord Deputy-General of the Marches, issued an order, in 1552, that the lands around all villages within the three Marches should be enclosed with "Hedges and Ditches, whereby may ensue much Wealth and Advantage to the People, both by Tillage and Pasture; and by straitening the Passes, much greater Security, the Watches for the future being more easy to be kept, to the great Safety, Comfort, and Profit of the People. . . all such portions thereof, as be convenient for Tillage, Meadows, or Grazing, to be inclosed with Ditches five Quarters in Breadth and six Quarters in Depth, and to be double set with quick Wood and hedged above three Quarters high."[2] The following local gentlemen were appointed "*Commissioners for Enclosures upon the* Middle-Marches. Between the Waters of *Cokett* and *Ayll* from *Lierchel*-burne to the Sea:—

Robert Lisle of *Felton.*
Thomas Swinburne of *Edlingham.*
John Bednell of *Lematone.*
George Fenwyke of *Brenk-burn.*
George Metcalfe of *Alnewycke.*
Harry Heron of *Alnewycke.*

"From *Lierchel-burne* to the March of *Scotland* between *Brunishe* and *Symondsyde :—*

---

[1] Hodgson's Northumberland, Part iii., Vol. ii., pp. 247-248.

[2] Traces of these enclosures are yet visible at Wreighill, in Coquetdale.

Sir George Ratclyff, Knight.
Cuthbart Musgrave of *Harbottell.*
Robert Collingwood of *Eslington.*
Robert Clavering of *Callehoe.*
Thomas Horsley of *Skyrnwod.*
Persevall Selbye of *Bytilsden.*
Edward Gallen of *Trewhytt.*
Persevall Clenell of *Clenell.*"[1]

Our beloved Borderland continued in this unsettled condition until the happy union of the Thistle and the Rose, when that extreme animosity which for centuries had existed between the two kingdoms gradually began to subside; the border strongholds were dismantled, and the inhabitants settled down to agricultural pursuits, for the success of which we need only look on the well-cultivated fields and fertile valleys to be seen on both sides of the old East, West, and Middle Marches; or to put it in the words of the Ettrick Shepherd :—

"Now we can ride the Border side,
And brethren meet at every turn,
But then the meed was hang and head,
To ravish, pillage, slay, and burn.

God prosper all the Border dales,
On both sides of our ancient line,
And never may rankling grudge prevail
For the doughty deeds of auld lang syne!"

(RAID OF THE KERS.)

[1] Border Laws, pp. 327-330.

CHAPTER II.

ALNHAM.

Various Spellings of Alnham—Its Owners—Situation—Surrounding Hills—The Vill in Norman Times—The De Vescys—Its Value in the Fourteenth Century—The Percies—The Castle Mound—Scottish Raids—The Pele Towers—Fray at Alnham in 1256—Field Names—Proprietors in 1663—Population—A Roman Causeway—Castle Hill Camp—The Rithe—Pigdon's Leap—Division of the Common—Mills—Duke's Cottages—Old Residents—Folk Lore—The False Alarm—Cockfighting—Wrestling.

ALNHAM, oftener called "Yeldom," and by one old writer "Yarwell,"[1] is also found in the following various spellings:—Alneham (1331), Alenham (1354), Elnam (1509), Alenam (1512), Alnem (1523), Alname (1541), Aylname (1550), Ayneham (1557), Aylneham (1567), Ailnham (1663). The village of Alnham consists of the vicarage, the church and schools, a farm house, and a long straggling row of detached houses, each standing within its own "toft and croft," the whole of which, with one exception, belong to the Duke of Northumberland. A small farm, called "Penny Laws," is a portion of the Harbottle Estate, formerly known as "Clennell's Lands." Alnham stands at the very foot of the southern outliers of the Cheviot range of hills, within six miles of Scotland. The highest of the hills which stretch from the west, close down upon Alnham, are Hogden Law (1,797 feet), Hazelton-rig Hill (1,655 feet), and Coldlaw (1,290 feet); while further to the west rise Wether Cairn (1,834 feet), and Cushat Law (2,020 feet). Delightful it is in summer time with a clear bright sky overhead, to wander over those breezy

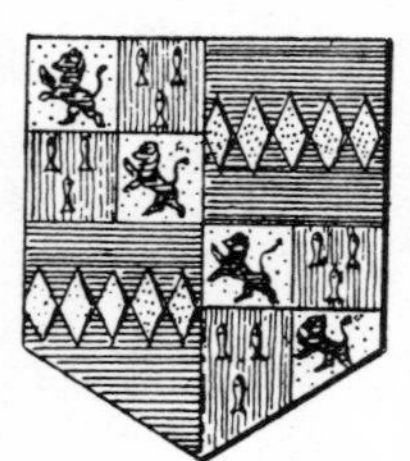

[1] Magna Brittannia, London, 1724, p. 629.

uplands, and to partake of the unbounded hospitality of the kind hearted shepherds of the Cheviots; but during the stormy days of winter it is a most perilous undertaking for the stranger to venture across their pathless wastes. Many a sad tale can the shepherds tell of severe winters and heavy snowstorms amid those mountain solitudes, of snow-slips and of the dangerous ground drift—storms accompanied with great privation, and frequent loss of life.

Horsley, in describing the "Valley of the Aln," in 1729, says:—"*Alnham, Prendwick, Great and Little Ryle.* The river Ale rises in the wild grounds above Alnham, more usually called Yeldom, another flagrant instance how strangely names may be corrupted and metamorphosed. It runs near Prendwick, belonging to Mr. Alder, and the Ryles, Great and Little, belong to a family of the Collingwoods."[1]

The now obscure village of Alnham was in far-off feudal days one of no small importance, as may be gathered from the cluster of ancient buildings, its castle mound, its pele tower, and its little Transitional Church. In the reign of Henry III. and Edward I. the vill of Alnham was part of the lordship and estate of William de Vescy lord of Alnwick,[2] of John de Vescy in 1289,[3] and has ever since continued to be a member of that barony.

At an inquisition made at Alnwick in 1289, it was found that John de Vescy died seized (amongst other possessions) "Of Alneham with shealings of this vill, and of a capital messuage, demesne lands, farms of free tenants, of bondmen, cotmen, and of mills, and of rents yearly—£51 7s. 6d."[4] And in 1368, at an inquisition made at Newcastle, Henry de Percy held the town of Alnham as part of the Barony of Alnwick. "The town of Alnham he held in his own demesne; and the site of the manor, with a garden and two

---

[1] Horsley's Northumberland, 1729, p. 53.

[2] Testa de Nevill, Hodgson's Northumberland, Part iii., Vol. i., p. 209.

[3] Ibid., p. 49.

[4] Tate's Alnwick, Vol. i., p. 88.

acres of meadow, render in herbage six shillings; one hundred and eighty acres of demesne land in the hands of tenants at will render sixpence per acre, and fifteen acres of demesne meadow twelvepence per acre; of eighteen bondagia, twelve are in the hands of tenants at will, each yielding thirteen shillings and fourpence, and other six are wasted and render in herbage twelve shillings; twelve cotagia in the hands of tenants at will render twenty-four shillings, and six, which are wasted, render in herbage twelve shillings; one water mill renders forty-three shillings and fourpence; and free tenants twenty-four shillings and threepence."[1]

The foundations of an extensive fortress are yet visible on a green knoll opposite to the church, shewing traces of a square tower and the remains of other buildings, probably the outer offices, the dwellings of the servants, and the wall of the barmekyn. Mr. William Brown, of Alnham, says that his father, the late Edward Brown, excavated a large quantity of stones out of the "castle mound," with which to build walls around the fields on the adjoining farms, and he himself remembers having seen a number of door heads, window heads, and mullions, along with other dressed stones, amongst the ruins. This is no doubt the remains of the fortlet described in the list of 1415, as:—"*Turris de Alneham, Comitis Northumberland*,"[2] while incorporated in the present vicarage is the stout pele of later times. From letters found in the State Papers we can gather that the village of Alnham and the surrounding district had suffered severely from the ravages of the Scots during the reign of Henry VIII. These letters were written by the Earl of Northumberland to the King. The first is from Alnwick Castle, dated October 22, 1532, when the Earl complains that "the Scottes of Tyvydail, with the nombre of 300 personages and above, Launce Carr beyng theyre governer, whiche is a deputye of the Marchyes, hathe not only brunte a

[1] Tate's Alnwick, Vol. i., p. 138.

[2] C. J. Bates, Border Holds, Vol. i., p. 17.

towne of myne called Alenam on Thursday, beying ye 10th day of this instanth monthe of Octobre, with all the corne, hay, and householde stuf in the said towne, and also a woman ;" and again on the 20th November, 1532, he writes to the King from Berwick with a further complaint that the Scots, numbering 3,000 men or more, under the leadership of the Kers, came across the Borders :—" After which so doone, and the bushment and forray met, thei did cast of two other forraies abowt 12 of the cloke of the day light upon the said Wednysday, and the oone forray did run down ye watter of Bremysch and ther tuke upe 4 townes called Inggram, Reveyley, Brandon, and Fawdon, and the other forray com to the watter of Aylle, and ther tuke upe two townes called Ryle and Prendwyke, which townes standes at the utter parte of your Highnes Middle Marchiez towards Scotland, and atheir of thaire said forrais was to the nombre of 200 men."[1] . . . . In perpetrating the raids just mentioned, the Scot was doing nothing more than paying back the noble Earl in his own coin ; because when an English warden's raid was being organised in the year 1523, the Earl then promised the King "to lett slippe secretlie them of Tindaill and Riddisdaill for the annoyance of Scotland. God send them all good spede ! "

The two border fortresses at Alnham had evidently received ill-usage at the hands of the Scots, for when Bowes and Ellerker make their survey of the Border in 1541, they say :—" At Alname be two lytle tovres whereof thone ys the mansion of the vycaredge and thother of the Inherytaunce of the kinges matie p'cell of the late Erle of Northumb'landes landes beinge scarcely in good reparac'ons."[2] Alnham at this time was held by Henry VIII. Henry, the sixth Earl Percy, died without issue ; and his brother Thomas—having been party to Ask's conspiracy, or the " Pilgrimage of Grace "—was beheaded in 1537 ; therefore, the Earldom of Northumberland

[1] State Papers, Record Series iv., iiii., p. 625.

[2] C. J. Bates' Border Holds, Vol. i., p. 43.

remained sometime dormant. The following interesting note is also found in "Border Holds," Vol. i., page 43:—"Alnham. The Lord hath there a faire stronge stone Tower of Ancient tyme builded & strongly vaulted over, & the Gates & Dores be all of great stronge Iron Barres and a good demayne adjoining thereto, the House is now ruinous and in some decay, by reason the Farmer useth to carry his sheep up the Stares and to lay them in the Chambers which rotteth the Vaultes, and will in shorte time be the utter decay of the same house if other reformacion be not had."—Stockdale's Survey, 1586, at Alnwick Castle.

The following incident, recorded in the early Assize Rolls of Northumberland, which took place at Alnham during the thirteenth century, gives us some idea of the character of its inhabitants and the state of society at that period.

"Adam Servaunt, of Alnham, had struck Richard Berii on the head with an axe so that within eight days he died. And the aforesaid Adam, after the deed, was harboured in the village of Alnham for half-a-year, and afterwards he fled and was suspected. Therefore, let him be driven out and outlawed.[1] The chattels of the said Adam are worth 9s. 6d., for which the Sheriff has to account. And William Wodester was in company with the said Adam, and struck the aforesaid Richard, and at the instigation of the aforesaid William the aforesaid Adam wounded the aforesaid Richard, and William forthwith fled and is suspected, therefore let him be driven out and outlawed. He has no chattels, and the township of Alnham did not apprehend the said Adam, therefore let it be amerced."[2] (40 Henry III., 1256.)

The field names of an old township like Alnham are not only of some interest, but of great service in recording its ancient manorial rights and customs, as well as preserving the

[1] During this year there are recorded 77 murders; only 4 of the murderers were justly punished, the remainder were simply outlawed.

[2] Northumberland Assize Rolls, Surtees Society. No. 88, p. 118.

names of the holders of its lands in past times. The following lands, whose names are yet extant in and around Alnham, throw some light on the history of the manor and its appurtenances :—

The Camp Hill Pasture.
The Millers' Close.
The Mill Ridge.
The Castle Middle Field.
The Dyers' Field.
Buddle's Upper Field.
Buddle's Middle Field.
Buddle's Low Field.
Tulley's Close.
Carter Knowle Field.
Hogden, Cobden and Hogspethford.

The "Rentals and Rates for Northumberland, with the Proprietors Names, in 1663," thus describes Alnham :—

Towns and Places.	Names of Proprietors.
Ailnham (T) & Moore.	Robt. Alder.
	Ra. Davison.
——— Vicaridge.	Vicar, for the Vicarage.
——— Rectory.	Mr. Chr. Ogle, for ½ the Rectory.
	Mr. Alex. Collingwood.
	½ Rectory.
Ailnham Mill.	
Cobdon.	Mr. Alex. Collingwood, of Ryle.
Hesledonrigg.	Mr. Tho. Selby of Bittleston.
Long Cragg & Frued's Moore.	
Prendrick.	Mr. Robt. Collingwood.
	Mr. Geo. Alder.
	Geo. Alder.
Scarnwood.	Sr. Thos. Horsley.
——— Tyth.	
——— Mill.	
Vnthank.	Mr. Robt. Vnthank.[1]

In 1664 the following persons were free tenants of the manor, in the barony of Alnwick, at Alnham :—

"Alexander Collingwood, Ralph Davison, John Hearon, Robert Alder, Alneham; George Alder, Prendicke."

The Parish of Alnham covers an area of 12,389 acres, and includes the townships of Alnham, Prendwick, Screnwood, and Unthank. The population of the parish in 1801 was 233

[1] Hodgson's Northumberland, Part iii., Vol. i., p. 263.

persons; in 1811, 211; in 1821, 269; in 1881, 266; and in 1891, 205 persons.

The farmers in the parish in 1827 were:—

"Stephen Atkinson, Alnham.
John Chrisp, Prendwick.
George Crawford, Alnham.
Anthony Marshall, Alnham.
John Pattison, Unthank.
Edward Simmons, Screenwood.
John Snowdon Screenwood.
John Collingwood Tarleton Esq., Collingwood House.
Unthank."[1]

The church at Alnham is said to be built "in the site of a small Roman camp, which most probably has been for a Centurion's guard, to protect their herds of cattle when grazing during summer in the rich pastures on the bank of the river Aln above Whittingham."[2]

In 1850, the Rev. G. S. Thomson (Vicar of Alnham) observed, while some men were cutting a drain near to Alnham, under a peat bog 9 inches deep, the paved stones of an ancient roadway, similar to the causeways made by the Romans, which may have been connected with the station at Alnham. On the Castle Hill, west of the village, there is a well-defined British camp, 100 yards in diameter, with double ramparts, commanding an extensive view ranging to the Simonside Hills south of the Coquet, Alnwick Moor on the east, with Beanley, Bewick, Ros Castle, and the Cheviots on the north and north-east. Within this strong camp are hut circles and other enclosures. The entrance is from the east.[3] In a very steep valley immediately west of this hill the "Rithe," a tributary of the Coquet, rushes in its noisy course towards the dark woods of Hazelton-Rig. A little further up the valley, where this mountain stream glides between two perpendicular rocks, a chasm is pointed out as "Pigdon's

[1] Parson and White's Directory, 1828.

[2] Arch. Æliana, Vol. i., p. 240. (Old Series.)

[3] History Berwickshire Naturalists' Club, Vol. x., p. 547.

Leap," which, tradition says, a cattle-lifter named Pigdon, pursued by a band of country people, cleared at one bound, and thus managed to escape.

Alnham Common was divided and apportioned in 1776,[1] when the only freeholders appear to have been the Duke of Northumberland; Thos. Clennell, Esq., of Harbottle; Mr. Byne, Prendwick; and the vicar of the parish. In former times there were two mills at Alnham, a fulling mill,[2] of which we find a trace in the name of the "Dyer's Field," and a corn mill, which, as we learn from the Church Register, was in existence in 1789. These mills were situated a little above the vicarage. There is also a tradition of a fair for the sale of black cattle having been held some time or another at Alnham. The "Duke's Cottages" were set apart about the beginning of the present century, the date "1800" being cut on the door-head of the house now in the occupation of Mr. Wm. Brown, in whose family it has continued since its erection. Mr. Andrew Tully and Mr. Thomas Brown also occupy "Duke's Cottages," which were the dwelling-places of

---

[1] ALNHAM DIVISION.—We, William Marshall, Simon Dodds, and George Chisholm, Gentlemen, the Commissioners appointed in and by an Act of Parliament, made in the 15th year of the reign of his present Majesty, for dividing and inclosing a moor, called Alnham Moor or Alnham Common, and also the in-field grounds of the township of Alnham, in the parish of Alnham, in the county of Northumberland, do hereby give notice that we do intend (by virtue of the power and authority given to, and vested in us, by the said Act) to put up to public sale or auction, on Monday, the 23rd day of September next, at one o'clock in the afternoon, at the house of Mr. William Donkin, innkeeper, of Great Tosson, all that Plot or Parcel of the said moor or common, as it is now ascertained and staked out, containing 125 acres or thereabouts, and boundered as follows, viz., by a part of the public high road leading from Alnham Townhead to Northfieldhead, and a part of Mr. Byne's allotment of the said common, on or towards the north-east; by a part of his Grace the Duke of Northumberland's allotment of common, on or towards the north-west; by a part of the said Duke's allotment of common, and a part of his allotment of in-field ground, on or towards the south-west, and adjoining the west end of the town of Alnham.—Dated 21st August, 1776. WILLIAM MARSHALL, SIMON DODDS, GEORGE CHISHOLME. N.B.—Mr. Ell. Reed, of Prendwick, will shew the said plot or parcel of ground.—*Newcastle Courant, August 24th, 1776.*

[2] The fulling mill was probably at Hazelton-Rig, as the "Dyer's Field" lies close to it.

their grandfathers, Mr. Andrew Tully being the third of that name. Previous to the erection of the "cottages," the greater part of the village of Alnham stood near to the ford through the Aln, at the junction of two roads, the Church road and the Netherton road, described in 1724[1] as follows:—"This Town, which is pretty large, takes its name from the River *Aln*, but of late has been called usually *Yarwell*." During the early part of the century there was a public-house at "Yeldom," kept by Fanny Fiddis, a well-known personage at that time. There also dwelt within the ancient manor, about the same period, several worthies whose names are handed down to us in the following amusing stories, which we here introduce as a piece of folklore:—

During the French War, at the beginning of the present century, Napoleon Bonaparte's ambitious scheme for the invasion of England caused great fear throughout the whole kingdom, a fear which was brought to the highest pitch in the February, of 1804, by an event now known as "The False Alarm," the effects of which not a district felt more, or was more in the midst of it, than the east coast of Northumberland. For the defence of hearth and home, there were in the valleys of the Breamish, the Aln, and Upper Coquet, three volunteer companies—The Coquetdale Rangers, the Cheviot Legion, and the Percy Tenantry Volunteers. It was late on that memorable Tuesday night, the 31st January, 1804, when the inhabitants of the valleys of the Breamish and the Aln were thrown into great consternation by the firing of the beacon on Ros Castle, a lofty hill in Chillingham Park, which was speedily responded to by the beacons in Alndale and Coquetdale. George Atkinson, yeoman, of Alnham, was "fotherin" when he saw the beacon fire on Ryle Hill, so he buckled on his armour, mounted his charger, and made for Caisley Moor, the rallying-point of the west countrymen. At Netherton there was great excitement. Tom Nevison, Capt. Smart's servant man, better

[1] Magna Brittannia, London, 1724, p. 629.

known as "The King i' the Causey," scoured round the outlying district and gathered all the stragglers in. Amusing excuses are said to have been given by several who did not care about going to the muster. For instance, Tom Bolam had "a pain iv his breest," but three glasses of whisky at the "Fighting Cocks" soon cured him, and then he was open to fight "Bonny" or any other man—so said his neighbours. Willie Middlemas was seized with a violent pain, which nervous folk are liable to have during a thunderstorm; but no sooner did it become known that the alarm was false than Willie at once set forth and joined the troop in time for dinner at Collingwood House. Jack Dixon's horse wanted shoeing. Whilst that was being done, the news came that it was a false alarm; nevertheless, Jack boldly mounted, and was also with his troop at dinner time. At Collingwood House there was plenty of good cheer, and, as it was wickedly reported, the troopers felt so much relieved that they had not to fight the French they partook largely of the eatables and drinkables set before them, and very soon their spirits rose beyond all bounds. Jack Dixon—the "Noodle," as he was called—became so elated that when he mounted he knew not right from left, and therefore took the wrong road home to Netherton, and went by Alnham instead of Yetlington. Old Geordie Buddle, of "Yeldom," was standing at his garden-gate, when he heard in the distance the sound of a charger coming by Hogspethford. Presently the trooper rode up and saluted Geordie, who, looking somewhat curiously at the Ranger, said, "An' what wad thou de, Jack, if the French was comin'?" "De!" exclaimed Jack, "'all sune let ye see what aa' wad de." Saying this, he drew his sword, and at one bound leapt off his horse into the garden amongst Geordie's winter cabbages, at the same time shouting in a commanding tone of voice, "Give point against infantry;" "Give point against cavalry." Singling out a nice big cabbage, he made a ferocious cut at it, saying, "If that had been a Frenchman, that's what aa' wad hae dune tiv him." In this manner he laid about him until the whole of poor Geordie Buddle's cabbages were cut into mincemeat, and then, puffing and blowing with the exertion, he boastingly exclaimed, "Aa've lettin' ye see what aa' can de." "Yes," observed Geordie, very quietly, "Yor a brave soldier, Jack; you'll sune be an officer." Tommy Readhead, the Netherton Miller, took a very matter-of-fact view of the whole affair. Tommy was drying oats on the high kiln when the news came that "Bonny" had landed; so on hearing the sound of the bugle, he shouted to his wife, "Come here, Mary, an' kill thur yetts, an' grind thim, an' if the French dis land at the mill, we'll let thim see she's not toom." Saying this he hastened off to join the gallant band of defenders.

It is interesting to note how strong the spirit of antipathy to the French showed itself amongst the rural population of North Northumberland for many years after the close of the French War. As in the olden days the cry was "Scotch and English," so at the period of which we are speaking the very children played at a game they called "French and English." But the most amusing manner in which this feeling showed itself was in the names our fathers and grandfathers gave to their game cocks—the custom of cockfighting being at that time universal. A notable cockfight was held some fifteen years after Waterloo, at Netherton, a little village about two miles south of Alnham, on which occasion the feathered warriors on one side were named after the English generals, and those on the other side after the French generals who had taken part in the Peninsular Campaign and Waterloo, whose names were then household words throughout the country. The match was arranged by James Blacklock, of Yetlington, a veteran of the cock-pit, and John Buddle, of Alnham, a Waterloo hero. The "Yeldomites," with Buddle as their captain, chose the names of the English generals, whilst the "Yetlingtonians," with Blacklock as their leader, adopted those of the French. Many of the persons present that day had vivid recollections of the "False Alarm,"—and not a few had served as volunteers in the ranks of the Coquetdale Rangers, the Cheviot Legion, the Percy Tenantry Volunteers, or had been drawn for the Northumberland Militia, whilst Buddle and several others had actually fought the French under the command of those very generals whose names they had assumed for their birds, and, as might be expected, the excitement was great. Amongst the company assembled on that eventful day were Jack Buddle, Bill Buddle, Tom Brown, Andrew Tully, Watty Fiddis, Stephen Atkinson, Jimmy Trummell, Jimmy Elshender,[1] Bob Hedley, Jim Blaaket, Bob Dodds; Dode Avery, Willie Middlemas, Ned Hibbert, Browell Robison, Willie Boag, Tom Taylor, Geordie Scott, Kit Mordue, Tom Mavin, Mark Aynsley, Tommy Balmbra, Wull Scott, Johnny Roberts. Nicknames were at that time very common amongst the people living in the upland districts of the Coquet and the Aln, therefore we find some of the spectators rejoicing in the following sobriquets:—Harry i' the Rig, Willie the Weaver, Jack the Theeker, The Teddin, Bottle Green'aah, Cleesh, The Buck, Tallyrand, The Scammeller, Young Renny, The Gravit, Bendigo, Brassy, Pilpan, and Billy the Butler. The main having been drawn, the birds fell together in the order, and with the results following:—

(1)

Jack Buddle's	Duke of Wellington BEAT
Dode Avery's	Murat.
Bob Dodd's	Marshall Ney BEAT
Jimmy Elshender's	Sir John Moore.
Stephen Atkinson's	General Wolfe BEAT
Ned Hibbert's	General Grouchy.
Jim Blaaket's	Napoleon BEAT
Jimmy Turnbull's	General Picton.

The second time:—

(2) Wellington BEAT Ney.
Napoleon BEAT Wolfe,

and, strange how history repeats itself, at the third and last time—much to the joy of the "Yeldomites"—

[1] Alexander.

(3) {Jack Buddle's ... ... Duke of Wellington BEAT
{Jim Blaaket's ... ... Napoleon.

The usual doggerel rhyme commemorating the event began thus :—

"Jim bagg'd Napoleon, and off he went
To Netherton cockin—the lad was bent ;
But Wellington lick'd him to his heart's content
That varra day."

Just before the third and last encounter between Wellington and Napoleon, it was agreed on all sides to adjourn to the "Fighting Cocks" and have a friendly dram. Whilst thus refreshing themselves, some one suggested "to hev a bit 'Warselin,'[1] 'Hip, Step, an' Loup,' and 'Fut Racin'" to finish up the day ; and, as the following description of the subsequent proceedings (by one who knew the characteristics of all the local celebrities) is too amusing to be lost sight of, we venture to give it :—"It was soon settled to have the sports, so the hat went round and the coins dropped in, and when counted over there was sufficient money to be divided into three prizes—for a hunt-the-hare footrace for boys, a hop-step-and-jump, and wrestling. The callants started from the "Fighting Cocks," up the town to the mill, round by the Half-way House, the Wellfield, down the Buller Bank, and home to the cock-pit. Young "Dock" won the race. The hop-step-and-jump was a severe contest, the Mountaineers—Cheviot Shepherds—leaping with two sticks in their hands, while the Lowlanders had a stone in each hand, which they threw away when finishing the leap. The competitors were Tom Temple (a grand jumper), The "Teddin" (Rob Young), Bob Lamb, Anty Anderson, and The "Gravit." After several ties, The "Teddin" came off the victor. "There noo," says he, "there's three brothers on uz. Mat for a shot, Geordie for a fight, an' me for a jump at "Truffet Races."[2] The wrestling was more a trial of strength than science. There was a good entry,

---

[1] Wrestling. [2] Low Trewhitt Races.

and the collar and elbow, the nipping and squeezing of each other's backs was amusing, the competitors resorting to all the tactics of the ring—such as throwing off the chest, hipping, the hank, cross-buttocking, tripping, and the cleek—but, for activity, sheer strength, and durability, none had the slightest chance with Watty Fiddis, of Yeldom, who cross-buttocked all his men and was declared the winner.

"For the Yeldomites are strong and bold,
They can stand the heat as well as the cold;
When once they grip they keep their hold,
Whatever you may try.
They'll fling you slap upon your back,
An' certie's there you'll lie."

CHAPTER III.

ALNHAM CHURCH.

Before and after its Restoration in 1870—Granted to the Monks of Alnwick Abbey by De Vescy—Value of the Living at various Periods—Oliverian Survey—Terrier of 1663—Communion Plate—Bell—The Registers—Churchwarden's Accounts of the Last Century—Monuments—Weddings and Wedding Customs—The Petting Stone—Riding for the Kail.

ALNHAM CHURCH is dedicated to St. Michael, the most popular Saint in North Northumberland, no less than eight churches in the Archdeaconry of Lindisfarne being dedicated to that Saint. The living is in the gift of the Duke of Northumberland. Mr. F. R. Wilson's valuable work, "The Churches of Lindisfarne" (1870), thus describes Alnham Church:—"In a pastoral district, bounded by undulating lines

of hilltops, near the source of the River Alne, where there are the remains of a great castle, and a pele tower, now occupied as the vicarage-house, stands, on a sloping site, a beautiful little Transitional Church . . . . The church consists of a nave, with a porch on the south side, and an arcade on the north side, proving the fact of a north aisle in previous centuries; north and south transepts, whereof the south only is part of the original fabric . . . . and a chancel, with an ancient Transitional arch. Four buttresses at the west end, and two at the north and south angles of it, give movement to the outline; and the preservation of some of the ancient windows maintains its general air of simple antiquity." On the chancel floor are inlaid six tomb slabs, on which are sculptured floriated crosses of much gracefulness. The font is ornamented with heraldic devices, which Mr. Wilson states associates it with the Percy family—as does the font in the church of St. Michael at Ingram. We may remark that a number of the fonts in Northumbrian churches are dated about the years 1662-4, which seems to denote that they were the restorations after the destructive period of the Great Civil War. Alnham bears the date 1664, Ingram 1662, Rothbury 1664.

The Builder thus describes the state of Alnham Church in 1862:—"Open the rickety church-door. The eye is met by a green flash from the damp, mildewed walls, and by streaks of sky seen through the unceiled slates. The western end, with its early transitional single light, has not been much disturbed; but the rest of the window openings have been modernised and filled with common sashes, which are rotten, and let in wind and rain. The east end has a small square sash, such as is ordinarily provided for a scullery or any inferior office. Three of the worm-eaten, mousy pews are square, with a table fixed in the centre of each; a fourth forms three sides of a quadrangle that is occupied by a stone. Fungi abound, and the pavement is sodden with damp. Ruin is imminent, unless precautions are taken to avert it." Precautions were haply taken to avert it, and in 1870 Alnham Church underwent a careful restoration under the supervision of the late Mr. F. R. Wilson, architect, Alnwick.

Excepting that its venerable walls tell us of the period in which it was erected, very scant indeed are the records relating to the early history of Alnham Church and its pre-reformation rectors. Like most of our ancient parish churches, it would be built and endowed by the early owners of the manor, but towards the end of the twelfth century, William de Vescy granted Alnham Church to the monks of Alnwick Abbey;[1] and as its style of architecture corresponds with that period, it would appear that the monastic brethren had then rebuilt the church, as it was their usual custom either to rebuild or beautify churches given to them.

We learn from the *Taxatio Ecclesiastica*—a tax made on all church property about 1291—that Alnham Rectory was valued at £31.[2] The *Nonarum Inquisitions* of 1340 gives it at £37 13s. 4d.[3] The procuration fees in 1357 of the Rectoria de Alnham, *non valet ultra* iiij*s*.[4] In the Kings books (Henry VIII.), the living was valued at £3 7s.[5] as a discharged vicarage. During the reign of Elizabeth it was also £3 7s., then in the gift of the Crown. "Bishop Barnes' Injunctions," 1575 to 1587, thus records it:—"Vic. Alneham iij*l* vij*s*. the Quene." The following interesting notice of Alnham Church is found in Tate's History of Alnwick, Vol. I., p. 289. It is part of a formal document written in 1597, by Henry, the ninth Earl of Northumberland, to Thomas Percy. For many years this Thomas Percy, called the conspirator, one of the leaders in the Gunpowder Plot, and who was slain at Holbeach on the 8th of November, 1605, was constable of Alnwick Castle, and auditor and commissioner to the Earl, who appears to have had great regard for his kinsman, when he writes thus:—

"The very true and undoubted patrone of the parishe and churche of Alnehame sending greeting in the Lord God Everlasting, graunts by his writing to my wellbeloved Cosyn Thomas Percy, his executors, and assignees, the first and next

---

[1] Tate's History Alnwick, Vol. i., p. 64.

[2] Hodgson's Northumberland, Part iii., Vol. i., p. 353.

[3] Ibid., Part iii., Vol. iii., p. xl. (Preface.)

[4] Ibid., Part ii., Vol. iii., p. 427.

[5] Ibid., Part iii., Vol. iii., p. xliv. (Preface.)

advowsone, donation, nomination, presentation and free disposition of the Rectory and Parsonage of the Parish Church of Alneham."

The Oliverian Survey of Church Livings, 1650, says:—"That the Parish of Alneham was formerly a Viccaridge, the Earle of Nòrthumberland Patron thereof, Mr. Thompson Viccar, and the value of the said Viccaridge worth twenty pounds p'annu,"[1] while the Rentals and Rates of 1663 show that the neighbouring landowners then held the rectorial tithes. Amongst the papers belonging to the parish now in the possession of the Vicar is:—"A Terrier of the Gleeb Land belonging to the Vicaridg of Alneham in the County of Northumberland and Diocese of Durham. Imprs.—There is a Vicaridge-house which is an old Tower but ruinous and so hath been these twelve years by past it fell in Mr. Thompson's time.

2dly. Another low house where the Clerk lives at present.

3dly. A Little Close called the Church Meadow joying the Church-yard and lying upon the North side of the Church.

4thly. A priviledge in Alneham Common.

Given under our hands at Alneham the Eight day of December 1663,

Archibald fforster X his mark }
Christopher Jamison X his mark } Church Wardens."

The old tower has been repaired, and is now occupied by the vicar; the house in which the clerk lived has disappeared, and the privilege in Alnham Common appears to have been lost.

In the Proceedings of the Newcastle Society of Antiquaries, Vol. iv. (New Series), p. 235, is found the following description of Alnham Church Communion Plate and Bell:—

"There is a small church here, consisting of chancel, nave, and two transepts. The nave had formerly a north aisle of three bays, as shewn by the walled-up arches; fragments of

[1] Hodgson's Northumberland, Part iii., Vol. iii., p. lxxvi. (Preface.)

two mediæval grave covers have been made use of in filling up. There are four mediæval grave covers forming part of the chancel floor. The chancel arch is of rude Transitional work. In the churchyard are three socketted bases of crosses. The communion plate consists of four pieces :—

I. CUP, 6⅝ inches high, 3¾ inches diameter at mouth, 3½ inches at base. Egg-shaped bowl, 4 inches deep. Plain incurved stem, reeded base. Five hall-marks under base: i., maker's initials, H. C.; ii., lion passant gardant; iii., leopard's head, crowned; iv., London, year letter *n*, for 1788; v., King's head. Inscribed on side—*The Gift of | Mrs. Collingwood | of Unthank | to | Alnham Church | Anno Xti., 1788.*

II. PATEN, 7 inches diameter, rim 1⅛ inch wide, with moulded edge 2 inches high. Open stand, 3¼ inches diameter. Three marks: i., maker's initials, E.E | B | J.W., for E. Barnard and Sons; ii., A.; iii., cross on shield; and No. 133. Inscribed in centre—PRESENTED | TO THE | PARISH OF ALNHAM | BY THE | REVD. G. SELBY THOMSON, M.A. | VICAR | 1853.

III. Small, straight-sided FLAGON, 7 inches high 8½ to acorn knop on lid. Spout, Diameter at mouth 2½ inches, at base 4 inches. Five hall-marks: i., makers' mark, H.W | & CO.; ii., crown, for Sheffield; iii., lion passant gardant; iv., Sheffield, year letter H, for 1875, and v., Queen's head. Inscribed round bottom edge—**Given to Alnham Church by the Congregation & Friends, 1875.—M. Lazenby, Vicar. W. Brown, Ch.-Warden.**

IV. BRASS ALMS DISH, 9¾ inches diameter. Inscribed round rim: "✠ Lay vp for yourselves treasures in heaven."

In the turret at the west end of the church is a bell, which Mr. Wilson (Churches of Lindisfarne) says is inscribed :—

ALNHAM NOV. 1759.

The Registers of Alnham, from which we give the following extracts, date from 1714. There must have been an older one ; but, as the living of Alnham was held for many years by the rector of Ilderton, owing, probably, to the vicarage tower of Alnham being uninhabitable, it is just possible that the older records may be incorporated in the registers of Ilderton :—

BAPTISMS.

1714, Dec. 28.—George S. to Mr. Robert Alder in Prendwick.

1766, May 14.—Margaret Daughter of Alexander Collingwood Esq. of Unthank.

1768, Feb. 19.—Isabella Daughter of Alex. Collingwood Esq. of Unthank.

1772, Oct. 20.—Elizabeth Daughter of Francis and Elizabeth Collingwood of Prendick.

1773, Jan. 19.—John Son of David and Jane Bolam of Unthank West Field.

1789, Oct. 11.—Adam Son of Thos. Towns Alnham Mill.

1792, Nov. 13.—James Son of Will[m] and Mary Green.

1795, June 9.—Ann Posthumous Daughter of Will[m] Snowdon late of Scranwood.

1804, Dec. 2.—William, Son of William Holmes of the 11th Regiment of the Army of Reserve and Anne his wife Unthank West Field.

MARRIAGES.

1717.—John Wood and Ann Burn Married the week after Martinmass 1717.

1720, Sept. 29.—Mr. James Gladstains and Mrs. Margery Alder were Married Sept. 29, 1720, in Alnham Church by Mr. James Allgood Rector of Ingram.
(Sep 29 St Michael & All Angels 1720)

1723, Nov. 28.—John Forster in Prendwick and Ann Hunter in Morpeth.

1732, Aug. 13.—Mr. Benjamin Adams in the Parish of Felton & Mrs. Elizabeth Collingwood of Little Ryle in Whittingham Parish.

1754, Dec. 11.—Walter Ker of the Parish of Chatton & Dorothy Collingwood of the Parish of Alnham were Married in Alnham Church by Licence December 11th in the year 1754 by me Geo. Lindsay, Vicar.

This marriage was solemized between us ... ... { Walter Ker. Dorothy Ker *alias* Collingwood.

In the presence of us { Thos. Collingwood. Thos. Cuthbertson.

1771, May 5.—The Banns of Marriage between James Davison and Mary Turnbull both of this Parish were duly published on Sundays the 14th, 21st and 28th of April anno. 1771 by me Willm Smith, Curate. The said James Davison & Mary Turnbull were Married in this Church by Banns on the fifth Day of May in the year of our Lord one thousand seven hundred and seventy one by me Willm Smith, Curate.

Witness { Thos. Dixon. James Turnbull.

This Marriage was solemnized by us { James Davison. Mary her X mark. Turnbull.

BURIALS

1727, May 12.—Geo. Elliot in Screnwood.

1729, Dec. 4.—Ann Relict of Christofer Davison of Alnham Burnhead.

1734, Mar. 26.—George Vint in Eslington.

1736, Oct. 19.—Mrs. Ann Alder in Prendick.

1741, Mar. 17.—Mary wife of Wm. Skelly.

1770, Jany. 2.—Mr. Percival Collingwood from Prendick.

1776, Jany. —Bilhah Vint from Islington.

1792, Mar. 9.—Mary Robinson from Unthank West Field.

From a mass of entries in the parish minute and account book, relating to parochial matters during the last century, we extract the following, which, in their own peculiar way, give us a side glance into the manners and customs of the older inhabitants of the parish, as well as giving us a list of old family and place names, several of which are yet well known, whilst some are nearly out of the remembrance of the present generation :—

1766. "Memo.—The Sequestration of the Vicarage of Alnham was read in Alnham Church on Sunday the 14th of Sep. Anno. 1766 in the time of Divine Service by

William Smith, Curate.

Witness—Thos. Dixon."

1775. May 15.—"Att a meeting of the Churchwardens and as many of the foure & twenty as thought fitt to Attend, Notice being duly Given itt is hereby Agreed that Francis Collingwood for Prendick Town foott and James Davidson for Mr. Clenels land be appointed Churchwardens for the Insueing year.

(Signed) John Bolam Churchwarden for Blackchesters.
John Brown being Appointed Churchwarden & Did nott appear or did nott serve in his office."

1775. May 29.—"Att a Meeting of ye fower & twenty, att ye sametime John Bolam ye Old Churchwarden after all Disbursments their is Returned into ye New Churchwardens hands — Francis Collingwood & James Davidson ye New Churchwardens ye sume of one pound fifteen shillinges.

(Signed) Fran. Collingwood.
Jas. Davidson.

Henry Ilderton. Thomas Snowdon.
John Errington. Martin his X mark Ilderton."

"Weddenesday For Easter Week

Aprile 7, 1779

Att a Meeting of the Churchwardens and as many of The fower and Twenty as thought fit to attend Notice Being Duly Given it is There by agreed, (&c &c).

For Licquer this Day 8s. 6d."

"Cash Received from the Parishioners of Alnham For the use of the Parish Church for the year 1783.

		£	s.	d.
Alexr. Collingwood Esqr.	7 antients	2	15	3
His complyment to the Parish		2	2	0
Henry Ilderton	...7 antients	4	6	11
Elly Reed ...	...7 antients	3	10	7
Edwd. Potts ...	...7 antients	2	16	0
Wm. Lumsdon	...7 antients	2	3	9
Jno. Storey ...	...7 antients	1	6	10
Wm. Foster ...	...7 antients	1	8	0
Esqr. Clennell	...7 antients	0	8	9
The Vicars		0	5	0
Cash in hand		0	2	6
		21	5	7
Thomas Snowdon		0	6	9
		£21	12	4

Cash Disburst for the Use of the Parish Church of Alnham for the year 1783.

	£	s.	d.
To George Lindsey for Workman Ship	8	5	11½
To Mr. Hay for Deals and Wood	6	16	1
To William Gill for Nails ...	1	1	7½
To a Cloath & Napkin for the Communion Table	0	11	0
Att the Michaell Court... ...	0	6	6
To Dinners Att the three Courts...	0	9	0
To Henry Ilderton for Caring home the Wood...	0	8	4
To Laying the Flags	0	8	0
To Court Charges May 6, 1784	0	8	6
To Getting a Licence for the Vicar	0	6	0
To Thos. Jobson for Carring home Deals	0	5	0
To Licquer	0	2	3
To four Pair of Bans	0	2	0
To Robert Moole	0	1	6
To John Potts	0	1	0
To Christopher Davison ...	0	1	0
To Surplus Wishing	0	3	0
To Thomas Snowdon	0	2	6
	19	19	3
To Glazing the West Window	0	1	6
	£20	0	9
2 Bussims 5.	21	1	2

In 1813, George Snowdon signs himself as "C.Wardner," and in 1815 the name of George Buddle is amongst the signatures in the Vestry books, while that of Andrew Tully, who was Parish Clerk for many years, is frequently met with.

We might here note that Mr. Wm. Brown, the present Clerk, Sexton, and Churchwarden, has held the office of Parish Clerk and Sexton for no less than 42 years, and that of Churchwarden for 22 years.

"Names of Occupiers in Alnham Parish liable to stand Churchwardens by regular rotation, as under, viz.:—

1819.—Stephen Atkinson, Alnham ... ... 1st.
1820.—John Chrisp, Prendwick ... ... 2nd.
1821.—John C. Tarleton Esq., Colld. Ho. ... 3rd.
1822.—John Snowdon, Screenwood ... ... 4th.
1823.—Anthy. Marshall, Alnham ... ... 5th.
1824.—Adam Atkinson Esq., Alnm. Moor ... 6th.
1825.—Geo. Crawford, Alnham ... ... 7th.
1826.—Aurther Storey, Heselton ... ... 8th.
1827.—Thomas Pattinson, West Unthank ... 9th."

Within the walls of the church, and on the green sward of the quiet "God's Acre" outside, are several quaint tablets and moss-grown gravestones, denoting the burial places of past generations of those who, during the last two centuries, were the "indwellers" of this remote hill parish. Our space, and, perchance, the patience of our readers, will only admit a copy or two of these interesting records. The first is the inscription on a mural tablet on the west pier of the south transept arch, erected in memory of the Collingwoods, who, in the parish of Alnham, as well as in the neighbouring parish of Whittingham, and other parts of the county, were, at one time, a numerous and important family:—

"Below this Voult lyes the Body
of William Collingwood of Prindick
who this life departed Sept. 18th
1763 in the 43d year of his age
Also Percival Collingwood of
Prendick died December 31 · 1769
in the 31st year of his age."

The other is laid on the floor of the church beneath the west window, and bears an inscription in fine old block letters, arranged in the following curious manner:—

ANOV
S ALDE
R DOVGH
TER TO I
OHN AL
DER. 1611.

In former years old social customs were observed with much spirit in the parish of Alnham. The following incident connected with Alnham Church may be given as illustrating the Marriage Customs of the past generations:—"June 12, 1840: Married at Alnham Church, by the Rev. G. Wood, William, second son of Mr. Michael Thompson, long topsman to Adam Atkinson, Esq., of Lorbottle House, to Ann, third daughter of Mr. William Taylor, head shepherd to the late Mr. Crisp of Prendwick, and then holding the same situation under his nephew, Mr. H. Crisp. Mr. Crisp regaled the bridal party, consisting of upwards of twenty couples, to breakfast; and, after the ceremony, a keenly contested race for the 'spurs' took place, from the church door to the bridegroom's house, which was won in grand style by a lady, although matched against some of the most celebrated sportsmen of the country."[1]

We supplement the foregoing account with a description of the wedding, as narrated to the writer by a spectator:—As a great number of the competitors in the race for the "spurs" at this wedding were hill shepherds, many of whom did not possess a horse, and therefore had to borrow, the whole country-side was scoured far and near for mounts. A Mr. Ogle, then farmer at the Follions, had a "misteched" thorough-bred mare which Nicholas Maughan, servant-man with Mr.

[1] Sykes' Locai Records.

Michael Thompson, secured for himself as being likely to win the "spurs" if properly ridden. Mounting at Prendwick, where the cavalcade met, they proceeded to Alnham. When *en route* for the church, several of the party set off at full gallop to the rendezvous, Mr. Stephen Atkinson's, at Alnham—where the quadrupeds had to be stabled during the ceremony—Nicholas and the thoroughbred leading the van; but Nicholas, not being quite so much at home on the "pig skin" as on his native heath, turned at too sharp an angle when entering the stableyard gateway, ran foul of the "sneck" and ripped the mare's shoulder open. Nothing daunted, he still persisted in the race, but this unfortunate accident lost him all chance of winning the "spurs." At Alnham a large concourse of people were assembled to witness the ceremony, besides the usual contingent of "hempy" callants, who first looked after the horses and then after the pennies which were "scammelled" at the church door. The wedding party having remounted their steeds—the bride on a pillion behind the bridegroom—away they went "helter skelter" over Prendwick Hill, through the flat by the Cross, past Cobden Old Walls, and when "Yeldom Moor" hove in sight the weddingers were welcomed by the good dame and her staff of assistants with a hearty cheer, accompanied by a chorus of barking collies and the firing of guns. The wedding dinner was of a substantial character and plenty of it, the cooking thereof having employed the mistress and the maidens for several days before the event; therefore the numerous guests—their appetites sharpened by the bracing air of the hills—did more than ample justice to the good things provided for them. After dinner, there was drinking of toasts, singing of songs, sports, dancing, and merry-making which lasted far into the small hours of the next morning.

The following description of another celebrated race for the "Kail," which took place at Alnham, may be of interest to our readers:—

On the 28th of December, 1849, Joseph, son of James

Turnbull, of Netherton, in the parish of Alwinton, and Mary, third daughter of John Amos, of Ewartly Shank, in the parish of Alnham, were married at Alnham Church. This being the marriage of a son and daughter of two of the oldest families in the district, the auspicious event was celebrated in the good old style with great rejoicings and festivities. The bridal party, consisting of about a dozen couples and ten gentlemen friends, accompanied by a fiddler, playing appropriate tunes, set out on foot from Ewartly Shank, the residence of the bride's father, to Alnham Church, a distance of three miles over the hills. The marriage ceremony was performed by the Rev. G. S. Thomson, Vicar of Alnham, and no sooner was the nuptial knot tied, than, in accordance with the old Northumbrian custom, the "best man"—on this occasion Robert Smart Turnbull—secured the "garters" by being the first to kiss the bride :—

> "He took the bride about the neck
> And kissed her lips with such a clamorous smack,
> That at the parting all the church did echo."

Then having duly jumped the "petting stones," the weddingers adjourned to the house of Stephen Atkinson, a well-known and much respected farmer, in the "Yeldom" of former days, where a sumptuous breakfast was provided for the whole company, presided over by the kind-hearted vicar, who, with his genial presence and merry laugh, was the very life and soul of the party.

> "A man he was to all the country dear,
> And passing rich with forty pounds a year."

Although yet early in the day, dancing began immediately after breakfast to the merry-going tune of "Tallygorum" (Tullochgorum), and it was not until past the hour of noon that the bridal party bethought themselves of returning to the "Shank." Thereupon, leaving the hospitable roof of Stephen Atkinson—their number now augmented to fifty or sixty persons—the joyous party proceeded to climb the hills beyond Alnham towards Ewartly Shank, which, we might inform our readers, is a shepherd's house in the centre of a large sheep farm situated amongst the Cheviot Hills, three miles north-west from the village of Alnham, and stands on the ridge between the Fore burn and the Shank burn, whose united waters flow into the river Breamish at Alnham Moor. Lofty hills surround the Shank on all sides—High Knowes (1,294 feet) on the south, Cushat Law (2,020 feet) and Hogden (1,797 feet) on the west, with Het Hill (1,063 feet), Scaud Knowe (1,500 feet), and Shill-More (1,734 feet) to the north. On reaching the elevated ridges of High Knowes—from which point the first glimpse of the Shank is obtained—the young men of the party began to prepare themselves for that important event in the day's proceedings—the running for the "Kail." Amongst the competitors—all of whom were "yald" young fellows belonging to the country-side—were Willie Amos i' the Shank, John Burn i' Yeldom Moor, Jock i' Linsheels, Robert Turnbull and Tom Chisholm i' Netherton. Just at that moment the excitement was greatly increased by seeing old Peggy Amos, mother of the bride, standing in front of the Shank, about a mile distant, waving a large bright-coloured silk handkerchief—the prize they were going to run for. The cry at once arose—"the Kail! the Kail!" and swift as a herd of deer the impatient hillmen started on their race to the Shank "o'er mountain, moss, and moor." Utterly regardless of the biting north wind which on that cold December afternoon came sweeping down from the lofty heights of the great Cheviot, those hardy Northumbrians "kept pitching off their duds as they ran," coats and vests, and the various etceteras of a gentleman's costume, flying in the wind, to be gathered up by the friends and spectators, who with all speed were following up the rear. At length, after a severe contest—and not without a considerable amount of scraffling through the bogs and open drains, accompanied with many a "killiecouper" amongst the bent and heather, not to mention numberless ludicrous mishaps, not altogether pleasant to the runners, but highly entertaining to the onlookers—the goal was reached by the breathless, coatless, hatless, mud-bespattered troop, amid the barking of dogs, the squealing of pigs, and the shouting of men, women, and children, and Jock i' Linsheels was acknowledged by all to be the winner of the "Kail," although the unlucky young chiel who had the misfortune to win the "mell" declared that the "race was won by a fluke." By the time the panting competitors had recovered their "wind" and resumed their outer garments, and otherwise made themselves fit for decent society, the gong was sounded for dinner :—

"At last the beef appears in sight,
The groom moves slow the pond'rous weight;
Then haste is made, the table clad,
No patience till the grace is said—
Swift to the smoking beef they fly!"

The dinner being excellent, the appetites of the guests being also excellent, it is needless to say that the viands vanished in a most remarkable manner, which astonished that worthy woman, Mrs. Amos. But such is the love of dancing amongst the hill population of Northumberland, that by the time the chairman had given the usual toast of "Bride and Bridegroom," the "Next Happy Couple," and so on, the feet of the young folks were itching for the floor, and the fiddler had already "roselet" his bow ready for action. At last :—

"—— All are full, the meat away,
The table drawn, the pipers play,
The bridegroom first gets on the floor,
And dances all the maidens o'er."

The dance, on this occasion, was led off by the "best man" and the bride to the tune of the "Keel Row." The fun and jollity continued with unabated spirit throughout the evening, and it was not until long past the "wee short hour ayont the twal," that the merry-makers—having sung "God save the Queen" in the most loyal and hearty manner—dispersed to their several homes, amid the lonely valleys of the Cheviots.

CHAPTER IV.

SCRENWOOD.

An Old Border Manor of Importance—Garrisons in Horsley's Tower at Screnwood—Probable Site of the Tower—Old Place Names—Early Notices of Screnwood—Part of the Barony of De Vescy, held by Walter Bataill and Thomas Bunte, 1252—William de Middleton, 1289—Sir John de Strivelyn—The Horsleys, from 1358—Roger de Horsley—Sir Thomas Horsley the Royalist—The Riddells of Felton—The Selbys of Biddleston—Fire at Screnwood in 1659—John Snowdon of Screnwood, a Northumbrian Character—Old Social Customs—Notice of Mr. Thomas Forster, of Screnwood, by "D."

THE ancient manor of Screnwood is about half-a-mile to the south of Alnham, and may be said to be on the boundary line that there divides the vales of the Coquet and the Aln. Screnwood House and hamlet of to-day stands on the north bank of the Rithe, just where that turbulent little stream issues into the open valley from between the steep slopes of the Castle-Hill and the Rig-Hill. During the troublous days upon the Borders, when the manor was held by the old Northumberland family, the Horsleys, Screnwood was, as one of the places of defence in the Middle Marches, of no small importance. An official report of the state of the Borders, made in 1509, says:—"Thomas Horsley of 'Skyrnwood' has 20 men;"[1] and a similar return, made in 1526, records that "John Horsley of Screnwood from Scotland 4 mile, and from Riddisdale 3 mile, may dispend of his father's land 10 pound by the year and in fee of my Lord of Northumberland 10 pound by the year. He may serve the King with 30 horsemen, and is a true wise borderer."[2] While in the Survey of 1541 we read—"At Scrynwood is a toure & a barmekyn of the Inherytance of John Horseley esquier kepte

[1] Hodgson Hinde's History of Northumberland, p. 340. [2] Ibid., p. 348.

in very good repac'ons."[1] Of this Border tower nothing now remains, but we are informed that some years ago the ruins of a large house, with walls of great thickness, having pointed doorways and mullioned windows, besides other old foundations, were standing in the green field east of the present Screnwood House. It is very probable that these were the remains of the Border tower and barmekyn of the Horsleys.

"Shirmounddene," "Shirmondesden," or "Chirmundisden,"[2] and "Helm Park," are old place or field names frequently found mentioned in connection with the manor in times past, but which have entirely disappeared, unless "Screnwood Park" be a survival of "Helm Park." Other notable field names at Screnwood are "The Town Green," "Pace Hill," "Chapel Knowe," "Slaughter Bush Field," "Early Dale," "Moffatt's Letch."

The manor of Screnwood first emerges from the mists of antiquity as one of the possessions of the De Vescys, the early lords of Alnwick. It is mentioned in the "Testa de Nevill," a document drawn up in the time of Henry III. and Edward I., which contains a list of landholders, with the names of their vills and manors, and the various tenures by which they were held, as being part of the barony of William de Vescy, who died in 1252, when it was held in subfeudation by Walter Bataill and Thomas Bunte, who hold "Sc'venwood" by the third part of one knight's fee. The same Walter Bataill also held half of Linnshiels from Gilbert de Umframville.[3] In 1289 the heirs of William de Middleton held "Scranewoode," but on the death of John de Middleton, a rebel, "Shanewode villa" was conferred upon Sir John de Strivelyn, a nobleman of Scottish descent, who held it until his death in 1378,[4] but before this date, viz., in 1358, the Horsley's also held lands in

[1] C. J. Bates' Border Holds, Vol. i., p. 43.

[2] Hodgson Hinde's History of Northumberland, p. 348.

[3] History Berwickshire Naturalists' Club, Vol. x., No. iii., p. 550.

[4] Escheats 2 Richd. II., Hodgson's Northumberland, Part iii., Vol. ii., p. 249.

Screnwood. Roger de Horsley, who, in 1320, was one of the Keepers of the truce between the English and the Scots, and in 1337-8 captain of Bamburgh Castle, died in 1358 possessed of the manor of Screnwood, and lands and tenements at Horsley. In 1509 Thomas Horsley was the owner of Screnwood; John Horsley in 1526 and 1541; and in the "Book of Rates and Rentals," 1663, Sir Thomas Horsley is recorded as the proprietor of "Scarnwood," of which the annual value was £100; this Sir Thomas Horsley was one of the Royalists, on whom Charles II. intended to confer the honour of "Knight of the Royal Oak." His name also occurs among a list of the gentry of Northumberland in "Blome's Britannia," 1673, of Long Horsley, Knt.[1] Eventually Screnwood came into the possession of the Riddells of Felton Park and Swinburn Castle. In 1827 it was the property of Ralph Riddell, Esq., of Felton Park, but now forms part of the Biddlestone estate, the ancient domain of the Selbys.

We learn from an entry in the Rothbury Church Books that a fire had taken place at Screnwood, in 1659. Many an interesting item of local history can be gathered from the pages of our old Parish Registers, which well repays all the tedious labour of research. The entry referred to says:—"1659 Thomas Moore of Scranwood had two shill:—out of ye Parish Sesse in Lieu of a Collection by order of Sessions to be made for repayre of his losses by fire." In those days ordinary dwelling houses were mostly covered with a thatch of straw or heather, therefore it was no unusual occurrence for a whole row of cottages to be burnt to the ground by a single spark from a chimney. When such a disaster did occur, collections were made by orders or "briefs" in all the parish churches in the county, for the benefit of those poor householders who had sustained any loss.

During the first quarter of the present century Screnwood was farmed by John Snowdon, an amusing character, of whom

[1] History Berwickshire Naturalists' Club, Vol. x., No. iii., p. 555.

the following incidents are related:—Scrainwood, with its old low-thatched farm house and offices *en suite*, its brook in front "wi' toddling din" from the "black moss," and the heights of "the rigg" refreshing its green haughs and filling the creel of the angler after a May flood—the peaceful home of John Snowdon, whose imperturbable temper and fund of humour were never ruffled by the freaks of fortune, which makes

> "The best laid schemes o' mice an' men
> Gang aft aglee."

Mr. Snowdon and Mr. Henderson, of Langleeford, were old familiar acquaintances:—

> "Monnie a night they'd merry been,
> And monnie mair they hop'd to be."

Mr. Henderson would at times relate from his inexhaustible store of anecdote. Being with Mr. Snowdon at Rothbury fair, and while the market night was growing late and Mrs. Snowdon humming at home "Jackey stops lang at the fair," Mr. Snowdon, whose weight was fully twenty stones, requested a grocer of the company to give him a receipt for twenty stones of sugar. On arriving home with Mr. Henderson, and finding Mrs. Snowdon's patience exhausted, her husband told her, as a solatium to her wounded feelings, that he had bought her twenty stones of sugar. "It shan't be brought into the house." Giving his wife a kiss, "It's a' here already, hinney." Thinking that her arrivals had had more than enough of what Neil Gow, with touching pathos, sings farewell to, the bottles were taken off the table. Mrs. Snowdon retired to bed, exemplifying that feminine ambition—

> "The high, the low, the great, the small,
> In poverty or riches;
> A common will pervades them all—
> 'Tis I shall wear the breeches."

Mr. Henderson's antipathies to uxorious despotic rule condemned what he termed an act of henpecking. "Keep quiet, Henderson; we'll soon have the bottle again," says Mr.

Snowdon, ringing the bell, and giving an order to George Howey, an old servant, to "saddle the mare; I'm going to set Mr. Henderson home." The maid, alarmed, runs up to her mistress, crying, "The maister's ordered George Howey to saddle the mare to set Mr. Henderson to Langleeford." "Take them the keys, and they may sit as long as they choose," replies Mrs. Snowdon. "Now, you see, Henderson, there's a way of managing a wife without flying in a passion," says his host.[1] For many years Screnwood was in the occupation of a member of the Forster family, of Burradon, of whose death, in 1878, we give the following notice, from the pen of a late well-known writer:—

"DEATH OF MR. THOMAS FORSTER.—Another link connecting the present with a past generation has given way under the weight of years. Mr. Tom Forster! a name synonymous in his sphere with authority; a prominent actor upon a wide stage in the character of 'guide, philosopher, and friend in the drama of rural life.' He was stern in the maintenance of opinions founded upon facts; Conservative of customs which bore the stamp of the wisdom of our ancestors, and an unmerciful enemy to shams. The *petit maitre* writhed under the caustic force of his sarcasm. Having seen many vicissitudes in men and manners, theories found little favour in Mr. Forster's mind till tested by experience. Faithful as a friend and valuable as a counsellor, his advice to explorers was always founded upon the maxims of the experienced pilot. Plausibility in vain attempted to falsify the quotients of his estimates. He was regarded as a mentor in arbitrations upon the farm, and as judge at stock sales—

> 'Poising the cause in justice's equal scales,
> Whose beam stands sure, whose rightful cause prevails.'

As tenant of Scrainwood for nearly half a century, and of other farms in Northumberland, besides his own estate, Mr. Forster's memory will live in Coquetdale. The very few remaining

[1] Reminiscences of Samuel Donkin, p. 20.

companions of his youth may cast a retrospective glance through the dim vista of eighty years, and exclaim—

> 'We sail the sea of life; a calm one finds,
> And one a tempest; and the voyage o'er,
> Death is the quiet haven of us all.'"

—D., in *Newcastle Journal.*

CHAPTER V.

PRENDWICK.

A Member of the Old Barony of De Vescy, held under the Tenure of Socage by William de Walays—Walter de Prendwyc—John de Unthanc—William Cocus and Gilbert de Glentedon—Granted by Edward III. to William de Emeldon, 1332—John de Coupland, 1344—Thomas de Motherby, 1370—Subsequent Owners—Alder and his "lytle toure newlye buylded," 1541—Collingwood, 1663—Byne—Carr, 1792—Carr-Ellison—Tenant Farmers—William Lumsdain, 1799—John Reed, 1811—John Chrisp, 1827, a Typical Northumbrian Farmer—Extent of Prendwick—Its Hills and Fells—Lost in a Snowstorm—Field and Place Names—Prendwick Lamb Sales—Harvest Supper—A Northumbrian Kirn.

PRENDWICK, which stretches along the base of the hills to the north-east of Alnham, was in early times, along with Alwinton, Biddlestone, Clennell, Netherton, Burradon, Sharperton, Farnham, Alnham, Screnwood, and other manors, a member of the extensive barony of the De Vescy's,[1] but unlike Alnham and Screnwood it was held by several persons under the more servile tenure of socage.[2] We find in the "Testa de Nevill," under "Socagium baronie de Vesci," that "William de Walays" holds one carucate[3] of land in "Prendwyc" for two shillings. "Walter de Prendwyc" holds one carucate for half a mark.[4] "John de Unthanc" holds thirty acres in "Prendwyc," and in "Unthank" one carucate of land, and half a carucate for half a mark. Walter the son of Edmund holds thirty acres for five shillings. While "William Cocus" holds thirty acres for one pound of pepper, and "Gilbert de Glentedon" also holds thirty acres in "Prendwyc"

[1] Hodgson's Northumberland, Part iii., Vol. i., p. 209.

[2] Service rendered by a tenant to his lord by the Soc (Soke) or ploughshare.

[3] A ploughland of about one hundred acres in extent.

[4] A mark was a coin of the value of 13s. 4d.

for one pound of pepper.[1] In 1309, the De Vescys ceased to be the lords of Alnwick, and shortly after Prendwick appears to have been severed from the barony, for in 1332 Edward III. entrusts William de Emeldon with the charge of certain lands and appurtenances in "Prendewyk;" and the same monarch in 1344 grants to John de Coupland, for good service rendered to the king, the lands in "Prendwyk;" also certain lands in "Magna Ryhill" (Great Ryle) and other Northumbrian manors; and again in 1370, Thomas de Motherby obtains a grant from Edward III. of lands and tenements in "Ryhull" and "Prendewyk."[2] The next record of Prendwick and its owners is found as follows in the Border Survey of 1541:—"At Prendyke ys lykewyse a lytle toure newlye buylded by one Thomas Aldye gent. thinherytoure of the same." The Muster Roll of 1538 contains amongst the names of the armed men of Alndale who met on Abberwick Moor, those of "Thomas Allder, Robert Allder, and George Allder, Prendyk." The Alders were owners of land in Prendwick for upwards of two centuries. In 1663 George Alder and Robert Collingwood were the proprietors, the annual value then being £138,[3] and in the Northumberland Poll Book of 1747, Robert Alder appears as a freeholder in "Prendick," but in the list of voters in 1774, Francis Collingwood is the owner of Prendick and resides there. Whilst the Alders are found in various parts of the country—Daniel Alder at Adderstone, John Alder in London, Caleb Alder in Newcastle, Charles Alder and John Alder at Longframlington, each of whom had an interest in the county.

In 1792 the whole of the Prendwick estate was purchased from the representatives of the families of Byne and Alder

[1] A pair of gloves or a pound of pepper was a frequent rent under socage tenure.

[2] Exchequer Rolls. Hodgson's Northumberland, Part iii., Vol. ii., pp. 308, 318, 332.

[3] Book of Rates and Rentals in 1663. Hodgson's Northumberland, Part iii., Vol. i., p. 264.

by Ralph Carr, of Dunston Hill, co. Durham, great grandfather of the present owner, Mr. John Ralph Carr-Ellison. Prendwick was at that time, or shortly before, two distinct farms—Upper and Nether Prendwick. The tenant farmer at Prendwick, in 1799, was named William Lumsdain;[1] in 1811, John Reed;[2] and in 1827 we find the name of John Chrisp,[3] whose descendants in the third generation are now in the occupation of the "acras and carucates of Prendwyc."

"The similitude of John Chrisp," says the late Samuel Donkin in his Reminiscences, 1886, "has not appeared upon the agrarian stage of North Northumberland during the last half century. Dilettanteism would fail in pourtraying his characteristics — the ocular obliquity of foppishness would diverge from the manly figure. Mr. Chrisp's motto — 'Business: sport after'—the sowing sheet round the shoulders at seed time, with 'the lark rising wi' speckled breast' from the daisy 'to greet the purpling east'—the fork in hand in the hay field—the hook in harvest—the shears at the clippings—the plaid, with the collie, at lambing time; nothing incited his ridicule more than the gloved grieve behind a band of field workers."

Prendwick farm, besides the rich tillage lands lying in the valley of the Aln, includes within its boundary a wide expanse of high ground stretching to the north over towards the valley of the Breamish, being part of the southern range of the Cheviot hills. This extensive tract of pasture land consists of high and exposed ridges, with acres upon acres of rough fell lands, bogs, and morasses. It was amid these lonely wastes one stormy, drifty afternoon in the December of 1863, that "Nellie Heron," of Hartside, a person well known and much respected throughout the valleys of the Breamish and the Aln, unfortunately perished in the snow, while attempting to cross the hills from

[1] Muster Roll of the Cheviot Legion Volunteer Cavalry, 1803.

[2] Subscribers' List. Mackenzie and Dent's History of Northumberland, 1811.

[3] Parson and White's Directory, 1828.

Alnham to Hartside. A stone marks the spot at the "Shiel Bog," on Prendwick ground, where Mrs. Heron was found. This memorial is a freestone slab, about thirty inches high by nine inches square, much resembling a march stone, and contains the following inscription:—"Ellenor Heron, Departed Dec. 3rd, 1863."

Some of the most interesting field and place names on Prendwick farm are West, East, and Middle Floats. These are low-lying fields along the banks of the Aln.[1] Willow Tree field, Dove Cote field, Mill-Dam field, Church field, Long Bank, and others, give their own derivation; while March Gutters, Black Middens, and Maylies fields are not so clear. Older and more expressive names are found on the higher lands amongst the hills—such as Hart Law, Crow Plantation, Old Stell, and Craw-Crook Well, on Gair's Syke. "Thief's Road" is evidently a continuation of the "thieves' road," or "salters' road," that crosses the Breamish near Blakehope. On the ridge of the hill is "Watch Cairn," probably the spot where the men of Prendwick kept watch and ward in the old troublous Border days, when "The Passages from Prendeke to Engram" had to be watched nightly by six men. Further out is the Chesters, a solitary shepherd's house, where are the remains of a strong British Camp, containing several hut circles, surrounded by a double rampart. On the extreme western boundary of the farm is that part of Alnham Common, consisting of 366A. 0R. 12P., allotted to Prendwick on the division of the Common in 1776.

A small tract of land on the hills between Great Ryle and the Chesters is named on the Prendwick plans as "Prickly Knowes." We give a copy of a curious sale bill announcing an auction sale to be held at this place about the year 1740, which is bound up in Vol. I. of the Harbottle Presbyterian Church Records, along with many other quaintly-worded documents, ecclesiastical and otherwise, relating to the district.

[1] Grass growing on swampy ground is in some parts called "Float Grass."

Printing at that time would be costly, therefore the notice of the sale is written on a small sheet of paper measuring 5½ inches by 7, which would be duly posted on the doors of Harbottle Meeting House, to be read on Sunday morning by the members of the congregation while having the accustomed weekly chat and interchange of domestic news before entering their place of worship. Having fulfilled its mission of proclaiming the roup, the piece of paper has been utilized by the economical deacon, who appears to have kept the church accounts, for the back of this primitive poster is filled with a list of church collections, expenditure, and other items connected with Harbottle congregation for the years 1740 to 1745. The following is a verbatim copy of the notice :—

"These are to give notice to all manere of parsons thare will be a Sale of goods by way of Roupe one the 17 day of this month of May. Consisting of fresh young Cowes owsen Stots & Quies, a Cople of good Stood Mars and fols and other horses. Credit to May day next Insuing upon Responsable Security according to the maner and mening of Roupe att ye Place Caled Pricklaw Knowes near Prendick."

Before the establishment of Cattle Marts in the various centres throughout the county, "Prendwick Lamb Sale" was an annual event of much importance to Northumbrian flockmasters, whilst amongst the rural population of the Vale of the Aln "Prendwick Kirn" was a festive event of no less importance. In those old harvesting days of hook and sickle, the whole country-side was invited to the feast of the ingathering at Prendwick, when a night of merriment and social enjoyment ended the labours of the harvest. This old-world custom, the "Kirn Supper," a social gathering of the people which helped to foster that kindly feeling so desirable between master and men, as well as the occasion of much pleasant intercourse amongst friends and neighbours, is yet observed here and there in Northumberland ; and we rejoice to say that that rustic festival "Prendwick Kirn" is still in existence, and is at the end of each harvest carried out in the same spirit of liberal hospitality as in former years.

We have early recollections of a Northumbrian Kirn of the good old type, of which we shall here venture to give a description for the benefit of those of our readers who have not had the same good fortune. It was a beautiful moonlight night in the autumn of one of the "fifties," when we set forth with pleasurable anticipations to our first "Kirn Supper." The last load of corn had been safely led in, and every stack in the well-filled stackyard was covered and secured for the winter. Word of mouth invitations had been sent out a full week before the event to a large number of the friends and acquaintances of the farmer and his family. Amongst those invited were several good fiddlers, whose services would thus be secured for the night. About six o clock the visitors—some in gigs and some in long carts full of straw, others on foot in pairs, singles, or groups of threes and fours--began to arrive, when there was much handshaking, and many hearty greetings given and returned. The first part of the festive proceedings consisted of tea and spice cake—just such delicious cakes as only a Northumbrian housewife can handle on the hot girdle. As a piece of diversion amongst the younger members of the company, there was a ring, a sixpence, and a button, concealed between various pieces of cake and placed on a certain plate which was handed round, and it was highly amusing to see the caution used by the lads and lasses in choosing their piece, for they assuredly believed whoever amongst them got the button was certain to be an old maid or a bachelor—those who got the ring would be rich, but not be beloved—whilst the happy he or she who was lucky enough to get the ring were as certain that they would be first married. By the time tea was over all the guests had arrived; therefore, about eight o'clock, the whole party proceeded to the granary—a long loft above the barn—which had been thoroughly swept, and gaily decked with corn stalks and party-coloured ribbons, and lighted with dozens of home-made dips arranged in tin sconces around the walls, a huge stable lantern being hung at the top of the outside flight of stairs leading to the granary to light the steps of the guests as they went to and fro. A large kitchen table. on which stood a couple of chairs planted against the wall at one end of the granary, served as a platform for the musicians. After the fiddlers had screwed and scraped and twanged their instruments into tune, the Kirn began with the Keel Row Country Dance, led off by one of the farmer's sons and a lady visitor. Then followed in quick succession—without the formality of a programme—Scotch Reels, Threesome Reels, Sylph Reels, and Country Dances. The Corn Rigs, Highland Laddie, The Soldier's Joy, The Morpeth Rant, The Haymakers, The Triumph, and Haste to the Wedding being amongst the most popular, in the figures of which there could be introduced with good effect a variety of step-dancing such as the "treble," the single and double "shuffle," the "cut," and the "Highland Fling," all of which are now nearly out of fashion, but which were considered the acme of good dancing by our grandfathers and grandmothers. During the evening one or two of the most expert or "teached dancers" favoured the company by dancing a hornpipe. Often during the excitement of a Scotch Reel, when the tune was more than usually merry and the dancers in good glee, they would snap their fingers, stick up their thumbs, and, giving an extra jump, shout "Hoo! wor side yet!" Then, if the fiddler happened to be a bit of a wag, he ran his finger down the first string, producing a shrill, squeaking sound, the signal for each swain to salute his fair partner with a kiss; when the fiddler did this, he was said to "squeak the fiddle." Just in the middle of a country dance great fun and confusion was created by the sudden entrance into the ball room of two grotesquely dressed figures, one attired as an old man, the other as an old woman, wearing a coal scuttle bonnet—characters known as "Bessie and Jimmie"—a custom evidently a relic of the mummers of olden times. The two figures never spoke, but quickly cleared the floor of the dancers, and, motioning to the musicians to begin, they each performed, in splendid style, a well-known but difficult hornpipe, afterwards going round the company with the hat, and collecting sixpence from each person for the benefit of the fiddlers. Shortly after this, two young men who had been amissing for some time, stealthily entered the granary. These were the two mummers "Bessie and Jimmie." During the course of the evening sandwiches and ale were served out *ad libitum*, a "steady hand" having charge of the beer barrel. For the accommodation of the older members, or those who did not care to dance, there was a corner reserved in the farm house, where they could enjoy themselves with a hand at whist, a friendly crack, or a quiet pipe. When the Kirn was drawing to a close, well on in the small hours of the morning, a young farmer who, during the evening, had acted as a sort of M.C., very quietly locked the granary door on the inside, put the key in his pocket, and announced the "Cushion Dance," at which there was no small stir, and strong expressions of disapprobation amongst the girls at so arbitrary a proceeding; but whether the opposition was real or pretended, the door was locked, and the dance began. The "Cushion Dance" is described as a country dance, in which one person held a cushion while the rest of the company danced in a ring singing :—

"The best bed, the feather bed,
The best bed ov' a';
The best bed i' wor hoose
Is clean pea straw."

At the end of the chant the cushion was laid at the feet of a favoured person and knelt on. The person thus saluted kissed the kneeling suppliant, and then took up the cushion in turn and danced round with it as the first had done, all singing, again and again, the refrain: "That dance of dances, the *cushion dance*." [1]

---

[1] Northumberland Words, by R. O. Heslop.

By the time the cushion dance was over, which brought to a happy conclusion the evening's festivities, the company were all fairly well paired, or in the words of the old May Pole Song:—

> "For every he has got him a she,
> And the minstrel's standing by,
> For Willy has gotten his Jill, and Johnny has got his Joan,
> To jig it, jig it, jig it, jig it up and down."

CHAPTER VI.

COLLINGWOOD HOUSE ESTATE.

GREAT RYLE.

Its Early Owners—Uchtredo de Rihul, 1177—Roger Fitz-Ralph, 1235—Collingwood, 1541—Lord Ravensworth, 1848—A Pele Tower at Ryle—Ryle and its Inhabitants Fifty Years Ago—Field, Place, and Hill Names—Incident on Ryle Hills during the Wars of the Roses, 1463.

LITTLE RYLE.

The Manor held by Richard of Ryle, 1295—By Henry, son of John, son of Henry, 1350—William Swan, 1429—Collingwoods, early in the Sixteenth Century—John Collingwood Tarleton, 1827—Lord Ravensworth, 1848—Collingwood House Dismantled—Bassel-House at Little Ryle—Tenant Farmers—Field Names.

RYLE MILL

The Mill of the Manor—Collingwoods in 1663—The Taits of Ryle Mill—Happy Memories of the Harvest Field at Ryle Mill—Place and Field Names.

COLLINGWOOD House Estate, as its name denotes, once belonged to the Collingwoods, but is now the property of Lord Ravensworth, and consists of the farms and hamlets of Great Ryle, Little Ryle, Ryle Mill, Collingwood House, and Unthank, all of which, with the exception of Unthank, are in the parish of Whittingham.

GREAT RYLE.

Great Ryle, or, as it is termed in old deeds, "Ryhull," "Richill Magna," and "Ryhille," was held in the reign of Henry III. by Roger Fitz-Ralph, the King's forester, who at the same time held the manors of Cartington and Ditchburn. An earlier record is found in the Pipe Roll of 23rd Henry II. (1177), where Roger de Stutevill, sheriff of the county, renders an account of "one mark of Uchtredo de Rihul." This was probably for drengage. The Royalty of Great Ryle was in the hands of Gilbert de Umfreville of Harbottle and Redesdale in the first year of Edward II., and eventually the manor came to be possessed by the famous Northumbrian family, the Collingwoods. In the list of Border Fortresses of 1415 there is no record of a tower either at Great Ryle or Prendwick, but in the Survey of 1541 we find a pele tower at both places, "newly buylded," the result, probably, of those harrying inroads committed by the Scots amongst the hills of Upper Alndale in 1532.[1] The Survey of 1541 says:—"At Great Ryle there hath one Thomas Collingewood, gent., newlye buylded a toure upon the Inherytaince of Robt. Collingewood And is mynded to buylde lykewise a barmekyn about the same as his power may serve thereunto." Not a vestige remains of the towers of Great Ryle or Prendwick.

The hamlet of Great Ryle, some forty or fifty years ago, consisted of several long, low-roofed thatched houses, scattered here and there along the green slopes of Ryle Hill. These primitive dwellings, with their stout, rough-hewn oaken beams and rafters, the ends of which, instead of resting on the walls, were carried down inside and let into the earth, to prevent the thrust on the mud-built walls, were at that time not uncommon in the district. The building was usually divided into two "ends" by a stout party wall, which contained the fireplace and the wide, open chimney.[2] There was only one outer door, which opened into one of the "ends," called the "entry." In this "entry" the cow was housed during winter. The cow and the family thus lived under the same roof, and both went out and in by the same door. On the right or left, as the case

[1] State Papers, Record Series iv., iiii., p. 625.

[2] It was the custom at that time for the farm labourers, or "Northumbrian Hinds," to carry with them from place to place their own iron bars and fire-stones to form the grate, as well as a large iron pot which had to be fixed in the fireplace; a few years before this they even carried their windows about with them.

might be, on entering the outer door, an inner doorway in the party wall led into the dwelling room of the family, the ceiling of which consisted of bass mats or strong calico. Across the middle of the floor, fronting the fireplace and dividing the apartment, stood the old-fashioned "box beds," with sliding doors, in which, notwithstanding the modern notions of sanitation and hygiene, there slept soundly and well many a hardy son of the soil. Behind the beds was a small space called the "in-bye," where often another bed was set up, and where articles of domestic use were also kept, such as flour, meal, bread, the Sunday clothes "Kist," and other goods and chattels. A single window of four small panes lighted the house, a single pane the "in-bye," whilst all the light needed in the cow-house and "entry" was admitted by the door. These old thatched houses at Great Ryle, in which many years ago lived Peggy Peary and Andrew, Wullie Laidler, Wullie Potts, Bob Reay, Sam'l Henderson, Jimmy Bowey, Jenny Chisholm, and Andrew Tait, have long since disappeared, and comfortable modern, well-lighted dwellings now occupy their place.

To the lovers of local lore field names are always of interest, therefore we here give the names of some of those at Great Ryle:—West Horsden Hill, Whinney Field, Middle Horsden Hill, North Hill, East Hill, The Croft, The Hill, Mere Burn Field,[1] Low Cow Hill, High Cow Hill, Garden Close, North Cow Close, Front Field, Middle Close, Leazes Field, South Leazes Field, Ox Close, Low Front Field, South Cow Close, Low Bank, Curry's Close, Little Field, Railey Lands, West Railey Lands, while the pond or mill-dam is known as "Puddle." The hills immediately behind Great Ryle, Chubden (653 feet) and Ryle Hill (917 feet)—sentinels of the Cheviots—contain many traces of pre-historic occupation on their south-eastern slopes.

---

[1] Mere Burn here probably means the old boundary line between the Eslington and Ryle estates.

The township of Ryle played its part in the stirring events of byegone times, as may be gathered from old county records.[1]

"William de Lindeseye, and Nicholas de Swynton and Thomas son of Gilbert de Ryel have slain Ralph Bende outside the house of Elias the miller in Eslington. And William and Nicholas forthwith fled and are suspected. And the aforesaid Thomas fled to the refuge (or sanctuary) of Karu (probably Carham) and having heard that the aforesaid William and Nicholas had absconded on account of the aforesaid death returned to the village of Ryel and was there harboured until the coming of the Justices, and afterwards absconded, and all are suspected, therefore let them be driven out and outlawed. The chattels of the aforesaid Thomas are worth 24s. 8d. for which the Sheriff has to account and the others have no chattels and the township of Ryel had harboured him therefore let it be amerced."—(40 Hen. III., 1256.)

The following extract relating to an incident which took place on Ryle hills during the Wars of the Roses, 1463, is also of great interest:—"Montagu reached Newcastle just in time to defend it against a sudden attack from Sir Ralph Grey. Several Lancastrians fell in a skirmish under the walls. The burghers of Newcastle also captured four French vessels, one of them being, it was supposed, a large 'carvile,' belonging to the Comte d'Eu. Grey and Breze then engaged on the siege of a castle near Alnwick, probably Warkworth, but they were compelled to abandon this on the advance of Montagu, who had been relieved at Newcastle by the arrival of Warwick with a considerable force. Notwithstanding this, Henry and Margaret, with the King of Scots and Breze, proceeded to lay formal siege to Norham about midsummer. 'Then,' says Gregory, 'my Lord Warwick and his brother, the Lord Montagu, put them in devoir to rescue the said castle of

[1] Northumberland Assize Rolls, Surtees Society, lxxxviii., p. 117.

Norham.' To do so they had to outflank the strong Lancastrian triangle, formed by the castles of Bamburgh, Alnwick, and Dunstanburgh. Being probably inferior to their combined adversaries in point of numbers, they appear to have determined to keep as far as possible out of their way to the west, and therefore to have chosen to march by Rothbury and Ingram. They seem, after crossing the Aln, to have found Queen Margaret with her French adherents and a large body of Scottish troops drawn up on the hill-side, in front of Great Ryle, in order to prevent their passing over into the Breamish valley. It would be difficult to find a more advantageous position for the purpose, but, anyhow, the Scots were seized with a sudden panic, and shamefully deserted the braver Frenchmen. In attempting to escape towards Scotland, Margaret was overtaken by a band of Yorkists, who laid hold of her royal jewels and other treasures. In spite of her piteous entreaties, they were quite prepared to cut her throat, when they began to fight among themselves over the rich booty. The Queen, seeing their attention thus distracted, besought an esquire who was there to take pity on her, 'for the sake of the Passion of Our Saviour Jesus Christ,' and assist her escape. 'Madam,' said he, yielding to her prayers, 'mount you behind me, and let my lord the prince get up in front, and save you I will or die, though death seems the more probable.' So the Queen and prince mounted, and the three rode off, while the soldiery were too much engrossed in their quarrel to notice their departure. Near the place where this occurred there was a wood, and into it they rode, in order to be lost to sight. To the terror-stricken Margaret every tree looked like a man with a drawn sword—not that it was her own life she cared for so much as for that of her son, in whom centred all her hopes of an ultimate restoration. The wood was indeed a favourite haunt of robbers, known to be merciless cut-throats; and as the Queen was deploring her fate, up came one of them, hideous and horrible to behold. He was about to attack the party, when Margaret boldly bade him approach," and beseeching him for help, ended her pathetic appeal thus:—"'Save my son, and keep him for me, and, if God grant his re-establishment, he will know how to reward a marvellous service such as never yet hath fallen to the lot of a man like thee to perform.' With these words, or something like them, Margaret so confounded the robber, that, seeing her tears and distress, and hearing that she was the Queen, he felt a deep sympathy for her. Touched by the Holy Spirit, who softened his heart, he even began to weep with her, and threw himself at her feet, declaring that he would die a thousand deaths and bear a thousand tortures rather than abandon the prince, whom he would bring to the haven of refuge in spite of everybody. He sought pardon for his misdeeds from the Queen, as though she still bore the sceptre in London, and vowed before God and the world never to relapse into his former ways, but to devote his life to acts of mercy. Then he quickly took charge of the prince, for Margaret was still in dread of being pursued and taken, and only yearned to know that her child was safely entrusted to God's guidance. For herself she felt no fear as long as her son was concealed, so, kissing the boy, who was all tears, she left him in the hands of the bandit, who honourably fulfilled his promises. Margaret, for her part, rode off, mounted behind the esquire, and, trusting to Providence, made her way without any guide towards the frontier, where she expected to find her husband."[1]

LITTLE RYLE.

While Great Ryle occupies an elevated site on the slopes of the smooth green hills, whose undulating lines bounds the valley on the north side of the Aln, Little Ryle stands in the bottom of the valley, on the south side of the river. From early times "Ryle Magna" and "Ryle Parva" were generally held by different owners. In the 23rd of Edward I. (1295),

[1] C. J. Bates' Border Holds, Vol. i., pp. 437, 443, Appendix.

Richard of Ryle held the Manor of Little Ryle,[1] and in the 23rd of Edward III. (1350), Henry, the son of John, the son of Henry—who then held Whittingham and other places round about it—had lands in "Ryhill Parva" and "Alburwyk."[2] In 1429, William Swan was the owner of Little Ryle, who also had lands in Snitter and Rothbury;[3] but during the early part of the 16th century both of the Ryles became the property of the Collingwoods. From the "Rentals and Rates" of 1663, we learn that Mr. Robert Collingwood was the owner of Great Ryle, Blakehope, and Ryle Mill, their annual rental being £186; and that Mr. Alexander Collingwood was the proprietor of Little Ryle and "Kairsley Houses," whose annual rental was £140. During the early part of the present century (1827), Collingwood House Estate belonged to John Collingwood Tarleton, who resided at the newly-erected Collingwood House, formerly called Unthank Hall; but in 1848 the estate was purchased by the Hon. Henry Thomas Liddell, the late Lord Ravensworth. The ancient hall of the Collingwoods, and the later mansion of Collingwood House, have entirely disappeared, but the neglected old carriage drive, the ruinous garden wall, the shrubberies and the plantations, all testify that there had stood, on what is now a perfect wilderness, a well-appointed mansion. But as Eslington House, the country seat of the Ravensworth family, is only two miles distant, Collingwood House was not required by its new proprietor, and consequently

[1] Escheats, Ed. i. Hodgson's Northumberland, Part iii., Vol. i., p. 51.

[2] Ibid., p. 76.

[3] Tate's History Alnwick, Vol. i., p. 247.

soon fell into decay, the stones being used a few years ago in building the new farm-house at Great Ryle. Incorporated in the farm-house at Little Ryle are the remains of the bassel-house of former times, or which may have been the residence of the Collingwoods of Little Ryle, the basement, now used as a kitchen, having a stone barrel-arched roof, and a small mullioned window, built up in the gable, of which we give a sketch. This class of building was common on the Borders during mosstrooping days, and although not so large as the towers that were built at Alnham, Great Ryle, or Prendwick, yet the walls of these fortified farm-houses were of great thickness — the roof usually covered with large grey-stone slates, fixed to the rafters with sheep-shank bones; therefore, when the stout oaken door was barred, the inmates were comparatively safe, for a time at least, from the clutches of any lawless riders who might favour them with a call when out on a plundering excursion.

In 1827, the farmer at Great Ryle was Anthony Pape; at Little Ryle, William Taylor; and at Unthank, John Pattison.[1] The following are some of the field names on the farms of Little Ryle and Unthank :—

LITTLE RYLE.—Caisley Moor, Night Fold, Caisley West Field, Kiln Field, The Seven Acres, Fanny's Burn, Beans Close, Bought Knowles, Horse Close, Quarry Field, High Hopes Close, The Half Moon, The Middle Field, The Four Acres, The Ten Acres, Low Hopes Close, West Intake, East Intake, The Haugh, The West Flowers, The East Flowers, Back Crosses.

UNTHANK.—Ormond's North Field, Waterside Close, Ruff Field, Cart Close, Well Close, Ormond's Hill, Coldside, North Red Meadows.

RYLE MILL.

Ryle Mill was no doubt the mill of the Ryle manor, for in 1663 it is mentioned amongst the possessions of Robert Col-

[1] Parson and White's Directory.

lingwood of Great Ryle. Ryle Mill has been for many years in the occupation of a much respected family, whose name, "the Taits of Ryle Mill," are as a household word in the vale of Aln. The present occupant is Mr. Job Tait, who resides at Eslington Hill. Pleasant are our boyhood recollections of many happy days spent in the old farm-house at Ryle Mill, for when Whittingham School broke up for the Harvest holidays, Ryle Mill was the happy hunting ground of the writer. Fishing in the Aln—the Harvest Field—the Irish Shearers, and the huge "Yetlin" full of oatmeal porridge, which smelt and tasted as never porridge before or since ever smelt or tasted—the impromptu dance in the kitchen at night to the music of the flute and Andrew Davidson's fiddle—the spinning wheel—the making of the cheese—curds and cream—float whey and yearned milk—delicious white cakes—fresh churned butter and creamy milk—and then on Sunday mornings the delightful drive over the hills in the family "Car" to Branton Meeting, to hear the Rev. James Blythe (now gone to his rest at the ripe old age of 85)—are visions that yet rise as pleasant memories of the happiness found under the roof of a Northumbrian farm-house some forty years ago, the remembrance of which, as years roll by, are looked back to as the happiest of days.

"Ah! happy years! once more who would not be a boy?"

The field names at Ryle Mill are:—The Haugh, Kiln Field, Middle Field, Stackyard Field, North Back Field, North Broom Hill, Low Leazes, High Leazes, Low Mere Burnside, High Mere Burnside.

ESLINGTON PARK, 1894.

CHAPTER VII.

ESLINGTON.

Its Site and Surroundings—The Lady's Bridge—Old Road—The Vill of Alan de Essinton, 1161—Held under Drengage by Addoch de Eselinton, 1187—Alano de Estlington by Military Scutage in 1203—Heselrig—Heron, 1362—Heselrig, 1415-1541—Collingwood, 1544—Will of Sir Robt. Collingwood, 1556—Border Exploits of the Collingwoods—Feud between the Selbys and the Collingwoods, 1586—Will of Thomas Collingwood, 1596—The Royalist Collingwoods, 1650—George Collingwood—The Jacobite Rising, 1715—List of Northumbrian Collingwoods, 1509-1810—Eslington purchased by Sir Henry Liddell in 1719—Circular of Sale—Sheriff's Precept, 1719—Eslington in 1729—The Liddells from 1719—The Hon. H. T. Liddell, the late Earl—Elections and Election Squibs of 1826—The Hon. H. G. Liddell, the present Earl—James Allan, the Piper, at Eslington—Eslington in 1835—Old House at Mountain—Eslington House, Gardens, Parks, 1894—Verses by James Wright—Extract from the "Lay of the Last Angler."

ESLINGTON, the country seat of the Earl of Ravensworth, stands on the north bank of the river Aln, at the southern base of the Ryle Hills, and two miles west from the village of Whittingham.

The ancient vill and manor of Eslington, with its fair broad acres and its sylvan glades, possess associations of more than ordinary interest. In early times it was held by a family who took the surname of Eslington; it afterwards passed through the hands of the Hesilriggs, the Herons, and the Collingwoods, who, residing within their strong manor house at Eslington, took an active share in all the warlike movements and expeditions in Northumberland during the Border wars. The first notice of this fortress is found in the Patent Rolls, 9th Edward III. (1335), where we learn that Robert of Eslington had a kernellated or fortified mansion at Eslington.[1]

[1] License to crenellate Eslington.—"20th Feb., 1335, Ed. III., at Newcastle, to Robert de Eslington for 'mansum suum apud Esselynton.'" C. J. Bates' Border Holds, Vol. i., p. 9.

Of this fortified mansion—the stronghold of the Eslingtons and the Hesilriggs—not a vestige remains, the only architectural relic being a fine Jacobean doorway, which probably belonged to an erection of the Collingwoods, now built into the north wall of the kitchen garden. For the active part George Collingwood, of Eslington, took in the Jacobite rising of 1715, he was executed and his estates confiscated. In 1719, Sir Henry Liddell, of Ravensworth, purchased the estates from the Crown Commissioners, by whom the present mansion was built about 1720. The entrance drive at that time, as the turf covered carriage road yet testifies, wound up the north bank of the Aln from the "Lady's Bridge," at the foot of Allerburn bank or Mountain field. This picturesque bridge—of one graceful arch, with its lichen covered parapets and its sylvan surroundings—forms the subject of a woodcut by Bewick. We here give a sketch of the bridge, taken on the spot expressly for this volume.

The earliest record we have of Eslington is in the Pipe Rolls[1] of 7th Henry II. (1161), under the head of New Pleas,

[1] Hodgson's Northumberland, Part iii., Vol. iii.

where Alan de Essinton renders an account of five marks to William de Vescy of Alnwick, then sheriff of the county. In 1187, 33rd Henry II., it was held by Addoch de Eselinton on the tenure of drengage, a species of service by which much land was held in the north. Early in the reign of John this tenure appears to have been changed, for in 1203 Alano de Estlinton held it under military scutage. It is afterwards held by Brian, the son of Alani de Eslinton, in 1271; Robertus de Eslington[1] in 1327; also by Ranulph, John, Roger, William, Almo, and Uctred, all of whom took the surname of Esclington, Estlington, or Eslenton, and who held the manor until the middle of the fourteenth century, when the various vills which now form the Eslington estate are for the first time associated with Eslington. In the escheats of 21 Edward I. (1293) it is found that John de Eslington had owned "Esselinton maner" and also held lands in Framlington and elsewhere; while Whittingham, Thrunton, and Ryle were held by Michael de Rihull;[2] but, in 1327, not only the manor of "Eslyngton" but the vills of Whittingham, Barton, and Thrunton,[3] are held by Robert of Eslington, with service attached to Bamburgh Castle.[4] His ancestor John de Eslington had, in the days of Edward II., held the office of constable of Bamburgh Castle. "There is nothing of moment," says Mr. Bates, "in Eslington's accounts which have been

[1] Names of Witnesses to an Inquisition taken at Rothbury, 21 King Edward I. (1293), proving Robert de Eslington, son of John de Eslington, to be the heir of the Eslington estates:—"Juratores dicunt super sacrum suum, viz., Henricus de Warton, Nicolaus de Warton, Walterius de Warton, juxta Rothbury, Johannes Gallon de Trevwick, et alii coram Roberto de Normanville apud Rothbury, die dominica et diei paschæ in tres Septimanas anno regni regis Edwardi vicessimo primo." (Wallis' Northumberland.)

[2] Hodgson's Northumberland, Part iii., Vol. i., p. 50.

[3] The Eslington estate of to-day includes Eslington, the village of Whittingham (which gives its name to the parish and township), the farms and hamlets of Mountain, Howbalk, Rothill, Barton, Thrunton, Thrunton Mill, Thrunton Low Field, Bridge of Aln, Mounthooly, Whittingham Lane, and part of Learchild.

[4] Hodgson's Northumberland, Part iii., Vol. i., p. 67.

preserved, except, perhaps, that the truncage[1] due to the castle from the several townships had by that time been commuted for the annual sum of £4 19s. 4½d., which appears to have been for the most part taken out in horses and swine. Eslington was taken prisoner at Bannockburn on the 25th of June, 1314, and owing to the extreme gravity of the crisis, the king, three days later, appointed Roger de Horsley constable of Bamburgh by word of mouth."[2]

About the year 1362, 'Esselynton' manor and the manors of Whittingham, Thrunton, and Barton, are held in equal parts by Elizabeth, the wife of Gilbert Heron and Donaldus de Heselrig.[3] Elizabeth was probably the sister and co-heiress of Heselrig. In 1415 Eslington was in the hands of Thomas Hessilrig, for in the list of Border fortresses, drawn up in that year, Eslington is thus described:—

"Turris de Eslington . . . . Thomæ de Hessilrige."[4]

The Itinerary of John Leland, the Royal Antiquary of Henry VIII. (1538), contains the following notice of Eslington:—

"Hasilrig of Northamptonshire hath about a. 50. li. lande in Northrubreland And Esselington wher is a pratie pile is Hasilrigges; and one of the Colinwoodd[es] dwellith now in it and hath the ouer site of his landes."[5]

Another survey of the Borders made in 1541 thus records it:—

"At Eslyngton ys a toure wth a barmekyn of the Inherytaunce of one . . . Heslerygge esquier. And in the tenor & occupaco'n of Robt. Collingewood esqui', who kepeth the same in good repac'ons."[6]

It is evident that for many years the Collingwoods were

---

[1] The service of carting logs to the castle.

[2] C. J. Bates' Border Holds, Vol. i., p. 243.

[3] Hodgson's Northumberland, Part iii., Vol. i., pp. 80-81.

[4] Border Holds, Vol. i., page 17. [5] Ibid., p. 25. [6] Ibid., p. 43.

tenants of the Heselriggs, at Eslington. In 1509 "Heselrigg" is the owner of the tower, and "Roberd Colyngwood" is the "inhabitant." In 1538 it is a "pile of Hasilrigges," and one of the "Colinwooddes" dwelt in it. In 1541 it is the "Inherytaunce of 'Heslerygge,'" but in the occupation of "Robt. Collingewood," while at the same time the Collingwoods were the owners of the tower at Whittingham, and part of the village of Whittingham — probably that portion of it clustering around their tower on the south bank of the Aln. Very shortly after this we learn that Eslington had become the manor of the Collingwoods. In 1544 Sir John Collingwood, of Eslington, was High Sheriff of the county of Northumberland, while Sir Robert Collingwood, of Eslington, in 1551, and Cuthbert Collingwood, of Eslington, in 1580 held that honourable office. In 1568 Cuthbert Collingwood, nephew and heir of Sir Robert Collingwood, of Eslington, was possessed of the mansions of Eslington and Bolton, Little Ryle, Great Ryle, and Titlington, part of the village of Whittingham, lands in Netherton, and the vill of Glanton; but Thrunton and Barton were still held by "Launc. Heselrige."[1]

The following extract from the will of Sir Robert Collingwood, contains much of local interest. The will is dated June 12, 1556, and begins with the words: "In dei Nominie I Robert Collingwood of Eslyngton in the County of Northumberland Esq.' and then follows the usual pious invocation to 'Our Lady Saint Mary the Virgin and all the whole company of Heaven.' He desires to be buried in the Parish Church of Whittingham, and wills that his lands in the County of Northumberland be divided into three parts. The one whereof to remain to his wife for her dower, and other to his executors for the payment of his debts, and the third part to descend to his heir. As to the third part, that Richard Loncaster should be receiver of the rents and to pay legacies. He wills that all

[1] Hodgson's Northumberland, Part iii., Vol. iii., p. lxx. (Preface). (Liber Feodarij, 10 Eliz., 1568.)

his Executors should meet at his house at Eslington and take a copy of the said Richard Loncaster's account, and that until such time as his nephew Cuthbert accomplish 21 years he should be under the order of his Executors, and if his lands could be obtained as he (the testator) had thereto promised the master of the wayrdes he willed should have the order and rule of the same. Willed that all leases for years as he had made to his tenants should remain in force. Also concerning all such lands &c. as his cousin Alexander Collingwood and he (the testator) had purchased of King Edward VI. should remain in full force Except the lands in Lyttell ryle which he had released unto the said Alexander. Also such wardship as he (the testator) had of the body and lands &c. of his nephew John Collyngwood his brother Henry's son, unto himself, to enjoy the same as soon as he attain 21 years his (the testator's) cousin of p. rylle (Little Ryle) and Robert Collingwood of Ettill to enjoy the same. Also where he had demised the erection of a cantaria for a priest to celebrate in the Parish Church of Whittingham at the Altar of Saint Peter. He willed that all the priests thereafter thereto nominated should during the time have and enjoy one Cottage and garth in Whittingham holden of Edward Steanson as also an annual rent of 4.l. out of his lands &c. in Tyttlyngton, Northumberland. Wills that his cousin Ralph Collingwood and Thomas Collingwood should enjoy such leases as he (the testator) had given of Tyttlington or Ryll to them for 60 years and that his cousin Ralph should have an annuity of 53s. 4d. Testator bequeaths his tithe corn of Whittingham parish and the town of Fenwick unto my nephew which should be heir God willing, until such time as he should come to his, his Executors to have the guiding and rule of the same. Testator gave all the leases he had of the towns of Fawdon, Bolton, Branton, Dissington, Wettesland . . . . Ingram and Lowick and the Cleugh in Northumherland unto his said nephew Cuthbert Collingwood. Testator appointed Robert

Collingwood of Bewick . . . . Collingwood of Ryle, Edward Bednell (Lemington) Raufe Collingwood of Titlington, and Sir Richard . . . . priest, supervisors of his will. Appoints his brother Percivall Fenwick . . . . Carr of Ford, John Carr his brother, Robert Horsle, John Bednell, Thos. Carlisle, and . . . . of Pangshawes."

Records of the Collingwoods and their doughty deeds in field of battle and Border fight have been handed down to us by history, tradition, and Border ballad. Those brave knights were ever found in the forefront of the English army during the French and Scotch wars, and when not engaged in active service abroad, they assisted the Wardens of the Marches in keeping order at home—repelling thievish marauders and administering justice amongst the unruly Borderers. In 1522 Robert Collingwood, as we learn from a contemporary record :—"Ys a wyes boerderar, a trew man well myendyt to justice." During the reign of Queen Elizabeth, Sir Cuthbert Collingwood, a knight renowned for his activity and gallantry, had the misfortune to be taken prisoner by the Scots, with several other English noblemen, at the Reidswire. A meeting of the Scotch and English Wardens was being held on the 7th of July, 1575, at the Reidswire (on the boundary between England and Scotland, near the head of Redewater), for the purpose of amicably settling disputes; but the proud and fiery chiefs, Sir John Forster, the English Warden, and Sir John Carmichael, the Scotch Warden, quarrelled over the case of a "fouled bill," and a skirmish took place between their armed followers, in which the Northumbrians got the worst of it. Sir Geo. Heron of Chipchase was killed. Sir John Forster, James Ogle, Henry Fenwick, and Cuthbert Collingwood were taken prisoners.[1] A ballad, written at the time, by a Scotsman, recounts the exploit, and speaks in high terms of Collingwood.

---

[1] "The Raid of the Reidswire."

> "But if ye wad a souldier search,
> Amang them a' were ta'en that night,
> Was nane sae wordie, to put in verse,
> As Collingwood, that courteous knight."

As might be expected, it was no uncommon event for the valiant Sir Cuthbert to have a brush with the Scots, and to fall a captive into their hands. The following curious letter, which we venture to give in full, informs us of such an occurrence, besides giving a graphic description of the lawless condition of the Borders during the reign of Elizabeth :—

"From Thomas Randolph (English Ambassador in Scotland) to Archibald Douglas (Scotch Ambassador in England).

"1586, July 3.—*Ex malo principio magna familiaritas conflata est.* Beginnings here have been very hard. I hope now that the end will be the better. We will do as we may and take what we can get. But, so long as your lands in Tividale and Liddesdale have so many thieves so their servants and tenants, we never look to have the borders in quiet, and whensoever you intend to put at them, upon warning, you shall have as good assistance as we can make you. The complaints that we have against you are so many, that, seek redress from what time ye will, all the thieves in Scotland are not able to satisfy the losses of England. But, what need I to babble or prate with you of this matter. You shall hear enough of them at your coming to London: how many of our men have been murdered and slain, how many maimed and hurt, how many spoiled and burnt: besides the goods and insight they have carried away. Woe is me for the gentle Mr. Archibald! How pitifully you will be 'coursed' and canvassed when you come there, and for nothing more than that the Carrs are not delivered, according to promise, by the King's self. If they be sent hither before my Lord of Rutland's departure, upon our lives and credits they shall be safely conveyed to Carlisle, and there safely kept as her Majesty hath promised. Whereof, at this time, Mr. Secretary Walsingham hath written unto you his mind. The delays breed suspicion. Where suspicion is, true love taketh no place. I have to blame you, and earnestly to reprove you, that did undertake to do so much as to procure the speedy delivery of Sir Cuthbert Collingwood; for whom I humbly crave favour at your King's hands, and from you a speedy answer. So far to discredit a gentleman of service, a knight, a servant in heart and will to your Sovereign, to satisfy the will of a number of such as the Bornes are, I leave it to your wisdom to consider. And so, good Sir, I do bid you heartily farewell.—Berwick, 3rd July, 1586."[1]

In the same year there appears to have been a quarrel between a son of Sir John Selby of Twisel and Sir Cuthbert Collingwood, for we find Sir John Selby writing thus to Archibald Douglas:—

"Touching the late fray[2] that happened betwixt Sir Cuthbert Collingwood and my son, whereof I have some-

[1] Historical Manuscripts Commission, 1889. Salisbury Papers, Part iii., p. 149.

[2] Regarding this affray, which proved fatal to one of Sir Cuthbert Collingwood's party, Mr. W. W. Tomlinson relates, in the *Monthly Chronicle* for 1890, p. 546:—"That on the 22nd Nov., 1586, a gallant company rode north from Newcastle. It consisted of Sir Cuthbert Collingwood of Eslington, with his lady and daughter riding on pillions behind two retainers; Thomas Collingwood, his heir; a younger son; Robert Clavering, the High Sheriff of Northumberland; his brother, William Clavering, and nine others. Sir Cuthbert Collingwood and Robert Clavering had been summoned to Newcastle, with other North Country gentlemen, to attend the Lord President of the North and to celebrate the Queen's Accession. On a moor beyond Morpeth they were met by William Selby of Berwick, and 12 or 13 of his associates, chiefly soldiers from the garrison at Berwick, who had been lying in wait for them. Everyone in Sir Cuthbert's company at once understood their intentions, for there had been a bitter feud between the Collingwoods and Selbys. Lady Collingwood threw herself from her seat, and on her knees begged Selby, with tears, to let her husband alone for that time. Clavering also tried to preserve peace, but to no purpose, for Selby and his company discharging their pistols shot Sir Cuthbert and young Clavering in the breast. Sir Cuthbert's wound was not fatal, but for William Clavering there was no hope of recovery. Selby fled, but four of his associates were tried at the assizes at Newcastle, and a verdict of manslaughter was returned against three, but the fourth was liberated. The Collingwoods and Claverings were still further incensed against the Selbys by this tragic event, and it was very difficult for those in authority to bring about a reconciliation. It was submitted to arbitrators, and afterwards the Lord Chamberlain undertook to end this trouble, but they absented themselves from Berwick on the day appointed for the hearing of the case."

what written in my former letters, the truth thereof was in this manner. Before my son came nigh the place where Sir Cuthbert was, not known of him, the said Sir Cuthbert was alighted in the way with his whole company, and divers of their swords drawn ; my son riding on his way, and perceiving them alighted, and standing in that manner with his company, alighted, and in his alighting they shot their pistols at him. Notwithstanding this injury offered, my son, loath to bring all that company in trouble, came to parley, and in a manner agreed to leave for that present. Notwithstanding in my son's return and his company to their horses some of Sir Cuthbert's company discharged two more pistols at him. The one of them struck a horse of one his company through the head, which was the only cause of that which happened, which chanced only in their own defence. There were divers of my son's company taken, who are by the shewing very extremely handled, and I fear that, through the persuasions of Sir Cuthbert and the Sheriff, my Lord Lieutenant will presently hold a gaol delivery for executing of them that are taken.

"I am informed that they try all the means they can to make Mr. Secretary their friend in this matter and that they incense his honour wrongfully with the cause. If the execution of the prisoners may be stayed while the assizes at Lammas, I doubt not but by good dealing the matter may be brought to some good end. The slaughter of the Sheriff's brother was by great chance, for he was my near kinsman, and it is well known through all the country that there hath always been great friendship betwixt our houses, and never before this any manner cause of controversy. I am therefore heartily to request you to be a mean to Mr. Secretary that the indifferency of the cause may be heard, and that the judgement may come before indifferent judges, and then I doubt not but the truth will take effect, and that there may be justice used according to deserving.—Berwick, 29th November, 1586."[1]

[1] Historical Manuscripts Commission, 1889. Salisbury Papers, Part iii., p. 198.

The well-stocked leas and pasture lands of Eslington must have been a favourite hunting ground for the Scots. In the time of Sir Cuthbert Collingwood, Eslington tower was stormed by a party of Scots, when several of Sir Cuthbert's retainers were slain whilst defending the fortress, and the knight himself barely escaped with his life. Again in 1587 Eslington was stormed and taken by no less a personage than the Duke of Buccleuch. Sir Thomas Fairfax, writing from York to the Earl of Rutland, at Nottingham, on the 8th of December, 1587, says:—"My brother (-in-law, Sir William) Bellasis has met with a misfortune which is a sorrow to us here. He was garrisoned at Eslington, and had a hundred soldiers dispersed through four towns. The Scots ran a foray, and before his people were assembled he was taken prisoner by the Lord of Buccleuch, as we hear. His brother James has not been heard of since, and James Godson and his ensign one Harte and fifteen soldiers slain. This was on the first of December."[1]

Thomas Collingwood was the owner of Eslington in 1596, whose will, dated Feb. 25, 1596-7, we quote as follows:—"Thomas Collingwoode, of Eslington, in the countye of Northumberland, esquier. To be buryed in my parishe churche of Whittingham. To my brother-in-lawe, Mr. John Swinborne, of Edlingham, esquier, towardes the education of his children, and to my sustor, Rebecca Collingwood, in token of my especiall love and goodwyll towardes them, and in requitall of there zealous affection extraordinary shewed to me, the sum of £20, to be paied yerlye for xiiij yeres, to be paied out of my chief tenementes and hereditamentes within the countye of Yorke. To my sonne, John, duringe his lyfe, all my landes in Titlington and Brome parke, allowinge and grantinge unto him full power to make joynter unto his wyef, if it please God he have one, to the valewe yearlye of 40£. To my daughter, Mary Collingwoode, towardes her education and in full satisfaction of her childe's part 500£. . . . . .

[1] Historical Manuscripts Commission, 1888. Rutland Papers, Vol. i., p. 232.

To John Clerke, of Alnwyke, burgess, in consideration of his faithful goodwyll, service and travale, usede to me, and my ancetors, and in hope of his zealous affection hereafter, to be shewed towardes my wyefe and children, 40s. yerely, duringe his life. To my servante Juliane Gower 20£. To my servante, Edmonde Collingewoode, 20£, and to his brother Martyne, my servante xx nobles. To my servante, William Smythe, xx markes, and to my servante, George Leslye, xx nobles, and the same to my servante Jeffray Hallyday. To my servant John Alder, my horsse callede gray Browne, and v markes. To my servante Robert Selby, and to Elizabethe, his wife 5£. To my nursse and servante Katherin Raynolds xx nobles. To all the reste of my servantes there duble yearlye wages. To my neace, Margarett Swinborne 10£. And for the better discharging of these my legacies &c. I doe gyve demise &c. to my brethren-in-law, Rauf Gray, of Chillingham, and Edward Gray, of Morpeth esquiers, all my landes &c. in the counties of Yorke and Duresme for the space of xiiij yeres . . . . .
I make my saide brethren-in-lawe, Rauf, and Edward Gray, esquiers, and my brethren, Mr. Francys Radclyfe and George Collingwoode esquiers, supervysors.

"INV. Thirtie fower kyne 56£ 13s. 4d., vj quyes 10£, xlij oxen 79£ 2s., iiij two-yere cattell 2£ 13s. 4d., xiiij skores of yowes 60£ 13s., vj skores of gymmers and dinmondes 19£ 10s., x skores of hogges 26£ 13s. 4d., vij horses and mares 20£. Houshold stuff 20£. In furniture for husbandry 6£ 13s. 4d., in corne in the felde and in the house, 45£, x younge cattell, of a yeare and a halfe, 3£ 7s. 6d. ✠ "[1]

The following extracts from the State Papers show the manner in which the estates of the Royalists were impoverished while the Parliamentarians were in power:—

"2nd March, 1650. Cuthbert Collingwood, Dalden co. Durham and claimants on his Estate (amongst others)—

Sir Art. Hesilrigge Bart. begs report of the Attorney-

[1] Durham Wills and Inventories, Vol. xxxviii, p. 268.—Note.

General to whom was referred his claim to lands in Eslington &c. co. Northumberland, sequestered from the Collingwoods Papists in arms, and decided by law to be his, but the Barons of Exchequer say they have no power to remove the sequestration."

"7th June, 1650. Nich. Ogle of Eslington, Northumberland."

"5th Jan. 1654. Rob. Stapelton and John Toung assignees of Cuthbert Collingwood beg to compound for the tithes of Whittingham Rectory, which are in the additional Act for Sale. Noted fine at $\frac{2}{6}$, £78 6. 0."

"24th April, 1656. The Treason Trustees give notice to the Committee for Sequestrations that there is to be a trial in the Common Pleas about Eslington, Whittingham and other lands co. Northumberland contested between Collingwood and Sir A. Hesilrigge and advize them to defend the State title therein."[1]

In 1628 we find a George Collingwood, at Eslington,[2] and in 1638 a Cuthbert Collingwood;[3] but during the Commonwealth Eslington would appear to have been, for a short time, in the occupation of a member of the Ogle family, who, in the struggle between Charles I. and his Parliament, joined the Roundheads, while the Collingwoods espoused the cause of the Royalists; therefore, as may be gathered from the following extract, there was ill-blood betwixt the two old Northumbrian families:—

"June 11th, 1657, Robert Ogle of Eslington, gentleman, gave information before the House of Commons that, Sir Robert Collingwood of Brandon inveighed against Robert Fenwick, Esq., a member of this present Parliament, saying:—'He was a base fellow; his father was hanged for felony, and he did wonder who sent him to Parliament.'"[4]

---

[1] Calendar of the Committee for Compounding, &c. (Domestic) 1643-1660, Part iii., pp. 2204-5 (Eslington).

[2] Arch. Æliana, Vol. ii. (Old Series), p. 316, &c. [3] Ibid.

[4] Hodgson's Northumberland, Part ii., Vol. ii., p. 351.—Note.

Again we find a George Collingwood, at Eslington, in 1663,[1] and in 1715 another of the name, the last of the Collingwood owners of Eslington.

The Jacobite rising of 1715, the last save one of those civil wars which have so often convulsed our land, was highly popular on both sides of the Tweed, and nowhere more so than amongst the Roman Catholic gentry of Northumberland. Therefore the Collingwoods—true to their political traditions, and adhering steadfastly to their hereditary faith—were staunch Roman Catholics and Jacobites to boot, and warmly espoused the cause of the Pretender. On the 6th of October, 1715, James Ratcliffe, the unfortunate Earl of Derwentwater, marched with sixty followers from Green Rig, in North Tyne, to Plainfield Moor, in Coquetdale, where he was joined by several Northumbrian supporters of the Jacobite movement. Staying all that night at Rothbury, they proceeded next day to Warkworth. We are not sure whether George Collingwood, of Eslington, joined his friend Derwentwater at Plainfield or not, but he was certainly with him at Warkworth. The Jacobites were under the command of General Thomas Forster, of Adderston and Bamburgh Castle, M.P. for Northumberland. At the battle of Preston, on the 12th and 13th of November, 1715, in which the Jacobites were totally defeated and the rising quelled, the Northumbrians were led by the Earl of Derwentwater and George Collingwood, whilst Charles Collingwood, his youngest brother, had command of the reserve, which was drawn up in the churchyard; but the chivalrous spirit of the Collingwood would not suffer him to stand inactive, and he impetuously dashed into the *melee.* The leaders of the movement, amongst whom were seven lords, besides 1,490 others were taken prisoners, many of whom were executed, including the Earl of Derwentwater and George Collingwood. Patten, in his History of the Rebellion,

---

[1] Hodgson's Northumberland, Part iii., Vol. i., p. 266.

gives the names of the following local gentlemen, who were taken at Preston :—

"John Clavering, a Papist of Northumberland.
John Clavering, brother to William Clavering, both Papists in Northumberland.
John Hunter, a farmer ar Callylee, in Northumberland, reputed very rich. He made his escape.
John Talbot of Cartington, in Northumberland, a brave young gentleman. He made his escape from Chester.
George Collingwood of Northumberland, a Papist of a valuable estate. He was ordered for London, but he was seiz'd with the gout at Wigan, and from thence he was carried to Liverpool, and there found guilty, and afterwards executed there, the 25th of February, 1716. He was a very pious Gentleman, and well beloved in his country."

In the song, "Derwentwater's Farewell," he is thus mentioned :—

"And fare thee well, George Collingwood,
Since fate has put us down ;
If thou and I have lost our lives,
Our King has lost his crown.
Farewell, farewell, my lady dear,
Ill, ill, thou counsell'dst me,
I never more may see the babe
That smiles upon thy knee."

Tradition says, like his friend, Lord Derwentwater, Collingwood was urged by his wife—a daughter of Lord Montague—to take the fatal step of joining the Jacobites in their unsuccessful attempt to place a Stuart once more on the English throne, and that when leaving Eslington to join the rebel army, he turned round on his horse when at Thrunton Crag End, an eminence a mile south of Whittingham, and, fondly gazing over his fair domain, felt a secret foreboding that he was looking upon it for the last time, and that never again would he sleep under the ancient roof tree of the Collingwoods at Eslington :—

"He passed
From out the massy gate of that old hall,
And mounting on his steed he went his way.
And ne'er repassed that hoary threshold more."

In the rising of 1745, the following shows that the old Jacobite spirit still burned within the hearts of the Collingwoods :—

"Northumberland.—Whereas Thomas Collingwood, son of ——— Collingwood of Thrunton, in this county, was committed on Wednerday last to the gaol in and for the said county, at Morpeth, for high treason, and made his escape from thence in the night between the 27th and 28th of this instant November (1745). These are therefore to give notice that if any person or persons shall apprehend the said Thomas Collingwood, and deliver him to the keeper of the said gaol, such person or persons shall have paid to him or them by the treasurer of this county, a reward of £50. N.B.—The said Thomas Collingwood is a person of middle stature, about 25 years of age, has a round face, and a short nose, and wore, when he escaped, a light-colour'd wigg, a dark-colour'd coat, and a silk handkerchief about his neck."[1]

He was re-taken, and tried at Carlisle, on the 19th September, 1746, but, as nothing could be proved against him, he was acquitted.

In connection with the Jacobite movement of 1715, we append the names of suspected persons, residents in the Vale of Whittingham in 1715 aud 1718:—[2]

Papists in ye North Division in Coquetdale Ward August 19, 1715—

Calleley	...John Clavering esq.
	—— Moodey.
	—— Moodey.
Yeatlington...	...Luke Blakelock.
	Wm. Avery.
	James Gardiner.
High Houses	...Mr. John Hunter.
Eslington	...Geo. Collingwood esq.
	Cuthbert Blakelock.
	John Wilson.
	John Ferry.
	Wm. Cowley.
	Mich. Brown.
	John Blagdon.
	John Perey.
	Christopher Perey.
	Wm. Robson.
Whittingham	...John How.
Mountain of ye Clay	...Mr. George Morrison.
Glanton	...John Heslipp.
Edlingham	...Alexander Himer.
Fawdon	...Thos. Snawdon.
	Wm. Snawdon.
	—— Snawdon, a Brother of ye same.

[1] *Newcastle Courant*, Nov. 30, 1745.

[2] Session Records, Northumberland.

The following persons were reported by the High Constable in 1718 as having been "concerned in the late Rebellion":—

John Hunter of Calliley high-houses.
Thos. Selbye of Calliley.
Jno. How of Whittingham.
George How of the same.
Henry Brown of Eslington Miln-house.
George Downey of Thrunton.

Besides the Collingwoods of Eslington there were numerous branches of that historic family established in different parts of the county during the sixteenth, seventeenth, and eighteenth centuries. To those of our readers who love to trace the line of old families, we trust the following list, compiled from various sources, of Northumberland Collingwoods may be of interest, consisting of knights, lairds, squires, and yeomen, with their places of abode, arranged in chronological order, but without any attempt at showing their pedigrees or degree of relationship:—

1509. Robert Collingwood, Esq., inhabitor of Eslington Tower.
1541. Robert Collingwood, Esq., owner of Whittingham Tower.
1544. Sir John Collingwood, of Eslington.
1550. Ralph Collingwood, of Titlington.
Robert Collingwood, of Bewick.
Henry Collingwood, of Ryle.
1551. Sir Robert Collingwood, of Eslington.
1556. Alexander Collingwood, of Little Ryle.
Robert Collingwood, of Etal.
1568. Cuthbert Collingwood, of Eslington.
1578. Roger Collingwood, Parish Clerk of Whittingham.
1585. Thomas Collingwood, of Little Ryle.
Cuthbert Collingwood, of Shipley.
1596. Thomas Collingwood, Esq., of Eslington.
Robert Collingwood, of Eslington.
John Collingwood, of Eslington.
George Collingwood, of Eslington.
1628. George Collingwood, Esq., of Eslington.
Thomas Collingwood, of Great Ryle.
Alexander Collingwood, of Little Ryle.
Francis Collingwood, of Thrunton.
1638. Cuthbert Collingwood, Esq., of Eslington.
Ralph Collingwood, Esq., of Branton.
Henry Collingwood, of Great Ryle.
Alexander Collingwood, of Little Ryle.
John Collingwood, of Reveley.
Ralph Collingwood, of Ingram.

(Circa.) 1650. Thomas Collingwood, of Glanton.
1660. Martin Collingwood, of Shipley.
George Collingwood, of Shipley.
1663. George Collingwood, Esq., of Eslington.
Robert Collingwood, of Great Ryle.
Alexander Collingwood, of Little Ryle.
Samuel Collingwood, of Barra.
Sir Robert Collingwood, of Branton.
Alexander Collingwood, of Hedgeley.
Edward Collingwood, of Eglingham Parish.
George Collingwood, of Eglingham Parish.
Luke Collingwood, of Kirknewton.
Cuthbert Collingwood,
John Collingwood,
Daniel Collingwood,
Robert Collingwood, } of Ingram Parish.
1695. William Collingwood, of Eslington.
1698. Edward Collingwood, of Byker.
1699. Robert Collingwood, yeoman, of Eslington.
Edward Collingwood, of Glanton.
1700. Thomas Collingwood, Esq.
1703. John Collingwood, of Eslington.
1706. Thomas Collingwood, of Eslington.
1711. Henry Collingwood, of Great Ryle.
1715. William Collingwood, of Whittingham.
George Collingwood, Esq. (executed Feb. 25, 1716), of Eslington.
1718. John Collingwood, of Eslington.
Robert Collingwood, of Eslington.
Charles Collingwood, of Eslington.
1724. Alexander Collingwood, of Shawdon.
1725. Alexander Collingwood, Esq., of Little Ryle.
1745. Thomas Collingwood, of Thrunton.
1747. Alexander Collingwood, of Chillingham.
Henry Collingwood, Esq., of Cornhill.
Henry Collingwood, Esq., of Westerheugh.
Thomas Collingwood, of Westerheugh.
Alexander Collingwood (Junior), of Little Ryle.
George Collingwood, Esq. (Lt. Gov. of Fort Augustus).
Edward Collingwood, Esq., of Chirton.
1774. Edward Collingwood (Junior), of Chirton.
John Collingwood, of Chirton.
Thomas Collingwood, of Cornhill.
Francis Collingwood, Parish Clerk of Ford.
Henry Collingwood, of Cornhill.
John Collingwood, Esq., of West Lilburn.
Francis Collingwood, of Prendwick.
Alexander Collingwood, of Unthank.
1787. Edward Collingwood, High Sheriff of the County.
1793. Henry Collingwood, High Sheriff of the County.
1810. Cuthbert, Lord Collingwood.

At the present day a much respected member of this ancient and honourable family resides in the parish of Whittingham — F. J. W. Collingwood, Esq., J.P., Glanton Pyke. Another of the name, E. J. Collingwood, Esq., D.L., is the owner of Lilburn Tower; while in the village of Whittingham there also lives a lineal descendant of this old Northumberland family. The crest and coat of arms, still used by the Squires of Glanton Pyke and Lilburn Tower, are the same as those borne by the brave Collingwoods of old. The Collingwood arms are: "Argent, a chevron between three stag's heads, erased sable, having in the mouth a leaf." Their crest is a stag at full gaze under an oak tree proper, respecting which there is the following old rhyme:—

"The Collingwoods have borne the name,
Since in the bush the buck was ta'n;
But when the bush shall hold the buck,
Then farewell faith, and farewell luck."[1]

We shall now bid farewell to the Collingwoods and the Jacobites to notice another link in the annals of Eslington, and that is the advent of that noble family who now possess its broad and fertile acres. As already mentioned, Eslington, the forfeited estate of the unfortunate George Collingwood, was purchased in 1719 by Sir Henry Liddell, of Ravensworth. We are enabled to place before our readers a copy of the circular announcing the sale—a most interesting document, which not only describes the estate, but gives the names of the tenants, and shows the value of land at that period. The endorsement reads thus:—

"Particular of the Eftate
late of GEORGE
COLLINGWOOD
To be Sold on Friday *the*
Thirteenth of February 1718
next at Nine in the Morn-
-ing. No (45)."

[1] Denham Tracts, Vol. i., page 100.

"Particular and Rental of the Eſtate late of GEORGE COLLINGWOOD, in the County of *Northumberland.*

To be Sold at Eſſex-Houſe *in* Eſſex-Street, *on* Friday *the Thirteenth of* February *next, at Nine of the Clock in the Forenoon.*

A Large Stone House sash'd, with Coach-House, Stables, &c. A Garden well wall'd and planted, with an Orchard, and other Conveniences, fit for a Gentleman.

Tenant	Premises	l.	s.	d.	l.	s.	d.
Mr Joseph Browne, a Mansion House, *&c.*					67	—	—
Mr Gilbert Parke, the *Croft* Mead, *&c.*					26	—	—
Robert Perry, *Eslington East* Farm					17	—	—
William Dixon	*Eslington West* Farms	11	5	—			
Cuthbert Blakely	*Eslington West* Farms	3	15	—			
John Collingwood	*Eslington West* Farms	7	10	—			
Robert Clark	*Eslington West* Farms	3	15	—			
William Cowly	*Eslington West* Farms	3	15	—			
					30	—	—
William Dixon, *per Eslington* Mill					10	—	—
—— *Morrison*, *Eslington* High House					262	—	—
Robert Hudson	*Whittingham*	15	—	—			
Henry Bell	*Whittingham*	15	—	—			
John Jackson	*Whittingham*	15	—	—			
James Anderson	*Whittingham*	18	—	—			
John Dodd	*Whittingham*	12	—	—			
John Nicholson	*Whittingham*	15	—	—			
					90	—	—
John Howe, *per Howe's* Farm					44	—	—
Gowen Hopper	*per Barton*	49	10	—			
William Ellison	*per Barton*	8	5	—			
Henry Todd	*per Barton*	8	5	—			
					66	—	—
William Collingwood	*Whittingham* Cottages	3	—	—			
Thomas Hall	*Whittingham* Cottages	—	10	—			
Thomas Anderson	*Whittingham* Cottages	1	—	—			
Edward Piles	*Whittingham* Cottages	—	5	—			
Adam Anderson	*Whittingham* Cottages	—	5	—			
Richard Curry	*Whittingham* Cottages	—	5	—			
John Hamm	*Whittingham* Cottages	—	10	—			
					5	15	—
Carry'd over					917	15	—

	l.	s.	d.	l.	s.	d.
Brought over						
William Mills	13	6	8			
John Pigdon } *per Rathill* Farm	13	6	8			
James Browne	13	6	8			
				40	—	—
John Elliot				23	—	—
Robert Whitham	12	16	—			
Robert Graham	12	16	—			
Robert Nicholson } *per Whitton Lee* Farm	12	16	—			
George Nicholson	12	16	—			
Matthew Mills	12	16	—			
				64	—	—
Andrew Dixon, *Thrunton South* Quarter				29	—	—
John Elliot, Ditto, *West* Quarter				30	—	—
Thomas Davison, Ditto, *Middle* Quarter				30	—	—
William Miller, Ditto, *East* Quarter				29	—	—
Andrew Dixon, The Corn Mill				14	—	—
				876	15	—
Whittingham Tithes being held by Lease for Twenty One Years, of the Dean and Chapter of *Carlisle*, value	50	—	—			
A Quit-Rent due from *Glenton*	—	18	—			
				50	18	—
				927	13	—
Claim'd and allow'd by the Commissioners and Trustees out of the said Tithes	25	6	8	} 25	7	3
Ditto, a Quit-Rent out of the Lands	—	—	7			
Total				902	5	9

Timber on the Estate to a considerable Value.

N.B. *There are Three Annuities charged upon and issuing out of the above Premises, viz.*

	l.	s.	d.
To *John Collingwood* (aged 62) for his Life	20	—	—
To *Robert Collingwood* (aged 60) for his Life	20	—	—
To *Charles Collingwood* (aged 56) for his Life	20	—	—"

Connected with the deeds relating to the purchase of the Eslington estate by Sir Henry Liddell in 1719, are three hazel tallies, one of which is 19 inches in length; another is 23 inches, having 10 notches; the third is much shorter, and has only 4 notches. The existence of these primitive forms of receipt and account is probably due to the fact that the estates of George Collingwood having been confiscated were then in the possession of the Crown; and Exchequer tallies were in use until the year 1834, of which we give the following description:—

"The Tallies used in the Exchequer answered the purpose of receipts as well as simple records of matters of account. They consisted of squared rods of hazel or other wood, upon one side of which was marked, by notches, the sum for which the tally was an acknowledgment: one kind of notch standing for £1,000, another for £100, another for £20, and others for 20/-, 1/-, &c. On two other sides of the tally, opposite to each other, the amount of the sum, the name of the payer, and the date of the transaction, were written by an officer called the writer of the tallies, and, after this was done, the stick was cleft longitudinally in such a manner that each piece retained one of the written sides, and one half of every notch cut in the tally. One piece was delivered to the person who had paid the money, for which it was a receipt or acquittance, while the other was preserved in the Exchequer."[1]

A document of great interest also accompanys the hazel sticks and the deeds, the endorsement of which reads:—"28th May, 1719. Copy of Commissioners Precept to Sheriff of Northumberland to deliver Sir Henry Liddell Possession."—

"*To the High Sheriff of the County of Northumberland.*"[2]

"In pursuance of an Act of Parliament Intituled an Act for vesting the Forfeited Estates in Great Britain and Ireland in Trustees, to be sold for the use of the Publick. And for giving Relief to Lawfull Creditors by Determining the Claims and for the more Effectual bringing into the respective Exchequers the Rents and Profits of the said Estates till sold. We Commissioners & trustees in the said Act named Do hereby Require and comand you to put Sr Henry Liddell of Ravensworth Castle in the Co. of Durham, Bart., into the possession of the Mannors of Eslington, Whittingham, Thornton & Barton, and the Messuages, Lands & Tenements & Hereditaments late of George Collingwood Esq. attainted of High Treason, lying in Eslington, Whittingham, Thornton & Barton, in the said County of Northumberland, sold and conveyed by us, or some of us to the said Sir Henry Liddell & his heirs by Indenture of Bargain & Sale.

---

[1] Knight's Pictorial History of England, Vol i., Book ii., chap. i., p. 116.

[2] William Cotesworth of Broomhouse, Esq. Mackenzie and Dent's History Northumberland, Vol. ii, p. 797.

Dated this 14th day of this inst. May according to the import of the said Indenture. And herein you are not to fail at your perill. Given under our Hands and Seals this 28th Day of May Anno Dom. 1719.

J. BIRD.
CHA: LONG.
JOHN EYLES.
HENR CUNINGHAME."

Horsley, who wrote in 1729-30, thus describes Eslington:—"Eslington stands also close by this river (Aln). It is a pleasant seat, and has been just now rebuilt by Sir Henry Liddell, the present owner of the estate. It had long been the seat of the Collingwoods, but Mr. Collingwood, the late proprietor of the estate, lost both it and his life by being unhappily concerned in the insurrection against his late Majesty King George. His fate was generally lamented and pitied, he himself having had the character of an inoffensive, peaceable gentleman."[1]

From the year 1719, when Eslington was first purchased by Sir Henry Liddell, of Ravensworth, the following members of that historic family have been its owners:—

Sir Henry Liddell, 3rd Baronet, 1719 to 1723.
Sir Henry Liddell, 4th Baronet, 1723 to 1784.
Sir Henry George Liddell, 5th Baronet, 1784 to 1811.
Sir Thomas Henry Liddell, 6th Baronet, 1812 to 1855.
Hon. Henry Thomas Liddell (late Earl Ravensworth), 1856 to 1878.
Hon. Henry George Liddell (the present Earl).

In 1821 Sir Thos. Henry Liddell, the 6th Baronet, was raised to the peerage, and a hatchment in the spandrill of one of the arches in the north arcade of the nave in Whittingham Parish Church tells that he died in 1855, at the age of 80. He was succeeded by his son, the Hon. Henry Thomas Liddell, the late Earl of Ravensworth, of happy memory—we say of happy memory, because who is there amongst the old Eslington tenantry but remembers with pleasure his noble form—his benevolent countenance—ever beaming with

[1] Horsley's Northumberland, p. 53.

that frank, genial smile, which won the hearts of all around him?

In 1878 the good old Earl died lamented by all on the Eslington estate, of whom a local poet wrote:—

"The kindly man, the dear, familiar face,
We miss from the accustomed place,
Where he was wont to kneel in prayer
As lowly as the humblest there."
. . . .
"A man of high and cultured mind,
He loved his country and his kind;
For Britain's rights, his country's good,
He like a patriot staunchly stood;
. . . .
Such was the man we miss and mourn."

(In Memoriam, by Jas. Thomson).

"In the memorable election struggles of 1826, Lord Ravensworth, then the Hon. Henry Thomas Liddell, played a prominent part; he was the popular candidate from the outset, and maintained his position to the end. As one of his admirers expressed it in sentimental verse:—

"Our strife is who shall love him most,
Who most behold, and near him tarry;
Our greatest pride, our country's boast,
Is gallant, noble, matchless Harry."

While another, less mellifluous, but more heroic, bade his fellows:—

"Strike, strike, Northumbria's harp again!
Exhaustless still the glorious strain
Great Liddell's worth inspires;
His honest heart, his judgment clear,
His eloquence to thousands dear
Each patriot's bosom fires."

Thus, through the scorching days of the hottest summer on record, the strife went on, till after a fifteen days' poll (from June 20 to July 6) the great election of 1826 came to an end, and the Hon. H. T. Liddell, who headed the lists the first day, and kept his position to the close, was triumphantly returned. The figures were declared to be for—

The Hon. H. T. Liddell	1,562
Matthew Bell, Esq.	1,380
T. W. Beaumont, Esq.	1,335
Viscount Howick (retired)	977"[1]

Liddell's colours were pink and white,[2] and his tune "Because he was a bonnie lad." Bell's colour was blue, and his tune "The bonnie pit lad." Beaumont's colour was white, and his tune "The white cockade." While Lord Howick's colours were blue and buff, and his tune "Orange and blue." Elections sixty years ago were very different affairs indeed to our uninteresting and matter-of-fact ballot-box system of the present day. Those were the days of husting speeches—open voting—processions and demonstrations—bands of music, stale eggs and bags of soot—feasting and drinking, fun and revelry, and big bills for the candidates. We have been told on good authority that during the fifteen days of the great general election of 1826, cartloads of voters and their friends out of the valleys of the Coquet and Aln travelled daily back and forward to Alnwick—the town where the election was held, a distance of from eight to ten or twelve miles—to be feasted and refreshed by the Tories one day—by the Whigs the next. After being feasted and refreshed at the expense of each party alternately, they voted for their man on the very last day of the poll, with feelings of regret that the glorious campaign had come to an end. When Mr. Liddell, after the election, went to Rothbury to thank his supporters there, a great crowd met him at the west end of Beggar Rig, took the horses out of his carriage, and dragged the successful candidate in triumph into the village. In doing so two men were unfortunately run over—one, John Mackay, was killed on the spot; the other,

---

[1] *Weekly Chronicle*, Jan., 1891, "Men of Mark 'twixt Tyne and Tweed," by Richard Welford.

[2] "When bright beauty's glance is beaming,
Lasses' love and lads' delight,
See young *Liddell's* colours streaming,
In a flood of *pink* and *white*."—(Surtees).

William Storey, was seriously injured. Mr. Liddell put up at the "Three Half Moons," then the principal inn at Rothbury, kept by Mr. David Maxwell. David was a staunch supporter of the Liddell party, and the glass goblets used in the "Half Moons" on that occasion, and during the whole time of the election, had engraved around them "Liddell for ever, and staunch promises." The late Mr. Anthony Oliver, gardener at Eslington Park, an old and faithful servant of the Ravensworth family, was at that time a young man in the service of the Hon. H. T. Liddell, and often related how, during the heat of the 1826 election, he had to run the gauntlet to reach a place of safety, where he was obliged to remain for several hours, to escape the fury of a Newcastle mob, who, exasperated by the pink and white rosette in his hat, were pursuing him "hot trod" through the streets of Newcastle.[1]

---

[1] Mr. Oliver lived until he was 80 years of age, being gardener at Eslington Park until the day of his death. He died in 1881, when the following notice of him appeared in the columns of the *Newcastle Daily Journal*:—"As will be seen in our obituary column, there passed away from our midst, on Monday last, at the ripe old age of fourscore years, one whom we may term an 'old standard,' one of the 'past generation'—Mr. Anthony Oliver, gardener, Eslington Park, near Whittingham. Mr Oliver, for the long period of fifty-eight years, faithfully filled the office of gardener to the noble family of Ravensworth, with whose members, both old and young, and at all times, he was a special favourite. Fifty-six of these years were spent at Eslington, having gone there in the eventful 1826, the year of the great General Election, in which his master, then the Hon. H. T. Liddell, took such an active part as Tory candidate for Northumberland, the whole county at that time being one constituency, and was returned at the head of the poll. Mr. Oliver was a great reader, had a retentive memory, and in his conversation had an amount of dry humour, mixed with good common sense, and was altogether a most intelligent man. In religious matters he was a consistent and one of the oldest members of the English Presbyterian Church at Branton. Having been married on Christmas day, 1826, after 55 years of wedded life, he leaves a widow and family to lament his loss. He at one time took a great interest in the local flower show of Whittingham, when his assistance and advice were much valued. He also for many years contributed to the *Alnwick Mercury* a series of well-written articles on 'Cottage Gardening,' which contained much useful information for amateurs, whom he always styled as 'Friends,' and many will yet remember the initials used by the old man, A. O. E. P. He has died full of years, and feelings of the greatest respect from all classes who knew him will follow him to the grave. His death will leave a blank not easily filled in the Vale of the Aln."—*Communicated.*

Numerous very amusing squibs and songs were written at the time of the election, for and against the different candidates, from which we select the following :—

FOR LIDDELL.

Liddell for ever!

Strike up in full concert, pipe, tabor, and fiddle!
Northumbrian Freeholders ; rejoice one and all,
You've called to your service your well-beloved Liddell,
And true to his word, he obeys the high call.
His star lately waning,
Th' ascendance is gaining
On high, see! it rises transcendently bright;
In mild glory beaming
Its radiance is streaming,
And the *rival orbs* twinkling are lost in its light.
O Liddell for ever!
Now lads, now or never,
Support him, nor heed opposition a straw!
If private worth charms ye,
If eloquence warms ye,
Then Liddell for ever!—Hurrah! lads, hurrah!

The Greenwich Receiver may hector and bluster,
Brave *Blenky* may boast of his promise the breach,
Little *Nunky* his troop may triumphantly muster,
The Parson a volunteer sermon may preach:
The Receiver we'll jeer at,
And *Blenky* we'll sneer at,
For *Nunky* the tears of compassion will spring;
The priest—heaven mend him;
His trumpet may lend him:
Still, with Liddell for ever! the welkin shall ring.
O Liddell for ever!
Now lads, now or never,
Support him, nor heed opposition a straw.
If private worth charms ye,
If eloquence warms ye,
Then Liddell for ever!—Hurrah! lads, hurrah!

The fair brow of Beauty no longer is clouded,
No more in her looks deep dejection we trace;
On her cheek, where the *lily* so lately intruded,
Behold the bright *rose* is resuming its place.
Her eye brightly glistens,
To Hope as she listens;
She whispers, "Soon Liddell triumphant you'll view!"
Th' emotion excited
Shall never be blighted,
For his friends and supporters all staunch are and true;

And soon, lads, at Alnwick
The *Blues* in a panic,
Shall see us the Hustings come pouring around;
Worth and *Honour* shall laud us
And *Beauty* applaud us
Whilst with Liddell for ever! the air shall resound.

Let Bell, to sweet Woolsington wisely retiring
Enjoy the delights of the *Bottle* and *Chase*,
Nor a seat in St. Stephen's think more of acquiring,
Where surely he'll find himself—out of his place—
For all understand Matt,
Is but a poor hand at
Speech-making—he's none of your eloquent Prigs—
Then why should we send him
Where nought can attend him,
But neglect from the Tories and scorn from the Whigs.
O Liddell for ever!
He's honest, he's clever;
And when in the Senate he raises his voice,
With many a loud *hear him!*
All parties shall cheer him,
And crown with high plaudits the man of our choice.

The following rhyme was composed by a person, named Elizabeth Wyndham, who was better known as "Betty Wundrum," of Percy's Cross:—

LIDDLE FOR ME!

Tune: "Jigging for Me."

By the margin of Tyne as I saunter'd along,
I heard an old woman lilt up a new song,
As she sat near a cot, with a child on her knee,
And the burthen was—"Liddell, brave Liddell for me!"

Chorus—
O Liddell, sweet Liddell, brave Liddell for me,
O Liddell, sweet Liddell, brave Liddell for me,
For a Parliament man he will suit to a T—
The bright star of Eslington—Liddell for me!

O Liddell and Bell are now running a heat,
The prize to the winner—a Parliament seat;
And Liddell's the man that will suit to a T—
The bright star of Eslington—Liddell for me!
O Liddell, sweet Liddell, &c.

Matt. Bell's a good shot, and can stand a good drink,
At the cry of the hounds he'll run off in a blink.

May the next fox he chases run into the sea,
And he follow after it—Liddell for me!
O Liddell, sweet Liddell, &c.

O Liddell cares little about a fox chase,
But Liddell has goodness and Liddell has grace,
And Liddell I'll love till the day that I dee—
The bright star of Eslington—Liddell for me!
O Liddell, sweet Liddell, &c.

May Liddell succeed with his aim in the end,
For Liddell has been our supporter and friend;
At a tale of distress the tear starts in his e'e—
The bright star of Eslington—Liddell for me!
O Liddell, sweet Liddell, &c.

Now the old wife arose, and entered her cot,
And more of this favourite song I heard not;
But her lilting made such an impression on me,
That all the way home I sang—Liddell for me!
O Liddell, sweet Liddell, &c.

For Bell.

Matt. Bell and Kenn'd Worth.

Tune: "Sing hey diddle diddle, the cat and the fiddle."

Sing hey diddle diddle,
Here's young Mister Liddell,
To Parliament wishes to go;
Then give us your voices,
And that will rejoice us,
How say you, freeholders?—No, no!

He's smart and he's natty,
He's tall and he's pretty,
Of very first water a beau;
At court and at gala,
He's sure without fellow,
How say you, freeholders?—No, no!

At waltz and quadrille,
He's quite sans pareil:
On fiddle he draws a good bow.
Then send him to London
That we mayn't be undone;
How say you, freeholders?—No, no!

No, no, Mr. Liddell,
Tho' you dance and can fiddle,
You won't do for us of the north;
Tho' your coat's the first fashion,
And your style very dashing,
We like better Matt. Bell, and kenn'd Worth.

On the death of his father, in 1855, the Hon. H. T. Liddell was called to the House of Lords, when: "Released from the responsibilties of political life in the House of Commons, Lord Ravensworth found more time to cultivate the gifts with which Nature had endowed him. For, outside of the political world, his lordship was a man of many and widely varied parts. An excellent classical scholar, he could use with great effect both brush and pencil; a poet of no mean order, he was equally at home in Natural History or Roman Antiquities; a fluent and effective orator, he wielded, at the same time, the pen of a ready and graceful writer. Lord Ravensworth's felicitous power of expression, and the rich garniture of classical imagery with which be studded his public addresses, were the delight of cultivated audiences. Rarely, during his later life, did a great public function occur in the North of England at which his lordship was not a welcome president, celebrant, or guest. Upon such occasions, he was singularly successful in winning the assent and enlisting the sympathetic concurrence of his hearers. On the 2nd of April, 1874, when he had entered his seventy-eighth year, his lordship was advanced a step in the peerage, being created Earl of Ravensworth and Baron Eslington. He died on the 19th of March, 1878, having enjoyed his added honours barely four years, and was buried among his ancestors at Lamesley."[1]

In 1878, the Hon. Henry George Liddell, the present Earl of Ravensworth, a worthy scion of a noble race, succeeded to the title and estates of his father. Born in 1821, and educated at Eton and Christ Church, Oxford, his lordship has throughout his long career held the esteem and admiration of those amongst whom he has passed his days, both in respect to his qualities as a gentleman, a public man, a sportsman, and a landlord. His youth saw Mr. Henry George Liddell promi-

[1] *Weekly Chronicle*, Jan., 1891.—"Men of Mark 'twixt Tyne and Tweed," by Richard Welford.

nent in the manly sports; he was a noted cricketer, a good shot, and a fearless rider to hounds.

When, at the General Election of 1852, Mr. Henry George Liddell came forward in the Conservative interest to seek the suffrages of the electors of South Northumberland, it was quickly made manifest to all that he must have devoted time and attention to the study of questions affecting the welfare of the commerce and industries of the North of England. The other candidates for the two seats were Mr. W. B. Beaumont, one of the retiring members, and Mr. George Ridley, both of whom were Liberals. Mr. Liddell's speeches were enlivened by the true spirit of patriotism with which they were invested, and this superiority to mere party questions he maintained when returned to Parliament, where he served his constituents with such earnestness and impartiality that, up to the time of his succession to the House of Lords in 1878, his seat was never contested. His first election address contained a declaration of his political views, and in this statement "Mr. Henry George," as he was then and for long popularly known to the people, said he was a decided supporter of Lord Derby's administration. Deeply attached by principle, by education, and by conviction to the Protestant Established Church, he desired to maintain her just rights in all their integrity, at the same time that he regarded all classes of his fellow-Christians in the spirit of universal charity and good-will.

At a meeting in Hexham, convened by the High Sheriff of Northumberland, Mr. Liddell was nominated by Sir Matthew White Ridley, of Blagdon, and seconded by Mr. J. B. Coulson, of Swinburne. In their speeches at Hexham the candidates spoke out freely on questions of the day and local matters. Mr. Liddell said that, short as his experience had been, it had sufficed to teach him who those men were to whom they had to look for the maintenance of those great principles, those rights, privileges, and liberties, which had raised England to the high position in which she stood—a position unequalled, and the envy of every country in the world. He looked to the Conservative Government of Lord Derby. "Free trade" was, he considered, a phrase which was a total fallacy; it was merely a system of free imports. At the poll Mr. Liddell was returned second on the list, the result being—Mr. Beaumont, 2,306; Mr. Liddell, 2,132; Mr. George Ridley, 2,033.

To celebrate the election of Mr. Liddell, a banquet was given to that gentleman in the Corn Exchange, Newcastle, on the 8th July, 1852. Speaking on this occasion, the newly-elected member said he went to Parliament with the conviction that great reforms were needed in our financial system; and he thought he might safely say that it was by these reforms only that relief could be afforded to those great interests which had suffered and were then suffering from recent changes in legislation. When he saw the rapid strides that the commercial, the shipping, the mining, the manufacturing, and agricultural interests were making in South Northumberland, then it became more apparent to his mind that these interests required the almost exclusive attention of their member.

This was the key-note of Lord Ravensworth's career in Parliament, and one of the first actions was to bring about a negotiation for an improvement of the commercial relations of Great Britain and France. The interest of British shipowners had the special attention of Mr. Liddell from first to last, in and out of the House of Commons, and later in the House of Lords. His services in this respect were indeed highly valued. For many years his lordship was President of the Institute of Naval Architects, and he continues to hold the important office of President of the North of England Steamship Owners' Association. To the present day his presidental addresses at the annual gatherings of this influential body are looked forward to with widespread interest, as authoritative utterance on the position of a vast branch of industry.

At a great meeting of the London Shipowners' Society, held in February, 1876, to consider the state of the laws in regard to merchant shipping, Lord Ravensworth—(then Lord Eslington)—was asked to preside. His lordship stated that the shipowners did not want a fussy, meddlesome, crotchetty interference with their business—they asked simply for a fair field and no favour, feeling confident of their ability to hold their own if that were granted them. They did not, however, want to see an artificial stimulus given to foreign trade; nor, above all, did they want to be legislated for in a spirit of suspicion. It was a national matter, and he was there as an Englishman; and as an Englishman he could not forget, and he would not ignore, what the merchant shipping had done for this country.

As a result of this meeting, Mr. Disraeli received a deputation of the shipowners, introduced by Mr. Goschen, and headed by Lord Eslington. The interview, happily, was productive of legislation, if not setting at rest the most difficult questions raised.

Lord Ravensworth acted as President of the North-East Coast Exhibition, held at Tynemouth, in 1882, and was President of the Council of the Newcastle Jubilee Exhibition of 1887, in which capacity his lordship had the honour of receiving, at the opening ceremony, His Royal Highness the Duke of Cambridge, and later in the season His Royal Highness the Prince of Wales.

About the middle of the last century William Allan, father of the celebrated James Allan, the Duke of Northumberland's piper, who then lived at Hepple, in Coquetdale, was often over at Eslington Park, where, with his favourite dogs, Charley, Phœbe, and Peachem, he would stay a fortnight or three weeks together, being employed by Lord Ravensworth to kill some otters which threatened to destroy all the fish in the pond at Eslington. At that time the river Aln, which flows close past the south front of Eslington House, was damned back and formed a broad sheet of water extending from bank to bank.[1] The sloping boat landing can yet be seen on either side. It was, no doubt, in this pond or lake where Will and his dogs hunted the otters, and with his rough and ready sayings afforded at the same time much amusement to his lordship. Will used to say—"When my Peachem gi'es mouth, I durst always sell the otter's skin." Once Mr. Bell, the agent, was told by his lordship to ask Will if he would sell him the dog Charley, and to fix any price he liked. His reply was—"His hale estate canna buy Charley." When at Eslington, Will was well entertained; he had whatever he could eat or drink, and always had a comfortable bed to lie on. But Will, probably accustomed only to a woollen rug wrapped around him, did not appreciate the privilege of clean sheets, and once gave the following account of how he spent a night at Eslington:—"And," says he, "when night cam on they put me in amang some things they ca' sheets; I slid, and I slid, and I slid about, and rolled first on ane side and then on the other, just iv all the warld as tho' I had been thrawn in to sleep amang salmon. At last I kicked out the things they ca' sheets, and fell in amang the blankets, where I got foothad, and slept till the mornin'."

Will died at Whitton, near Rothbury, in 1779, while attempting to play the tune, "Dorrington Lads Yet," on the bagpipes. The Reedwater minstrel thus describes him:—

"A stalwart tinkler wight was he,
And weel could mend a pot or pan,
And deftly Wull could thraw a flee,
An' neatly weave the willow wan'."

---

[1] This lake has long since disappeared, but it was probably that "piece of water" referred to in the following extract from the itinerary of a journey made in 1835 by James and Hannah Bell, from Preston in Lancashire to Harbottle in Northumberland:—"June 12th, 1835, Whitingham.—Refreshed ourselves and Dapper (the horse). Day rather foggy, yet pretty fine. Had a pleasant drive thro' a beautiful fertile country; passed the seat of Lord Ravensworth, a pretty Hall, with a fine piece of water in front and plantation, which give it a pleasing appearance."

About a mile to the north-east of Eslington is the Mountain farm, where there stands the quaint seventeenth century house, now covered with "Red Pan-tiles"—once the farm-house—of which we here give an engraving.

While in the garden of the modern farm house there is the door-head of another house of much interest, for thereon is cut the letters "G. C. 1709," the initials of the unfortunate George Collingwood who forfeited his life and estates in the fatal rising of 1715. This was probably the doorway of a house that stood on the same site, which for many years after the death of the head of the house of Eslington, was the residence of two of the Collingwood family—the Misses Collingwood.

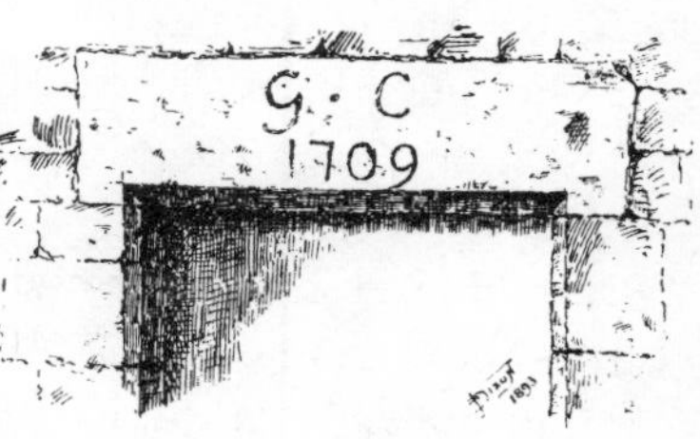

On an acclivity to the north of Eslington, in a thick plantation, stands a building known as "Dunse Castle," a name it derives from the fact of having been the stable of a celebrated steed called "Dunse."

Eslington House is a massive quadrangular block of warm-coloured freestone, erected, as already stated, about the year 1720, which (standing, as it does, in a charmingly sheltered situation, surrounded by tastefully laid out gardens and shrubberies, pleasant lawns and a well wooded park, stocked with a fine herd of fallow deer) forms a perfect ideal of an Old English country mansion. A sheet of water in the park, west of the house, is a spot full of the greatest interest to the botanist, the naturalist, and the ornithologist. Amid a tropical-like growth of Bulrushes, Greater Reed Mace *(Typha latifolia)*, Purple Loosestrife *(Lythrum salicaria)*, Great Hairy Willow Herb, Queen of the Meadow, and the large flat leaves of the White Water Lily *(Nymphea alba)*,[1] may be seen darting hither and thither the Coot, the Tern, aud many other species of water fowl, in whose movements and preservation the noble owner — in a true Selbornian spirit — takes the most lively interest. The garden at Eslington Park has ever been famous for the luxurious beauty of its flowers, the perfection of its fruits and vegetables, as well as for the splendid order in which the shrubberies and gardens have for many years been kept under the fostering care of two generations of the Olivers — the late Anthony Oliver, and his son, Mr. Joseph Oliver, the present gardener. Mr. Oliver is an eminent and most successful florist, having propagated several very excellent varieties of Dahlias, Hollyhocks, and other plants, his latest development being two superb Penstemons, which he has named the Earl and the Countess. The gardens abound not only in the best specimens of our modern flowers, but one's eyes are gladdened by the sight of an endless variety of those good old-fashioned herbaceous plants and flowers which have always been the glory of our English gardens. Here we see dense masses of the Lythrum, whose pyramidal

[1] Amongst many other interesting specimens of English Wild Flowers growing in the immediate vicinity of Eslington, are the Marsh Violet, Yellow Mimulus, Marsh Cinquefoil, Birds'-nest Orchis, Yellow Toad-flax, and Enchanter's Nightshade.

spikes of lovely purple flowers mingle with the golden yellow of the Solidago and the bright purple of the Monkshood, while rich borders of Begonias, Calceolareas, Violas, and the deep clear blue of a Lobelia—one of Mr. Oliver's seedlings—are intermixed with pleasing effect, each plot evincing the greatest care and skill in their arrangement.

A fine Arborvitæ, standing on the lawn, is cut and trimmed into the shape of a large peacock, a relic of the conventional gardening of fifty years ago. Several handsome Spanish Chestnut trees, of somewhat peculiar growth, are also of some interest; while scattered throughout the park are clumps of magnificent Sycamores, Beeches, and lofty Firs—one noble specimen of the silver fir having reached the altitude of one hundred and twenty-four feet.[1]

The beauties and attractions of Eslington have often been sung, and we here append a copy of a broadsheet published some time between 1840 and 1850:—

ESLINGTON.

A SONG OF ALNSIDE.

By JAMES WRIGHT, *Comedian.*

The high-flown Muse, on soaring wing,
May foreign castles praise;
To Eslington my humble voice,
In grateful notes I'll raise.

Then come ye sons of Alnside,
None ever can ye blame,
Come sing in praise of Eslington,
And Liddell's honoured name.

Thy crystal waters, murmuring low,
Reflect the solar beam;
The speckled trout in all its pride
Sports wanton in the stream.

Then Alnham and the sister Ryles,
You all must feel the same,
Come sing in praise of Eslington,
And Liddell's honoured name.

The bounding roe and fallow deer
Trip o'er thy verdant lawn,

[1] This and other trees in the park were blown down in the gale of Saturday, December 29th, 1894. (See Appendix.)

The stately buck, with antlered head,
The doe and timid fawn.

Then canny lads of Whittingham,
Come join with loud acclaim,
And sing in praise of Eslington,
And Liddell's honoured name.

Improvements such as these we see
Proclaim the owner's taste,
An earthly paradise is made
Of wilderness and waste.

Then Barton and the Bridge of Aln,
Your voices here I claim,
Huzza! for bonny Eslington,
And Liddell's honoured name.

Though shady bowers and streams without
The Poet's praise may win,
We'll not forget those lovely forms
That grace thy hearth within.

And now accept a toast from me,
The best my heart can frame,
The noble House of Ravensworth,
And Liddell's honoured name.

The late Hon. and Rev. Robert Liddell (uncle to the present Earl of Ravensworth) was, some thirty or forty years ago, a frequent visitor at Eslington. He was an enthusiastic and expert angler, and we feel assured that the following lines, descriptive of a fishing excursion to the north, written by the rev. gentleman, with which we shall conclude this notice of the charming vill and manor of Eslington, will be read with interest by those of our readers who are acquainted with the district:—

COMPENSATION.[1]

The summer passed by more sunny and dry
In the north than old folks could remember,
And unless I forget, there was not the least wet
Till about the thirteenth of September.

I had visits to pay, and had promised to stay
At Eslington first, in my outing:
Though Lord R. wrote me word, it was simply absurd
To expect in the Aln any trouting.

[1] "The Lay of the Last Angler," by the Hon. and Rev. Robert Liddell, formerly Vicar of St. Paul's, Wilton Place, London.—Rutherford, Kelso, 1884.

The stream at the time was a streak of green slime,
  Without over-statement or blether;
Nor did he once care, all the weeks he'd been there,
  To put his trout tackle together.

Now here was my run of good fortune begun
  (For I wasn't delayed by this panic);
As we started by train, a magnificent rain
  Went with us from London to Alnwick!

And when the chaise stopped—as "at home" we were dropped—
  To be welcomed by Harry, dear fellow!
The Aln had "gaen oot" abune half a foot,
  Quite as thick as pea soup, and as yellow!

Next day she'd run in, pale-coloured and thin,
  With east wind a nice ripple producing;
And a drizzling rain just now and again,
  Which proved to the trouties seducing.

Nor is there a doubt that, after long drought,
  When fish have grown feckless and lazy
The very first shower has magical power
  To drive them all perfectly crazy.

So I fancied to try if they'd look at the fly;
  My nephew'd gone out for some shooting,
Letting "Uncle Rob" stay to go after his prey—
  They call me "Rob-water" for looting!

There's a limited space just in front of the place
  Scarce the fourth of a mile in extension,
'Twixt a foot-bridge and lane, and the "cauld" of grey stane
  (Border term for dam-head, I may mention).

Then the burn's from the door sixty yards and no more,
  Where we oft wet our line at beginnings;
But I little thought such a lot would be caught
  In such a small distance for innings.

It proved the good scheme of fishing *up* stream,
  And more than rewarded my labours;
For each bonnie trout was drawn downwards and out,
  Without ever disturbing his neighbours.

They were rising so fast, there was scarcely a cast
  But one took the first fly he might chance see—
(I put on but two, and I'll tell 'em to you,
  A "hare's lug," and at tail "Hoffland's Fancy.")

The result was a score of five dozen and more
  (Baker's dozens they were, if you ask it),
And, weighing all round three or four to the pound,
  They made a respectable basket.

In that evening the rain came in earnest again,
 And continued all night without stopping,
So the next day at eight we'd a furious spate,
 All the banks to some distance o'er-topping.

'Twould be two days from hence ere water so dense
 To a normal condition subsided,
And in four at the most I must leave my kind host,
 Which none could regret more than I did.

But what of the third ?—if by luck it occurred
 That the weather would quietly settle,
The Aln in that time would clear off its slime,
 And for fly be in excellent fettle.

When that day was at hand the river was grand !
 For our purpose it scarce could be better ;
But white clouds in blue sky, and hot sun in one's eye,
 Were scarce angling signs to the letter.

'Tisn't easy to say which is best in its way—
 A full water or suitable weather ;
And 'tis only in dreams that a fisherman seems
 To secure both conditions together.

'Tis better, indeed, we are mostly agreed,
 That Providence rules this proceeding ;
But if I had my cboice, I should always rejoice
 At high water in course of receding.

Fish are on the *qui vive* from morning till eve
 When a river is flushed in its running,
And they're mostly so keen for what they can glean,
 That their appetite conquers their cunning.

As sods break away from the edge of the brae,
 Worms and larvæ are dropped in the eddy ;
And each little prize is noted by eyes,
 And mouths to devour them are ready.

On food they will gloat till they're full to the throat,
 And the mass tumbles out of their gullet ;
Yet still they will rise at the succulent flies,
 As an epicure plays with a pullet.

But after two days of glut in such ways
 They become rather careless and saucy,
And unless they are hit by a tempting tit-bit,
 They don't or they *won't*, any more see.

We walked up a mile, past the mill of Great Ryle,
 Before we began our campaigning ;
For there we could find many pools to our mind,
 Dark-coloured, but clearness regaining.

To counteract glare, a westerly air
  Gave the flies a nice undulous motion,
Inviting the trout to be on the look-out,
  If on feeding they had the least notion.

To make my tale short, we had excellent sport,
  Though they wanted some little persuasion ;
Yet they rose pretty fast, and we numbered at last
  Just the same as on th' other occasion.

Thus ended my bout with the Eslington trout,
  For a burn 'twas sufficiently fruity ;
But for salmon I burned, and to Scotland adjourned
  In hopes of some weightier booty.

. . . .

. . . .

CHAPTER VIII.

CALLALY.

Callaly, an Ancient Estate of the Claverings—Held under the Tenure of Drengage and Truncage—Old Forms of Spelling Callaly and Yetlington—The Vill of William de Callaly in 1247—Gilbert de Callaly in 1261—Robert Fitz-Roger in 1271—John Fitz-Robert (Clavering), 1332—Notable Members of the Family—Clavering's Cross—Sir John Clavering, the Royalist, 1644—Sequestration of Callaly Lands, 1653—William Clavering, the Old Jacobite Squire of Callaly, taken Prisoner, 1715—Edward John Clavering, the last of the name, 1876—The Estate Purchased by A. H. Browne, the present owner, 1877—Wills of Gawin Clavering, 1580; Robert Clavering, 1582; William Clavering, 1586—Callaly Castle, 1415-1541—An Old Tradition—Recent Erections—Museum—Dining Room—The Garden and Stables—Callaly Village—Camps at Callaly.

LEAVING Eslington, with its many interesting associations, and crossing about a mile to the south, we come upon Callaly, another of those ancient estates whose history carries us far back in the annals of Alndale, and which for upwards of six centuries and a half was held by the old and honourable family of Clavering.

Callaly,[1] like Eslington, was held in early times under the tenure of drengage[2] by men who took, as was then the general

[1] The various spellings of Callaly given below shews the gradual change into its present form :—Calyalea (1161), Kaleweléé (1219), Calewele (1227), Kaleweley (1230), Calveley (1247), Caluwel (1256), Kalveley (1261), Calvely (1271), Kailoule (1271), Calverley (1306), Calnly (1307), Caluley (1325), Calonly (1327), Calouley (1329), Calyeleghe (1330), Calonly (1361), Callole (1394), Kaloule (1415), Calely (1426), Callalye (1541), Calloley (1568), Callalie (1582), Callaley (1662), Calhalee (1715). The spelling of its sister manor of Yetlington has also undergone many changes :—Yachelinton, Yaclinton (1204), Jakelinton (1211), Yetclinton (1220), Yatlington (1221), Jackelinton (1241), Jackelington (1242), Jachilton (1245), Jaclinton (1253), Jetelinton (1261), Yhetlyngton (1394).

[2] "From some time in the reign of the Conqueror the lands of Callaly and Yetlington were held by a tenure that comprised the duty of sending a cart to Bamburgh with the trunk of a tree for the King's hearth every other day between Whitsuntide and Lammas."—History of Northumberland, Vol. i., p. 24.

CALLALY CASTLE, 1826.

CALLALY CASTLE, 1894.

custom, the surname of the place at which they lived. Therefore, towards the end of the twelfth century and beginning of the thirteenth, it was the vill of William de Callaly, and afterwards of his son and heir, Gilbert de Callaly, both of whom also held the adjoining manor of Yetlington; but Gilbert, "whose father and he had only recently gained emancipation from the old tenure, and the honour of knighthood, unable to redeem his debts, sold Callaly and Yetlington to a Jew, who again disposed of it to the family of Fitz-Roger, lord of Warkworth and numerous other manors, who subsequently took the surname of Clavering from their principal estate of that name in Essex."[1] This change of ownership would appear to have taken place towards the end of the thirteenth century, for in the Charter Rolls, 31 Henry III. (1247), "Willus de Calvely holds Calveley et Yetlington."[2] In the Originalia, 45 Henry III. (1261), Gilbert, the son and heir of William, has Callaly from the King *in capite*;[3] but ten years later, in the Charter Rolls of 55 Henry III. (1271), we find that Robert, the son of Roger, the son of John, has lands in Callaly and Yetlington.[4]

The "Fitzes," or Claverings, were a numerous and powerful family of noble extraction, and claimed to have derived their descent from Charlemagne. The old family name was de Burgh. At the Conquest, Serlo and John, two sons of the Norman baron, Eustace de Burgh, accompanied William Duke of Normandy on his expedition into England; and, as many other Norman barons did, settled down in the manors of the conquered Saxons, which were granted to them by William the Conqueror. Serlo died without issue, and his brother John became possessed of all his lands, who was in turn succeeded by his son, Eustace Fitz-John, Richard Fitz-

[1] History of the Berwickshire Naturalists' Club, Vol. xiii., p. 44.

[2] Hodgson's Northumberland, Part iii., Vol. ii., p. 390.

[3] Hodgson's Northumberland, Part iii., Vol. ii., p. 283.

[4] Hodgson's Northumberland, Part iii., Vol. ii., p. 392.

Eustace, Roger Fitz-Richard (1178)—the first baron of Warkworth—Robert Fitz-Roger (1214), John Fitz-Robert (1240), Roger Fitz-John (1249), Robert Fitz-Roger (1310), and John Fitz-Robert, who assumed the name of Clavering. The arms of the Claverings of Callaly were the same as those borne in 1268 by their great ancestor, Robert Fitz-Roger, lord of Warkworth, namely:—Quarterly, or and gules, a bend sable. The crest of the late family was a cherub's head with wings erect, and their motto—"Ad coelas volans."

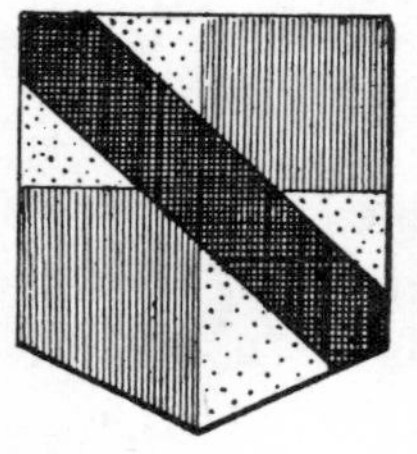

It is worthy of note that, amongst the descendants of Eva, Baroness Clavering, who was four times married, first to Thomas de Audley, Ralph Lord Neville, Ralph de Ufford, and Robert Benkale, there were the following persons of distinction:—"A king of England, a queen of England, a Duchess of York, a Duchess of Clarence, a Duke of Bedford, a Marquis of Montacute, an Earl of Westmoreland, an Earl of Northumberland, an Earl of Salisbury, an Earl of Kent, the celebrated Earl of Warwick, a Lord Latimer, a Lord Abergaveny, an archbishop of York, and an Earl Marshall of England."[1] John Fitz-Robert, Lord Clavering, his cousin Eustace de Vescy of Alnwick, and Lord Robert Fitz-Walter, all of whom were Claverings, were amongst the twenty-five barons who compelled John to sign *Magna Charta* at Runnymede. Lord Robert was the leader, and thus rendered himself most obnoxious to the King. In 1332, John de Clavering, baron of Warkworth and Clavering, died without male issue, and the estates became the property of the Percies, but Callaly appears to have remained in the hands of a branch of the family, for in the 17 Richard II. (1394), "Callole et Yhetlyngton" were held by Robert Clavering, Knight;[2] and, although

[1] Mackenzie's Northumberland, Vol. ii., page 28. (Note.)

[2] Escheats of 17 Richard II., Hodgson's Northumberland, Part iii., Vol. ii., p. 259.

the Claverings took a leading part in nearly every civil commotion, down to the rising of 1715, yet they continued to hold Callaly for six centuries and a half in unbroken descent.

In the midst of the tumult and turmoil that existed in Northumberland during the stormy days of the Tudors, in which the Claverings usually contrived to be mixed up, it is not surprising to us to find that many of the male members of that family did not die in their beds, but in some way or other met with violent deaths in field of battle or Border brawl. Localities where these frays took place (frequently linked with a tradition of the death of some person of note who was in the fight) are to be found all over the county, such as: "Percy's Cross," Malcolm's Cross," Russell's Cairn." Another of these sites is known as "Clavering's Cross," at Stanton, near Morpeth, respecting which there is the following account:—"On the Limekiln flat, about a quarter of a mile north of the village, a stone cross still stands in a field, on the east side of the way, which the tradition of the neighbourhood says was set up in memory of a gentleman of the name of Clavering being slain on the spot in an encounter with a party of Scots.[1] Though what is left of the cross is apparently older than 1517, yet it may have obtained its name from the fact that on the 10th April, 1517, Edward Horsley of 'Scranwodd,' came to the Cathedral Church of Durham and sought immunity for feloniously striking a certain Chr. Clavering of 'Calyle' upon the head and in other parts of the body with a sword at Goorfen, between Morpeth and Horsley, on the 2nd April then inst., from which he died on the same day; as also did Chr. Horsley for similarly striking John Carr of Hetton, at the same place and time, with a sword and dagger."[2]

Affrays amongst underlings, as well as lordly feuds, were very common events in the everyday life of our ancestors.

---

[1] Hodgson's Northumberland, Part ii., Vol. ii., p. 111.

[2] Proceedings of Society of Antiquaries, Newcastle-on-Tyne, Vol. vi., p. 208.

We here record an incident which took place some three centuries before the encounter just related, which vividly illustrates the rude and savage manners of the burly Northumbrian borderer of the thirteenth century:—"William the forester of Callaly had slain Alan Foders within the vill of Eslington, and forthwith had fled and is suspected, therefore let him be driven out and outlawed. His chattels are worth 36s., for which the Sheriff has to account. Afterwards it is shown that Alan—a certain quarrel having formerly arisen between them—had assaulted the aforesaid, and the said William fled to the house of a certain Peter the baker and shut the door; and Alan followed and broke open the door upon him, wishing to kill him, so that the said William seeking to defend himself, for that one or other of them, was not able to avoid his own death, struck the aforesaid Alan with a certain staff on the head, so that he died from that cause." (7th Edward I., 1279.)[1]

During the Great Rebellion of the seventeenth century, Sir John Clavering, of Callaly, with his three sons, Sir Robert, Ralph, and Thomas, stoutly supported the king's cause, not only with men and money, but in personal services in the field:—

"He has doffed the silk doublet the breastplate to bear,
He has placed the steel cap o'er his long-flowing hair;
From his belt to his stirrup his broadsword hangs down—
Heaven shield the brave Gallant that fights for the Crown!"

"For the rights of fair England that broadsword he draws,
Her King is his leader, her Church is his cause;
His watchword is honour, his pay is renown,—
God strike with the Gallant that strikes for the Crown!"

In 1644 the brave Sir John was taken prisoner by the Roundheads and conveyed to Yarmouth, thence to Norwich, and finally to London, where, after having been "barbarously used in many prisons and common gaoles, dyed a prisoner in London in the latter end of 1647." Of his son, Sir Robert,

[1] Northumberland Assize Rolls, Surtees Society, 88, p. 322.

Sir Marmaduke Langdale, the commander of the Royalist army in the north, thus speaks in his certificate of service, dated 1660:—"His eldest sonne, Sir Robert Clavering, in the beginning of the said troubles, at his own chardge, raised a regiment of horse and another of foote, with some troops of dragoones; with these he often eminently served his late maiestie, as appeared by their many engagements, more particularly at Anderton Moor fight, where he (commanding the forlornè hope) was very instrumental in gayning that greate victory which then made us masters of the north."[1] These Border men, who formed part of the "Loyal Duke of Newcastle's" army, were known wherever they went as "Newcastle's Whitecoats," from the colour of their doublets; and it is recorded of these hardy Northumbrians that at Marston Moor, even when completely overpowered by numbers, they stood like a wall until shot down, and after the battle a long white line showed where the brave regiment had so steadily fought, in whose ranks were doubtless found many a sturdy yeoman out of the vales of the Breamish, the Coquet, and the Aln. For their loyalty to Charles I. the Claverings lost High Trewhitt. In 1652 it was sequestrated by Parliament, and some ten years after it was in the possession of a member of an influential Parliamentarian family in Coquetdale named Potts, and it was only by the payment of heavy fines that John Clavering, son and heir of the unfortunate Royalist, Sir John Clavering, retained possession of the paternal estate and manor of Callaly, an account of which is found in the State Papers, as follows:—

"JOHN CLAVERING.—Recusant, Callaly, Northumberland and the Claimant on the Estates of his Father Sir John Clavering."

"21 June. He begs ⅓ of his estate, sequestered for his recusancy."

---

[1] Mackenzie's Northumberland, Vol. ii., p. 31. (Note.)

"21 June. The County Committee of Northumberland are to certify why they do not allow him ⅓ of his estates."

"7th Nov. They report that it was sequestered for the delinquency of his father Sir John Clavering, now dead, who was Commissioner of Array and active in the first war, and that, as no composition has been made, he can only claim $^1/_5$."

"3d. Nov., 1653. John Clavering begs to compound for Whittingham Rectory, which is surveyed and in the late Act of Sale."

(He pays the fine and gets ⅓ of Callaly Manor, &c.)

"9th Dec., 1653. Allowed ⅓ of Callaly Manor and other lands and his mansion house for habitation with arrears from 1649."

"16th Sept., 1653. Discharge from sequestration of houses &c. Upper Trewhet, Rothbury, Northumberland, forfeited by SIR JOHN CLAVERING, &c."

"17th Feb., 1654. NICH. OGLE of Eslington Northumberland begs confirmation of a contract of 23 Aug. 1653 for 4 years with the County Commissioners of ⅔ of Callaly Farm sequestered for recusancy of John Clavering, rent £44 13s. 4d., being let according to instructions and at full value. Noted the County Commissioners to certify the contract and sealing of the lease."[1]

In the calendar of prisoners confined in the dungeon of the Castle at Newcastle-upon-Tyne, waiting their trial at the Assizes, to be held in July, 1629, we find several to have been committed by Sir John Clavering, Knight. On the 19th January, 1628, he committed :—

"George Bourne of Aylneham moore, for the felonious stealeing of two sheepe w[ch] vpon his examinac'on he hath confessed being the goodes of one Robert Wright of Ingram, Webster."

"George Tate, for the felonious stealing of five sheepe, the goodes of William Kirsopp of Ingram."

---

[1] Calendar of the Committee for Compounding, &c. (Domestic), 1643-1660 Part iii., pp. 2340-2 (Callaly).

"3rd April, 1629. John Burne of Snytter, for the murthering & killing of Robert Lawson, late of Snytter, his Maister, wch upon his examinac'on he hath confessed."[1]

Robert Clavering, Esq., was the owner of Callaly and Yetlington in 1663, when the annual rental was £288. Callaly Mill at that time belonged to Ralph Clavering, Esq., and the rental of it was £5 10s.

The Claverings were deeply involved in the Jacobite rising of 1715; and for the leading part they took in that unfortunate affair, William Clavering of Callaly, and his brother, John Clavering, were taken prisoners at Preston fight and conveyed to London. It was only through the benign influence of Lady Cowper, the beautiful Mary Clavering of Chopwell, wife of Lord Cowper, High Steward of England, that her kinsmen—the Claverings—and others of our north country squires, with the exception of the gentle George Collingwood of Eslington, were acquitted and allowed to return to their Northumbrian homes, sadder and wiser men. Lady Cowper in her diary thus speaks of the arrival of the prisoners in London:—"This week, the prisoners were brought to town from Preston. They came in with their arms tied, and their horses (whose bridles were taken off) led each by a soldier. The mob insulted them terribly. The chief of my father's house (William Clavering of Callalee) was amongst them. He was about seventy years old. A desperate fortune had drove him from home in hopes to have repaired it."[2]

The Claverings of Callaly were connected by marriage with many of the principal families in the counties of Northumberland and Durham. Various of its members, during successive generations, married into the families of the Heatons, Fenwicks of Fenwick Tower, Greys of Horton Castle, Riddells of Gateshead, Swinburnes of Capheaton, Lambtons of Lambton, Middletons of Stokefield, Widdring-

---

[1] Arch. Æliana, Vol. i. (Old Series), pp. 157-8.

[2] Lady Cowper's Diary, p. 62.

tons of Widdrington, Selbys of Biddlestone, Erringtons of Haughton, and the Collingwoods of Eslington. Robert Clavering married Mary, daughter of Sir Cuthbert Collingwood, "that courteous knight," who held Eslington during the reign of Queen Elizabeth. "In his will, dated April 21, 1600, Robert Clavering desires burial in the church of Whittingham. He leaves his horse—grey Blackstone—to Hugh Gregson of Berwick."[1]

In 1791 John Clavering, Esq., of Callaly, married Christina, daughter of Sir Edward Swinburne of Capheaton. She died in 1818, and he married as his second wife Catherine, daughter of John Selby, Esq., of Biddlestone. On the 3rd of July, 1838, Edward John Clavering, Esq., the last of the Clavering owners of Callaly, married Jane, only daughter of John Carr, Esq., of Bondgate Hall, Alnwick. He died in 1876, leaving an only daughter, Augusta, Lady Bedingfield, the wife of Sir Henry Paston Bedingfield, of Oxburgh, Norfolk; and in 1877 the estate was sold. Thus, after an ownership of six centuries, the historic name of Clavering was severed from the paternal lands of Callaly, and we cannot, without some feelings of regret, contemplate the breaking up of this old and respected family who, in the heyday of their greatness, were amongst the chief of the landed gentry in North Northumberland.

On the 6th of June, 1877, the ancient estate of Callaly was purchased by Alexander Henry Browne, Esq., J.P., a descendant of an old Northumbrian race, who in days gone by, are said to have owned all the lands lying between Cheviot and the sea. And those who have the weal of their county at heart, must admit that the change in ownership has been a happy one, for a wealthy and resident landlord is beneficial to all classes.

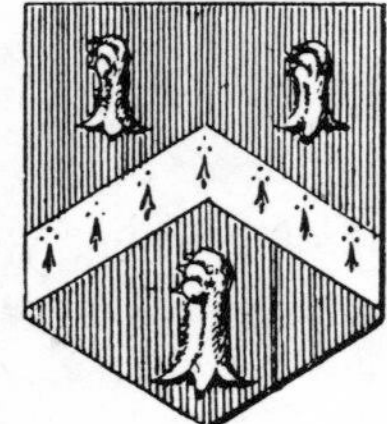

[1] Durham Wills and Inventories.

The following extracts from the wills of the Claverings,[1] besides being curious, will give an idea of the articles of furniture contained in a country mansion three hundred years ago, and also the value of grain and farm stock at that period. The first quoted is the will of Gawin Clavering, "a member of the house of Callaly, who appears to have farmed under the head of his house at Duddoe, and perhaps at Callaly. The numerous legatees under his will were all relations of the family of Clavering":—

"TESTAMENTUM GAWINI CLAVERING.

Nov. 19, 1580. Gawine Claveringe of Callaly, in the parishe of Whittingham, gentleman. To be buryed in the parishe churche of Whittingham. To Robert Claveringe, the elder, esquier, three angells. To my mistresse, his wiffe, one old angell. To Robert Claveringe the younger, an old riall. To James Ogle of Cawsey Parke, one old angell of gold. To Thomas Bradforth of Bradforth, the elder, one old angell of gold, and the same to Thomas Bradforth, the younger. To Elizabeth Foster of Bruntone, one old angell of gold. To John, sonne of James Ogle of Cassey Parke, two angells of gold; the same to George, Cuthbert, Robert, and Charles, his brothers, and Jane and Agnes, his sisters. To William, sonne to Mr. Robert Claveringe, £3, and to Thomas, his brother, 40s. To Thomas Selbye of Bittelston, one angell of gold, and the same to Beill, his wife. To Robert Selbye his sonne, 20s, and to Agnes and Barbarye, his daughters, 5s a pece. To Jane, wife of Thomas Errington of Haughton, one angell. To my cosinge Thomas Claveringe, one gray meare, and one stott at Oldakeris, and all the stottes at Bittleston and Duddaye. To the servantes of the house of Callaly 3s 4d. To William Claveringe of Oldakeris and his wife all the right, &c., which I have in my lease of Wynnynshall, in Biwelle lordshippe, except they provide themselves a better lease, at the expiracion of the lease of Oldakeris. To Raphe Claveringe one old angell, to be paied him at the laste paiement of his farme. To Edmon, sonne to the said Raphe Claveringe, 5s. To the poore, 20s. To the churche of Whittinghame so much as will bye a cloth of green for the table in the queare. I make John, James and Cuthbert Claveringe executors. (Proved Aug. 4, 1581.)"[2]

The second is the will of Robert Clavering, the head of the house:—

"TESTAMENTUM ROBERTI CLAVERING ARMIGERI.

Nov. 30, 1582. Roberte Clavering of Callalie, within the countie of Northumberland, esquier. I committ my bodie to be buried in the Christian buriale, within

[1] Durham Wills and Inventories.

[2] Durham Wills and Inventories, Surtees Society, Vol. xxxviii., p. 94.

the parish churche of Whittinghame, upon the southe side of the quear, next the wall before my wive's seat. To my wel-beloved wief, Ann Claveringe, my maner house of Callalie, with my demayne and milne, together with the whole towne of Callalie, &c. . . . . . Inventorye appriced bye Luke Ogle of Eglenhame, gent, and Richard Satterthwat, vicar of Whittenhame, at Callelye, the last daye of Januarye, 1582. *At Callelye*—Eightene oxen, 20*l*. A bull at *Yetlentone*, 20s. viij. oxen at *Yetlentone*, 8*l*. iiij. stirks ther, 30s. xxiiij. kyn and their folowers, whereof x. of the same kyne and ther folowers be 11*l* 13s, and the other xiiij. kyn and ther folowers, 14*l*. ix. stirks, 3*l*; on branded bull, 20s. On whyt meare at *Yetlenton*, 16s. Tenne score ewes, price of everye on 3s 4d, 33*l* 6s 8d. Thre score gymmers and dynmonts, every on 3s, 9*l*. Six score hogges, 12*l*. viiij. tupes, 24s. xlvj. ewes, 7*l* 13s 4d. Two tupes, 6s. xx. gymers and dynmonts, 3*l*. xxviij. hoggs at 2s the piece 56s. Two meares, 3*l* 6s 8d. On whye with calfe, 20s. Two wheat stacks of xx. boules, 8*l*. Two stacks of beare, of xx. boules, 4*l* 13s 3d. v. stacks of otes, of fourscore boules, 10*l* 13s 4d. xxxiij. boules of wheit sawne at *Callelye*, price of every boule is 8s, 13*l* 4s. Two ruckes of herdcorne at *Yetlenton*, and iiij. boules and a bushell, 20s. lx. thraves of otes, of xx. boules, 53s 4d. xx. thraves of beare, of iij. boules, 14s. Sawne at *Yetlentone*, x. boules of herdcorne, 4*l*. Mor sawne at *Yetlentone* in fermold, v. boules, 40s. iiij. boules of herdcorne at the same fermold in *Yetlenton*, 28s. xl. thraves of otes, of xij. boules, ther at *Yetlenton*, 32s. On heystacke, 5*l*. *The household implements.*—Tene silver sponnes, 15s. On silver salt, 20s. ij. garnishe of puder vessell, 3*l*. On blacke clocke faced with taffetye, 40s. A long gown furred, 46s 8d. A paire of hangings for a bedde, 10s. Five coverings of bedds, 40s. xxviij. payre of course sheits, 4*l* 13s 8d. xix. payre of lynen sheits, 7*l* 12s. Two webes of lynen clothe, contayning fiftye yerds, 50s. viij. puder candlesticks, 13s 4d. v. chamber potts, 3s. iiij. chists, on counter, ij. cofferes, and on cupbord, 26s 8d. On quilt, 6s. On covering of a bedde lyned, 30s. *In the lawe chamber and the highe chamber, at the haule end.*—Four bedsteids, 10s. On basin and on ewer, 4s. x. quissions, 10s. xv. pair of blancots, 3*l*. Thre carpete clothes, 12s. *In the two chambers at the neyther end of the haule*—Foure bedsteids, 10s. Five buffette stooles, 2s 6d. Two pressers, 6s. xxv. pladds, 41s 8d. xvj. coverlets, 48s. Four fetherbedds and four bolsters, 53s 4d. xij. flocke bedds and pillowes, 42s. xiij. pillowbeares, 16s. xiij. bolsters, 17s 4d. *In the kytchin.*—Two new pannes, 12s. Thre kawdrones, 30s. Fyve brasse pottes, 20s. Foure iron speits, 5s. Two dropping pannes, 16s. Two frying pannes, 2s. On payre of racks, 2s 8d. On morter and a pestell, 5s. Fyve swermes of bees in the garding, 10s. On trunk, 5s. xij. swyn, 30s. *In the butterye.*—Foure small table clothes, 13s 4d. Thre round table clothes, 6s. Two dusin table napkynes, 4s. Thre cupbord clothes, 7s. xxxvj. stones of lynt, at 4s 8d every stone, 8*l* 10s 4d. viij. stone and seven pound of Englishe irone, at 16d a stone, 11s 5d. Two firkynes of sope, 20s. On berrell of terre, 12s. Two long waynes, 26s 8d. Thre short waynes, 30s. Thre plughes, with their furnitoures, 10s. vj. boules of ote malt, 24s. The lease of the teith corne of *Callelye*,

19s 9d. The haye at *Yetlentone*, 20s. The increase of xxxiij. boules of wheat, sawn at *Callelye*, by estimation, 21*l* 8s. The increase of x. boules of herdcorn, sawen at *Yetlenton*, by estimation, 8*l*. The increase of v. boules of herdcorn, sawn at *Yetlenton*, by estimation, 4*l*. Corne sould after 12s a boule, as by ther names appeareth in my booke. Of wheat xxij. boules, 13*l* 4s. Beare at 7s the boule, xxx. boules, 10*l* 10s. Otmeile, at 10s the boule, xvj. boules and a kening, 8*l* 1s 6d. Otes, at 4s the boule, xvj. boules and a kening, 3*l* [illegible]s. Malt, at 6s the boule, vj. boules, 50s. Corne owing. In beare, xxiij. boules and a kening, 4*l* 13s. Wheit, vj. boules, 42s. Otes, xxxiiij. boules and a bushell, 3*l* 9s. Of rye, v. boules, 30s. For buter, chease, and malt, 4*l* 15s 9d. Summa totalis, 376*l* 19s 9d. *The debts which Robert Clavering is owing.*—To the queen, 10*l*. To Roger Nycolson, 10*l* 13s 3d. To Thomas Hopper, 4*l* 7s 4d. To the vicare of Whitenham, 66s 8d. To Thomas Reivley, 3*l* 6s 8d. To Robert Caryslaye, 18s. To Cuthbert Clavering, 7*l*. To D. Skerne, 6s. To S. Thompson, 9s. ✠ "[1]

The third is the will of William Clavering of Duddoe. He was the third son of Robert Clavering of Callaly, whose will has just been quoted. He was killed at a Border encounter with the Scots, and probably made this will on the field of battle:—

"TESTAMENTUM WILLELMI CLAVERING.

Memorandum.—That in the latter parte of November, anno 1586, or thereabouts, William Claveringe, late of Duddoe, within the parishe of Norhame, gentilman, beinge of perfect mind and memorie, thoughe verie craysed and sore wounded in his bodye, did make his will noncupative, in manner following. He did geve to his eldest brother, Mr Robert Claveringe, one angell, and to his said brother's wife two angells. . . . . To the poore people of the parishes of Whittingham and Norhame 40s., and he willed that certaine of his shepe should be given to the poore of Duddoe and Tilmouth. All the rest of his goodes, &c., he did legate unto John, James, Cuthbert, and Thomas Clavering, his fower younger brethern whom he made executors. (Proved July 21, 1587.)"[2]

Callaly Castle, the residence of the owners of Callaly, is situated in a charmingly secluded spot at the foot of the well-wooded slopes of Callaly Castle Hill, whose craggy peaks rise on the south some 800 feet above the sea level. Incorporated in the modern building are the remains of an ancient Border tower, the stronghold of the Claverings. A tower was described in the list of 1415 as—"Castrum de Kaloule vet':

---

[1] Durham Wills and Inventories, Surtees Society, Vol. xxxviii., p. 56.

[2] Ibid, p. 151.

Johes Clauerin Chlr.;"[1] and, says the Survey of 1541, "At Callalye ys a toure of thinheritaunce of Claverynge in measurable good repac'ons." If north country tradition is to be relied upon, this was probably the tower which owed its erection on its present site, the level green sward of the "Shepherd's Shaw," to a difference in opinion on that point between the lord of Callaly and his lady in days long gone by, which gave rise to the well-known local rhyme:—

"Callaly Castle stands on the height,
Up i' the day an' doon i' the night;
If ye build it on the Shepherd's Shaw
There it'll stand an' never fa'."

The following version of the legend was given by Mr. George Tate, F.G.S., in an article on "Whittingham Vale," contributed to the *Alnwick Mercury* in 1862:—"A lord of Callaly, in the days of yore, commenced erecting a castle on the hill; his lady preferred a low, sheltered situation in the vale. She remonstrated, but her lord was wilful, and the building continued to progress. What she could not obtain by persuasion she sought to achieve by stratagem, and availed herself of the superstitious opinions and feelings of the age. One of her servants, who was devoted to her interests, entered into her scheme; he was dressed up like a boar, and nightly he ascended the hill and pulled down all that had been built during the day. It was soon whispered that the spiritual powers were opposed to the erection of a castle on the hill; the lord himself became alarmed, and he sent some of his retainers to watch the building during the night and discover the cause of the destruction. Under the influence of the superstitions of the times those retainers magnified appearances, and when the boar issued from the wood and commenced overthrowing the work of the day, they beheld a

---

[1] "Kaloule vet, *i.e.*, Old Callaly, probably refers to the Castle Hill, and not the Tower of Callaly. Sir John Clavering of Callaly died 4 Hen. VI." (1426).—Note, Border Holds, C. J. Bates, Vol. i., p. 14.

monstrous animal of enormous power. Their terror was complete when the boar, standing among the overturned stones, cried out in a loud voice—

> Callaly Castle built on the height,
> Up in the day and down in the night;
> Builded down in the Shepherd's Shaw,
> It shall stand for aye and never fa'.

They immediately fled and informed the lord of the supernatural visitation; and, regarding the rhymes as an expression of the will of Heaven, he abandoned the work and, in accordance with the wish of his lady, built his castle low down in the vale, where the modern mansion now stands."—J. H.[1]

For our description of the architectural features of Callaly Castle we are indebted to an article from the pen of the learned Dr. James Hardy[2]:—"The mansion is of a castellated form, and is of various ages. The western end encases an old peel tower, and has within it a turnpike stair ascending to the roof, and another stair of the same construction embedded in the interior of the building. The oldest date, 1676, is on the dial, which probably belongs to an older structure, with the motto, 'VT HORA SIC VITA.' Beneath it the Clavering motto, 'AD COELAS VOLANS,' is on the scroll of the escutcheon. There are two dates on the front, one central, facing south, with the monogram of R.M.C. and the date 1707; the other on the western face of the eastern wing, with the same initials and date. The age of the main part of the building is thus ascertainable. Above a door on the back part of the house is a shield of a date 1727, with the initials R.C.; this portion is, therefore, of more recent construction. The inscription on a stone dug from the foundation of the apartment that formed the chapel, now being re-built[3] owing to the building having threatened to collapse, underneath an incised dedication cross, is:—

---

[1] The Denham Tracts, Vol. i., p. 324.

[2] History of the Berwickshire Naturalists' Club, Vol. xiii., p. 43.

[3] This was written in 1890.

AN : SAL : MDCC. ? II.
RODVL. CLAVERING
POSVIT.[1]

Beneath this, and freshly cut :—

MDCCCXC.
A. H. BROWNE
RE-POSVIT.

Ornamenting the middle portion of the front there is a ric display of finely cut sculpturing, harmonising with the hand some escutcheon which quarters the family alliances of th far-descended race of the Claverings." . . . . "Within the mansion the rooms are richl furnished with old carved furniture, bureaus, chests, chair and sideboards ; and decorated with statuary, old chin pictures, prints, Indian swords, armour, and ornament Some of the hangings are of the finest Cashmere and India lace ; and the couches are covered with flowered Indian silk The tapestry, representing the conversion and martyrdom St. Paul, was wrought by Belgian nuns."

The spacious saloon in the old portion of the mansion unique and worthy of note. This fine apartment measures 4 feet in length, and is 23 feet high, with a minstrels gallery each end, supported by large pillars, and profusely decorate with beautiful and artistic stucco work. The recent additio to the already imposing pile is the re-building of the easte portion of the structure, and the erection of a museum an central hall of lofty dimensions. The architecture of t additional eastern portion is copied from that part of t mansion erected during the seventeenth century, and consis of a splendid dining room, billiard room, and the museu in which is arranged the very fine collection of antiquiti brought together by the late Mr. William Henry Forman,

[1] Another reading of this inscription is given in our account of St. Mary Whittingham.

Pippbrook House, near Dorking, which a few years ago came into the possession of his nephew, Major Browne. As a private collection it stands almost unrivalled.

For a summary of the contents of the museum we quote from the Proceedings of the Newcastle Society of Antiquaries[1]:—

"The upper room is reserved for the finer and more valuable specimens. Arranged in cases around its walls is a very large number of Greek vases, varying in height from the smallest size to about two feet, decorated with mythological subjects in red on a black ground, and *vice-versâ*. Of these there are more than 800 examples, above 160 of them being Archaic. Many of them are from the Rogers collection. In the same room there are also some beautiful specimens of ancient glass, both plain and variegated, of Greek and Roman manufacture, some of them being highly iridescent, consisting of *amphorae*, *unguentaria*, ribbed bowls, alabastrons, beads, *armillae*, buttons, &c. Where there are so many objects it is somewhat difficult to particularize, but one long Roman glass bottle in the form of a fish is said to be unique; another is like a sword in its sheath; there are spindle-shaped bottles, one 21 inches long; a Roman light green vessel of glass has a spiral thread round the neck. Many are from Cologne, Colchester, London, &c. Amongst other objects are a curious glass ball, of Roman date, formed of cuttings of canes of coloured glass similar to Venetian glass, found in Norfolk; many fragments of variegated glass cups; a number of paste cameos, with heads of Jupiter, Mars, Hadrian, &c., and intaglios; some fine Roman cinerary urns of glass, with and without covers; a large number of glass vessels of different colours, some indented at the sides; a number of gems having various Gnostic devices, &c.

The gold personal ornaments were not seen, as they are amongst the objects on exhibition at Hanley, but they are very numerous and valuable, and are to be kept in octagonal cases in the centre of this room. The most noteworthy are a pair of *armillae* terminating in animals' heads, weighing 3 oz.; two large *fibulae*, with pomegranate and griffins at the ends; a bulla from the S. Rogers collection (inscribed HOST HOS), with chain attached; an Etruscan circular ear ornament, engraved with a triangular pattern; a Greek *fibula*, in form of a couchant lion, of granulated work; earrings terminating in lions' heads; a cup 2 oz. in weight; a ring, with Greek inscription; a necklace formed of thin plates of gold *repoussé*; oval beads with honeysuckles and seven pendants of Victory in a biga (also from the Rogers collection); a necklet of beads of emerald matrix and gold rosettes between; ten gold objects bearing various devices (discovered at Kertch); necklace of open-work beads; ten small pendants of Cupids' heads, and one larger in

---

[1] Meeting of the Society, held at Callaly Castle, on Monday, August 31, 1891. Vol. v., p. 92. (Proceedings.)

centre; a funeral wreath of leaf gold, consisting of three large flowers and leaves *repoussé*, with veins, at each end of the band is a griffin; splendid Greek funeral wreath, weighing more than 8 oz., composed of two separate stalks of ivy leaves and berries; another weighing nearly 5 oz., of myrtle leaves and berries, the end of the stem, ornamented with granulated work, terminating in rings. In one of the centre cases are two fine Merovingian brooches, one being circular and inlaid in rosettes and vandyked with variegated glass on the outer border; the back, ornamented with anulets, has the hinge and sheath for a pin. There are also some Mexican and Peruvian objects of gold; a number of Celtic ring money; Saxon *fibulae*, silver figures, ivory ticket for Colosseum at Rome, two Roman silver clasps, of horse-shoe form, plated with gold, &c. Of Egyptian objects there are portions of mummy cases, large bronze figures of cats, hawks, &c., a large number of alabastrons, ushabtis, scarabs, &c. There are many inscribed Babylonian cylinders and cone seals; also a large number of bronze objects discovered at Chiusi, consisting of figures of animals, &c., and a Roman sacrificial axe of bronze from a temple in Thessaly.

In the lower room there is also a miscellaneous collection of objects of all ages. There are seven Roman *cippi* of marble; with the exception of number 3, which is cyclindical, all are square with pedimented tops. One or two have the remains of the body still in them. The top of one, sloped like a roof, is ornamented with a tegulated pattern. All bear inscriptions.

1 :—SERGIA SEDATA | SERGIAE LAIDIS LIB | FILI FECERVNT ET | SIBI. Above inscription two figures, a man and woman, standing holding hands; three lines before erased. All in sunk tablet surrounded by leaf moulding.

2 D · M | CLAVDIAE VICTORIN | E · CLAVDIA · PRISCA · ET CLAVDIVS · SABINVS | MATRI PIENTISSIMAE.

3 A round cippus with vine leaves, rams' heads, and birds in relief. DIS · MANIBVS | TI CLAVDI | SATVRNINI | TI · F · VII · VIR | EPVLON.

4 In a sunk tablet: DIS · MANIBVS | FABIAE · D · L | FELICVLAE; surrounded by ivy leaves and flowers.

5 DIS MANIB | ANNIAE P · F · ISIADI · VIXIT · ANNIS | XVI · MENSIB II DIEB XVII | CORNELIVS · P · L · MAMERTINV | VIR · INFELICISSIMVS | FECIT | CONIVGI DVLCI FIDELI PIAE | CONIVGALI ET SIBI. in a square sunk panel; at each side a figure standing on an animal's head (ram) holding a festoon of leaves and fruit, two birds pecking; in angle of lid, an ox head, a cornucopia at each side.

6 In sunk moulded panel:—L · MVNIVS · L · F · PRISCVS | · ALLIAE · PRISCAE · FILIVS | ARTEMAE NEPOS. Coped top tegulated.

There are also two large leaden *ossuaria* containing bones. On a piece of leaden pipe in one of the cases is the inscription C. POPPAEI · AVG · I · HERMETIS. On a piece of coloured marble, 6ins. long, TINATIALI | THYMELE.

Other objects in this room are nine Greek helmets of bronze, Roman bronze ewers, *paterae*, saucepans, dishes, mirrors, strigils, etc.; a large head with earrings in ears; a large number of small bronze figures of gods, etc.; *fibulae* of different shapes, keys, combs, modelling implements, *lingulæ*, *styli*, pins, etc. An armlet of bronze, inscribed CVMAGVHFR; Roman lamps from different places, with names STROBILI, ANCHIAI, EYT, VETTI | CRISPIN | VS, etc.; a quantity of pseudo-Arretine ware; objects of bone, such as combs, dice, pins, etc., found in London and elsewhere; medieval objects from the Thames, etc. Amongst the later antiquities is a bronze mortar 6⅛ diameter, bearing the inscription around it PTRVS VAN DE GHEN ME FECIT MCCCCCLII. While at the bottom of the staircase are some fine Etruscan, Greek, and Roman sarcophagi, one sculptured in high relief with the rape of Helen."

Within the castle there is also a very fine collection of pictures, many of which are of great interest and value. There are examples of the works of Wilkie, Morland, Lawrence, Watteau, Hogarth, and several other eminent painters. Selby's celebrated collection of birds, and several antiquarian relics discovered on the estate, have also found a place in the museum.

A few hundred yards north-west of the mansion stands an imposing block of buildings, forming a quadrangle, having a handsome clock in the turret over the entrance gateway, whose pleasing "Westminster" chimes is the timekeeper for the numerous retinue of menservants and maidservants, foresters and gardeners, employed on the estate. In this range of buildings are the stables, which contain a most complete arrangement for the stabling of upwards of one hundred horses. A glass-covered verandah, projecting over the stable and coach-house doors, runs round the whole range, thus protecting both men and horses while undergoing the usual washing down. Within the quadrangle, besides the stables and coach-houses, over which are the hay-lofts and granaries, the men have their apartments, their dining rooms, sleeping rooms, and comfortable reading rooms, well supplied with current literature, newspapers, sporting and otherwise, as well as chess and draught boards, cards, and all kinds of games. Here the men can sit and read or smoke and chat during their leisure hours, and on winter evenings. In this portion of the appurtenances of Callaly Castle, Major Browne and his family take a very great interest.

The whole of the mansion, the stables, and several cottages are lighted by electric light, the motive power being a pair of splendid nine-horse power engines by Marshall of Gainsborough, and a pair of dynamos by Kapp capable of putting out 85 amperes, running at 900 per minute. Besides those in the stables and the cottages, there are over 700 lamps in the castle, varying in size from eight-candle up to 100-candle power. There are two accumulators, one for the lights, and the other for the passenger lift, organ bellows, and fan-blast for taking the hot air out of the kitchens. At the engine house there is a small accumulator for the stables and the cottages, which also drives two lathes. The engine room, and other buildings connected with the electric light, are contiguous to the stables, and everything pertaining thereto is kept in the most perfect order by an experienced electrician.

The gardens, on the north side of the burn, are laid out with herbaceous and shrubby borders in the old style, and contain many plants that botanists delight to look upon "Of old plants there are Solomon's Seal, Lilies of the Valley, Double Rockets, a wealth of White Narcissi, Hemerocallis (various sorts), thriving plants of the intensely bright blue *Mertensia prostrata*, Rosemary bushes, and a spreading bush of goodly size of the Teesdale *Potentilla fruticosa*. Besides flowering Rhododendrons and Azaleas—always charming to look on—are two youthful *Abies Douglassi*, and a goodly Cedar of more mature age. The chinks of the garden walls and the bridge are full of the Wall-rue Fern—*Asplenium Ruta-muraria*; *Sisymbrium thalianum* grows on a wall-top near the public road; there is much *Lychnis dioica* in the plantings, besides outcast Rockets and Columbines, and the *Hypericum quadrangulum* and *Geum rivale* in the ditches. The plants most noticeable in the greenhouses are Ferns, Calceolaries, and Clerodendrons. Good Roses are grown here.

An old vine, a black Hamburgh, which nearly fills one of the houses, was planted by one of the Claverings a hundred and fifty years ago."[1]

Callaly was once a considerable village; but, like many of our oldest and most interesting villages, it has dwindled down to three or four cottages and the agent's residence. During the early part of this century it had its joiner's shop, a school, a public-house, besides several other houses and cottages; it could also boast of an Alnwick carrier, the last of whom was well-known on the road; but of late years the houses were allowed to fall into decay, and gradually this ancient village became nearly depopulated. Our engraving shows the only

remaining bit of old Callaly. Since the advent of Major Browne many improvements have taken place. The farm steadings throughout the whole estate have been re-built on the most approved modern plans, and no expense has been spared to make them as perfect as possible. The village of

[1] History of the Berwickshire Naturalists' Club, Vol. xiii., p. 45.

Callaly also bears marks of being cared for. Callaly Avenue, a picturesque arcade of fine spreading beeches, extends from the village to the eastern limits of the Callaly estate,[1] underneath whose leafy shade the traveller from Rothbury passes on his way to Whittingham, and at length, emerging from the shady grove, he obtains the first sight of the church tower, the snug vicarage, and the quaint red-tiled housetops of the interesting old village of Whittingham.

It was at Callaly, on the 16th May, 1801, that Lewis Proudlock, the original Coquetdale poet, was born. Amongst his earliest effusions are the following lines on his native place :—

"All hail ! ye blest Callalian shades,
  Of various trees so fair and tall ;
Surrounding fine the peaceful glades
  Where stands yon close sequester'd hall.
O, may its grandeur never pall,
  Its honour in no age decline ;
So still esteem'd it ever shall
  B' adorn'd by Clavering's noble line.

The arbours, grots, and dens around
  May many a tedious hour beguile ;
E'en heath-clad hills the scenery crown,
  And give the dale a sweeter smile.
Who can but dallying muse the while,
  Or joy entranc'd, unthinking stay,
Beneath the branches many a file
  Wide bow'ring o'er the pleasant way."

In the harvest days, when shearing the corn with the sickle was the only mode known, poor people were allowed by the farmer to "gather" the fallen corn behind the reapers into small bunches, or "singles." In this manner as much was gathered during harvest as would serve a poor family for several months. By and by the less charitably inclined farmers introduced stubble rakes, which called forth from Lewis the following address :—

[1] A stone may be observed in the old park wall, about midway through the avenue, on which is cut the date 1704, evidently the work of William Clavering, the Jacobite squire of Callaly.

"To the Stubble Rake.
Thou famine maker 'mang the poor
That dost our harvest stubble scour;
How can I be but vext and sour,
To see thee, thief!
I look fu' hatefully and doure
On thy grim teeth,
Wi' which thou dost fields harshly harrow,
And tear dejected hearts wi' sorrow,
And gars them tine the vera marrow
Off a' their banes,
Sin' thou leaves nought on rig and furrow
But dirt and stanes.

. . . .

"Callaly is remarkable for its camps, of which there are three, if not four—one at the High Houses, one at the Rabbit Hall, and one on the hill above the Mansion House. That at High Houses is on the farm of Cross Hill (Cross Hill probably denotes the site of a boundary cross, or where one stood at cross roads; such crosses were erected in former ages as guides for travellers). It is on high ground, and commands the Vale of Whittingham, particularly towards the west. It is nearly ploughed down, but its form can still be seen; it was an oval, about 110 yards east and west, 90 yards north and south, defended apparently by a strong rampart and deep ditch. The spot is about a mile north of our line (the Roman Road).

"Rabbit Hall (or Hill) Camp is on much lower ground, and about 350 yards on the south of our line. It is so destroyed in parts that its shape originally is scarcely discernible. It is about 1,100 yards on the north-east of Lorbottle House, and close to the old road to Callaly. It was an oval, the north-east and south-west diameter about 90 yards, and the north-west and south-east about 65 yards.

"The Camp on the conical-topped hill, called the Castle Hill, is covered with wood, briers, and ferns, so that it is very difficult to ascertain the shape properly. The shape of the inner ward of the Camp is nearly a semi-circle, with a diameter of about 100 yards, which coincides nearly with the outcrop of strata. The area of the inner part may be about three-quarters of an acre. Three of the sides are very precipitous, so much so that the second rampart has not been continued all round; but on the other side, towards the west, where the slope is not so rapid, an outer line is continued, forming a sort of outer baly. The ditch towards the west appears to have been excavated out of thc rock, and when made was about 40 feet wide; altogether it must have been a very strong post, and from its extensive command of view, both in a west and east direction, along the line of the Roman Way, must, it is imagined, have been occupied by that people, though probably not originally constructed by them. This supposition is strengthened by the fact of its also commanding a view of the junction of Roman roads about two miles distant. The Roman Way runs close under the hill on the north side; and the spot near the present entrance (south) lodge was occupied till lately by some cottages which were known by the name of Street Way.

"In addition to these three camps in these townships, there are traces of another in a field about 650 yards north of the mansion, called 'Old Hag.' It was on the north side of the brook, was small, its interior not more, possibly, than about 30 yards, and circular in shape; it is, however, nearly destroyed. There was a larger part, indistinctly visible, projecting towards the west, and leading to a supposition that it was a temporary place of strength before the building of the ancient part of the present mansion. It is possible that the present road from the lodge (south) at Callaly is on the Roman line, and that the present road into the wood on the south side, at about 500 yards east from the lodge, was the original up to the camp on the top of the hill. At about 400 yards beyond this, eastward, it seems possible that the Roman Way left the present road, the vegetation indicating it; and about 50 yards before we reach the small cottage, called

Reynard's Lodge, it is plainly seen in the present old cartway; and we have local evidence that it was ploughed up on the north of the cottage. From this point it will have run straight . . . . to about 60 yards south of St. Ninian's Well, falling into the Devil's Causeway below Thrunton." . . . . . .—*MacLauchlan's Memoir.*

The field names of Callaly of which we give a selection are, many of them, of great antiquity and interest. YETLINGTON LANE FARM has Big-Hops Close, Low Floats, West, High, and Low Charters, Tongues, Haver Acres, Ox Close, Snowden's East Close, High and Low Thornlees. CALLALY HIGH HOUSES—Gills Well, Nesbitt's Close, Four Nicked Close, High Folly. CROSS HILL FARM—Ox Close, Mare Meadows, East Cow Hill, East Pea Law, West Pea Law, Box-hill Field, High Camps, Low Camps, Ewe Layers.

CHAPTER IX.

LORBOTTLE.

Lorbottle held by Alexander de Lilburn in 1177—Held in 1191 by Sawel, along with Nafferton and Matfen—By Philip de Ulecote, 1213—William de Felton and the Bertrams of Bothal in 1291—Sir Robert Ogle, 1407—Robert Lord Ogle, 1544—Cuthbert Lord Ogle, 1568—Marquis of Newcastle, 1663—Earl of Oxford, 1724—Lorbottle Lordship in 1724—Its Field Names and its Tenants—Scottish Raid, 1532—Royalist Dragoons taken Prisoners at Lorbottle, 1648—Folk Lore.

ADJOINING the Callaly estate, on the south-west, is that of Lorbottle, which, although not occupying so prominent a place in the historical annals of the county as Callaly, is yet an ancient and important manor. In the Pipe Roll[1] of 23 Henry II. (1177), the sheriff of the county renders an account of thirty-five shillings and sixpence for "Luverbota,"[2] which was the land of "Alexander de Lilleburn." It then appears to have been in the hands of the Crown, and continued to be until 1191, when Sawel, the king's serjeant, obtained a grant from Richard I. of the manors of Matfen, Nafferton, and Lorbottle, and for many centuries these manors remained linked together under one owner. On the death of Sawel, King John, in the 14th year of his reign (1212), granted the same manors to Philip de Ulecote, who had been advanced by the king from the constableship of Chinon, in

[1] Hodgson's Northumberland, Part iii., Vol iii., p. 27.

[2] The mode of spelling Lorbottle has undergone many changes, as may be seen from the following examples:—Levboda 1177, Luverbota 1177, Luerbotle 1178, Liverbotle 1179, Luvebotle 1182, Luwerbotr 1201, Lowarbetr 1213, Luerbott 1256, Loubothill, Lowerbothell, Loverbothill, Loverbottle, Louirbotdil, West Liverbothill 1272 to 1300, Lourbotill 1327, Lourbotell 1333, Lourbodill 1369, Lourebothyll 1406, Lourebottill 1417, Lowerbotle 1568, Lurbottle 1663, Larbottle 1724.

Touraine, to be his forester in Northumberland, and as such held Matfen, Nafferton, and Lorbottle.

In the 19th Edward I. (1291), William de Felton held part of Lorbottle, and had free warren there,[1] besides holding other manors throughout the county, while in 1341 a portion of the manor of Lorbottle was in the possession of the Bertrams,[2] of Bothal; but eventually the whole of it appears to have come to the old Northumbrian family of the Ogles. Sir Robert Ogle[3]—a hero of Otterburn fight—held it in 1407, who, on the decease of his mother, Eleanor, daughter and sole heir of Sir Robert Bertram, of Bothal, had livery of her lands, the manor of Lorbottle and of twelve husband lands[4] and twelve cottages there, with respite of homage.

In 1544, Robert Lord Ogle, having received the King's command to invade Scotland, in case he was slain, made his will and arranged his affairs. He, however, came safely back, but was killed at the battle of Ancrum Moor in the following year. One of the items in his will reads :—

> "I give and bequeathe to my sonne Thomas Ogle all my singular lands and tenements within the towne of lourbattell with all commodites profittes thereto belonginge during his native life of the afornamed Thomas paying thereto to thomas Ogle now of lourbattell vij$^{l.}$ vj$^{s.}$ viij$^{d.}$ by yeare during his native life out of the same towne and after the discease of the said Thomas now of lourbottell then to remain to my sonne thomas duringe his life. And after the discease of the forenamed Thomas to remayne to my heyres."[5]

Cuthbert Lord Ogle, brother to the last-named, in 1568 held certain lands in Lorbottle,[6] and in 1663[7] it was held by

---

[1] Hodgson's Northumberland, Part iii., Vol. ii., pp. 393-394. (Charter Roll.)

[2] Ibid, p. 371. (Patent Rolls.)

[3] White's Battle of Otterburn.

[4] "The *husbands* of land mentioned so frequently in deeds respecting Northumberland, contained twenty acres, and at times twenty-four or thirty.—"Northumberland Words," by R. O. Heslop.

[5] Wills and Inventories, Surtees Society Publications, Vol ii., p. 120.

[6] Hodgson's Northumberland, Part iii., Vol. iii. (Liber Feodarij), p. lxiii. (Preface.)

[7] Ibid, Part iii., Vol. i., p. 266. (Rentals and Rates of Northumberland, 1663.)

the Marquis of Newcastle—the loyal duke—a descendant of the Ogles, who at the same time had lands in Hepple, Great Tosson, Flotterton, Sharperton, Warton, and Sheepbank, all of which remained long in the possession of this important family.

Henrietta Cavendish Holles, only daughter of the Marquis of Newcastle, married, in 1713, the 2nd Earl of Oxford, whose family name was Harley, and it was from him the nation got the Harleian MSS. He had an only child, Lady Margaret Cavendish Harley, who, in 1734, married the 2nd Duke of Portland. A manuscript survey of the baronies and manors belonging to the Earl of Oxford and Mortimer in the County of Northumberland, in 1724, gives a full description of the Ogle lands in Coquetdale, including Lorbottle, of which it says:—

"LARBOTTLE LORDSHIP in the Parish of Whittingham consists of sixteen Farms[1] and two cottages. Pays Tythe in kind and a modus for hay. Limestone on the ground seven miles from bole.[2] Divided at present into two parts the East and West End. Improvable by inclosing.

1724. Tenants of the East End that farm the West End.

George Trewhit	1½ Farms.
Thomas Swan	1 ,,
John Swan	1 ,,
Mary Swan	1 ,,
Roger Story	½ ,,
James Dunn	1 ,,
John Hogg	½ ,,
Michael Swan	½ ,,
Thomas & Wm. Robson	1 ,,

[1] Within the last few years the term "farm" has been found to have had a very different meaning from the present general acceptation of the word, and further, that every township or lordship was divided into so many equal parts, each part being termed a "farm;" thus we find that Lorbottle, in 1724, consisted of sixteen equal parts called farms, and two cottages. For a fuller account of these ancient divisions of land, we refer our readers to an able paper in Archæologia Æliana, Vol. xvi., p. 121, entitled "The Ancient Farms of Northumberland," by Frederick Walter Dendy.

[2] Seven miles from the limekiln.

Tenants of the West End that farm the East End.

Robert Story junr	1	Farm.
Robert Brown	1	,,
Edward Wilson	1	,,
Geo. Dunn	1	,,
Walter Scot a Cottage		
Wm. Swan	1	,,
Robert Story senr [1]	1	,,
Geo. Hogg	1	,,
Mich. Swan	1	,,
John Nicols a Cottage.		

LARBOTTLE.

				A.	R.	P.
	A.	Back Close	A.	1	2	17
S.	B.	Long-bank	M.	122	3	0
	R.	Watter Leys	P.	44	0	25
O.	P.	Long Faugh [2]	P.	156	3	0
	Q.	East Faugh or Field	A.	114	0	0
	I.	Great Field Flatt	A.	10	3	18
	K.	Great Flatt	A.	15	0	32
	C.	... ...	A.	4	0	16
	D.	... ...	A.	8	0	13
	N.	Cottage Close	M.	1	1	0
	E.	Back Close	A.	4	3	32
		House & Croft	P.	0	2	8
		House & Garths...	P.	0	3	4
		The East End		485	0	5

			A.	R.	P.
V.	West Pasture & Grey-stone Moore ...	P.	443	2	0
G.	South Crofts	A. M.	23	3	33
F.	South Flatt	A.	4	0	19
H.	South Flatt	A.	15	2	18
L.	Ditto	A.	7	0	8
M.	Prumpley...	A.	18	2	0
	Cottage Hose & Garth	P.	0	2	16
	The West End		513	1	14
	Larbottle Common	P.	1208	2	00"

[1] In the Session Records of October, 1701, the house of Robert Story, of Lorbottle, is one of the houses licensed to be used as a meeting-house for Protestant Dissenters.—Arch. Æliana, Vol. xv., p. 154.

[2] Faff—Fallow Land.

During the early part of the present century, Adam Atkinson, Esq., was the owner of Lorbottle, and resided at Lorbottle House; but in 1886 the estate was purchased by A. H. Browne, Esq., of Callaly Castle. Lorbottle House stands in an airy and pleasant situation facing the south, opposite to a range of picturesque crags called the "Maiden Chambers."

It is difficult to decide the site of the old town of Lorbottle, which was ravaged by the Scots in 1532, "uppon Sonday at nyht, being the 13th day of this instant monthe of October, came in on the close nyght a hundreth lyght horsemen, and toke up a towne called Lowrebotell, twenty horses, and all the insyght of the said towne;" such was the report of the Lord Warden of the Marches to Henry VIII;[1] while the following verse records a tradition of another Scotch foray, said to have taken place in 1549:—

"Mark Ker rode on, and Mark Ker rode on,
But never a hoof or horn saw he
Till he came to the ford of Larbottle burn,
Where a dainty drove lay on the lea.—*Raid of the Kers.*"

The property of the Ogles—staunch Royalists during the Great Rebellion—Lorbottle, was on Friday night, the 30th of June, 1648, the quarters of a troop of Cavaliers, who, having ridden far in great haste, were taken during the night, tired and fast asleep, by Major Sanderson and a party of Roundheads, who writes thus:—"The first towne we fell into was Tossons, where wee took a lieutenant and sixe of his dragoons, all in bed; the next towne was Lurbottle, where we took 60 horse and 60 men, all in bed.[2]

The following incident is recorded, not only as being connected with Lorbottle, but as presenting a striking picture of the gross ignorance and superstition at one time prevalent in Northumberland. Towards the end of the 17th century there lived at Edlingham a poor old woman named Margaret

[1] State Papers. [2] Skirmish in Northumberland.

Stothard, a reputed witch, who was accused of having been the cause of much mischief in the neighbourhood. Depositions to that effect were made by several persons before Henry Ogle, of Eglingham, Esq., one of his Majesties Justices of the Peace for the County. We here give a copy of "*The information of Jacob Mills of Edlingham Castle*"—"Informing sayth that upon Satterday last the 20th of Jan. 1683, one Alexander Nickle of Larbottle and his wife told this Informant, that about eight years agoe or there abouts they the said Alexander Nickle and wife had a childe dyed and before ever it was any thing unwell to there knowledge there came into the house one Margaret Stothard of Edlingham, and the said Alexander's wife being in the house among hir children the said Margaret asked hir almes of hir and the woman being afraid of her by the ill fame she bore in the country that she was a witch this informant is not possitive whether she refused to give hir almes or that she had it not to give hir, soe the said Margaret Stothard went away, and after she was gone one of the childer said to her mother, did not you see what the woman did to you when she went away, and the woman answered noe: so the childe said she, to wit, the said Margaret Stothard, did wave at her mother a white thing three tymes, and the mother said she did not care for hir what she did, for she hoped the Lord would protect hir from any such as she was. But next morneing before day the childe grew unwell and continued all the day very ill, still crying out the woman that waved the white thing at you is above me pressing of me and lieke to bricke my backe and press out my hart, and so the childe continued still cryeing out in that manner, untill next morning againe about cocke crow, and then dyed soe that they veryly believe she was the death of the said childe, and further sayth not."

Alexander Nickle,[1] *the father of the child, deposed to the*

[1] The following entry is found in the register of Rothbury Church. Baptism:—"1677, April 29th. Willm. fil Alex. Nickle, Lurbottle."

same effect, adding further: "That, seeing the childe in the sad condition, went up to Cartenton to my Lady Widdrington, and told hir the childe's condition, and the Ladye's answer was, that she could not understand any distemper the childe had by the circumstances they told her, unless she to wit, the childe was bewitched."[1]

Lorbottle has a place among the records of Northumberland Folk Lore. A class of people are said to have lived at Lorbottle during the early part of the century who were described as the Lorbottle "Cubs," "Kebs," or "Coves," who were reported to be great eaters, which gave rise to the following:—

"Yorr as bad as the Kebs of Lorbottle,
Ye'll eat nineteen penny loaves to a pint
Of ye'll, and cry for more stuffing."[2]

Whether true or not, they were credited with many stupid notions and actions—for instance, it was said they never knew when it was raining until they saw the drops falling on the surface of a pond called "Puddle," and if at the dinner hour a few of those curious individuals happened to be sitting resting on a gate or wooden fence, they were unable to distinguish between their own limbs and feet and those of their neighbours; and, again, to secure the comforts and enjoyment of a perpetual summer, they attempted to build a wall around the cuckoo, thinking by thus preventing her departure they would succeed in having fine weather all the year round; and the moon at her full, slowly rising behind the Long Crag, was transformed in their eyes to a huge red cheese, and imagining they could haul it down, set off to the hill with "wine ropes"[3] to do so. They got a weather-glass, and, seeing the mercury fall, they hid it, and put out tubs to see if it was raining, as they could not decide otherwise.[4] One of them went a fishing

---

[1] Mackenzie's Northumberland, Vol. ii., p. 35.

[2] The Denham Tracts, Vol. i., p. 18.

[3] Wain ropes. [4] The Denham Tracts, Vol. i., p. 37.

in the burn close bye, but instead of catching trout, caught a huge eel. Taking it home, nobody knew what the monster was, so they thought the best thing to do with it was to throw the beast into "'Puddle,' an' droon him." Many other incredulous tales are told of this peculiar people — how the stories originated one cannot possibly tell—probably they were fabricated to annoy certain of the inhabitants of Lorbottle at that time, and then became popular tradition.

CHAPTER X.

THE CRAGS.

Their Formation—Extent and Aspect—Fauna and Flora—View from the Summit—British Remains—Camps—Cists and Tumuli—Castle Hill—Macartney's Cave—Wedderburn's Hole—Black Monday Rock—Coe Crag—Long Crag—Rimside Moor—Folk Lore—Jamie Macfarlane.

A RIDGE of coarse sandstone hills, belonging to a series known as the "Simonside Grits," extends from Lorbottle on the south-west to Thrunton on the east, and forms a portion of the southern boundary of the Vale of Whittingham. These hills are severally called Lorbottle, Callaly, and Thrunton Crags, which rise from 800 to 900 feet above the level of the sea. Along their whole northern face huge masses of bold precipitous cliffs rear their lofty heads, which to the south slope gradually away, forming on the summit a plateau of bog and moorland. The northern slopes of the hill are thickly strewn with large lichen-covered blocks, which have, during the course of centuries, become detached from the main mass and rolled down the steep, whose :—

". . . rocky summits, split and rent,
Form turret, dome, or battlement."

The eastern part (Thrunton Crag) is clothed to the summit with a dense plantation of firs. Callaly and Lorbottle hills are not so thickly planted. Numbers of beech and birch trees are growing along the base of the hills, while the bird cherry *(Prunus padus)*, the wild cherry *(Prunus avium)*, and mountain ash *(Pyrus aucuparia)*, the rowan tree of the north, of which it is said :—

"That witches have no power
Where there is Rown-tree wood,"

are all found growing in many a thicket throughout the whole range; there is also a thick undergrowth of "blaeberry bushes," the "bilberry," or whortleberry *(Vaccinium myrtillus)*, whose pretty green foliage spreads over the greater part of the north side of the hill. The fruit, which is ripe in July and August, here attains to perfection, and large quantities of it are often gathered by the people living in the neighbourhood for the purpose of making jellies and preserves for winter use. And many a merry party from the surrounding villages has wandered over these crags in search of the juicy blaeberry, who, with the poet, could say :—

> "And here are rich blaeberries, black and wild,
> Beneath the beech-trees' thickest branches growing;
> This makes me once again a wayward child,
> A pilgrimage into the woodland going.
> The haunt of squirrels and of wood-mouse knowing,
> And plucking blackberries all the day,
> Till eastward mountain-shadows night was hurrying,
> And sending me upon my homeward way,
> Fill'd both in soul and sense with the old forest grey."

The rarer cowberry, or red whortleberry *(Vaccinium Vitis idæa)*, with bright evergreen box-like leaves, and the cranberry, or marsh whortleberry *(Vaccinium oxycoccos)*, are also found growing here and there if carefully looked for, while the black crowberry or crawcrook *(Empetrum nigrum)*—a plant entirely unknown in the south of England—grows plentifully on the drier parts of the hill. The fruit is too acid for domestic use, but it affords excellent feeding to the moor game which here abound in such numbers that the name of "Blackcock" is given to a plantation in the locality. In damp mossy spots on the summit of the hill are found those singular-looking plants—round-leaved sundew *(Drosera rotundifolia)* and the common butterwort *(Pinguicula vulgaris)*—both of which are partially insectivorous, and on the moors around the downy heads of the hare's tail cotton grass *(Eriophorum vaginatum)*, wave in the summer breeze like tufts of cotton wool. The ravines and dells at the base of the hills are filled with a luxuriant growth of ferns and mosses—there the common bracken, the broad buckler *(Lastrea dilatata)*, the sweet mountain buckler *(Lastrea montana)*, the male fern, and the graceful fronds of the lady fern, mingling with beds of velvet bog moss *(Sphagnum)* of every hue, from the brightest green to the deepest crimson, all add their charms to the beauty of this wild mountain scenery.

On the crags the botanist will also find the pretty white star-like flower, tinged with pink, of the Chickweed Winter-green *(Trientalis Europœa)*, Heart leaved Tway-blade *(Listera-cordata)*, and the pretty yellow bloom of the Petty Whin *(Genista Anglica)*. In the open drains, and similar damp places, are Hairy Sedum *(Sedum villosum)*, the attractive spikelets of the Bog Asphodel *(Narthecium ossifragum)*, and the lovely Grass of Parnassus *(Parnassia palustris)*, while in some of the old grass lands that trend along the base of the hills on the Lorbottle side grow the Frog Orchis *(Habenaria viridis)*, Adder's tongue *(Ophioglossum-vulgatum)*, and Moon-wort *(Botrychium lunaria)*.

Three varieties of heath and heather cover the whole of this range of hills, *Calluna-vulgaris* (Common Heather), known as "Bee Heather," *Erica tetralix* (Cross-leaved Heath), *Erica cinerea* (Fine-leaved Heath). The two *Ericas*, of which there is much less than the *Calluna*, are locally known as "ling."

In the almost inaccessible recesses of the crags is found the lair of the badger and the fox, and within the last ten or fifteen years a colony of squirrels have established themselves amongst the beech trees in Callaly Avenue. The owl, the goatsucker, and the hawk, as well as the peregrine falcon, and an occasional eagle, finds covert in the fastnesses of Thrunton and Callaly Crags. In the open glades the harmless slow worm *(Anguis fragilis)* and its dangerous neighbour, the common adder *(Vipera berus)*, are frequently met with. A pool of water on Callaly Crag is the favourite resort of the dragon fly, and on a fine summer day numbers of these magnificent insects can be seen darting quickly to and fro on the surface of the water. In the darksome depths of the pool is the water newt *(Lacerta aquatica*, Linn*)*, while the nimble little form of his much prettier companion, the lizard *(Lacerta agilis)*, is seen amongst the heather and shrubs on the hill. Both are known under the local name of "Ask," from Gaelic *asc*. Newt and Eft are the old Saxon names.

A popular belief once prevailed that these harmless little reptiles were venomous.

The view from the highest part of the crags—

> "Where once the wild boar and the fox
> Sought their prey 'mong Thrunton rocks—"

is of great extent, embracing the whole of the Vale of Whittingham, with its numerous villages, hamlets and ancestral mansions, several miles of sea coast, the adjacent Vale of the Breamish, Ros Castle and Chillingham on the north and north-east, with the hills at Coquet-head, from the lofty Thirlmoor down to Harbottle, and the distant fells of Redesdale in the far west. While on the north-west, about twelve miles off, are the Cheviot Hills—the old boundary line between Scotch and English ground, on which in past centuries much brave Border blood was spilt. The nearer hills being those of Biddlestone, Alnham, Prendwick, and Ryle. Immediately in front, divided from the crags by a deep ravine, are Humbleton and Castle hills, both of which are clad in a gloomy covering of pine trees. The latter is the site of one of the most important pre-historic hill fortresses in the Vale of Whittingham, for a description of which we again quote Dr. Hardy's report:—"It is not intended to dwell on the excavations of the old Camp, so obligingly prosecuted by Major Browne, at much cost and labour of men, preparatory for this Club Meeting, which, when time and circumstances permit, may probably be resumed, and plans and correct measurements may be obtainable. This much has been revealed: that within the area of the British encampment there are the foundations of a medieval building of an oblong shape, apparently constructed of ashler stones laid with mortar, and that the occupants had strengthened the interior wall of the old Camp with a facing of mortar-laid ashler, of which two courses at least are still preserved; that they had also strongly re-built the walls of the main gateway, and, while quarrying for materials to execute these operations, had deepened the ditches. It is just possible that this newly-discovered edifice may have been the 'Castrum de Kaloule vet,' the Castle of Old Callaly of 1415, from which afterwards the owners may have removed to a more sheltered and better watered situation in the vale below. That there was in 1415 a 'New Callaly' is apparent from 'Old Callaly' being specified in the return of the fortalices of that period."[1]

The old march dyke between the Callaly and Eslington estates leads in a straight line, north and south, from the crag down a narrow gorge, and, threading its way between the Castle Hill and Humbleton, continues on by the White Knowe towards Whittingham wood.

> "Unfrequented woods
> I better brook than flourishing peopled towns;
> Here can I sit alone."

In one of the large upright blocks of sandstone standing on the side of Callaly Crag a small cave has been neatly cut, having a well formed gothic entrance. This cave, whose secluded situation is admirably fitted for the oratory of a recluse, is said to have been hewn by a chaplain at Callaly Castle, named Macartney, as a quiet retreat wherein to pursue his studies, and is yet known as "Macartney's Cave." Mid-way up the face of Thrunton Crag, to the east of a bridle path the "Hunter's Road," there is also a cave called "Wedderburn's Hole," a memento of mosstrooping days, said to have been the hiding place of a notorious cattle lifter named Wedder-

---

[1] History Berwickshire Naturalists' Club, Vol. xiii., p. 52.

burn, who doubtless made levy upon the flocks and herds of the neighbouring farmers in the vale of the Aln.

Black Monday Rock is a huge block of sandstone, standing on the western slopes of Callaly Crag. No trace can be found of how it got this name. On a ridge of the hill lower down, near Rabbit Hall—an old house in ruins—there are the turf-covered mounds of a British Camp, and not far off, facing Dancing Hall, is seen a Fairy Ring—that mystic circle where, according to local tradition, the tiny forms of the fairies might have been seen enjoying their revels by the bright moonlight, in those days when—

> "The king of elves and little fairy queen
> Gamboll'd on heaths and danced on every green,
> And where the jolly troop had led the round,
> The grass, unbidden, rose and mark'd the ground."

Set up amongst the heather on the moors are several rough stone slabs having an incised circular cross cut thereon, probably old boundary stones. Similar stones with incised crosses are found on the moors stretching between Coquet and Redewater. Further to the south, on Lorbottle ground, are some sheepfolds and the ruins of a building called Prince's House—once occupied by a person of the name of Prince. Beyond, again, are the rugged heights of the Long Crag, Coe Crag, and Rimside Moor.[1] Capping the summit of many of the hills of this range, and scattered over the moorlands, are numerous cairns and tumuli, the burial places of the ancient occupants of the surrounding camps. The eastern termination of the range is known as Thrunton Crag End, around which winds the old coach road; and on the northern slopes of the hill, down towards the Howe Moor and the Swine-burn—a name suggestive of the British wild boar—several cist-vaens, and the spear heads already recorded, were found; while

[1] In the rising of 1745, Rimside Moor was the spot fixed upon by the Jacobite leaders on which they intended to give battle to General Wade's army.—*Newcastle Courant*, Nov., 1745.

near to the hamlet of Thrunton there is a remarkable spring of water, called St. Ninian's Well.

The "Blackcock," famous for the number and size of its adders, which infest the banks of the little burn whose waters flow from the Coe Crag eastward, through Thrunton Moor is a piece of the wildest mountain scenery in the district Here, early in the present century, there lived, in a miserable hovel, Jamie Macfarlane, a besom maker. Jamie had a daughter, Peggy, a very tall, uncouth woman, who went about amongst the country folks selling the heather-besoms and scrubbers her father made. Peggy was a well-known character, not only in Whittingham Vale, but throughout North Northumberland, and was generally considered to be a sort of a half-wit.

The following is recorded of her in the "Denham Tracts," under the head of "Popular Sayings as to Indecision":—

"YE'RE LIKE MEG MACFARLANE WHO HAD A TWENTY HUNDRED MINDS WHETHER TO GO FOR THE NIGHT TO WHITTINGHAM OR TO FISHES STEAD (or Fishers-Stead)."

Meg was a tall, stout woman, who sold throughout the country the heather-besoms manufactured by her father, Jamie Macfarlane, who, during summer, dwelt in a peage or divot-hut, on Belford Moor, where he found sticks for handles in the woods for nothing; he had an alternative place of residence likewise on Rimside Moor. Jamie, a long, lank man, had his wits about him, and had a remarkable knowledge of the Scriptures; but Meg could rarely decide for herself. The question was put to her, about mid-afternoon at Fowberry Newhall, "where she was bound for to-night?" To which she replied as above. Both places are about twelve miles distant. Fishers-stead is said to be in the Norham district. The saying is frequently adduced for the benefit of those who hesitate in coming to a decision. There is another saying about Meg or Peg, that, having friends both at North Sunderland and Fountain Crag, she sat down on Belford Moor, for a long time quite puzzled which she should visit, hence the saying, "As sore puzzled as Peg Macfarlane, who didn't know whether to go to North Sunderland or to Fountain Crag." [1]

One morning poor Jamie Macfarlane was found dead in his hut on Thrunton Moor, and for several years after this painful event that stretch of lonely moorland road, leading from Thrunton Crag End to Rough Castles, where it crosses the Coe-burn by "Elliots-bridge," was the dread of belated travellers, for it was said that Jamie's ghost was always to be seen at midnight standing beside the gate on "Elliots-bridge," with a "buzzom-shank over his shoulder." Frequently have we ourselves, with nervous step and furtive glance at tree trunk and gate post, passed this lonesome spot at the eerie hour of midnight, and have more than once been startled by the sudden whirr of the moorcock or the plaintive bleating of the solitary snipe, but never did we see the ghost of Jamie Macfarlane. Therefore, "I say the tale as't was said to me," for:—

"Some have mistaken blocks and posts
For spectres, apparitions, ghosts,
With saucer-eyes and horns, and some
Have heard the devil beat a drum."

[1] The Denham Tracts, Vol. i., p. 18.

CHAPTER XI.

WHITTINGHAM.

Its Site and Surroundings—Anglo-Saxon Township—Old Spelling—Synod at Twyford—Possession of Ceolwulf, 737—Owners after the Conquest—A Thirteenth Century Brawl—Old Names, 1538—Freeholders in the Parish, 1628—Royalist and Roundhead, 1648—Owners in the Parish, 1663—Villagers in 1718—Whittingham in 1729—Villagers in 1811-1821-1845-1855—Field Names—Population—The Village, 1828—Whittingham Fair—The Tower.

THE charming Old English village of Whittingham occupies a pleasant site on the banks of the Aln—a little Northumbrian burn—which, flowing through its midst, divides the village into two parts, the connecting links being a wooden foot bridge and a neat stone bridge of four arches. The church, the vicarage, and the schools stand on gently rising ground on the north side of the burn. The old pele tower, the police station, the post office, and the village inn are all on the south side; while picturesque cottages, standing for the most part within neatly kept gardens, fill up the intervening spaces. A fine plantation of beeches near the river, and the well-wooded hedgerows—luxuriant during summer in wild roses and a profusion of other lovely wild flowers—show the rich quality of the soil, and add to the beauty and sweetness of the landscape. The whole of the village and its surroundings are the property of the Earl of Ravensworth, who is also lord of the manor.

Undoubtedly the village of Whittingham is of Anglo-Saxon origin, as its name would infer, and which is also shown in the remains of Anglo-Saxon masonry seen in the lower courses of the church tower; and although Whittingham only now goes to form part of the Eslington- estate, yet it is the parish town, has for centuries been the principal township,

WHITTINGHAM.

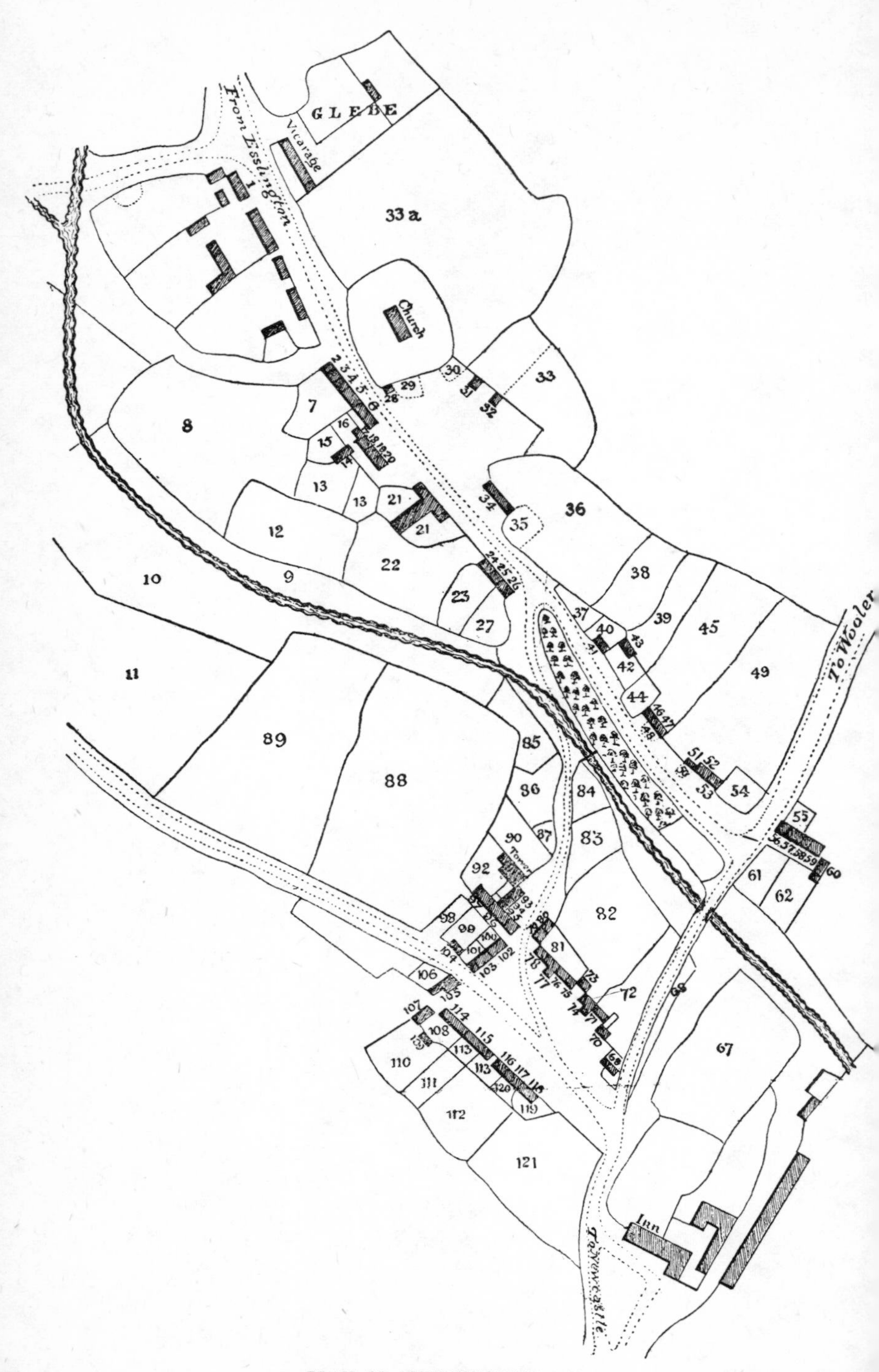

PLAN OF WHITTINGHAM, 1826.

and gives its name to the Vale. The following examples are amongst the earliest forms of spelling Whittingham:—Huting-ham; Hwytingham; Huyttingha; Whitingham, 1201; Wit-ingeha, 1209; Wytgha, 1229; Witinchop, 1241; Wytingham, 1253; Wintingham; Qwitingham, 1279; Witincham, 1290; Wytingeham, 1291; Whityneham, 1357; Whityngham, 1386; Wittynggam, 1509; Whyttyngame, 1541.

As early as the seventh century we read of a place in Northumberland called Twyford, thought by some to refer to Whittingham; others give the preference to Alnmouth. Both villages answer to the description given by Bede:—

"A.D. 664, it happened that a great synod was assembled in the presence of King Egfrid, near the river Alne, at a place called Twyford, which signifies 'the two fords,' in which Archbishop Theodore, of blessed memory, presided. Cuthbert was, by the unanimous consent of all, chosen bishop of the church of Lindisfarne."[1]

And then we read that in the ninth century, A.D. 882, a King of Northumbria was chosen out of the famous Vale of Whittingham, which is thus related:—

"The army which, under the command of Alfdene, the king of the pagans, had invaded Northumbria, had for some time been without a leader, in consequence of the slaughter of Alfdene and Inguar by the thanes of king Alfred but now, having subdued the inhabitants of the country, they took possession of it, and began to take up their abode there, and to inhabit the districts of Northumbria that they had before laid waste.

Upon this, Saint Cuthbert, appearing in a vision to abbat Edred, commanded him to tell the bishop and all the army of the English and the Danes that, paying the price of his redemption, they must redeem Cuthred, the son of Hardicanute, whom the Danes had sold as a slave to a certain widow at Wintingham, and when redeemed must make him their king. This was accordingly done in the thirteenth year of the reign of King Alfred."[1]

Of the owner of Whittingham at the Conquest we have no record; but this we know, that it was part of the possessions with which king Ceolwulf endowed the see of Lindisfarne,[2] when, in A.D. 737, he "received Peter's tonsure, and gave his

[1] Bede's Ecclesiastical Hist., Book iv., ch. 28. (Giles.)

[1] Annals of Roger de Hoveden, Vol. i., p. 51. (Riley.)

[2] Ibid, p. 53.

kingdom to Eadbert, his uncle's son."[1] But as the Domesday Book of William the Conqueror—completed in 1086—did not include the county of Northumberland, there is no trace of its later Anglo-Saxon lords. The earliest notice of Whittingham is found in the Pipe Rolls 7 Henry II., 1161, where "Uhtred de Witingeham"[2] renders an account of twenty marks for drengage, under which tenure he held the vill or part of it. The vill of Whittingham appears to have been held by various owners, for in the Pipe Rolls 5 John, 1203, we find that "Vincentio de Whitingham"[3] pays forty shillings scutage (a knight's fee instead of personal service in the field); and at the same time William de Flammavill also holds lands there —for which the first of the name had got a charter—changing the service from drengage to the rendering of one or more sparrow hawks. Robert Fitz-Roger in 1209,[4] and John Fitz-Robert in 1219[5] pays to the King forty shillings for Whittingham, and for the custody of the heirs of William de Flammavill. In 1254, Whittingham was held by Michael, the son of Michael, with Thrunton, Barton, and Ryle.[6]

During the thirteenth century, the manor of Whittingham becomes linked with Eslington. In the escheats of 49 Henry III., 1265, we find that John de Eslington held the manors of Eslington and Framlington, Mitford Park, Whittingham, Thrunton, Barton, and lands in Glanton.[7] After this Eslington appears as the principal manor, perhaps from it being the owner's residence, and eventually the manors of Eslington, Whittingham, Thrunton, and Barton became known as the Eslington estate. About the middle of the fourteenth century

---

[1] Anglo-Saxon Chronicle.

[2] Hodgson's Northumberland, Part iii., Vol. iii., p. 5.

[3] Ibid, page 84.

[4] Ibid, page 103.

[5] Ibid, page 118.

[6] Escheats, Hodgson's Northumberland, Part iii., Vol. i., p. 43.

[7] Hodgson's Northumberland, Part iii., Vol. i., p. 44.

the Hesilriggs became the owners of Eslington, followed by the Collingwoods, for, in 1568, Cuthbert Collingwood was possessed of the manors of Eslington, Bolton, Little Ryle, Great Ryle, and Titlington, with a moiety of the vill of Whittingham, with land in Netherton and the vill of Glanton.[1]

As we may judge from the following extract, fierce and uncivilised must have been the indwellers of Old Whittingham :—"Robert de Ryel killed William Kiverur in coming from the tavern (or cottage) of Wytingham in the road beyond Wytingham. And Agnes, wife of the said Robert Ryel, the first discoverer, comes and is not discredited. And Robert forthwith fled and is suspected. Therefore let him be driven out and outlawed. He had no chattels, and Agnes forthwith raised the hue and cry, and the township of Wytingham did not pursue, therefore let it be amerced." (7th Edwd. I., 1279.)[2]

It is of interest to note the names of the inhabitants who dwelt in the Parish of Whittingham some three hundred and fifty years ago. In 1538, to ascertain the number of men he would be able to call into the field from Northumberland, Henry VIII. commissioned Sir Cuthbert Radcliffe, of Cartington, and Robert Collingwood, Esq., of Eslington, to muster all the able men with horse and harness, and able men on foot, out of Alndale and Coquetdale, on Robert's Law, near High Trewhitt, and on Abberwick Moor. At this muster, which took place on the 17th and 18th of April, 1538, there were present the following numbers of armed men belonging to the parish :—Glanton, 22 ; Shawdon, 7 ; Barton, 5 ; Thrunton, 12 ; Whittingham, 29 ; Callaly, 16; Yetlington, 20; Eslington, 19 ; "Meykle" Ryle, 12—making a total of 142 men ready for active service. Amongst the names on the

[1] Hodgson's Northumberland, Part iii., Vol. iii., p. lxx. (Preface.) (Liber Feodarij, 10 Eliz., 1568.)

[2] Northumberland Assize Rolls, Surtees Society, 88, pp. 116-7.

muster roll are found George Reid, John Reyd, Edward Reyd, Richard Hopper, John Hopper, James Smyth, and Roger Nycholson, out of Glanton; Thos. Collingwood, Thomas Pigdon, Roger Pigdon, Rycd. Pigdon, James Pigdon, Jno. Butiman, Thos. Butiman, and Roger Brown, out of Whittingham; Thos. Clavering, John Atkinson, Henry Whytwham, and Cristo, out of Callaly. The most numerous surnames are Collingwood, Pigdon, Butiman, Nycholson, Alder, Hopper, Reid, and Dychburn. The Herons seem to have disappeared, as the name does not occur once in the Whittingham list. The principal Christian names are Roger, Gilbert, Richard, Cuthbert, Henry, Edward, Thomas, James, John, and William; while Peter, Lawrence, Andrew, and Rynon are occasionally met with.

A list of the freeholders in the parish of Whittingham for the years 1628 and 1638, shewing by whom the various lands were owned, cannot fail to be of interest to the reader:—

FREHOULDERS IN NORTHUMBERLAND, 1628.

COOKEDALE WARDE.

Sr. John Clavering of Callaly Kt.
George Collingwood, of Eslington, esq.
Thomas Collingwood of Great Ryle, gent.
Alexander Collingwood of Little Ryle, gent.
Thomas Unthanke of Unthanke, gent. (Alnham Parish)
Robert Clavering of Leerchild, gent. (Edlingham Parish)
Jeffrey Procter of Shawdon, gent.
Francis Collingwood of Thrunton, gent.

COC-DALE WARDE, 1638.

Sr. John Claveringe of Calloleye Knight.
Cuthbert Collingwood of Eslington, esq.
Henry Collingwood of Great Ryle, gent.
Alexander Collingwood of Little Ryle, gent.
Thomas Unthank of Unthank, gent.
George Alder, of Prendick, gent. } (Alnham Parish)
John Collingwood of Revely, gent.
Robert Collingwood of Ingra, gent. } (Ingram Parish)
Robert Clavering of Leirchild, gent.[1] (Edlingham Parish)

[1] Archæologia Æliana, Vol. ii. (Old Series), page 316.

Echoes of the dreadful civil wars of the seventeenth century, when the fair lands of England were stained with the blood of Cavalier and Roundhead, are found to exist in the vale and village of Whittingham. A letter in the State Papers, written by Clavering, of Callaly, giving information to the Royalist head-quarters that the Scotch troops, under General Leslie, had crossed the Borders into Northumberland, says:—

"Aug. 25, 1640.—About 400 horse ordered breakfast at Whittingham; they came from Brandon hills, singing psalms all the way. They behaved civilly, and paid for everything; they quartered that night at Lemington and at Edlingham New Town."[1]

There used to be an old tradition in Whittingham of a troop of soldiers having passed through the village many years ago, who required an extraordinary number of loaves of bread, which were supplied to them from the village bakery. Whether this tradition refers to those Scotch dragoons, or to an incident of the later Jacobite movement of 1715 or 1745, we cannot say; but the remains of a large baker's oven was discovered a few years ago, while W. Dixon and Son, merchants, were making some alterations in an old seventeenth-century house adjoining their premises, in Whittingham. This was probably the public oven which supplied the troopers with the bread. Again, in the summer of 1648, Whittingham was visited by Cromwell's Roundheads, at a time when the fortunes of war were much against the Cavaliers in Northumberland. A troop of Roundheads, under the command of a Major Sanderson, made a forced march overnight from Chollerton, in North Tyne, into Coquetdale and the vale of the Aln, and finding the tired Royalist troopers in bed, took some hundreds of them prisoners. They came by way of the Simonside Hills, Great Tosson, Lorbottle, and Callaly. Major Sanderson, in his report to Head-quarters, gives some interesting details.

"Friday, 30 Junii.—According to agreement we rendevouzed about eleven of the clocke, at Chollerford, three miles north of Hexam. We hasted away that

[1] State Papers.

night, and marched sixteen miles from Hexam to Harterton ; bated our horses two houres ; then mounted again and marched from thence. I had the command of the forlorne hope. The first towne we fell into was Tossons, where wee took a lieutenant and sixe of his dragoons, all in bed ; the next town was Lurbottle, when we took 60 horse and 60 men, all in bed. The next quarter was Carlile (Callaly), where Col. Grey, Lieu. Col. Salkeld, and many others were taken, with 80 horse. The next quarter was Whittingham, where Lieut.-Col. Millet, and many considerable men, with 200 horse. The next was, at one time, an engagement upon Eslington, where were 100 horse, at Glanton ; in Glanton were 180 horse, most of them were taken with the officers and souldiers in that quarter. At Eslington was taken Sir Richard Tempest, Major Troulop, and many others. Wee advanced on towards Branton, but finding that wee were cloyed with prisoners and horse and booty, wee retyred towards Whittingham, where Col. Lilburne was labouring to rally into a firme body: for there appeared about Shawton four bodies of the enemies' horse, who had taken the alarme and got together ; but all the rest wee tooke before they could mount. The victory was beyond all expectation, God working it for us. Wee had got but one horse shot dead, and one man shot through his thigh, and of the enemy there was five slain, and Capt. Smirk run through the body, and some others wounded. The enemies' bodies of horse that appeared at Shawton retyred from us northward ; and when they were gone out of sight, two miles, wee drew off to Newtown, staid two houres, withdrew to Morpeth, disposed of our prisoners as well as we could. Wee brought to Morpeth 309 that were droven a-foot; because wee wanted horses to carry them on ; there were many officers and gentlemen amongst them ; and wee brought 42 of them on horseback, so that we had 351 prisoners, besides many that escaped. Wee took about 600 horse, but the souldiers drove them away towards Newcastle, and sold them at high rates. Sunday, July second.—Wee brought our prisoners to Newcastle ; but Sir Richard Tempest escaped from Morpeth after he had brok his fast on Sunday morning. Wee have received information that the enemies' forlorne hope are advancing now about Long Framlington. Wee are drawing our horse together, and shall advance so soone as we can. Wee have ten troopes of horse come to us this night under Col. Harrison ; they are to meet us at Meldon. The enemy have about 600 horse left yet, and three troopes of dragoones. They brag of the Scots comming in to-morrow into England. If the Scots come not in, we shall, by God's helpe, free this country of these blades." (Signed, JOHN SANDERSON, Newcastle, July 3, 1648.)

Not only did these deplorable internecine conflicts affect the bulk of the rural population of the valley, for many of them were in the rank and file of both parties, although the majority appear to have joined the Royalists, but it was the leaders—the Cavaliers—who suffered most ; their estates were sequestrated, and they were heavily fined. The loyal vicar of

Whittingham was ejected from his living, and a minister, appointed by the sequestrators, placed over the parish. A Parliamentarian officer occupied for some time the mansion of the Royalist squire of Eslington. while the gallant Sir John Clavering, of Callaly, was taken prisoner by the Roundheads, and died in prison.

From the "Rentals and Rates" of 1663 we give the names of the then proprietors, with the value of the land throughout the parish of Whittingham, from which we can see that most of the King's party had got their own again :—

Place	Proprietor	£	s.	d.
Barton	Geo. Collingwood, Esq.	£50	0	0
Callaly & Yetlington	Robt. Clavering, Esq.	£288	0	0
Callaly Mill	Ralph Clavering, Esq.	£5	10	0
Eslington				
Eslington Mill	Geo. Collingwood, Esq.	£200	0	0
Eslington tithe				
Glanton	Names of Proprietors under Glanton	£150	0	0
Glanton tithe		£24	0	0
Lorbottle	Marquis of Newcastle.			
Lorbottle tithe				
Great Ryle & Blakehope	Mr. Robert Collingwood	£180	0	0
Great Ryle Mill		£6	0	0
Little Ryle	Mr. Alexander Collingwood	£140	0	0
Caisley Houses				
Shawdon				
Shawdon Wood House	Mr. Robert Brandling	£100	0	0
Shawdon Mill				
Thrunton and				
Barton	George Collingwood, Esq.	£64	0	0
Tithes		£20	0	0
Thrunton Mill		£20	0	0
Whittingham	George Collingwood, Esq.	£200	0	0
Vicarage	Mr. Henry Talentyre, Vicar	£70	0	0
Tithe	Dean & Chapter of Carlisle	£24	0	0

If one could but imagine the appearance of the village of Whittingham in the early decades of the eighteenth century, what a quaint old picture it would present to our view, with its low thatched cottages standing here and there, each with its own garth and croft attached. The best we can do is to place before our readers the names of the inhabitants during the last years of the Collingwood ownership, 1715, which are taken from the particulars of the sale of the estate in 1718:—Robert Hudson, Henry Bell, John Jackson, James Anderson, John Dodd, John Nicholson. William Collingwood, Thomas Hall, Thomas Anderson, Edward Piles, Adam Anderson, Richard Cury, John Hamm, Robert Whitham, Robert Graham, Robert Nicholson, George Nicholson, Matthew Mills.

Whittingham is thus briefly described by Horsley in 1729: "Whittingham has a church at it, and a yearly fair on the 24th of August. This town belongs now to Sir Henry Liddell, and, since the estate came into that family, considerable improvements have been made in it. The river Ale[1] comes through the town."[2]

"Marks' survey of Northumberland," 1734, says:—"This parish comprehends 1,000 families,[3] and thirteen villages, the principal of which is Whittingham (the church town), Glanton, Great Ryle, Eslington, Yetlington, Harbottle (? Lorbottle), Callaley, Thropton (? Thrunton), Barton, and Shawdon. Whittingham is situated on the south side of the river Aln, about two-miles-and-a-half from Ingram, and five miles from Alnwick, and five north from Rothbury. The valley is considerably large and populous. The church is in very good order, having lately had the addition of a new chancel, built at the charge of the lessees of the great tythes. Before the year 1715, the manor of Whittingham was part of the estate of the Honourable George Collingwood, Esq.; but, unfortunately, engaging himself in the Pretender's interest, lost, in consequence, both life and estate, to the great regret of all that knew him. There is a very good fair kept here once a year

---

[1] Aln. The Vale of Aln is sometimes called "Yelwater" or "Alewater" at the present day.

[2] Horsley's Northumberland, p. 54.

[3] This can scarcely be correct. Marks' was a somewhat cursory survey of the county; while a more reliable authority says that in 1730 there were 235 families.

on St. Bartholomew's Day, for all sorts of cattle and other goods, but has not any weekly market."[1]

From the Subscribers' List to Mackenzie and Dent's History of Northumberland in 1811, we give those belonging to the district of Whittingham :—

"Edward Anderson, Esq., Glanton.
Adam Atkinson, Esq., Lorbottle House.
Rev. Newton Blythe, Branton.
Capt. Bullock, Great Ryal (Ryle).
William Clark, schoolmaster, Whittingham.
John Clavering, Esq., Callaley.
Thomas Claxton, tinman, Callaley.
Thomas Common, millwright, Whittingham.
Selby Curry, seedsman, Glanton.
Robert Curry, farmer, Branton.
T. Greenshill, joiner, Glanton.
Rev. James Kirton, Glanton.
Wm. Lynn, Whittingham.
Rev. Jas. Manisty, B.D., Long Edlingham.
Miss Nicholson, Whittingham.
James Pigdon, farmer, Glanton.
S. Robertson, painter, Whittingham.
Peter Stephenson, butcher, Whittingham.
Henry Stobbs, farmer, Glanton.
Thomas Story, farmer, Fawdon.
Joseph Waterman, innkeeper, Whittingham.
George Watson, miller, Callaley Mill."

We here give an exact copy from the "Eslington Estate Book" of the plan of Whittingham, showing the position of the houses in 1821, as well as a list of the village tenants at that time. Besides the names of the tenants in 1821, we also give the names of the various occupiers circa. 1845-1855, which we hope will be of interest to our indulgent readers :—

North Side of the Aln.

	1821.	1845–1855.
No. 1	Isabel Dodds.	Luke Weatheritt, Farmer.
,, 2	Dr. Crea.	John Harrison, Woodman.
,, 3	Overseers of the Poor.	John Harrison, Woodman.

[1] Marks' Survey of Northumberland (1734), p. 83.

	1821.	1845–1855.
No. 4	Andrew Thompson.	William Riddell, Labourer.
,, 5	Thomas Thompson.	William Suthren, Joiner.
,, 6	Matthew Alder, Senior.	William Baston, Quarryman.
,, 17	Matthew Alder, Senior.	Outhouse.
,, 18	Henry Bolam.	Robert Grieve, Foreman Drainer.
,, 14	Henry Bolam.	Outhouse.
,, 19	Charles Patterson.	James Tait, Tailor.
,, 20	Mary Anderson.	John and Ellen Anderson.
,, 31	John Biggs.*	John Biggs, Millwright.
,, 32	Mary Carr.	John Biggs, Millwright.
,, 34	William Clark.	William Ternent, Schoolmaster.
,, 21	Dr. Crea.	Hannah Crea, Draper and Grocer.
,, 24	Thomas Alder.	Robert Ord, Carrier.
,, 25	John Henderson.	Robert Ord, Carrier.
,, 26	John Robinson.	Mary and Susan Robinson.
,, 41	John Walker.	Thomas Watson, Stone Mason. Edward Watson, Grocer.
,, 43	Overseers of the Poor	Outhouse.
,, 46	Thomas Hudson.	(Disappeared).
,, 47	William Dickinson.	(Disappeared).
,, 51	John Hudson.	Edward Hudson, Shoemaker.
,, 52	William Dickinson.	John Thompson, Kilnman.
,, 53	John Hudson.	Albert Errington, Head Forester.
,, 56	Overseers of the Poor.	Robert Gray, Tailor.
,, 57	Andrew Thompson	Robert Gray, Tailor.
,, 58	Joseph Waterman.	Adam Young, Carrier.
,, 59	William Dickinson.	Adam Young's Stable.
,, 60	Joseph Waterman.	Peggy & Nelly Hornsby.

South Side of the Aln.

	1821.	1845-1855.
No. 69	John Turnbull.	Miss Wealleans.
,, 70	Robert Henderson.	Robt. Clark's Blacksmith's Shop.
,, 71	Robert Henderson.	Christopher Thompson, Cooper and Grocer.
,, 74	Ralph Dodds.	Ditto ditto
,, 73	Alexander Liley.	Stable.
No. 75	Alexander Liley.	Bella Lawson.
,, 76	Alexander Liley.	George Robinson, Carter.
,, 77	Sybil Copeland.	John Hudson, Shoemaker.
,, 78	Phillis Vint.	George Dixon.
,, 79	Sybil Copeland.	Stable.

	1821.	1845–1855.
No. 80	Phillis Vint.	Stable.
,, 91	(The Tower) William Dickinson	Almshouses. Occupants in 1885: James Pigdon, William Watson, Joseph Davidson, Robt. Grey.
,, 93	Richard Mavin.	Matthew Morrison Dickinson's Farm Buildings.
,, 94	William Dickinson.	
,, 95	Richard Mavin.	
,, 96	George Hudson.	Francis Taylor, Post Office.
,, 97	Matthew Collingwood.	
,, 102	George Henderson.*	George Henderson.

Our engraving shews Cottages Nos. 76, 77, 78, 79, and 80, as they appeared in 1860.

	1821.	1845–1855.
No. 103	Matthew Alder, Junior.	Robert Clark, Blacksmith.
		Mrs. Moffat and Miss Wilson.
,, 104	George Henderson.	George Henderson's Cow Byre.
,, 105	Joseph Waterman.	James Hall, Butcher.
		John Ewart, Labourer.
,, 107	Joseph Waterman.	James Wright, Labourer.
		Walter Redpath, Labourer.
,, 109	Joseph Waterman.	James Hall's Killing Shop.
,, 114	Joseph Waterman.	John Scott, Labourer.
		George Dunn, Labourer.

	1821.	1845–1855.
No. 115	William Dickinson.	Matthew Morrison Dickinson, Farmer and Overseer.
,, 116	William Dickinson.	William Dixon, Draper and Grocer.
,, 117	William Bowden.	James Chambers, Shoemaker.
,, 118	Mark Vint.	Jane Dixon, Grocer.
		George Vint, Saddler.
Castle Inn	Joseph Waterman.	Adam Pile, Innkeeper.

It may be noticed that John Biggs* and George Henderson* are the only tenants of 1821 who still held the same cottages and lands in 1855. Old George Henderson died at Whittingham in 1885, in his hundredth year, while Mary Biggs, the relict of John Biggs, also lived to be a centenarian. She died at Whittingham in 1889, in her 102nd year.

The farmers in Whittingham in 1821 were Joseph Waterman, William Dickinson, Andrew Thompson, and George Thompson. Joseph Waterman, besides being Innkeeper, held Rothill, High Barton, East Lane Head, South Whitton Lea, and Whittingham Inn farms. William Dickinson had South Whitton Lea, Limeworks, &c. Andrew Thompson had Middle Whitton Lea, and Andrew and George Thompson had West Whitton Lea.

We here give a list of the most interesting field names on the various farms mentioned :—

West Rothill.—Tod's Headlands, Hawklemass, Ellen Steads, Tile Kiln Fields, Bradford Piece, Turf Moor.

East Rothill.—North Camp Field, North Rumpeth, Pasture Davridge, Broomy Stobs, South East Field (often called Whittingham Field).

High Barton.—Green Side, Night Folds, North Duck Field, North Eshet Lands, East Raveledge, South How Meadow.

East Lane Head.—Middle Close, West Close, East Mill Close, Aller Field, Spire Leazes.

South Whitton Lea.—North Tire Carlings, South Tire

Carlings, Wester Bank (now called the Green Field), Strenkle Bank (Nicholson's Hill), Lime Kiln Field, Middle Intake, West Intake (Reynard's Lodge), East Whitton Lea (Waterman's Field).

WHITTINGHAM INN FARM.—Crook Bank, West Pedlar Close (Ross's Haugh), South Middleton, Camp Field (The Shay Field[1]), Easter Bank.

MIDDLE WHITTON LEA.—Nine Wells, Gourleys, West Wood Head, West New Close (White Knowe).

WEST WHITTON LEA.—The Woodside, North Long Bank, West Brown's Close, Whittingham Haugh, South Spittle Dowes.

The fields and crofts, lying contiguous to the village of Whittingham, were let to the villagers in the same manner as they are at the present day. Dr. Watson now holds the Lea-side, and the same fields as Dr. Crea did in 1821, with the exception of the field up the back lane, known as the "Doctor's field," which is now in the possession of Robt. Scott, butcher. The vicarage field, behind the churchyard, was held by William Clark and Henry Bolam. Errington's field (now William Dixon's), was, in 1821, William Dickinson's. Rogerson's field was John Henderson's. Henderson's field was Matthew Alder's. Pile's field, in 1821, was Robert Henderson's.

FIELD NAMES—and almost every field has its distinctive name—are often derived from some ancient usuage or form of tillage, or from the name of an early occupant as well as from the shape, size, or some physical peculiarity, the study of which is not only full of interest, but of information to the lover of local history. We therefore add a further list of characteristic field names on the Eslington Estate:—

MOUNTAIN FARM.—White Leazes, Rein Deer Close,[2]

[1] Where the Postchaise occasionally stood in coaching times.

[2] The field where the Reindeer brought from Lapland by Sir Henry Geo. Liddell, in 1786, were kept.

Raven's Crag, The Twist, Mereburn Close, Kellet's Close, Cat Gallows, West Mill Close, Cow Loan,[1] Carn's Piece, Allerburn Bank (The Mountain Field), East Thorney Bank, North Spittle Dowes, Coney Warren.

HOWBALK (GRANGE FARM).—North Brown Cow, Middle and East Brown Cow, East, South and West Breadless-haugh.

ESLINGTON BANK TOP.—South Well Close, North Hopesburn Field, East Peary's Close, North Well Close.

ESLINGTON TOWN FARM.—Broom Rigs, Mill Close, Ox Close, Horse Close, Dovecote Close, Calf Close, East Field.

MOUNTHOOLY FARM.—West Well Close, East Well Close, East Peat Pots, West Peat Pots.

LOWFIELD FARM.—Wanless Crooks, Spittle Field,[2] Jockey's Dike Nook Field, The Payn.[3]

LEARCHILD FARM.—Ben Acres, Crookhill, Ox Close, High Bannock Close, West Field, East Field, Well Close.

THRUNTON MILL.—North Harepark, South Harepark.

THRUNTON FARM.—Wellywise Field, Threap Moor, North Stob Bank, Cumber Croft, Ox Close, Midrig, Mill Field, Dam Field, Little Allers, Saint Illian's (Ninian's) Field.[4]

The population of the parish of Whittingham in

1801	was	... ...	1,465 persons.
1811	„	... ...	1,862 „
1821	„	... ...	1,749 „
1871	„	... ...	1,928 „
1881	„	... ...	1,575 „
1891	„	... ...	1,512 „

It is a well-known fact, as the foregoing census record shows, that the population of our rural districts has for the last twenty years been rapidly decreasing. Various causes tend to bring about this continued exodus of the younger members of the

---

[1] A sheltering place where the cows were brought to be milked.

[2] Probably hospital lands.

[3] "Payne," a field or plain.

[4] A fine spring of water on Thrunton farm is known as "St. Ninian's Well."

families of our peasantry. Some years ago, when times were good, it was the "big money wage," given by employers in large towns and in colliery districts, that induced many to leave their native valley for the busy turmoil of those great centres of industry. And then of late years, owing to the large tracts of land being "laid away" to grass, only a tithe of the number of farm labourers are employed to work the small amount of acreage under tillage. On many farms where six draughts, or pairs of horses, were kept, with a corresponding number of field workers—women and lads—only a half or a third of that number is now required. As an example we quote High Barton,[1] a farm "onstead" connected with Rothill farm. There are at the present time only two families, where, about the year 1830, there were seven families, as follows, each supplying their quota of field workers:—

James Watson, Mason.
William Davidson, Mason.
Elizabeth Grey, Bondage House.
John Young, "Jobber" (Cattle Dealer).
Margaret Mills, Bondage House.
Robert Young, Shepherd.
William Black, Shepherd.

Again, the doing away of small holdings and the amalgamation of several farms into one is also another cause of the depopulation of agricultural districts. During the seventeenth, and early in the eighteenth century, we have certain evidence that the lands around our villages and hamlets were for the most part let off to a number of tenants in equal lots or parts called "farms." As we write we have before us a list of the farms and the names of the tenants in the lordship of Lorbottle in the year 1724, and find that Lorbottle then consisted of sixteen farms and two cottages,[2] while from the list of persons holding the village of Whittingham in 1718, it would also

[1] Barton (A.S.) The demesne lands of a manor; the manor-house itself; the outhouses and yards.—Wright's Glossary.

[2] Survey of "The Ogle Lands," 1724, quoted at page 146.

appear to have been divided in the same manner. As a class, the farm servants, who form the greater part of our rural population—the hinds and shepherds of Northumberland—are famed for their frugal and industrious habits, their high integrity of character and superior intelligence. "Physically, the Northumbrian hind is a tall and handsome man. The head of middle formation, neither brachycephalic nor macrocephalic, but perhaps inclining to the latter, if anything. His hair oftener light brown or dark brown than either white or black, or cold grey. His eyes very often hazel, often dark blue, often grey; not often light blue. His complexion ruddy and sunburnt. His gait a long active stride, less martial than the walk of the Scot, but totally unlike the heavy waddling roll of the Southern peasantry."[1] The average height of fourteen husbandmen is given as 5 feet 10·30 inches.[2] "The corn and cow kept as wages in North Northumberland have been highly advantageous to the hind fortunate in the possession of an industrious wife. . . . But the great secret of the superior moral and social status of the Northumberland hind is his sobriety and abstinence from those stimulants which, in the form of beer and cider, are swallowed in such enormous quantities by the farm labourers of the Southern counties."[3] No doubt the lack of industries, other than those connected with agriculture, helps to thin the ranks of our husbandmen, and the loss of such a population is much to be deplored, for:—

"—a bold peasantry, their country's pride,
When once destroy'd can never be supplied."

As an excellent illustration of a typical Northumbrian hind, we quote the following account from a local newspaper[4]

---

[1] The Northumbrians between Tyne and Tweed, by Ralph Carr, Hedgley.—History Berwickshire Naturalists' Club.

[2] The stature of native Northumbrians, by Geo. Tate, F.G.S.—History Berwickshire Naturalists' Club.

[3] The Agricultural Labourers of Northumberland: Their Physical and Social Condition, by Samuel Donkin, 1868.

[4] *Alnwick Guardian*, December 31st, 1892.

of a countryman and his wife, who during a long term of service in the Vale of Whittingham were always held in the highest esteem both by their masters and fellow-workmen :—

"WHITTINGHAM.—On Saturday last, the golden wedding of Mr. and Mrs. Telford was celebrated in a manner thoroughly befitting an event which so rarely happens. Mr. and Mrs. Telford, or 'Robin and Jenny,' as they are locally called, are generally respected throughout the district, and by all who have had the pleasure of their acquaintance. Although they have been 'toilers and spinners' for the most part of their lives, and have passed the threescore years and ten, they are still hale and hearty, and look as if their happy union might be prolonged for many years to come. They began their married life at Lorbottle fifty years ago, and, curious to relate, although 'Robin's' occupation often compelled them to shift from place to place during that period, they have never crossed the boundaries of the parish of Whittingham. During the afternoon they had their photographs taken, together with their family—seven sons and one daughter ; and in another group, including five grandchildren and two daughters-in-law. They received various presents, all suitable for the occasion, but the most characteristic of the event was that of their children, which was presented in the course of the evening in the most affectionate terms by their eldest son, Mr. John Telford. The memento was a handsome marble timepiece, the inscription, which was richly engraved on a gold plate with a neatly cut border, being as follows :—

'Golden Wedding
of
ROBERT AND JANE TELFORD.
Their children greet them.
Time flits ; affection stays.
Dec. 24th, 1892.'

Several friends were invited to the evening festival, and after ample justice had been done to a splendid supper, the presentation already referred to took place. Mr. Ross, in a few well-chosen remarks, proposed health and happiness to the honoured couple, which met with a hearty musical response. The remaining hours were spent in homely chat and cheerful song, concluding with 'Auld Lang Syne,' when the stroke of the midnight hour ushered in Christmas Sunday, exactly as it had done half a century ago when Robin and Jenny made their first appearance as husband and wife in the church at Great Bavington."

The village of Whittingham, divided as it is by the river Aln, was in former times known under two different names. A manuscript account, of 1730, says : "Whittingham is situated on the south side of the river Aln, and the other part is called the Church Town." During the fourteenth century, when the village was held by two owners, Hesilrigg and Heron (1362), it is probable that the south side belonged to the Herons, and the north side to the Hesilriggs, for in 1415 Whittingham tower, which is on the south side, was in the possession of William Heron. The villagers at the present day, living on either side of the Aln, speak of the opposite side as "over the water," or in Whittingham vernacular, "ower the witter." The stone bridge connecting the two parts was erected during the first decade of the present century, when stage coaches and other vehicular traffic began to supersede the old pack horse system of our great grandfathers; the ford by which they crossed the Aln being a few yards east of the bridge, where traces of the old road leading to the ford may yet be seen in a field, formerly known as "Pile's field," on the south side of the Aln. This old road was the main turnpike and coach road between Newcastle and Edinburgh, and came through from Morpeth by Weldon Bridge, Framlington, Rimside Moor, Thrunton Cragend, Whittingham, Glanton, Wooler, Milfield, Blue Bell, and on to Cornhill. In the old coaching days, when the "Wellington" passed and re-passed on its way to and from Edinburgh and Newcastle, there would always be a good deal of stir and bustle at the "Castle Inn"—the posting house kept by Joseph Waterman, afterwards by Daniel Ross, where the horses were changed at 11 a.m. *en route* for Edinburgh, and at 5 p.m. for Newcastle. About 1840 the "New Road" was made, which left the old coach road half a mile to the south of Rimside Moor House, and took a straight course through Roughlee Wood, Bridge of Aln, where a neat posting house was built, known for long amongst the inhabitants as "The New Inn," on through "Crawley Dene," rejoining the old road at Powburn; but very shortly after the formation of this road the coaches ceased running, in consequence of the opening, in 1849, of the east coast line of railway from Berwick to York, and for many years it might have been said of the Bridge of Aln that "its occupation was gone." Now-a-days, however, it is a busier and a more important place than it was in the old coaching days, for, on September 5th, 1887, a branch line of rail was formed from Alnwick to Cornhill, passing through the vale of Whittingham, which it enters at Learchild, and following for some distance the course of the Roman Causeway and the newer line—the coaching road—proceeds through Crawley Dene, by Powburn, to Wooler, and thence to Cornhill.

The following lines were composed whilst riding on the coach over Rimside Moor on a very cold morning[1]:—

He who o'er Rimside Moor hath past
Whilst mingling hail and rain pour'd fast,
Which by the bleak and wintry blast
Full in his face was driven:
That man, when safe the Castle Inn
He shivering reached—wet to the skin—
Might surely say, devoid of sin,
Now, now, I've got to Heaven!

Or he who rides o'er this drear scene,
What time prevails the hoar frost keen,
A blue tipt nose is his I ween,
And his two rosy ears.
His toes and fingers tingling ache,
His teeth a woeful chattering make,
And lo! iced o'er like some bride cake,
His frigid form appears.

But when to Waterman's he gets,
Benumbed with cold, no more he frets,
Down by the fire himself he sets,
And soon is in a glow;
Then should an angel to him say,
To Heav'n I'll bear thee straight away,
O'er Rimside, if the journey lay,
He'd flat refuse to go.

An old road, which was probably the original road previous to the erection of the stone bridge, leading to Eslington, the Ryles, Alnham, and Netherton, branched off from the Callaly road in the middle of the village of Whittingham on the south side, went past the tower, down the tower bank (generally called the "brae"), through the ford a little above the present

[1] Newcastle Literary Magazine, January 1st, 1824.

wooden foot-bridge, and on past the Church. The village stocks stood at the bottom of the "brae," near to the "Pit Well," a small spring, so-called on account of the blackness of the mud that surrounds it. Many years ago its brackish water was relished by certain of the old villagers, who thought there was some special virtue in its nauseousness, and which was also reputed to be "an excellent good remedie" for weak eyes. A little further up the "burn," on its south bank, there is a spring of delightful water, the "Cocks Well," whose name would seem to indicate the existence in bygone times of a Cock Pit, although there is no record or recollection to be found in the village of Whittingham of that once most popular village sport. The "Cocks Well" is situate in a charming little dene called the Leaside, whose steep green braes and moist bottoms are in summer a perfect wealth of wild flowers. There in early spring is found the Early Purple Orchis, Cuckoo Flower, the pale Primrose, and the Violet blue, besides—

> "There are spots where nestle wild flowers small,
> With many a mingling gleam;
> Where the broad Flag waves, and the Bullrush tall
> Nods still to the thrusting stream."

The local carriers in 1827 were:—Ralph Greason, from Callaly to Alnwick, every Saturday; James Davison, from Glanton to Alnwick, every Wednesday and Saturday; John Nicholson, from Whittingham to Alnwick, every Saturday.

Thomas Taylor was postmaster; and letters from Morpeth and the south arrived at 9 a.m., and from Edinburgh at 4·30 p.m.

Amongst the residents in the village of Whittingham in 1827 were John Clark, steward to J. C. Tarleton, Esq., of Collingwood House; Joshua Crea, surgeon; Geo. Henderson, tailor; Rev. Edmund Law, vicar; Rev. Joseph Law, curate; Thomas Taylor, clogger; George Vint, saddler; William Dickinson, farmer; Andrew Thompson, farmer and overseer;

William Clark, schoolmaster; Eleanor Vint, schoolmistress; John and Robert Henderson, blacksmiths; Isabella Bell, Hannah Crea, and William Wightman, grocers; John Biggs, millwright; William Reed, joiner; William Bowden and Thomas Hudson, shoemakers. In those days, besides the "Castle Inn," there were two public houses in Whittingham, the "Masons' Arms" and the "Hole-in-the-Wall," of which a sketch is given. The "Mason's Arms" stood on the spot now occupied by the Police Station, the hostess thereof for many years being Sybil Copeland, best known as "Aad Sib Copeland." A story is related of a west country carrier who once attempted to bamboozle poor old Sib in her reckoning. The carrier called on the Saturday morning, on his way to Alnwick, and had a glass of ale, saying. "Aa'l pay ye at night, Sib." Calling again on his return at night, he had another glass, which he drank off with the remark, "There noo, Sib, maw woman, we'll just let the tyen stand for the tother." The "Hole-in-the-Wall" was kept by Tom Dickinson, a well-known character, whom the villagers often called "Dang it." For many years he was head gamekeeper to Lord Ravensworth, at Eslington, and therefore for his sign adopted the symbol of his profession—a pointer dog. The old house is yet standing on the right hand side of the road, after crossing the stone bridge on the way to Glanton, with its original flight of outside stone stairs leading up to the door in the west gable. Respecting this old hostelry, a village rhyme says :—

"If ever you go to Whittingham Fair,
Be sure an' call at the 'Hole-in-the-Waa',
For there you get whisky for nowt
An' brandy for nothing at aa'."

Whittingham Fair, some fifty or sixty years ago, was an event of great importance amongst the people of the Aln and surrounding district; but the old statute fair, with its rows of refreshment tents and gingerbread stalls, troops of mountebanks, strolling players, and boxing booths; gangs of hucksters and muggers displaying their varied assortment of merchandise, boots and shoes, hats and caps, sickles, cheese, and crockery ware; its crowds of fresh-coloured country lads and lasses, enjoying their annual holiday—

> "His corn and cattle were his only care,
> And his supreme delight a country fair;"

its herds of cattle and droves of sheep; its free fights amongst the scores of shearers fresh from the Emerald isle; the village constable—Bob Clark, the blacksmith—hauling off the breakers of the peace to the "Kitty" in Ned Watson's stable; the riding of the Fair to the merry strains of Ned Hudson's fiddle, whose famous bow hand was ever in requisition at Kirn Supper or Merry Night—are now memories of the past, for the old village fair has degenerated into gymnastic games. Whittingham Fair was held on the 24th of August,[1] St. Bartholomew's Day, the patron Saint of Church and village. In early times dedication services were held annually on the Saint's day to whom the Church was dedicated, and then followed the village feast; and country people, taking advantage of meeting each other, gradually fell into the custom of bringing their goods and chattels for barter. In course of time the lord of the manor obtained a charter from the King to hold the fair and levy tolls. This is the origin of most of the old statute fairs,

---

[1] In 1734 the fair was held on the 24th of August, St. Bartholomew's Day, which was no doubt its original day; but in 1775 and 1785, as we learn from the columns of the *Newcastle Courant*, the fair was then held on September 4th. This date must have again been changed some time towards the end of the last century or at the beginning of the present one, for in 1810 the fair was again held on St. Bartholomew's Day. Probably the change in the Calendar from the "old style," which took place in 1752, may have had something to do with the temporary departure from the old date.

which are now fast becoming obsolete. Probably the dalesmen who came to the fair in those days were armed with sword and dirk, and, true to the old saying—

"Northumberlonde, hasty and hot,"

with them it was the word and the blow; therefore, we can understand the need of the following proclamation which we have heard so often read aloud on the morning of the fair by William Ternent, the bailiff:—

"O, yez! O, yez! O, yez! These are in Her Majesty's name, and in the name of The Right Honourable The Earl of Ravensworth, lord of this present Fair: strictly to charge and command, all and every person, coming to or resorting at this Fair, quietly and peaceably to behave themselves, as well in their Host-houses as without. And all persons liable shall pay their toll and stallage to William Ternent Bailiff of this Fair; or to any person he shall appoint, without let, molestation or interruption. And further if any person or persons shall expose to sale any horse or mare, colt, or filly; that the buyer, as well as the seller shall repair to the Bailiff, and with him, enter all such horses, mares, colts, or fillies, as shall be sold or exchanged with sufficiency for the same. Also, if any person or persons shall use any violence, by drawing any weapon, or shedding any blood shall forfeit to the Lord of the Manor 100 shillings.

GOD SAVE THE QUEEN AND THE LORD OF THE MANOR."

In riding the fair, a long cavalcade of horsemen, consisting of the tenantry and others, assembled at the Castle Inn, from whence they proceeded, led by the bailiff, and accompanied with the music of Ned Hudson's fiddle, who was often assisted by his two sons, William and John, all of whom were excellent musicians. After perambulating the whole extent of the village, on both sides of the water, the fair was proclaimed in an open space, under the shadow of the old tower, on whose lofty flagstaff floated, on St. Bartholomew's Day, the flag of old England. An adjournment was then made to the Castle Inn, where liberal refreshments, provided by the lord of the manor, were served out to those who had joined in the ceremony.

At the time we speak of, there were publicans' refreshment tents from Alnwick, Eglingham, Rothbury, Snitter, Thropton, Netherton, Harbottle, Alwinton, Long Framlington, and Glanton ; numerous huckster's stalls from Alnwick, on which "Shanter Jack," "Ailee Canair," "Dutch Billy," and many others offered for sale nuts and oranges, apples and claggum, gingerbread, sherbet, and gooseberries. There were hardware and cutlery stalls from Kelso ; hats, caps, and sickles from Rothbury ;[1] boots and shoes from Alnwick ;[2] and "cow cheese" by the score from the hilly districts of the Breamish and the Aln.

One part of the "toon gyet," near where the pant stands, now planted with trees, was entirely taken up by the "muggers," with their extensive display of useful and ornamental crockery ware—a welcome sight to the housewives of the parish, who annually replenished their stock at Whittingham Fair. The figures of old Duncan Angus and his wife Bella, Ben Pope and Mrs. Pope, Mally Young and Tom Young, Mally Campbell and old Jack Campbell (the horse couper), are still fresh in the mind of the writer. On the green, in front of "Morry Dickinson's," there was usually exposed for sale a large quantity of tar, in kegs, which was purchased by the Cheviot shepherds, who came down with carts to carry it to their various herdings amongst the hills ; this tar was used for "laying"[3] the sheep

[1] From an old account book of a Rothbury tradesman, dated Aug. 24, 1820, we quote the following:—"Sold at Whittingham Fair 23 dozen hooks; took £18."

[2] "For many centuries the Cordwainers or Shoemakers of Alnwick held the monopoly of the trade in this district. As late as 1701, Jeremiah Feugues, of Eslington, was bound under a penalty of £20 not to take an apprentice, nor to come nigher to Alnwick to make or sell shoes than the place he now lives at excepting for two families within the borough of Alnwick. This monopoly ceased in 1785." The Cordwainers Company of Alnwick had also control of leather goods sold at fairs in the county. "The searchers and sealers of leather, officers in the employ of the Company, visited all the fairs held in the neighbourhood :—

1774 Nov. 1st. Searching Rothbury Fair, 5s:
,, Sep. 4. Searching Whtttingham Fair, 5s.

These visitations were discontinued in 1803."—Tate's History of Alnwick, Vol. ii., pp. 331-332.

[3] "The Cheviot shepherds of the present day know nothing of 'tarry woo',' nor of the process of the smearing or 'laying' of the Cheviot sheep, the only ovine species known to their forefathers, who held a belief that an 'unlaid' sheep would suffer in condition. October, according to the temperature of the weather, which might protract the operation, was the time of its performance. The ingredients

at the back end of the year. In former years large numbers of cattle were sold at Whittingham Fair; these occupied the whole of the wide strip of green waste land that then existed on each side of the road, in front of the Castle Inn. The horses were "shown off," and bought or "couped," "through the lane," or on the road in front of the inn, where many a haggle took place over the sale of a broken-winded horse in the days of old Jack Campbell, his son Mark Campbell, Bill Curry, Jimmy Angus, Andrew Barclay, and others of that ilk. Amongst the usual tag-rag and hangers-on about the horse fair were "Ned the Mayor," Jack the Horse," "John Martin," and "Peter the Bear."

Hundreds of Irish reapers attended the fair, seeking to be hired for the harvest. Drinking and fighting were their favourite pastime; therefore, with their sickles under their arms, they always formed a dangerous element in the fair, and were much dreaded by the "fair folk." On one occasion the Irish "took the fair," when they in their drunken excitement played havoc amongst the hucksters' stalls and the muggers' crockery, smashing everything that came in their way, the terrified people fleeing before them, afraid for their lives, until—as the story goes—a brave-hearted joiner came on the scene, who, snatching a rail out of the nearest fence, he charged the mob, mowing the "Paddies" down right and left, and very soon cleared the fair. This startling event was often talked about in the writer's early days as "that year the Irish took the fair." This was long before the days of our present

were tar and butter, or the best of grease, the quality of which affected the value of the wool. At Ingram it was the practice, when the best of grease was scarce, to mix (or what was called 'menging') the tar with the contents of a dairy of the finest butter, which placed the Ingram 'clip' of wool in a higher position in the market. The cow byre being the theatre of performance, a lot of sheep were housed, the 'laying stools' and tubs of tar of proper consistency placed in juxtaposition, the shepherds 'bratted' in sheep skin, the sheep laid upon the stool, the wool regularly shed (separated) longitudinally, and dips of tar deftly drawn up the sheds, and the work was complete. From dark till ten o'clock light derived from candles looped in a yarn line over the heads of the 'layers,' the process went on."—Reminiscenses of Samuel Donkin, p. 4.

splendidly organised County Police Force. Then the only guardian of the peace was the village constable, who, on the fair day, frequently had the assistance of Derrick Ormond, the constable, from Alnwick; and generally before the day was over, the vaulted chamber of the old tower, then used as a lock-up, was fairly well filled with "drunk and disorderlies." To witness the untrained village constable taking an unruly prisoner to the "Kitty" was a scene not easily described. Much struggling, kicking, and tripping; much strong language on both sides; then the final hug and the roll over amongst the dust and dirt in the middle of the road; the unavailing attempts of the constable to put on the handcuffs, until one of the numerous highly amused bystanders helped him, was very often the programme. "Davie the Soldier," a sergeant of the line, was usually in attendance at the fair, who, having treated the company in a refreshment tent, persuaded some luckless country wight to take the "Queen's shilling," and don the rosette. Then followed a heartrending scene outside—father, mother, sisters, and sweetheart pleading, with tears in their eyes, the inexorable son of Mars "only to let him off," but all in vain, for the lad had taken the Queen's shilling, "an' listed for a souldier." The amusements of the fair were as numerous and varied as "Vanity Fair," and suited to the age. The famous Billy Purvis, the Showman,[1] and James Wright, the Comedian, often had their performances at Whittingham fair. Then there were nine pins, three sticks a penny, roley-poley, and the wheel of fortune, at the stalls; "penny a trial, no blanks, all prizes," shouted the vendors. Having paid the

---

[1] The following notes relating to his visit to Whittingham, which would probably occur from 1820 to 1840, are taken from T. Arthur's "Life of Billy Purvis":—"At Whittingham they put up at the only inn, kept by a Frenchman, who, allowing no smoking in his house, they were compelled to retire to the blacksmith's shop for a smoke." (Page 40.) "At Whittingham fair he bought a little horse for three pounds fifteen shillings, and at Glanton a bridle and saddle for fifteen shillings—four pounds ten the lot. He performed three nights at Whittingham in a butcher's shop, having good houses, or say well stocked shops." (Page 66.) William Purvis was born in 1784, and died in 1853.

penny, and had a trial, the result was oftener the reverse, "all blanks and no prizes." Boxing booths, jugglers swallowing flaming tow, and bringing out yards of ribbon, blind fiddlers, and tight rope dancers; while quoiting on the green, and fights—which always drew a good company—added to the entertainment of that eventful day in the annals of Alndale some fifty years ago.

WHITTINGHAM FAIR.

Are you going to Whittingham fair,
 Parsley, sage, rosemary, and thyme;
Remember me to one who lives there,
 For once she was a true love of mine.

Tell her to make me a cambric shirt;
 Parsley, sage, rosemary, and thyme;
Without any seam or needlework,
 For once she was a true love of mine.

Tell her to wash it in yonder well,
 Parsley, sage, rosemary, and thyme;
Where never spring water nor rain ever fell,
 For once she was a true love of mine.

Tell her to dry it on yonder thorn,
 Parsley, sage, rosemary, and thyme;
Which never bore blossom since Adam was born,
 For once she was a true love of mine.

Now he has asked me questions three,
  Parsley, sage, rosemary, and thyme;
I hope he will answer as many for me,
  For once he was a true love of mine.

Tell him to find me an acre of land,
  Parsley, sage, rosemary, and thyme;
Betwixt the salt water and the sea sand,
  For once he was a true love of mine.

Tell him to plough it with a ram's horn,
  Parsley, sage, rosemary, and thyme;
And sow it all over with one pepper corn,
  For once he was a true love of mine.

Tell him to reap it with a sickle of leather,
  Parsley, sage, rosemary, and thyme;
And bind it up with a peacock's feather,
  For once he was a true love of mine.

When he has done and finished his work,
  Parsley, sage, rosemary, and thyme;
O tell him to come and he'll have his shirt,
  For once he was a true love of mine.[1]

In the old mosstrooping days there were at Whittingham two towers, or peles, for the safety and protection of the villagers against the marauding attacks of Border freebooters. As for household goods or "insight gear," the poor Borderer, living within his miserable hut, built of sticks and mud, possessed—with the exception of his sheep and cattle—but very little to attract the notice of the "lifter." One of these towers still exists, an interesting relic of domestic architecture, a memento of:—

"Those days of yore, before the birth of order,
When rapine was the warden of the Border;
When will was law, craft wisdom, and strength right,
And the best plea for doing wrong was might."

The Border towers of Northumberland form so prominent a feature in the history of the county, that an able and exhaustive treatise on the subject has lately been written by

---

[1] This is an example of the enigmatical *duolinear* ballad, popular in the north and west of the county of Northumberland. It is also known in several parts of England, but is sung usually as a nursery ballad."—Northumbrian Minstrelsy, p. 79.

Mr. Cadwallader J. Bates, entitled "The Border Holds of Northumberland," from whose erudite and carefully-written pages we have gathered much valuable information, and from which we have freely quoted.

The first notice we have of a pele tower at Whittingham —which shows that there had existed at an early period a stronghold on the banks of the Aln—is found in the following note, at page 11, in "Border Holds":—"The *pila* of Whittingham and Bolton were taken from the partizans of Gilbert de Middleton in 1317."

On this occasion three prisoners were taken, for in 1318 there was a "petition to the King and Council by David de Langetone and Thos. de Hetone showing that Roger Purvays who was taken with two others in the 'piles' of Bolton and Wytingam resisting the King by the garrisons of Bamburgh Alnewick and Werkworde is an open traitor and one of the greatest evildoers in the March, and begging that he may be hanged and drawn, and asking the King's pleasure in regard to the others."[1] This *humane* request was quite characteristic of those stirring times on the Borders. The three men were evidently adherents of the hostile Scots, and had taken possession of the towers at Bolton and Whittingham. In the list of fortlets on the Borders in 1415 Whittingham tower was thus described:—"Turris de Whittingham—Willimi de Heron."[2]

Whittingham tower stands on the south bank of the Aln, and occupies a commanding position on the brow of a steep green knoll overlooking the river, and presents a most picturesque bit of Border scenery to the tourist as he passes along the highway towards Glanton. The tower is now surmounted by a modern corbelled battlement of *merlon* and *crenelle*, whilst a sort of enlarged bartizan at the north-eastern angle contains a lofty flagstaff, from which on village fetes and festivals, or when the lord of the manor is in residence at Eslington House, the Union Jack flaunts gracefully in the breeze, where erstwhile the cresset showed forth on the midnight sky the lurid glare of the beacon fire.

Unfortunately no engraving of the tower is extant to show its appearance previous to its restoration in 1845, but those who can remember the old tower describes it as a large square block, having a double roof running from east to west, covered with red pantiles, and a projecting spout to carry off the water from the gutter between the two roofs. The basement of the tower—where the walls are 8½ feet in thickness—yet retains some of its original features in the stone-vaulted roof and the sturdy arched doorway in the south wall, an engraving of which forms the title page to this volume. There are no loopholes or slits observable in the external angles of the structure, nor any sign of the existence of a spiral stair; but, judging from the internal masonry, there would appear to have been a straight flight of stairs in the thickness of the

[1] Chronicles and Memorials of Scotland.

[2] C. J. Bates' Border Holds, Vol. i., p. 17.

east wall, to which access would be gained by an inner door leading off to the right from the passage on entering the original south doorway, while another doorway leading straight forward gave ingress to the basement. The springer of this arched doorway is yet to be seen *in situ*. There has been no manhole in the roof of the basement to communicate with the upper story, as the inmates could go out or in without let or hindrance by the inner doorway.

The other tower, which was occupied by the vicar, stood at the west end of the village near the church, and does not appear to have been built until some time after Heron's tower, for we have no record of its existence until the survey of Border towers in 1541, which says:—

"At Whyttyngame bene two towers, whereof the one ys the mansion of the vycaredge and thother of the Inheritance of Rb't. Collyngewood, esquier, & bothe be in measurable good repac'ons."[1]

Therefore the tower standing at the present day is undoubtedly the old tower of the Heron's and the Collingwoods, while the parson's tower probably became incorporated in the old vicarage which stood close to the road at the west end of the village, and was removed when the present vicarage was built. In 1845 Whittingham tower was restored, the interior modernised, and converted into an almshouse for four elderly couples, man and wife, or brother and sister, connected with the estate, each of whom receives a pension of £10 per annum and a supply of coal. A tablet above the new doorway, broken through the east wall, contains this inscription:—

"By the munificence and piety of Lady Ravensworth this ancient tower, which was formerly used by the villagers as a place of refuge in times of rapine and insecurity, was repaired and otherwise embellished for the use and benefit of the deserving poor. A.D. 1845." "Blessed is he that considereth the poor and needy. The Lord shall deliver him in the time of trouble."

Although we cannot give the original height of the tower, its present measurements are as follows:—In form, rectangu-

[1] C. J. Bates' Border Holds, Vol. i, p. 42.

lar; exterior from east to west, 42 feet; from north to south, 36 feet; interior basement, length of vault from east to west, 25 feet; width from north to south, 19 feet; width of original doorway in south wall, 3 feet 10 inches; height of tower, 40 feet. There are several mason's marks on the stones of the original building.

Around the tower there would probably be a high wall; within this enclosure, called the barmkin, the cattle were secured at night. The walls of the tower would be pierced with loopholes and small windows, through which the inmates discharged arrows, hurled stones, and other missiles to defend their little stronghold against the attacking party. It was a common practice for the besiegers to pile green brushwood and wet straw against the outer door, which being set on fire, sent forth dense volumes of smoke; and, unless prevented by a second inner door, the fumes permeated the whole building, suffocating the unfortunate inmates. This cowardly proceeding is noticed by Mr. Crawhall in his admirable Border ballad :—

THE HOT-TROD.

Wae's me—God wot—
But the beggarlie Scot
Through the 'bateable land has prickit his waie
An' ravaged wi' fire
Peel, hau'din' an' byre—
Oor nowte, sheep, an' galloways a' tae'n awae :
But—by hagbut an' sword—ere he's back owre the Border,
We'll be het on his trod an' aye set him in order.

Nae bastles or peels
Are safe frae thae deils,
Gin the collies be oot, or the Laird's awae—
The bit bairnies an' wives
Gang i' dreid o' their lives.
For they scumfish them oot wi' the smoutherin' strae:
Then—spear up the lowe—ca' oor lads thegither,
An' we'll follow them hot-trod owre the heather.

Weel graith'd—sair on mettle—
Oor harness in fettle—
The Reivers we sicht far ayont "the Wa'."

Gin we bring them to bay
Nae "saufey" we'll pay
Weel fangit—syne hangit, we'se see them a'—
Then—on lads, on—for the trod is hot,
As oot owre the heather we prod the Scot.

We'll harass them sairly—
Nae "hoo" gi'e for parley,
Noo the spur's i' the dish 'fore their hungrie wames,
To your slogans gie mouth
An' we'll sune lead them south—
Gra'merce—gin we cross them—we'll crap their kames:
Then—keep the lowe bleezin' lads—ca' to the frae—
Syne we're up wi' the lifters we'll gar them pay.

Fae to fae—steel to steel—
Noo the donnert loons reel
An' catiff—cry "hoo"—but it's a' in vain:
Sec a clatter o' thwacks
Fa's on sallets an' jacks,
Till we've lifted the lifters as weel's oor ain:
Then, wi' fyce to the crupper they'll ride a gaie mile,
To their dance frae the woodie at "Merrie Carlisle."

CHAPTER XII.

WHITTINGHAM PARISH CHURCH.

Dedication—Foundation—A Manorial Church—Its Norman History—Its Early Rectors, 1294-1307—List of Vicars, 1373-1881—Its Value at various Times—Oliverian Survey, 1650—Its Anglo-Saxon Architecture, as described by Rickman—Monuments—Windows—Gallery—Barrel Organ—The Churchyard Stile—Early English Porch—Tombstones—Bells—Clock—Communion Plate—Registers.

THE Parish Church of Whittingham—dedicated to St. Bartholomew—is, as we have already stated, of Anglo-Saxon foundation, and was probably erected on the very spot where, in previous ages, the "tun moots," or meetings of justice, had been held :—

"It was at the church door as in the moot that banns were proclaimed, marriages or bargains made ; even the fair or market was held in the churchyard, and the village feast was held on the day of the saint to whom the church was dedicated." [1]

Whittingham Church may be classed amongst those termed manorial churches, which in early days were erected and endowed throughout our land by the owners of the soil on their own estates for the service of their dependants, the extent of whose spiritual jurisdiction was at first coincident with that of the estate itself, and where, within the precincts of the sacred "God's acre," under the shadow of the church, the people living within the "Kirkshire" began to bury their dead, instead of on dreary moors and wind-swept heights, as they had done in those days when they worshipped Woden and Thor. It was probably during the early days of Christianity, when the isle of Lindisfarne was the centre of religious

---

[1] Green's English Conquest.

life in Northumbria, that the holy rood was first set up within the Anglo-Saxon vill of "Huyttingham." It may have been in a building rudely constructed of wood and wattles, to be followed as time went on by a church of stone built "after the Roman manner." The exact date when this church of stone was erected cannot with certainty be fixed. The chancel of Jarrow Church, one of the earliest examples of Anglo-Saxon ecclesiastical architecture in the North of England, was built by Benedict Biscop during the latter part of the seventh century.[1] Therefore, allowing for the few years which would elapse before the building of stone churches became general in the outlying districts, we may venture to assign the eighth century as the probable date of the foundation of Whittingham Church. One thing, however, is certain, the fine old church as we know it to-day, in which there is found Anglo-Saxon, Early English—and at one time Norman—architecture, stands upon exactly the same ground as the church in which our ancestors offered up their prayers and praises; therefore its venerable associations carry us back over a period of not less than a thousand years.

The Norman history of Whittingham Church is much the same as that of Rothbury. In the year 1090 the tithes of Whittingham were given to the monks of Tynemouth, by Robert de Mowbray, Earl of Northumberland, but early in the next century Henry I. granted the churches of Warkworth, Corbridge, Rothbury, and Whittingham, to his chaplain, Richard de Aurea Valle, for the use of the Priory of Black Canons, which the King had founded at Carlisle; and, whilst the patronage of Warkworth and Rothbury have changed hands, Whittingham and Corbridge remain to the present day in the gift of the Dean and Chapter of Carlisle.

Until the beginning of the fourteenth century, the living of Whittingham was a rectory. The name of "Alanus de

[1] Arch. Æliana, Vol. x., p. 195. (New Series.)

Easingwold persona medietatis ecclesiæ de Whitingham" occurs in the records at Durham, October 18th, 1294. The last rector was John Kirkeby, 1307. After this date its parsons are called vicars, the first being Thomas de Penreth, 1373. We here give as complete a list of the rectors and vicars of Whittingham as our researches up to the present time enable us:—

Alanus de Easingwold		occurs	1294
John Kirkeby		"	1307
Thomas de Penreth		died	1373
John de Overton		occurs	1373
John de Berey		"	1410
Henry Waddyng...		"	1428
William Farleham		died	1536
Thomas Anglionby		occurs	1536
Richard Kitchin [1]		"	1556
Richard Saterthwait		occurs	1574
Clement Stephenson		"	1625
Henry Tallentire...	1633	to	1666
Thomas Wemys	1667	to	1697
Joseph Nicholson	1697	occurs	1703
Thomas Nevinson ... occurs	1731	to	1744
Erasmus Head, M.A.	1744		
Charles Ward, M.A.	1763		
John Law, M.A.	1773		
B. L. Sclater	1798		
Edmund Law	1804	to	1834
Robert William Goodenough, M.A.	1835	to	1880

William Shield, B.A., formerly vicar of Mansergh, Kirkby Lonsdale, the present vicar, came to the living in January, 1881.

---

[1] WILL OF RICHARD KITCHINGE, VICAR OF WHITTINGHAM.

"In the name of God amen. The xxv day of february yeare of our Lord God 1573. I Richard Kitching clerke Vicar of Whittingham sicke in body but whole in soule & of p'fitt memory thanks be to Almighty God maketh this my last will and

In those disturbed days following on the Reformation (1538) the parochial clergy of Northumberland were, many of them, ignorant and unlettered, as a perusal of "The Injunctions and other Ecclesiastical Proceedings of Richard Barnes, Bishop of Durham, 1575 to 1587,"[1] will tell us. We there learn that the Bishop, at his annual visitation, required the clergy to repeat the Gospel of St. Matthew either in Latin or the mother tongue, or give an account of it in writing. At a general chapter, held at Alnwick on the 30th July, 1578, the following results were recorded :—

"The Gospel of St. Matthew. Task duly performed by William Sorroby, curate of Rothbury (and others).

---

testament in manner and form folowing. Fyrst I bequithe my soull to Almyghti God and my body to be buried in the queare of Whittingiame. Also I giue to ye Jnco'bent two cowbords a sidbord an almerie in the hyetowre carts wans & all other implements wangeare in ye hye tour v stand beds a bruing cawdorn in the fornac the lantern boxs[2] wthout any troble. Also I gyv vnto nycholas tindall the elder gray mare also I giue to annas graye a cowe & to nycholas tyndell the youenger a qui. Also I giue to thomas kytchyng ye gray horse. Also I giue to John Kytchyng my brother's son the read bawson horse. Also I giue to John Tindals wyf the worst of the iiij° fetherbeds wth the clothes belonging therto. Also I gyv to Jane tyndell another of the fetherbeds wth the clothes belonging therto iiijer stotts. Also I gyv to John Kytchyng the son of Richart Kytchyng a cow & to annas dotesone a nother cowe. Also I gyv to the forsayd John Kytchyng the best brass pott. Also I gyve to his brother olyver the secownd brass pott. Also I give to John Kytchyng my best gowne forred wth cunne & to dorratte Kytchyng a nother of my gownes. Also I gyv to robert Kirbe a gowne a Jacatt a dowblett & a payer of hosse. Also I gyv to John Wolson a fetherbed wth the clothes beloning thereto seven oxen. I gyv to Annas gray a goune and to Jane Wolso a fring pane thre pecs of pouder vessell a chafendishe & a candelstike & bed coveringe iij par of shets iij towells iiij pilloberes and a lininge bordeclothe ij corches and a lininge aprone & a pair of silver croks and other two pair of crouks of letten iij rings. Also I make executors of this my last Will and Testament Jane Wolson she to pay my detts & discharge my legaces and for movabls she to vse as she shall think most expedient for hur discharge & for ye healthe of my soull I give to richard hondsons children a qui to John Kichinge a silver spone. Also I giue to robert claveringe a cawdron in witnes herof will'm heron george henmerrs richard warrey. Also I make sup'rices of this my last will & Testament to se my executor maintaines her right robert claveringe. Witnesses Richarde satterwik Jhon gibson roger aicheson thomas aicheson."—Wills and Inventories, Surtees' Society Publications, Vol. ii., p. 391.

[1] Surtees Society, 1850.

[2] Lent books.

"No account of task given by Richard Satterthwaite, vicar of Whittingham (and others).

"The excused were[1] Thomas Talentire, rector of Rothbury (and others).

"The sick and infirm were George Levinston, a Scotchman, curate of Allanton; Edmund Willy, curate of Brenckeburne, an old man."

NOTE.—At the end of this Visitation of Northumberland it is worthy of remark that in many parishes or chapelries in which was settled a house of old descent, and note and coat armour, we have one of the same family-name acting as parish clerk . . . . . The following list . . . . . leads to the conclusion that either the persons here specified were in such circumstances as to even make a parish clerkship acceptable, or that they thus officiated because no parishioner of the humbler class was able to read:—

"Ralph Thornton (parish clerk)...			Netherwitton.
Ralff Ogle	,,	...	Horsley.
George Hall	,,	...	Elsdon.
Roger Collingwood	,,	...	Whittingham.
Robert Taylor ...	,,	...	Rothbury.
Roland Wilkinson	,,	...	Alwinton."

In the list of Roman Catholic Recusants of Northumberland, 1677, those who would not attend their parish church, but held to their old faith, were "George Collingwood, of Eslington, Esq., and Ralph Clavering, of Callolee, Esq."

About the year 1291, "Wytingeham" rectory was valued at £50, and in the valuation of 1346 it was £100. The procuration fees at the visitation in 1357 of the "Rectoria de Whityneham, non valet ultra, xxxjs," and it was valued in the King's book, 1535, at £12 11s. 4d.

The Oliverian Survey, of 1650, says of Whittingham:—"That the Parish of Whittingham is a Viccaridge, the late

[1] William.

Deane and Chapiter of Carlisle Patron thereof; Mr. Henry Tallentyre, a preaching minister, the Viccar; and the value of the said Viccaridge fifty pounds p. annu., beside a Lease from the said Deane and Chapiter of Carlisle to the said Mr. Tallentyre of thirtye pounds p. anu." A much fuller account of the living is found in the *Survey of the Lands of Deans and Chapters*, also made in 1650. "The rectory of Whittingham and the advowson of the vicarage belonged to the Dean and Chapter of Carlisle, which is the reason of the value of the vicarage appearing in the survey of their possessions. Of these the Government had seized, and were, therefore, careful to know their true value."

"THE VICARAGE OF WHITTINGHAM.

	£	s.	d.
All that the vicarage-house, with one byer, one barn, a stable, a court yard, a fold garth, a garden, and one close on the back side, part arable, called the vicar's close, abutting on a close called Staine Acres on the east, and upon a parcel of ground called the *Ould Righte* on the west, contains 14 acres	4	10	0
One close of pasture ground, called Pasture Leases, abutting upon Thrunton Field on the south, and the Mill Close on the north, contains 5 acres	1	0	0
Two closes within the fields of Barton, one part arable, abutting upon the lands of Jane Barker on the east, and the lands of Thomas Gibson on the west, contain 16 acres	3	0	0
Four ridges of meadow ground abutting upon Wittonley on the south, contain by estimation 3 acres	0	8	0
Three ridges of arable land, abutting upon the land of Thomas Whitton on the south, and the lands of William Gowerley on the north, contain 2 acres	0	5	0
One parcel of meadow ground, lying in Whittingham Houghe, abutting upon Mr. Collingwood's lands south and west, contain 3 acres ...	0	10	0
One pasture close on the moorside, Mr. Collingwood's land lying about it, contain by estimation 3 acres	0	7	6
Sum total of the acres, 51	10	15	6
The tithes, calfes, wool, and lambs of the above said place, worth communibus annis	36	0	0
The Tithe hay and Prescription Money paid for tithe hay communibus annis	5	0	0
The Easter Book Tithe of pigs, geese, hens, milk, oblacions, mortuaries, and all other small dues are worth communibus annis	10	6	8
Sum total of this and the other side	£62	2	2

During the Commonwealth, sometime between the years 1650 and 1654, Henry Tallentire, the vicar of Whittingham, was ejected, and a Presbyterian minister, named Abraham Hume, occupied his place, which he continued to do until St. Bartholomew's Day, 1662, when, refusing to conform to the Church of England rites and form of government, he in turn was also ejected, and the old vicar, Henry Tallentire, was re-instated in the parish, and died in 1666 at the age of 73. We here give an interesting account of Abraham Hume, who appears to have been a superior man; but we must not forget that the writer—Edmund Calamy—was the son and grandson of two "Bartholomew Confessors," and to get at something like the real state of affairs prevailing during that unfortunate period in our history when such calamities were inflicted by one set of men who called themselves Christians upon another, it would be well to peruse not only "Calamy's Life of Baxter," but "Walker's Sufferings of the Clergy":—

"WHITTINGHAM.—Abraham Hume, M.A.; born in the Merse, Scotland; educated at St. Andrew's; chaplain to the Countess of Hume. Duke of Lauderdale married daughter of Countess; went with Duke to Paris and Geneva. Lauderdale, a ruling elder, appointed to Assembly of Divines at Westminster. Hume came to London with him; was called to Benton, Newcastle; ordained in London 20th April, 1647. Being a fixed Presbyterian, and zealous for the King and Royal Family, was turned out by the Government, chiefly through the influence of Sir A. Heselrigge, who pursued him till he was banished out of England; retired into Scotland till Oliver Cromwell was settled in the Protectorship. Then had a call to Whittingham, where the same Sir Arthur had an estate; sensible of the injustice he had done him before, concurred with others in calling him thither, and afterwards treated him with great respect. No temptation could ever induce him to own Oliver Cromwell as head of the Government; his unaffected and exemplary piety, conduct, and converse so endeared him to persons of all denominations that he became universally esteemed, and had great influence in that country. This gave him the opportunity of getting the vacant parishes in the neighbourhood filled with men of his own principles, both as to loyalty to the King and firmness to the Presbyterian form and rule; but though he had done and suffered much for the King and his interest, he was as soon turned out, as others, after the Restoration, because he would not conform to the Prelatical Government and forms. On leaving Whittingham he was invited by Lauderdale to his fiamily, where he continued till the Five-mile Act drove him away; was pressed by Lauderdale to conform, but was unmoveable; Lauderdale grew cool towards him. Travelled again to France in 1669; friendship with Mons. Claud, the famous minister of Charenton. Returned to London; was chosen pastor to a Society of Dissenters at Bishopsgate Without; soon scattered. Preached privately at Theobald's till King James's liberty. He was called to a congregation in Drury Lane, where he continued till his death, 29th January, 1706-7."[1]

The following brief and curious description of the parish of Whittingham is given in Bishop Chandler's notes of his visitation of the Deanery of Alnwick, supposed to be in 1736:—

"V. WHITTINGHAM.

	Tho. Nevison	li	Fam. 235
	value	120	57 Presb.
Residt.			42 Papists.
			Mass house at Callaly.
			Mr. Turner Preist.
			4 Petty Schools.
			Cat. in Lent and other times wth Lewis."

In 1774 George Morrison was parish clerk of Whittingham.

CHARITY.—"Matthew Hedley of Thrunton by his will, dated March 6, 1827, left £100 to the churchwardens of Whittingham for the benefit of the poor. This sum was invested in Government securities, and the interest (£21 3s. 4d.) is distributed yearly at Christmas."[2]

Judging from what remains of the Anglo-Saxon Church of Whittingham, the original structure would probably consist of a chancel, terminating at the east end with a semi-circular apse, a nave, seventeen feet wide, lofty in proportion to its width, having a heavy round-headed chancel arch, round-headed windows of a single light, without glass, but provided with wooden shutters to keep out the weather, and a square tower at the west end. The ground plan of the tower is only of small dimensions, the chamber in the basement, now used

[1] Calamy's Life of Baxter, Vol. ii., p. 511 (Second Edition, 1713).

[2] Bulmer's History of Northumberland, Vol. ii., p. 931.

as a vestry, being eleven feet square. The tower rises straight from its foundations without base or plinth; its lower stages yet remain intact, showing the characteristic work of those early builders in the "long and short" quoins seen at its angles, as well as in the return angles of the nave on both the north and south sides. A portion of the masonry in the south-east angle of the wall, at the junction of the chancel and the nave, may also be part of the original structure. Nearly on a level with the belfry floor, traces are visible in the east wall of the rude imposts and *voussoirs* of the tower arch, much defaced and discoloured as if from the action of fire. This arch appears to have been built up by the Early English restorers, who, when they did so, formed the fine pointed doorway, two feet eight inches wide, leading from the church into the basement. During the twelfth century a north aisle was added to the Anglo-Saxon edifice by an arcade of four Norman arches. These Norman arches were, unfortunately, taken down when the alterations were made in 1840, and replaced by the present arcade of four pointed arches to correspond with the original Early English arcade on the opposite side, which was erected in the thirteenth century, when the south aisle was added as well as the fine old south porch. At the west end of this aisle, now the baptistry, there is a small but charming Early English light, filled with stained glass, representing St. Bartholomew the tutelar saint.[1] The window next the pulpit in the north

[1] A brass underneath contains the following:—"To the Glory of God and the Memory of the Rev. W. R. Goodenough."

transept contains an interesting fragment of Early English architecture, the upper portion of the light being formed of one stone.

"This window belongs to that period of Early English architecture, when the lancet began to be superseded by combination of lights, and before the adoption of geometric tracery. Flat roofs were given to both nave and transepts, probably in the last century, when the gables of both were left standing exposed as in a ruin. In the repairs of 1840 the flat roof of the nave was removed, the walls heightened, and a clerestory added. On the east gable of the nave the marks of these three pitches of the roofs are visible. The chancel was not touched in the repairs mentioned; but it would have been well if it had been pulled down instead of the upper part of the Saxon tower, and the whole of the Norman arcade, for it belongs to the worst era of architecture."[1]

The chancel, with its round-headed wooden sash windows of square panes, as mentioned by Mr. Wilson, was built about the year 1725 at the charges of the lessees of the great tithes. However, in 1871 the chancel was thoroughly restored in the decorated Early English style, under the careful supervision of Mr. Wilson, at the expense of the lay rector, the late Earl of Ravensworth;[2] and at the same time the chancel arch was restored to its original height by the parishioners, assisted by

---

[1] Churches of Lindisfarne, F. R. Wilson, 1870, p. 95.

[2] Inscription on the brass erected in the south wall of the chancel, after its restoration in 1871:—

Cancellum.
hujus veteris Ecclesiæ
Pietate majorum extructum
Recentiori manu infeliciter reparatum
HENRICUS THOMAS BARO DE RAVENSWORTH,
In honorem Dei.
Sumptibus suis restituendum curavit,
A.D. MDCCCLXXI.

the Dean and Chapter of Carlisle.[1] It is said the preservation of the lower portion of the Anglo-Saxon tower is only due to the fact that while the masons of 1840 were doing their utmost, with the aid of gunpowder, to level to the ground this fine relic of the eighth century, they found they were endangering their newly-built north arcade, and were happily obliged to desist in their operations.

A few years ago, when the large old-fashioned box pews were being taken out to be replaced with the comfortable modern benches now in the church, a fine Early English piscina was discovered in the south wall of the south transept, which shows that previous to the Reformation it had been a chantry, or private chapel having its own altar, at which mass would be said daily for the souls of the founder and his family. All trace of its founder, or the saint to whom it was dedicated, seems to have been for many years lost sight of; but in the will of Sir Robert Collingwood of Eslington, reference is made to this chantry, which we find is dedicated to St. Peter. Judging from its architecture, and from the trefoil headed arch of the piscina, yet *in situ*—an interesting relic of the ancient services of the church—this chantry was probably founded during the last half of the thirteenth century, when Eslington and Whittingham were held by the family who had taken the

[1] Inscription on chancel arch brass :—

1871.
This Arch was Heightened
and restored
at the expense of the Parish,
aided by
the Dean and Chapter of Carlisle.

surname of Eslington, one of whom may have built the south aisle and founded the chantry. In 1547 (1 Edward VI.), all chantries were suppressed, and the lands belonging to them sold by the King to private persons. The lands pertaining to this chantry, therefore, were purchased by the Collingwoods of Eslington. When, in 1554, Queen Mary re-instated the Roman Catholic religion this chantry was probably then re-endowed, for in the will of Sir Robert Collingwood of Eslington, dated 1556, he demises, amongst other lands purchased of King Edward VI., 'The erection of a cantaria for a priest to celebrate in the Parish Church of Whittingham at the Altar of Saint Peter'; and 'that all the priests thereafter thereto nominated should, during the time, have and enjoy one cottage and garth in Whittingham, holden of Edward Steanson, as also an annual rent of £4 out of his lands &c. in Tyttlynton, Northumberland.'"[1]

The following description of Whittingham Church from Rickman's "Ecclesiastical Architecture" describes the interior as it existed previous to the restoration of 1840, just as our engraving shows the exterior at the same period:—

"On buildings supposed to have been built before the year 1000.

1.—WHITTINGHAM CHURCH, NORTHUMBERLAND.

This church has a Tower, and the west end of the aisles and one arch on the north side, all appearing of the same early style. There are Norman portions, but they are clearly of a different and later date, and parts of the church are even later still, with some modern mutilations.

---

[1] From the most laudable motive of perpetuating the history of this chantry, and in memory of a distinguished ancestor, Mr. F. J. W. Collingwood, of Glanton Pyke, caused the east window in the south aisle to be filled with glass, representing St. Peter; and a brass underneath contains its dedication, as follows:—"To the Glory of God, and to the Memory of Sir Robert Collingwood, of Eslington, 1556."

The corners of the tower and exterior angles of the walls of the aisles are clearly of long and short stones of a very strong coarse gritstone, and the whole walling being of the same stone as the quoins, and no plaster required, the construction of the masonry is very conspicuous. The battlements, and a part of the upper story of the tower, appear to have been altered; but the upper aperture has a rude balustrade between the two windows, thus presenting two feathers, generally the most striking and constant in these early build-

ings. One arch of what appears to me to be the original nave remains; it is very plain, has a large rude abacus, or impost, and a plain, square pier; it is now stopped, and forms part of the vestry. The next arch, eastward on the same side, is a common Norman one, with the usual round pier and a capital, with a sort of bell and a square abacus. The remainder of the church is later, and of little comparative interest."

The church now consists of a nave, measuring, in round numbers, 52 feet in length by 42 feet in width, inclusive of north and south aisles; width between north and south arcades, 20 feet; extreme width at north and south transepts, 77 feet. The restored chancel, 35 feet long by 16 feet wide; width of chancel arch, 11½ feet, with baptistry, south porch, and western tower.

The hatchments of the neighbouring old county families, the Liddells of Eslington, Claverings of Callaly, Atkinsons of Lorbottle, and the Pawsons of Shawdon, hang on the walls of the church, while several marble slabs to the memory of local persons also adorn the interior of the sacred edifice. One of these, inserted in the north wall of the chancel within the sanctuary rails, bearing the Collingwood arms, over which is an escutcheon of pretence of the Browns, contains the following :—

This Marble is sacred
to the memories of
ALEXANDER COLLINGWOOD,
of Collingwood House, Esqre.,
and MARGARET his wife
daughter of
Nicholas Brown
of Bolton, Esqre.
The former of whom departed this life
the 26th of September, 1795;
And the latter on the 9th of September, 1807,
and is erected
In pious and grateful remembrance
To the best of parents
By their afflicted
And disconsolate daughters
Margaret Michell
and
Isabella Tarleton.

The east window, consisting of five lights and geometric tracery, is filled with glass, to the memory of R. W. Goodenough, the late Vicar. In the centre light is pourtrayed the Good Shepherd; the other lights contain representations of the four Evangelists, while along the base are the symbolic figures of the Pelican, in the centre, with the Angel, Lion, Ox, and Eagle displayed two on either side. The general design of the window is bold and unique, and the deep rich colour of the glass has a pleasing effect in subduing the somewhat harsh light in the chancel. A brass contains this inscription :—

"To the glory of God and in Memory of R. W. Goodenough, Vicar of this Parish, 1836-1880. By his parishioners and friends."

A second brass bears the text:—

"Cast thy bread upon the waters; for thou shalt find it after many days."

On the east wall of the north transept a very handsome marble monument records the death of the son of the late Vicar, who fell during the Crimean war. Under a trophy and shield, with the motto "Ad Sanguinem," is the following inscription:—

To the Memory of
REGINALD CYRIL GOODENOUGH
Aged 18
Lieutenant of the 97th Regiment of Foot
First born son of
The Rev. Robert Goodenough, M.A.
Vicar of Whittingham
He fell mortally wounded within the Great Redan battery
Sebastopol
On the 8th of September 1855
Having led on his soldiers to the assault
In the first storming party
This monument
Is erected by his sorrowing friends
Inhabitants of this
His native parish and the immediate neighbourhood
Who witnessed his early promise
And mourn his untimely death.

"I know that my  Redeemer liveth"

The small organ gallery, now at the west end of the nave, replaced the larger one of 1840 that contained, besides the old barrel organ,[1] sittings for the townships of Lorbottle, Glanton, and Glanton Pike. Some few years ago this barrel organ was enlarged, and a manual substituted for the barrels. There were three barrels in the old organ, each of which played ten

[1] "In addition to the extensive alterations and improvements in Whittingham Church, a powerful-toned new barrel organ has been built by Mr. Brown, of York, which, from the volume and sweetness of harmony produced in assisting that part of our Church Service, so frequently neglected, has in this instance given great satisfaction to the parishioners."—*Newcastle Journal*, May 23rd, 1840.

tunes. This was long before the days of "Hymns, Ancient and Modern," and the Hymnal used in Whittingham Church, on the cover of which was printed in large type:—"This book belongs to Whittingham Church, and must not be removed," was entitled "Psalms and Hymns selected from the Book of Common Prayer.—Alnwick, printed by M. Smith, Bondgate Street, MDCCCXL." The first pages of the Hymnal contained tables to show what tunes would be played each Sunday; and as barrel organs in churches are now a thing of the past, a copy of these tables may not be out of place:—"There are three Barrels in the Organ, and each Barrel has ten Tunes set upon it. The Barrel will be changed the first Sunday Morning in every month, and the annexed Tables will shew what Tune will be sung on each Sunday in the month (arrangement being made for five Sundays). At each time of Singing during Morning and Evening Service, and also which Barrel will play for each month:—

Barrel. 1	January.	April.	July.	October.
2	February.	May.	August.	November.
3	March.	June.	September.	December.

FIRST BARREL.

Sundays in Month.	1	2	3	4	5
MORNING SERVICE: Morning Hymn ...	Truro.	Truro.	Truro.	Truro.	Truro.
After Litany	Fonthill.	Oldham.	Abingdon.	St. Mary's.	Oldham.
After Communion.	Gainsbro'.	St. James's.	Wareham.	Lydia.	Abingdon.
After Sermon	St. Mary's.	Lydia.	Gainsbro'.	Fonthill.	Wareham.
EVENING SERVICE: Commencement ...	Wareham.	St. Mary's.	St. James's.	Abingdon.	Fonthill.
Before Sermon ...	Abingdon.	Fonthill.	Oldham.	Gainsbro'.	St. Mary's.
Evening Hymn ...	Mount Moriah.	Mount Moriah.	Mount Moriah.	Mount Moriah.	Mount Moriah.

SECOND BARREL.

Sundays in Month.	1	2	3	4	5
MORNING SERVICE : Morning Hymn ...	St. Michael le Belfry.	St. Michael le Belfry.	St. Michael le Belfry.	St. Michael le Belfry.	St. Michael le Belfry.
After Litany	Devizes.	Sundridge.	Manchester	Luther's Hymn.	Sundridge.
After Communion	St. Anne's.	Lincoln.	Bath.	Darwell.	Manchester
After Sermon	Luther's Hymn.	Darwell.	St. Anne's	Devizes.	Bath.
EVENING SERVICE : Commencement...	Bath.	Luther's Hymn.	Lincoln.	Manchester	Devizes.
Before Sermon	Manchester	Devizes.	Sundridge.	St. Anne's,	Luther's Hymn.
Evening Hymn ...	Devonshire	Devonshire	Devonshire	Devonshire	Devonshire

THIRD BARREL.

Sundays in Month.	1	2	3	4	5
MORNING SERVICE : Morning Hymn ...	Warrington.	Warrington.	Warrington.	Warrington.	Warrington.
After Litany	Tottenham.	St. Bride's.	Abridge.	Duke Street	St. Bride's.
After Communion	St. George's	Irish.	Old 100.	Walworth.	Abridge.
After Sermon	Duke Street	Walworth.	St. George's	Tottenham.	Old 100.
EVENING SERVICE : Commencement...	Old 100.	Duke Street	Irish.	Abridge.	Tottenham.
Before Sermon ...	Abridge.	Tottenham.	St. Bride's.	St. George's	Duke Street
Evening Hymn ...	Rockingham.	Rockingham.	Rockingham.	Rockingham.	Rockingham.

For many years old George Henderson played the barrel organ, and pulled out the stops according to the signs made in his Hymn Book by the vicar, Mr. Goodenough. Sometimes the machinery went wrong, and then there was no singing. The clerk, sitting in the lower tier of the three-decker pulpit, gave out the Psalm or Hymn to be sung in the following fashion: "Let us sing to the praise and glory of God from the 23rd Psalm," and then proceeded to read out the first two lines of the verse. The old type of parish clerk that flourished in the days of the duet between the priest and the clerk is now extinct, but we can remember of three who filled that office in Whittingham Church—William Reed, James Grieve, and Edward Hudson. During the vicarship of Mr. Edmund Law, even before the barrel organ period, the singing in Whittingham Church was accompanied by a string band—fiddles and clarionets—in which four brothers, who were noted in the parish for their musical talent, were the principal performers, Thomas Hudson, George Hudson, John Hudson, and Edward Hudson.

An ancient stone Latin cross, which may have been a boundary or churchyard cross, was found in the north wall of the churchyard at the restoration of the church in 1840, and now stands, as seen in our sketch, a picturesque object on the wall near to the east stile. As in many other country churchyards, two public footpaths wind through amongst the tombstones in Whittingham Churchyard, and, for the convenience of pedestrians, without having to throw open the church gates, there are two stiles which are thus spoken of in *Chambers' Journal*:—

"Church stiles, with their steps up from the ground, their barrier to be stepped over at the top of them, often a stone slab fixed on end, and their steps down again on the other side into the churchyard are more common. They do not always take this form, being also often scarcely more than bars in some places of various ingenious contrivance. Whittingham churchyard, on the Alne, may be mentioned as a representative specimen. It has two of these stone stiles, one at the eastern angle and the other at the western, as though an old-time footpath running through the ground was thus protected. The river winds through the village, which is pleasant with trees, fountains, and a peel-tower. There are at both ends of the churchyard, placed at gaps in the wall, a few high narrow steps ; and in the gaps stone slabs are fixed edgeways ; and the steep steps are so arranged as to afford good footing whilst crossing these stones, and to form a second set of steps by which to descend to the level of the pathway on the other side. The church has a Saxon tower and Saxon angle-stones at the west end of the nave ; and it had a Norman arcade of four arches, only taken down within remembrance. It has much more work still standing of the thirteenth and fourteenth centuries ; and these stiles are still the means, in these Victorian days, by which the honest country-folk enter the sacred precincts that were reared so long ago, and have been so much to so many generations."[1]

Another object of some interest, of which we give an engraving, is the fine Early English porch with the Sun-dial on the gable over the entrance. These early horologes are often to be met with on a church porch or on the wall or buttress of the chancel, near to the priest's door. The porch has its original high-pitched vaulted roof. The external roof covered with stone flags, and the old stone seats on each side. The date (1687) may be noticed, cut on the first pillar on the right hand on entering the church; whether this was in commemoration of a national event or of some local event we cannot trace. A tradition, that smacks of the old Border days of feud and foray, used to be current in the parish of Whit-

[1] "In our Churchyards."—*Chambers' Journal*, July, 1893, p. 357.

tingham. A villager was being pursued by a mosstrooper, fully bent on taking his life. The church was the nearest place of refuge, whose doors in those days were always open, and where the fugitive could take sanctuary and be, for a time at least, safe from the vengeance of his pursuer. The villager succeeded in gaining the church door, and secured himself within the vestry in the basement of the tower, while the mosstrooper, enraged at being baulked of his prey, fired his pistol at the vestry door. In this there is every probability of truth, for a bullet hole was clearly to be seen in the stout oaken door of the old vestry, which was removed in 1840.

Scattered throughout the churchyard are several very old gravestones, some with curious epitaphs, others with rude carvings of cherub's heads, grim death's heads and cross bones —those symbols with which our forefathers were so fond of decorating their tombstones. One contains a rude representation of a cross within a canopy, an hour glass, a death's head and cross bones, while a bradawl, compasses, and saddler's knife denote the trade of the person buried; another has an hour glass and the legend FUGIT HORA cut thereon. A cherub's head, and the inscription "*memento-mori*," is cut on another old tombstone. In his early days the writer, and his Sunday school companions, could repeat the following, and many another of the inscriptions found on the old tombstones in Whittingham churchyard, which they learned by heart while sitting in the churchyard on fine summer Sunday mornings, waiting for the bells to ring for service:—

"HERE LIES
The Remains of SARAH MORTON
Wife of Tho. Morton of Whitting-
ham Lane, who departed this life
the 20th of Febry 1782 Aged 23 years
Also the Remains of ELEANOR MORTON
His daughter, who departed this life
the 22nd of March 1782 Aged one Month
Weep not for us Relations dear
We are not dead but sleeping here.

Our days are past, my Tomb you see
Prepare in time to follow me.
her surviving husband as the last respect
that can be paid, has caused this Monument
to be erected 1784."

"In memory of NICHO-
LAS HOGG, Shepherd
in Hartside who died
Dec. 22th 1802 Aged 50
Years.
Affliction sore six days i bore
Physicians were in vain, till
God was pleased by death to
ease. And take away my pain."

"In Memory of
RALPH RUTLEDGE who died at
Barton sept 1st 1765 aged 60 years
also his son WILLIAM RUTLEDGE who
died December 20th 1782 aged 45
years also his wife MARGRET RUTL-
EDGE who died october 1st 1790,
aged 35 years. Also 9 small
Childron."

There are two bells in the church tower, neither of which are inscribed. One measures 20¾ inches in diameter and 21½ inches from lip to top; the larger one, on which the "Jubilee Clock" strikes, measures 24 inches in diameter and 22½ inches in height. The clock was erected in the tower in 1887 in commemoration of the Queen's jubilee year, which was subscribed for by the parishioners and their friends. After the dedication service in church on Jubilee Day, June 21, 1887, the clock was set in motion by the twin sons of the late Hargrave Pawson, of Shawdon, and the brass plate containing the following inscription was also unveiled by the Hon. Mrs. Hargrave Pawson:—"This clock, a monitor of passing time, was placed in the tower of this ancient church on June 20th, A.D. 1887, by the inhabitants of Whittingham

Parish, in commemoration of the Jubilee of Her Gracious Majesty Queen Victoria, as a humble but earnest token of their love and loyalty to the best, wisest, and most constitutional and deservedly revered of English Sovereigns."

We shall conclude this chapter by describing the Communion Plate, and giving a series of extracts from the Parish Registers, and will only add that Whittingham Parish Church is one of the prettiest and most interesting churches in the Archdeaconry of Lindisfarne.

"The Communion Plate consists of the following:—

I. Silver bell-shaped CUP with lip, 8½ inches high, 4⅜ inches diameter at mouth, 3¾ inches at base; bowl gilt inside, 4½ inches deep. Five hall-marks: i. maker's initials E E / B / J W; ii. lion passant; iii. leopard's head; iv. London year letter *n* for 1828; and v. king's head. Band in centre of stem, plain ogee reversed base. Inscribed round base:—"*PRESENTED TO THE PARISH OF WHITTINGHAM BY THE HONBLE. H. T. LIDDELL, M.P. FOR NORTHUMBERLAND | A.D. 1829.*" *I H S* irradiated on side of bowl.

II. Silver PATEN, 9 inches diameter, with moulded edge, 3 inches high, on open stand, 3¾ inches diameter; I H S irradiated, surrounded by ornamental scroll work, in centre. Four hall-marks: i. London year letter courthand 'S' for 1713; ii. Britannia; iii. lion's head erased; and iv. maker's mark G with A within, for Francis Garthorne (O.E.P. 3d ed., p. 336). Same inscription on back as on cup.

III. FLAGON (electro-plated), 9½ inches high. 12½ inches to top of knop on lid. 3⅜ inches diameter at mouth. 6⅛ inches at base; handle double curve, spout. Inscribed on bottom:—PRESENTED TO WHITTINGHAM CHURCH BY R. W. GOODENOUGH, VICAR, 1862, and JAMES DIXON & SONS | SHEFFIELD, and marks E P B M.

IV. Pewter 'FONT.'

V. Pewter ALMS DISH.

Roger Collingwood was parish clerk in 1578."[1]

The following extracts are taken from the interesting pages of the Parish Church Register, which begins in the year 1658:—

BAPTISMS.

1667.—Augusti quarto, Joannes filius Jacobi Ru(ther)ford de Yetlington, baptizatus erat.

(John, the son of James Rutherford, of Yetlington, was baptized August 4th, 1667.)

1697.—Elizabeth, daughter of Mr. John Proctor, of Shawdon, March 1st.

1699.—Prudence, daughter of Mr. Edward Collingwood, of Glanton, April 27.

1702.—George, son of George Vint, of Calloley High Houses, Nov. 8.

1703.—Mary, daug. of Jno. Collingwood, of Eslington, March 17.

1703.—Chas. filius Josephi Nicolson, Vicarii hujus Ecclesiæ, June 8.

1703.—George, son of Thos. Hudson, of Whittingham, Nov. 12.

1707.—John, son of William Dixon, of Eslington, June 28.

1707.—Richard, son of Jno. Eliot, of How-baulks, Aug. 12.

1711.—Robt., son of William Collingwood, of Whittingham, April 30.

1711.—Anne, daugh. of John Hunter, of Calloley High Houses, June 23.

1711.—Isabel, daughter of George Collingwood, of Eslington, Esq., Aug. 22.

1711.—Henricus filius (Nothus) Hen^ci.^ Collingwood de Magna Ryle, Sep. 6.

1712.—Barbary, daughter of Geo. Collingwood, of Eslington, Esq.

---

[1] Proceedings of the Newcastle Society of Antiquaries, Vol. iv., p. 245.

1712.—John, son of John Hunter, of Calloley High Houses, June 3.

1713.—George, son of John Hunter, of Calloley High Houses, June 25.

1714.—Margaret, daughter of John Hunter, of Calloley High Houses, July 15.

1715.—Elizabeth, daughter of Wm. Collingwood, of Whittingham, Oct. 2.

1718.—Thomas, son of John Hunter, of Calloley High Houses, May 25.

1724.—Alexander, son of Mr. Alexander Collingwood, of Shawdon, Jan. 4.

1727.—Thos., son of Alex. Collingwood, of Unthank, Jan. 17.

1738.—Priscilla, daughter of James Hargrave, Esq., of Shawdon, Apl. 1.

1777.—Edward, son of Anthony Alder, of Royal Hill, April 16.

MARRIAGES.

1659.—John Bell, senior, of Whittingham, and Anna Stot, of the Myle-house, both of this parish (after lawful publication three several Sabbaths, in the Parish Church), were married at Whittingham, by Mr. Hume, Minister of the plase, the 17th day of May, 1659.

1716.—George Reed, of Hethpool, in ye parish of Kirknewton & Mrs. Sarah Collingwood, of Little Ryle, married Nov. 22, 1716.

1737.—Abraham Southern & Margret Gibbison, June 7, 1737.

1744.—Adam Crawford, Allenton, & Elean[r] Buoy ye Parr, Oct. 12, 1744.

BURIALS.

1658.—John, sonne of Matthew Wardell, of Calaly. Buried April the 3rd, 1658: age 12 dayes.

1666.—Mr. Henry Tallentire of Whittingham, Late Minister of the parish of Whittingham. Departed this life upon Thursday the 26th of Aprill, and his Corps Lieth interr'd Saturday The 28 of the said moanth, being

Lawfull Minister of this place Thirtie and Three yeares, Aged Seaventie & Three yeares X 1666.

1669.—July (Ingespu?) primo Joannus Collingwood de Glanton, Sepultus est.

1669.—August 21die Robertus Collingwood of Great Rile was buried in ye quire.

1669.—Nov. 30 ye lady Clavering was buried in ye quire.

1671.—Margaret Talentire, widow, buried in ye chancell, Januay 21, 1671.

1697.—John, son of Mr. Thos. Proctor, of Shawdon, Feb. 20.

1697.—Mr. Thomas Weames, Vicar of Whittingham, Feb. 25.

1698.—Mary, daughter of Cuthbert Blakelock, of Eslington, Sep. 28.

1699.—Robt. Collingwood, of Eslington, yeoman, Dec. 4.

1700.—John Pigdon, of Whittingham, April 8.

1700.—Madam Mary Clavering, of Calloley, June 10.

1700.—Isabell, wife of Thos. Collingwood, of Eslington, March 4.

1706.—Mr. Thos. Collingwood, of Eslington, Dec. 17.

1711.—Mary Collingwood, of Eslington, Feb. 5.

1711.—Robert, son of William Collingwood, of Whittingham, Mar. 8.

1718.—Jane, wife of Edward Anderson, of Glanton, aged 100 years; married to her husband 83 years, & dyed the same day on wc. they were married, viz., the Epiphany.

1727.—John, son of Ralph Clavering, Esq., of Callely, April 19.

1738.—Priscilla, wife of James Hargrave, Esq., of Shawdon, April 1.

1744.—Revd. Mr. Thos. Nevinson, Whittingham, Jar 17.

1746.—Alex. Collingwood, of Little Ryle, Esq., Jan. 7.

1803.—James Mather, of Ryle Mill in this Parish, Miller. According to the Coroner's verdict he was accidentally, casually, & by misfortune killed by the kick of a certain Bay Mare (aged 30), Oct. 20, 1803.

1804.—Samuel James Mackfarlin, of Thrunton in this Parish,

son of James Mackfarlin, Besom Maker, Oct. 9th, 2 yrs., 1804.

The following records of baptisms of the Claverings of Callaly are found, entered in one handwriting, on one page of the Register:—

John Aloyzius, son of Ralph Clavering, of Callaly, Esquire, by Frances, his wife, born 22nd of July, 1765.

Mary Eleneora, daughter of Ralph Clavering, of Callaly, Esq., by Mary, his wife, born August 5, 1768.

Ralph Edward, son of Ralph Clavering, of Callaly, Esq., by Mary, his wife, born Aprl. 28, 1771.

Lucy Ann Catherine, daughter of Ralph Clavering, of Callaly, Esq., by Mary, his wife, born August 10, 1772.

Frances Catherine, daughter of Ralph Clavering, of Callaly, Esq., by Mary, his wife, born April 7, 1774.

Edward John Henry, son of Ralph Clavering, Esq., by Mary, his wife, born Sep. 28, 1775.

Monica, daughter of Ralph Clavering, Esq., of Callaly, by Mary, his wife, Oct. 18, 1776.

The following are the names of the "Four and Twenty" of Whittingham, as they stood a century ago:—

"EASTER MONDAY, 1796.

The Vicar of the Parish.
The Curate of the Parish.
Sir Thomas Liddell, Bart.
Wm. Hargrave, Esqr.
J. Clavering, Esqr.
Geo. Collingwood, Esqr.
Mr. Anderson.
Mr. Mills.
Mr. Hatkin.
Mr. Pigdon.
Mr. Hopper.
Mr. Vardy.
Mr. Geo. Bell.
Mr. Adam Atkinson.
Mr. William Atkinson.
Mr. Whitham.
Mr. Bolton.
Mr. Renton.
Mr. Tomlin.
Mr. Donkin.
Mr. Gibbon.
Mr. Geo. Stephenson.
Mr. R. Bolam.
Mr. W. Nicholson."

An entry of much interest is found in the Churchwarden's book for the year 1798, which shews the patriotism of the parishioners at that time. A subscription had been set on foot in the parish to raise funds to help the Government in their straits at the beginning of the French War, when the sum of £162 15s. was collected, which is recorded in the the following manner:—

> "N.B.—In a Voluntary Subscription this year (1798) in Aid of Government ye following sums were contributed in this Parish, & our example was adopted afterwards by many Northumberland Parishes."

Then follows a list of subscribers and the sums given, which range from one shilling upwards, making a total of £162 15s.—"a sum which was reported not to be equall'd by any country parish in the North of England."

> "We linger on our eastward way,
> Where Twyford's steeple, old and grey,
> Skyward rears its lofty head."
>
> —JAS. THOMSON.

ST. MARY'S, WHITTINGHAM.

Turnbull Dixon
1894.

CHAPTER XIII.

THE CHURCH OF ST. MARY'S.—OUR LADY IMMACULATE.

Its Site—Erected in 1881—Removal from Callaly—Roman Catholic Recusants, 1677—English Catholics in Alndale—A Catholic Schoolboy, 1654—Confirmation by Bishop Leyburne, 1687—Number of Catholic Families, 1736—Local List of Papists and Nonjurors, 1685-1696-1715—Priests at Callaly, 1729 to 1877—At St. Mary's, 1881 to 1894—The Chapel—Solemn Opening, 1881—Interior Arrangements—Altar—Reredos—Memorial Window—Communion Plate—Clavering Monument—Extracts from Register.

MIDWAY between the villages of Glanton and Whittingham stands the Roman Catholic Church and Presbytery of St. Mary's, a charming block of buildings pleasantly situated amid its gardens and shrubberies, its shady walks and fern-grottos. It was in consequence of Callaly Castle—where there had been a priest since the twelfth century—having passed, by sale, into non-Catholic hands in 1877, that the present Church and Presbytery were erected for the use of the Catholics residing in the district. Here it may be as well to attempt a short sketch of the history of the English Catholics in the upper valley of the Aln from the period of the Reformation. As already stated, there had been a priest at Callaly from very early times, whilst after the edicts of Henry VIII., and during the many years that the heavy penalties and Parliamentary restrictions laid upon English Catholics continued in force, Callaly appears to have been the centre and place of resort for the Alndale adherents to the faith of their forefathers, where mass would, no doubt, be daily said by a priest in hiding. The Depositions from York Castle inform us that "George Collingwood, of Eslington, Esq., and Ralph Clavering, of Callolee, Esq.," were presented, in 1677, in the list of "Northumbrian Roman Catholic Recusants." The following incident, occurring, as it did, in the Vale of the Aln during the Sectarian days of the Commonwealth, tells its own tale :—

"1654.—In the village of Abberwick, a 'Catholic' boy, nine years old, went to a school in which he was the only Catholic. Some itinerant Protestant ministers had sent word to the master of the school that they intended to come and catechise the children, and requested him to keep the boys in the school till they came. The Catholic lad, hearing this, asked leave to go home. The master refused it, being determined that he should hear the intended instruction. The boy took the first opportunity to slip out of the school, and though the master and the other boys called out to him to come back, he ran home. The next day he fearlessly returned to the school, where he was severely flogged. The master asked him, tauntingly, whether it would not have been better for him to have stayed and heard the preachers the day before. The little Confessor answered, 'No; for, if he had willingly listened to the false doctrine of these teachers, he would have been liable to eternal punishment in hell.' The child said nothing of all this to his affectionate parents, who learnt it accidentally a fortnight after, and immediately withdrew him from the school."[1]

In 1687 Bishop Leyburne visited the northern counties of England to administer the rite of confirmation, when during the months of July, August, September, and October he confirmed 20,859 Catholics, of which number the following belonged to this neighbourhood :—

"August 13, 14.—Netherton and Witton, confirmed 243.
,, 15.—Cartington ,, 146.
,, 16.—Callaly ,, 282."[2]

[1] Records of English Province of the Society of Jesus, Series v.-viii.—Residence of St. John Evangelist, p. 124.

[2] The Episcopal Succession in England, &c., 1400-1875, by W. Maziere Brady.

According to Bishop Chandler's notes of his visitation of the Deanery of Alnwick, supposed in 1736, there were in the Parish of Whittingham "42 Papist Families. Mass house at Callaly, Mr. Turner, Preist."

From the pages of the Session Records of Northumberland of 1685 we quote the following extract, which shows the unsettled state of society, and the general distrust that prevailed in North Northumberland at that time. From it we also gather the names of the inhabitants, their residence, and their social position, which is always of value to the local antiquary and historian :—

"At the General Sessions of the peace held at Morpeth on the 29th April, 1st James the 2nd, Anno Dni 1685. The following persons who had been presented as Papists or Non-jurors were severally and respectively bound in the sum of 20£ on the following conditions—'That you shall render yourself when you shall be thereunto required by the proclamation of our S^d^ Soveraigne Lord the King or by his Maties Signification of his pleasure therein . To his Attorney Generall for the time being or otherwise as his s^d^ Maties shall thinke fitte'—

Johes. Clavering de Callalee, Ar.
Radus. Clavering de Callalee, Ar.
Jacobus Gardener de Yetlington, yeom. in x £.
Johes. Gardner de Lemonden, yeom.
Willm. Hall de Yetlington, yeom.
Lucas Gardner de Callalee, yeom.
Roger Snawdon de Callalee, yeom.
Johes. Moody de Callalee, yeom.
Robert Moody de Callalee, yeom.
Thomas Gibson de Yetlington, yeom. in x £.
Thomas Swann de Callalee, yeom.
Robert Collingwood de Eslington, yeom.
Johes. Swinhoe de Thrunton, yeom.
Thomas Davison de Thrunton, yeom.

Johes. Hall de Whittingham, yeom. in x £.
Jacobus Morrison de Eslington, yeom.
Radus. Pery de Eslington, yeom.
Andreas Curry de Eslington, yeom.
Johes. Browne de Callalee, yeom.
Cuthbert Blackelocke de Yetlington, yeom.
Andreas Hunter de Callalee, yeom.
Robtus. Moody de Callalee, yeom.
Georgius Todd de Callalee, yeom.
Richard Dobson de Alneham, yeom.
Thomas Riddle de Alnham, yeom. in xx £."

Again, in 1696, seven years after the accession of William and Mary, and just at the time that Sir John Fenwick, of Wallington, was committed to the Tower for being implicated in the Rye House Plot, Northumberland was looked upon with much suspicion by the Government, and we find the Roman Catholics, Nonjurors, &c., entering into recognizances at the Midsummer Sessions of 1696. Those in the vale of Whittingham were :—

Gibson, Thomas de Yetlington, Gen., 50£, May 11th. (Thos. Collingwood.)
Johannas Hunter de Callalee, High Houses, gen., his surety in 50£.

Johannas Hunter de Callaley, High Houses, gen., 50£, May 11. (,,)
Thomas Gibson de Yetlington, his surety in 50£.

Morrison, Georgius de Eslington, yeom., 50£, May 11, 1696. (,,)
Johannas Pow de Whittingham, his surety in 50£.

Pow, Johannas de Whittingham, yeom., 50£, May 11. (,,)
Georgius Morrison de Eslington, his surety in 50£.

Gardner, Johannas de Edlingham, gen., 50£, May 11. (,,)
Johannas Hunter de Callaley, High Houses, his surety in 50£.

It is amusing to notice that one person stood bond for the other almost in every instance, *vice versâ*.

We also give a list of the "Roman Catholics, Nonjurors, and others" belonging to the neighbourhood who, after the Rising of 1715, refused to take the oaths to George I. This list is of interest, as it gives their places of residence and the annual value of their lands :—

"*John Heslopp*, of Glanton	£12	0	0
Charles Collingwood, of Eslington, Gent.—Annuity ...	£20	0	0
Margaret Brown, of Bolton, Widow—Annuity ...	£120	0	0
Alexander Rotherford, of Burraton, Yeoman	£0	6	0
The Hon. *Katherine Collingwood*—Annuity	£200	0	0
James Selby, of Allenton, Gent.	£1	0	0
George Rotherford, of Bidleston, Gent.	£10	10	0
John Clavering, of Calleley, Esq.	£660	18	8
John Collingwood, of Eslington, Esq.	£889	16	2
Edward Widdrington, of Colt-Park, Gent.	£176	0	0
John Talbott, of Cartington, Gent.	£433	4	10"[1]

PRIESTS AT CALLALY.

"Henry Widdrington, S.J., died 16 Nov., 1729, æt. 61, at Callaly Hall, near Alnwick, the seat of the Clavering family, whose Chaplain he was."—Records of English Province (S.J. Series), v.-viii., p. 129. . . . Turner, circa. 1736.—Bishop Chandler's Visitation.

FROM SIGNATURES IN REGISTER.

	First Signature.	Last Signature.
Nic. Gilbert	———	5 Sept., 1796
Thos. Stout	20 Nov., 1796	———
Thos. Gillow	27 Aug., 1797	30 May, 1821
Edw. Crane	20 Aug., 1821	17 Nov., 1824
And. Macartney	21 Dec., 1824	24 Nov., 1825
Walter Maddocks	2 Feb., 1826	18 June, 1827
Nic. Brown	21 Mar., 1828	9 Apr., 1833
Jas. Abbot	———	29 Apr., 1833
Jos. Curr	7 June, 1833	13 Jan., 1836
And. Macartney (returned)	7 Dec., 1836	22 Oct., 1837
C. Brigham	4 Mar., 1838	8 Apr., 1838
Wm. Henderson	———	27 Apr., 1838
Jos. Howard	7 May, 1838	27 Oct., 1839
Thos. Ord[2]	23 Nov., 1840	22 Oct., 1865
Pat. Thos. Matthews	21 Jan., 1866	30 May, 1867

[1] Cosins' List of Catholics and Nonjurors, 1715, pp. 86-9.

[2] Father Ord is now at Thropton, having removed there on leaving Callaly in 1865.

Mat. Wm. Gibson	15 Aug., 1867 ...	9 Aug., 1871
Jas. Farrell	31 Dec., 1871 ...	13 Oct., 1872
Aloysius Hosten	12 Oct., 1872 ...	2 Feb., 1873
Jos. Arguis	——— ...	23 Aug., 1874
Jas. Stark[1]	6th July, 1875 ...	24 Dec., 1876

PRIESTS AT ST. MARY'S (OUR LADY IMMACULATE), WHITTINGHAM.

Chas. Ickenroth	March, 1881 ...	left Jan., 1882
Pat. Walsh	——— ...	left July, 1886
Wm. Taylor ... ... came	1 Sept., 1886 ...	———

The Church of St. Mary's is built in the Norman style of architecture, measures 55 feet in length by 21 feet in width, fitted with moveable benches of pitch pine. The entrance for the congregation is by a large doorway in the east angle of the south wall, the altar being at the west end.[2] The church was opened for divine service in March, 1881, the Rev. Charles Ickenroth being the first priest. The solemn opening took place on Sunday, September 11th, 1881, by the Right Rev. James Chadwick, Bishop of Hexham and Newcastle.

The altar and reredos of solid oak, a superb piece of wood carving, designed and made by Charles Beyaert, Bruges, was completed in the early spring of 1894. The formal opening took place on Trinity Sunday, May 20th, 1894, when the preachers were the V. Rev. James Canon Stark, of North Shields (formerly of Callaly), and the Rev. Fr. Stebbing, C.SS.R., Rector of the House of Redemptional Fathers at Perth. Other Priests present were—Rev. Edw. Rigby, Lowick; Rev. Robert Kerr, Biddlestone; and the Rev. Wm. Taylor, the Priest of St. Mary's. At the evening service the church was filled to its utmost limit, every inch of standing room was occupied, many being unable to gain admission. The new altar and reredos is 10 feet 6 inches in length, by about 10 feet in height. An elevated canopy in the centre of the reredos

[1] Father Stark left Callaly 1 Oct., 1877.

[2] The Architects were Messrs. Dunn and Hanson, Newcastle-on-Tyne.

contains the crucifix and tabernacle, while the space on either side is each divided into two single and a double canopy. The altar frontal consists of three large panels. The centre panel has the sacred monogram, I H S. The other two the symbolic figures of the Pelican and the Agnus Dei carved in high relief. The cost of this work of art was defrayed by private subscriptions, and, in such high esteem is Father Taylor—who at present fills the office of Priest at St. Mary's—held by all classes of the community, that Catholics and Non-Catholics heartily co-operated to bring to a successful issue the laudable scheme he had initiated.

The west window over the altar is composed of three lights, filled with very fine stained glass from the studio of Duhamel Marette, Prentre-Verrier, Evreux. The crucifixion forms the subject of the centre light, which has been treated in a most judicious manner, while the dexter contains a representation of St. John the Evangelist, and the sinister of St. Edward the Confessor. An inscription in glass along the bottom of the window runs as follows:—"Of your charity pray for the soul of Edward John Clavering, of Callaly Castle, who died November 3rd, 1876, R.I.P., to whose memory this window has been erected by his widow, Dame Clavering."

The general aspect of the interior is rendered very pleasing by the tasteful disposal of paintings and figures on the walls and in niches throughout the church. The duly-vested altar, bright with vases of lovely flowers, ornate ornaments, and the symbol of our faith, gives to its sacred precincts a charm and a solemnity at once soothing and refreshing, for

> "Religion crowns the statesman and the man,
> Sole source of public and of private peace."

CHALICE NO. 1 measures 6⅛ inches in height; diameter of bowl at top, 3¼ inches; depth of bowl inside, 2⁵/₁₂ inches; diameter of sexfoiled foot, 3¾ inches; no hall marks. This chalice is the same shape, and has the same form of ornamentation—four nobs around the stem, and six rays extending from the stem up the bowl—as the Heworth Pre-Refomation chalice, which is figured and described at pp. 48 and 221, Vol. iii. (N.S.), Proceedings of the Newcastle Society of Antiquaries, as follows :—" Mr. Hope says that he and Mr. Fallow found six or eight similar ones (all in the north), with flame-like rays up the bowl, as in the present instance. They are not English, but foreign ; may or may not be mediæval; are all made with a screw to take to pieces ; are mostly in Roman Catholic hands, and believed to have been made for recusant priests, to be taken to pieces for concealment." This they assign to the beginning of the sixteenth century. "Canon Franklin said the paten and chalice now in use in the Catholic churches were just the same as those exhibited" (p. 48).

CHALICE NO. 2, known, according to Fr. Stark, who was practically the last priest at Callaly, as the *new* chalice. Height, 9¾ inches ; diameter of bowl at top, 4 inches ; depth of bowl inside, 3¾ inches ; diameter of flattened cinquefoiled foot, 6 inches. No hall marks, as probably foreign. Under the base is the inscription :—

" Memento Janæ et Mariæ Clavering."
1671.

Immediately outside the church, near the door on the south side, stands a handsome monument to the memory of the last Clavering Squire of Callaly. The memorial consists of an Iona cross of freestone, with shortened shaft, filled in with carved diaper work in two rows, with I.H.S. at the juncture of the arms and shaft, and at equal distances are medallions containing the symbols of the Evangelists—Eagle (St. John), Ox (St. Luke), Lion (St. Mark), Angel (St. Matthew). A shield on the base at the front contains the arms of the Claverings—" Quarterly, or and gules, a bend sable." Around the base of the south-east and north sides is the inscription :—

"Pray for the souls of Edward John Clavering, Esq., of Callaly Castle, who died 3rd Nov., 1876, and of Jane, his wife, who died 13th Feb., 1881. This cross was erected to their memory by their daughter, Augusta Lady Bedingfield.

Buried under: Jane Clavering, 67. 19th Feb., 1881.—(J. W. Bewick, D.D.)

Edward John Clavering, removed from Whittingham Church and re-interred 9th June, 1881.—(C. Ickenroth.)"

In the course of improvements at Callaly Castle, on May 15th, 1890, the foundation stone of the chapel was exposed to view on the north-east corner, on which is cut:—

✠

AN: SAL: MDCCL
RODUL: CLAVERING
POSUIT

= Anno salutis MDCCL Rodulphus Clavering posuit
= In the year of Salvation 1750 Ralph Clavering laid (this stone).

The oldest register at St. Mary's begins in 1796, from which we give extracts. An older register, containing, no doubt, entries of the greatest interest, has unfortunately been lost.

BAPTISMS.

"LIBER BAPTIZATORIUM

5 Septembris 1796

Die 5 Septembris anno 1796, natus et baptizatus fuit Christopherus Peary filius Christopheri et Mariæ Peary (Olim

Born) Patrinus fuit Christopherus Bolam et Matrina Francisca Snowdon, in pago qui vulgo dicitur Branton A.Me

Nich. Gilbert, Miss: Apost:

1796 Sep. 5.—Christopher Peary, son of Christopher & Mary Peary, of Branton. Sponsors, Christopher Bolam & Frances Snowdon.

1797 July 13.—Mary Avery, daughter of Stephen & Barbara Avery. Sponsors, James Blacklock & Barbara Dodds.

1797 Aug. 27.—George Gibson, son of Ralph & Barbara Gibson. Sponsors, James Dodds and Mary Forster, of Callaly.

1798 April 12.—James Blacklock, son of James & Grace Blacklock, of Yetlington. Sponsors, Christopher Every & Mary Snowdon.

1800 Dec. 28.—Mary Protluck, daughter of George & Dorothea Protluck. Sponsors, Thomas Smith, Margaret Young.

Obituary of Callaly Congregation, 1797.

1797 October 27.—George Snowdon, of Dancing Hall, aged 67.

1798 Dec. 24.—Ann Snowdon, of New Town, aged 86.

1806.—Mary Gallon, of Fawdon, aged 90.

1813.—Mrs. Eliz[th.] Frankland, of Glanton West Field, at Alnwick, aged 20.

1815.—No one died in this Congregation during this year. Sit nomen Domini benedictum.

1817 June 1.—Mary Blacklock, Callaly Village, aged 89.

CHAPTER XIV.

GLANTON.

Salubrity of Glanton—Its commanding Site—Extensive Views—Glanton Pyke—Pre-historic Camp—Cist—Cinerary Urns—Bronze Celt—A Sixteenth Century Knife—Lands in Glanton held by William de Flammavill, 1200—Michael, son of Michael, 1227—John de Eslington, 1265—De Ros (circa), 1300—Robert de Glanton, 1304—John, son of Hugo, 1305—Robert, son of Alice, of Thrunton, 1313—John de Lilburn, 1356—William de Lilleburn, 1372—John de Lylleburne, 1399—Henry Lilburne, 1411—Thomas Lilleborne, 1439—Cuthbert Collingwood of Eslington, 1568—Arch. Forster, 1568—George Harbottel of Tuggel, 1627—Freeholders in 1747, 1774, and 1826—Tradesmen, Farmers, and others in 1827—Glanton in 1825—Traces of Old Field System—Old Roads—Market Cross—Keppin Well—Glanton of To-day—Schools—Presbyterian Church: its Pastors and its History—Folk Lore—False Alarm, 1804—Local Volunteers, 1803—Coquetdale Rangers inspected, 1806—Donaldson, the Glanton Poet, 1809.

THE salubrious little village of Glanton stands on the southern brow of the ridge that divides the valleys of the Breamish and the Aln, about two miles north of Whittingham.

From its commanding position, a magnificent panoramic view of many miles in extent is obtained. Right in the forefront lies the charming Vale of Whittingham, with its broad acres of green meadows, pasture lands, and well cultivated fields. The woods of Broom Park, Shawdon, Whittingham, Eslington, and Callaly, adding to the diversity of the scene, and the beauty of the landscape, which, with the dark pine clad heights of Callaly and Thrunton Crags, and the upland

heaths of Rimside Moor as a background, a pleasing contrast in lights and shades is produced, forming, withal, a somewhat sombre setting to so fair a picture. Beyond, to the right, are seen Simonside and other hills in Coquet-water, with the fells of Redesdale in the far distant west. On the east and south-east the view is bounded by the thickly wooded ridges of Alnwick Park and Brizlee Tower, the rising grounds of Lemington, Alnwick Moor, Corby Crags, and the hills lying around Edlingham, with a wide stretch of intervening country mapped out by luxurious hedgerows, and dotted with numerous farm-houses, hamlets, and family mansions; each ancient township being brimful of historic associations, and rife with old Border story, over which we shall give a hasty glance. At Battle Bridge and Garment Edge, towards the close of the ninth century, Saxon and Dane fought in deadly conflict for the fair valleys of Northumbria. Lemington Hall, a deserted mansion on the slopes of the adjoining hill, was once the fortress home of the Bednells, the "Turris de Lematon" of William Bednell, in 1415. Edlingham and its quaint old Norman church and mediæval castle, squatted in the valley below. Newtown, where, in 1640, the Scots on their way south, under General Leslie, camped for the night. Learchild and Thrunton, through whose now fertile fields once passed the Roman causeway from Tyne to Tweed. Bolton, the site of a hospital for lepers, dedicated to St. Thomas the Martyr, near which Surrey's army lay before the battle of Flodden. Shawdon, the "Castrum de Shawden" of Thomas Lilburn in 1415, the rallying point of the Royalist troops during a skirmish with the Roundheads in the summer of 1648. Crawley Dene, a sylvan retreat—its damp mossy dells the very joy of the botanist, and Crawley Tower, standing within a prehistoric camp that crowns the summit of the eastern bank of the ravine. Glanton Pyke, the beacon hill in the days of Border foray; while standing in the bottom of the valley is the old village of Whittingham, with its church of Saxon foundation, and its Border pele tower; with Eslington and Callaly nestling amid the greenery of their trees, the old homes of the Claverings and the Collingwoods; or, to put it in the more graphic words of a late well-known writer, "*Shawdon*, *Bolton*, and *Broompark*—a translucent trio of squire-archial harmony. *Eslington*, the palace of the Aln—with the arms of Ravensworth emblazoned on its shield—parks and preserves, cascades inviting the nymphs of the floods to sport in the limpid pools. *Callaly*, diversified in features, ornate with full-grown timber, pine-clad acclivities, rocks and ravines, horizons of purpling heath, haunts of the red grouse, are in picturesque contrast to the landscape of fertile fields and smiling homesteads. *Glanton Pike*, the Pisgah of the vale, and the horn of the altar of the Lares and Penates of *Glanton*, exultant upon the medium of intercourse with the world at its elbow. The romantic ravine of Crawley Dene, its northern end being crossed by the Roman road of Antoninus. *Crawley Tower*, upon an eminence near, whose history has so lately been elicited by a learned *coterie*[1] of Antiquarians."[2]

Glanton village is protected on the north by the rising ground, forming the apex of the ridge already noticed, which swells up behind it, the conical form of Glanton Pike rising on the north-west 695 feet above the level of the sea. Although the village does not present any of those picturesque fragments of ancient architecture usually sought for by the antiquary and the tourist, yet it is a place of considerable antiquity; and doubtless there existed on the slopes of the hill a primeval population long before the lower parts of the valley—such as the spots where the villages of Edlingham, Whittingham, and Alnham now stand had become the clearings of the Anglo-Saxon settlers—for in the immediate vicinity of Glanton are found distinct traces of those camps and earthworks generally

[1] Newcastle Society of Antiquaries met at Crawley, on June 30th, 1887.

[2] Topographical Sketches on the Alnwick and Cornhill Railway, by Samuel Donkin.—*Newcastle Daily Journal*, Sept. 1887.

ascribed to the Ancient British period. An old Northumbrian historian informs us that, "As a mason was digging for stone near Deer Street, beside Glanton Westfield, in the year 1716, he discovered an empty stone chest, upwards of three feet in length, and two in breadth, with a stone cover. Some time afterwards, three more chests of a similar form, with covers, were discovered at the same place. There were two urns and some fine earth in each, with some charcoal and human bones, on which were the marks of fire. Near these were two other urns, one large and the other very small. They were of ordinary pottery, and on being exposed to the air, fell into pieces. An ancient urn was also found more recently in ploughing a field near Glanton . . . ." Mr. Wallis says: "that a British *Securis*, or *Celt*, of the old mixed brass, was found in making a fence, about a quarter of a mile north from Glanton Westfield."[1] And Mr. MacLauchlan in his Memoir writes:—"It is probable that there has been a camp at Glanton; there are apparently the remains of one to the north of the village, and traditional evidence avers that they extended to the south.[2] Again, at the east end of the village, close to the road on the south of it, are remains of an enclosure, somewhat quadrangular in shape; but we could make out nothing satisfactory. Probably it has been a British settlement."[3]

A curious relic of a much later age than the foregoing—a brass repoussé knife handle, representing a bag-piper—was found at Glanton a few years ago, and is now in the possession of Mr. Bolam, Ravensdowne, Berwick-upon-Tweed, which the Baron de Cosson, in a letter to Mr. Bolam, thus describes:—"The figure of the piper is most curious. I find it difficult to offer any very definite opinion with respect to its date, but my

---

[1] Mackenzie's History of Northumberland, Vol. ii., p. 25. (A.D. 1825.)

[2] A portion of the road, midway between Glanton and St. Mary's Church, is known as the Camp hill, and the adjoining field eastward as the Camp field

[3] MacLauchlan's Memoir, p. 22.

own impression is that it belongs rather to the sixteenth than the fifteenth century. It is certainly a knife handle; and in the South Kensington Museum there is a complete knife with a handle much of the same general form, but with—if I remember rightly—a grotesque animal's head in the place of the piper."[1]

Glanton has, from an early period, been so much divided, and held by so many different persons, that it is a somewhat difficult matter to trace the various ownerships. Its first recorded owners, after the Norman Conquest, are found in connection with the "soke" of Whittingham, which, during Anglo-Saxon times, appears to have been the principal township in the upper valley of the Aln.

In the reign of John (1200), a Norman baron, William de Flammavill, renders, in the Pipe Rolls, an account of fifteen marks to the sheriff of the county for the lands lately held by Uhtred, the son of Gamel, in Whittingham, Thrunton, Barton, and Glanton. These lands continued to be held by the Flammavills until about the year 1223, and in 1227 the same vills and lands were held by Michael, the son of Michael.

Towards the middle of the thirteenth century there is a new owner of Glanton, or part of it, in John of Eslington, who, in 1265, died possessed of the manors already mentioned and the Glanton lands. In the "Testa de Nevill," circa 1300, a moiety of Glanton is there recorded as part of the barony de Ros. This was probably the eastern portion of the vill and township, as Shawdon was also a manor of that barony, while certain tracts of land in the west and south-west were, at the same period, the patrimony of the lords of Eslington. Again, in 1304, "Robertus de Glanton died seized of three-parts of Whittingham, 17 acres of land in Thrunton, and part of the vill of 'Glantindon.'" In 1305, John, the son of Hugo, had two parts of the manor of Whittingham, and part of the "villa" of Glanton; while in 1313 Robert, the son of Alice, of

[1] Proceedings Newcastle Society of Antiquaries, Vol. v., p. 122.

Thrunton, and in 1321 Isabella, the wife of John, the son of Hugo, held the lands in Glanton, which were evidently the Eslington portion. The following, however, refers distinctly to the barony de Ros. In the escheats of 29 Edward III., 1356, John de Lilburn died, holding the manors of Belford, "Wolloure" and "Schawden," with lands in Glanton as part of the "baronia de Werk;" which, in 1372, were held by William de Lilleburn; in 1399, by "John de Lylleburn, chevalier;" by Henry Lilburne in 1411; and in 1439, by Thomas Lilleborne. In a list, compiled 10 Elizabeth, 1568, of Northumbrian freeholders who held their lands *in capite*, are found Cuthbert Collingwood, of Eslington, and Arch. Forster as holding lands in Glanton.

In 1627, George Harbottel, of Tuggel hall, had certain lands in Glanton; but the "Rentals and Rates for Northumberland, 1663," only states the rental of the town of Glanton to be 150£, but does not give the names of the proprietors. We learn from the Whittingham Parish Register that in 1669 there was a John Collingwood in Glanton, and in 1699 Edward Collingwood. The Andersons were also very old owners in Glanton, as will be seen in the extracts from the Parish Register, under "Burials," 1718. The following list of residents and freeholders in the village and neighbourhood of Glanton, taken from the Poll Books of 1747, 1774, and 1826, gives the names of the owners:—

Freeholders' Names.	Residence.	Freeholds.
	1747.	
James Archbold	Beanley	Wark.
Nicholas Grey	Titlington	Akeld.
James Nesbit	Titlington	Wooler.
George Anderson	Glanton	Glanton.
Nicholas Brown, Esq.	Bolton	Bolton.
John Mills[1]	Glanton West-field	Glanton West-field.
Robert Stamp	Bilton	Glanton.

[1] The Mills family owned Glanton Pike, which was carried to the Collingwoods by the intermarriage of Margaret Mills with Henry Collingwood of Lilburn.

Freeholders' Names.	Residence.	Freeholds.
	1747.	
Robert Burrell, Esq.	Broom-park	Broom-park.
John Hopper	Alnwick	Glanton.
Roger Moffit	Shawdon	Sharperton.
James Hargrave, Esq.	Shawdon	Byker.
	1774.	
John Sprunston	Shawdon	Calf-close.
Matt. Forster, Esq.	Bolton	Brunton.
Daniel Alder	Adderstone	Glanton.
Edward Anderson	Glanton	Glanton.
Alex. Brown	Branton	Branton.
William Garrett	Battlebridge	Alnwick.
Richard Hadkin[1]	Glanton	Glanton.
Geo. Heslop	Glanton	Glanton.
John Mills[2]	Glanton West-field	Glanton West-field.
Jos. Mills	Glanton West-field	Glanton.
Jacob Pearson, Esq.	Titlington	Titlington.
William Shadford	Beanley	Glanton, annuit.
John Story	Beanley	Alnwick.
James Tannacky	Glanton	Glanton.
	1826.	
Thomas Allison	Powburn	Powburn.
Walter Allison	Powburn	Powburn.
Newton Blythe, Cl.	Branton	Alnwick.
Ralph Carnaby	Shawden	Rothbury.
Alexander Dunns	Chatton	Glanton.
John Frankland, Esq.	Glanton	Branton.
George Hughes	Middleton Hall	Glanton.
Andrew Holborn	Glanton	Glanton.
John Hopper	Glanton	Glanton.
Joseph Hughes	Glanton	Glanton.
James Pigdon	Glanton	Glanton.
John Turnbull	Glanton	Glanton.

[1] The Hadkins were ancestors of the wife of Sir George Bruce, and owned lands lying between Glanton and Greenville, now called Hopper's Hill. (Notes by J. C. Hodgson, on Branton Meeting House.—Arch. Æliana, Vol. xv., p. 156. (New Series.)

[2] On the doorhead of a house, standing on the north side of the road at Glanton Pike, are cut the following initials, which are, doubtless, those of John Mills:—

M.
I. M.
1750.

Freeholders' Names.	Residence.	Freeholds.
	1826.	
John Tewart, Esq. ...	... Glanton ...	... Glanton.
George Vint	... Whittingham ...	... Glanton.

In country districts, as a rule, old names die hard, but a perusal of the foregoing list shews that during the last fifty years great changes have taken place in the population of Glanton and its immediate vicinity, while in Glanton itself not a surname on the freeholders' list of 1826 is now to be found; such is the mutability of ownership. The tradesmen, farmers, and others in the village and township in the year 1827 were:—

William Curry, Cooper.
Jane Brown, Milliner.
James Dick, Baker.
James Lamb, Slater.
Isaac Matthewson, Draper.
Ralph Coxon, Blacksmith.
James Davison, Grocer.
George Dippie, Draper and Grocer.
George Paxton, Grocer.
Sarah Vint, Grocer.
William Dryden, Joiner.
Robert Mavin, Joiner.
John Thompson, Joiner.
George Hudson, Shoemaker.
John Patterson, Mason.
John Turnbull, Butcher.
Alex. Henderson, Surgeon.
John Hopper, Farmer.
Joseph Hughes, Farmer.
James Pigdon, Farmer.
George Weir, Farmer.
Robert Swanson, Red Lion Inn.
William Farmer, Nag's Head Inn.
Christopher Hills, Schoolmaster.
Rev. James Kirton, Presbyterian Minister.
Jacob Mills, gentleman.
John Tewart, Esq.
Major John Frankland, West Glanton.
Lieut. Robt. B. Reed, Powburn.

William Jobson, Farmer, Mile End.
George Stephenson, Farmer, West Glanton.
Ann Potts, Plough Inn, Powburn.
Thomas Allison, Joiner, Powburn.
John Mitchell, Stonemason, Powburn.[1]

Glanton is thus described in Mackenzie's History of Northumberland (1825), Vol. ii., p. 24:—"GLANTON is a fine pleasant village, situated on the turnpike road about two miles north of Whittingham, and nine miles west-by-north from Alnwick. It has recently been enlarged by the erection of several handsome houses, and is at present one of the most promising villages in the county. Here are two public-houses and a Presbyterian meeting-house. This fine village belongs to several proprietors, amongst whom are Henry Collingwood, John Tewart, George and Joseph Hughes, John Hopper, and Daniel Alder, Esqrs., and Mr. James Pigdon. Above Glanton, on the west side of the road, *Glanton Pike*[2] rears its lofty head. This mount is of a conic form, and commands a most extensive prospect, the hill called *Duns Law*, in Scotland, having been seen from it on a clear day. Formerly there was a beacon upon the summit to alarm the country in times of danger. *Glanton House*, the residence of Major Franklen, of Branton, is finely seated on the south side of the Pike, and is the property of Henry Collingwood, Esq."

This pleasantly situated country mansion, now in the occupation of its present respected owner, Mr. F. J. W. Collingwood, a lineal descendant of the old Northumbrian Collingwoods, stands on the southern slopes of the hill, embosomed amidst its rare and lovely trees. The view from the lawn, in front of the house, embraces a spacious expanse of the valley of the Aln, backed by the dark hills of Thrunton and Callaly. The green-houses and well arranged gardens,

---

[1] Parson and White's Directory, Vol. ii., p. 492.

[2] "Cymric, *pig;* Anglo-Saxon, *peac;* Norman-French, *pic;* peak or pointed hill. Example—Glanton Pike."—Place Names of the County of Northumberland, by John V. Gregory. Arch. Æliana, Vol. ix., p. 68. (New Series.)

under the care of Mr. Harris, the gardener, at Glanton Pike, contain many plants of interest. We glean the following interesting details from Dr. Hardy's Notes in the History Berwickshire Naturalists' Club, Vol. xii., No. iii., pp. 437-8 (May 29th, 1889.) "Mr. Collingwood has favoured the Club with some data of the height of the best of the Ornamental Trees :—

	ft.	in.
Araucaria imbricata	43	1
Deodar, Cedrus	43	3
Abies Morinda	42	0
Wellingtonia	45	4
Wellingtonia	49	7

. . . .

In the interesting museum there were noticed a Flying Fish, a small Crocodile, a stuffed Otter, a Night Heron, Waxwings, shot at Glanton Pike; also, *Thalassidroma Leachii*, and several other birds, which I believe are recorded in early volumes of the Club's Proceedings. Among the collection of weapons were a Russian Musket, taken at the capture of Sebastapol, 8th September, 1855, and an Assegaie from Ulandi, 4th July, 1879. There was not time to do more than glance at the literary stores in the library, which appeared to be valuable."

Mr. Collingwood, who is the oldest member of the Berwickshire Naturalists' Club, having been elected in 1840, communicates year by year to its proceedings the rainfall at Glanton Pike, and other scientific observations.

Two place names near Glanton, "The North Field" and "The West Field," are both of them indications of the old village community system of cultivation, when the lands around a village were divided into three common fields, cultivated in rotation, and allotted each year amongst the villagers. Of this ancient method of cultivation Mr. F. W. Dendy, in a most interesting paper on "The Ancient Farms of Northumberland,"[1] says:—"Beyond and around the village was the arable land, divided into great fields or flats, usually three in number. In that case they were worked on a three field rotation of crops, one being appropriated for autumn sown corn (*i.e.*, wheat or rye), one for spring sown corn (*i.e.*, barley or oats), or for peas and beans, and one was left fallow. These fields were again sub-divided into *furlongs* or *squares* or *shots*, placed very often at right angles to each other, with *headlands* or *headriggs* between them, on which the plough turned, and by which access was gained to these smaller areas. Each furlong was divided into acre or half-acre strips, separated from each other by *balks* of unploughed turf, and these acre or half-acre strips were usually known in the south as *sellions* or *stitches*, and in Northumberland, Scotland, and Ireland as *rigs*. . . . . The strips were distributed in equal proportions amongst the cultivators in such a manner that each man's holding was made up of a number of acre or half-acre strips lying apart from each other in the several square or oblong furlongs of which the three fields were composed, and these strips were so dispersed amongst similar strips held by his neighbours that no man, while the system remained intact, held two contiguous strips. Each individual holder was bound to cultivate his strips in accordance with the rotation of crops observed by his neighbours, and had rights of pasture over the whole field for his cattle after the crops were gathered."

The road to Powburn, which leads out of the north-west end of the village, probably follows pretty nearly the boundary between the North and West Fields. This road was the main turnpike in the older coaching days, before the new coach road was made through Crawley Dene, and was—with the exception of Rimside Moor—the highest part of the roadway between Morpeth and Wooler. Morpeth Bridge is 85 feet, Horsley Moor 461, Linden Hill 461, Weldon Bridge 149,

[1] Arch. Æliana, Vol. xvi., pp. 125-6. (New Series.)

Rimside Moor 816, and Glanton Hill road 518 feet above the level of the Quay of Berwick-upon-Tweed.[1]

Glanton of to-day is formed of one long street, running east and west, consisting of well-built houses, several of which stand within their own grounds, back from the main thoroughfare. Of late years this pretty village, with its pleasant surroundings and salubrious air, has developed into a favourite health resort; and since the opening of the Alnwick and Cornhill Railway—thus giving increased travelling facilities—visitors to the village are each year becoming more and more numerous, while the many places of interest within easy access also add greatly to its attractions—Chillingham, Alnwick and Wooler, Crawley Dene, Crawley Tower, Shawdon, Glanton Pike, Whittingham, Eslington and Callaly, the Cheviot Hills, trout fishing in the Breamish, as well as many delightful walks by hill and hedge-rows.

Glanton once possessed a market cross. Not a vestige of it now remains; but it is said to have stood about the centre of the village, on a slight knoll facing the Whittingham road. There is also a tradition of a chapel and a burial ground having been somewhere to the south of the village. The "Keppin Well," at the west end of the village, is a well-known institution, respecting which we cull the following from the Notes of Dr. Hardy:[2]—

"Glanton has a famous well, with imaginary salubrious qualities. It was the common well of the villagers, and lies near the base of a slope beyond the present school-house, and the water issued from a pipe. I am told that it was once customary for parents to take their weakly children to it in summer to be strengthened by the application of its refreshing waters. They were wrapped up in blankets and placed under the spout. It was called the *Keppin* or *Keppie Well*, owing to the water having to be caught or 'kepped' in pails or skeels or

[1] Hodgson's Northumberland, Part ii., Vol. ii., p. 105.

[2] History Berwickshire Naturalists' Club, Vol. xii., No. iii., p. 437.

jugs, with which the townspeople resorted to it in the morning to take their turn in carrying home the domestic supply for the day. It might thus become a metaphorical 'Keppin Well,' which people resorted to for gossip, or converted it into a place of assignation. 'Glanton green' is the name of a special variety of gooseberry raised at Glanton."

There is, or was, another well of delicious water at the east end of the village, which gave its name to the Playwell-lane, a picturesque lane leading down to the Dene-house and Crawley Dene.

A little way out of Glanton, on the Pike road, are the Board Schools and master's residence, an imposing and commodious block of buildings erected in 1873. These took the place of the old village school which stood in a corner, back from the main street, near to the chapel, where, long before the School Board era, the three R's were taught by Mr. Hills and Mr. Lowrey, both of whom for many years wielded the birch amongst the Glanton juveniles.

Glanton Presbyterian Church is not only the most prominent building in the village, but its interests form one of the most important factors in the history of the village during the past century.[1] We therefore give an account of the Glanton Congregation and its Pastors:—

"The congregation was formed in 1781, and the church was erected in 1783, as a stone above the entrance bears witness. The first minister was the Rev. Dr. Young, from 1781-1784, when he was appointed to the parish of Foulden in Berwickshire. In 1786, Dr. Young was succeeded by the Rev. James Young, whose ministry lasted till the close of 1797. Whether he died, or removed elsewhere, there is nothing to show. The Rev. James Kirton began his ministry in succes-

---

[1] In the Session Records, amongst the houses licensed for Divine Worship is found the following entry:—"1710. The house of Timothy Punshon at Glanton was *registered*."—Branton Meeting-House, by J. C. Hodgson. Arch. Æliana, Vol. xv., p. 154. (New Series.)

sion to Mr. Young in January, 1800, and continued till 1834, when he was followed by his nephew, the Rev. Wm. Kirton, who left for Pathhead, Kirkcaldy, in 1843. The Rev. James Kirton died in Edinburgh, but is interred in Whittingham Churchyard, where a stone marks his grave. The Rev. Wm. Kirton died a few years ago in New Zealand. In 1844, the Rev. Duncan Lennie was inducted into the charge, and continued till his death, which took place in 1858. Mr. Lennie was, according to his wish, buried at Bolton, where a stone erected by the congregation, with a suitable inscription, marks his resting place. In 1859, the Rev. David Fotheringham was ordained minister of Glanton, from whence he removed to Tottenham in 1864, where he still remains. During his incumbency much was done in the way of organization, and the congregation materially increased. The work done by Mr. Fotheringham was of a solid and permanent nature, and he was much esteemed by the congregation."

The Rev. R. H. Davidson succeeded Mr. Fotheringham in 1865, and is still in charge. On the 31st of March, 1891, Mr. Davidson's semi-Jubilee was made the occasion of a great demonstration, and a public clock was placed in the east end of the church to commemorate the event. The committee formed for the carrying out of the scheme consisted of the office bearers of the church, which then were James Dryden, William Haddon, John Haddon, John McLain, and William Oliver, elders; Thomas Miller, James Reid, Christopher Thompson, William Thompson, and John Tarbitt, deacons; while from amongst the congregation were John Dryden, William Douglas, James Dixon, James Greig, Thomas Huggan, Henry Taylor, Edward Utterson, Andrew Thompson, John Purvis, Robert Pallister, and Dr. Robertson. The appeal of the committee for subscriptions was liberally responded to by all classes, and soon a handsome sum was raised; and when Mr. Davidson, in a most unselfish manner, wished the memorial to be in a form that would be a public benefit, rather than a personal gift to himself, it was unanimously decided to erect a good clock. The clock is placed in the east end of the church, and chimes the hours and quarters on two fine-toned bells, for the accommodation of which a turret was erected on the roof, proving a decided embellishment to the somewhat severe building.[1]

During the pastorate of Mr. Davidson the Presbyterian cause has prospered at Glanton, and many great improvements have been made in the fabric and internal arrangements of both church and manse. In 1867, the church was re-fitted and furnished anew; and instead of the entrance by a narrow lane, porches were built and access obtained from the main road. The church is well-lighted, and heated by an improved hot-water apparatus.

The following are the first twelve entries in the Baptismal Register of Glanton Presbyterian Church:—

"A Register kept to insert the Births and Christnings of children born and baptized within the bounds of the Protestant Dissenting Congregation of Glanton, in the County of North$^{d.}$, by virtue of a licence obtained by the Rev$^{d.}$ James Young, from Joseph Roberts, Esq$^{r.}$, collector of stamp duties for the district of Morpeth, according to Act of Parliament. The licence bears date October first, one thousand seven hundred and eighty-five.

1. That Thomas, son of John and Margaret Dobson, of the Mile, parish of Whittingham & County of Northumberland, was born 1st, and baptized 6th Sept., 1786, by the Rev$^{d.}$ Dr. Young, then Minister of Glanton, now of Foulden, is attested by—Matth$^{w.}$ Trotter, Elder.

2. Robert, son of John and Ann Glaholm, of Brandon Whitehouse, and parish of Eglingham and County of Northumberland, was born Aug$^{st.}$ 28th, and baptized by the Rev. Dr. Young, then of Glanton, now of Foulden, is attested by—

Ann: Dom: 1786.

---

[1] *Alnwick Guardian*, March 28, 1891.

3. Isabella, daughter of John and Ann Hindmarsh, of Glanton, parish of Whittingham and County of North[d.], was born the 26th day of May, 1786, and baptized by me on the fourth day of June, 1786—by me, James Young, Protestant Dissenting Minister.

4. Robert Atkinson, son of Adam Atkinson and Isabella his wife, of Great Ryle, in the parish of Whittingham & County of Northumberland, was born the seventh day of May, 1786, and baptized the ninth day of May, 1786—by me, James Young, Protestant Dissenting Minister.

5. Thomas Hume, son of Tho[s.] Hume and Hanna his wife, of Glanton, parish of Whittingham and County of North[d.], was born June 28th day, 1786, and baptized the sixteenth day of July, 1786—by me, James Young, Protestant Dissenting Mins.

6. John Thompson, son of John Thompson and Mary his wife, of Callaly Mill, in the parish of Whittingham and County of Northumberland, was born on the 31st day of August, 1786, and baptized on the 17th day of Sep[r.], 1786—by me, James Young, Protestant Dissenting Minister.

7. Margaret Black, daughter of James and Margaret Black his wife, of Little Ryle, in the parish of Whittingham and County of North[d.], was born the 23rd day of August, 1786, and baptized the 28th day of August, 1786—by me, James Young, Protestant Dissenting Minister.

8. Rachel Alder, daughter of John and Alice Alder, of Glanton, parish of Whittingham and County of North[d.], was born on the 28th day of July, 1786, and baptized on the 6th day of August, 1786 — by me, James Young, Protestant Dissenting Minister.

9. Robert Kennedy, son of John Kennedy and Jane his wife, of Great Ryle, parish of Whittingham and County of Northumberland, was born on the 17th day of Sep[r.], 1786, and baptized on the 28th day of September, 1786—by me, James Young, Protestant Dissenting Minister.

10. Isable Rutherford, daughter of William Rutherford and Jane his wife, of Oovertharts, in the parish of Edlingham and County of Northumberland, was born November the twelfth, 1786, and baptized on the 14th day of the same month and year—by me, James Young, Protestant Dissenting Minister.

11. Elizabeth Kent, daughter of Alexander Kent and Mary his wife, of Little Ryle, in the parish of Whittingham and County of Northumberland, was born November the 1st, 1786, and baptized November the 10th day, 1786—by me, James Young, Protestant Dissenting Minister.

12. Ralph Rutherford, son of John Rutherford and Jane his wife, of Glanton, in the parish of Whittingham and County of Northumberland, was born December 27th day, 1786, and baptized on January the 14th day, 1787—by me, James Young, Protestant Dissenting Minister."

During the great French War, at the beginning of the present century, when Bonaparte's threatened invasion was foremost in the thoughts of all England, and elaborate arrangements were made to meet the expected attack,[1] Glanton was the centre fixed upon by the military authorities as the place of rendezvous for the volunteers in Glendale, Alndale, and Upper Coquetdale. Therefore that memorable night of Tuesday, January 31st, 1804, when the alarm was

---

[1] We have before us as we write a schedule of "Proposals for rendering the Body of the People Instrumental to the General Defence in case of Invasion," issued about the year 1800, which contains the following plan of defence under eight different heads:—

"1st. Driving the Country within Fifteen miles of the Coast.
2d. Bearing Arms and engaging to assemble when an Enemy has landed.
3d. Service as Pioneers (these to be provided with Pick-Axes, Spades, Bill-Hooks, and Felling-Axes).
4th. Service as Guides.
5th. Subscribing to find Carts, Waggons, &c.
6th. Millers engaging to aid the Supplies of the Army, if required.
7th. Bakers engaging to aid the Supplies of the Army, if required.
8th. Subscribing to furnish Barges or Boats upon Navigable Rivers and Canals."

given that "Bonny had landed," is famous in the annals of Glanton. Often has the writer, when a boy, heard from the lips of the past generation of Glanton folks recitals of scenes, pathetic and ludicrous, enacted on the night of the "False Alarm;" whilst vivid recollections of the firing of the beacons, the shrill calls of the bugle, the roll of the alarm drum, and the riding in hot-haste of troopers hither and thither through the darkness of the night, lingered for long in the memories of the older inhabitants of Glanton.

> "Then beat to arms the rolling drum, and many a darting light,
> Through open door and window small, gleam'd flickering on the night;
> While little girl and mother kind, and matron growing old,
> Gave ready aid, as if their hearts were made of sternest mould."

During the whole of that night troopers belonging to the Coquetdale Rangers and the Cheviot Legion Volunteer Cavalry came galloping in from all parts. The Rangers, being more widely scattered, did not get forward so quickly; but by day-break there was a full muster, to a man, of the Cheviot Legion, who, for its loyalty and despatch, henceforth received the name of the "Royal Cheviot Legion." After a night of great excitement, authentic news arrived early in the morning that the French had not landed and that it had been a false alarm. Therefore the troopers spent the remainder of the day at Glanton in that social and jovial manner for which our yeoman ancestors were so famous, and it was near nightfall ere many of them reached their homes. Late in the afternoon, three Coquetdale Rangers, returning home to Rothbury, were crossing Rimside Moor, when they espied Jamie Macfarlane, the besom maker, whom we have already noticed; whereupon the three troopers thought it would be a good joke to make Jamie believe they were the French, and take him prisoner. So, putting spurs to their horses, they galloped across the moor with drawn swords towards poor Jamie; but the besom maker was more than a match for the valiant Rangers. As they approached him, he suddenly turned his back to the foe, stooped down, and, looking through betwixt his legs, ran backwards towards them, shouting all the while at the utmost pitch of his voice. The horses, unaccustomed to such an extraordinary spectacle, reared and plunged, and would on no account face the charge of Jamie Macfarlane. The cavalry, therefore, beat a hasty retreat; at which the victorious Jamie triumphantly shouted after them, "Hey! thre' bonny Sodgers, canna tyek a buzzum maker!"

The following is a list of those persons belonging to Glanton and the Vale of Whittingham, whose names are found in the Muster Roll of the Royal Cheviot Legion Cavalry in 1803, commanded by Lieut.-Col. Horace St. Paul:—

OFFICERS.	When Enrolled.		
Capt. Edward Anderson	—	Farmer	Glanton.
Capt. Thomas Selby [1]	—	——	Biddlestone.
Lieut. William Bolton	—	Farmer	Mountain.
Lieut. William Wilson	—	Farmer	Heppell.
Lieut. John Mills	—	——	Glanton Pike.
Cornet John Howe	—	——	Lemmington.
Cornet Thomas Smith	—	——	Woodhall.
TROOPERS.			
Thomas Anderson	—	——	Mount Hooley.
John Anderson	1803	——	Glanton.
George Atkinson	—	Husbandman	Little Ryle.
James Blacklock	1803	Farmer	Yetlington.
John Brown	1803	——	Whittingham.
Charles Brown	—	——	Alnham.
Joshua Crea	1799	Surgeon	Whittingham.
Selby Curry	1803	Gentlemen	Glanton.
William Gibson	—	Farmer	Thrunton.
Caleb Hastings	1803	Miller	Thrunton Mill.
William Lumsdain	1799	Farmer	Prendick.
Robert Moody	1803	——	Yetlington.
B. Murton	—	Farmer	Titlington.

[1] Capt. Selby was in Edinburgh on the night of the False Alarm, and a mounted messenger was sent post-haste for him, and it is said that the gallant Captain never recovered from the effects of his long and rapid ride from Edinburgh to Glanton.

TROOPERS.	When Enrolled.		
Joseph Orde	—	Farmer	Branton.
Andrew Peary	—	Blacksmith	Branton.
John Stephenson	1803	Farmer	Yetlington Lane.
Henry Smith	—	——	Callely High House.
George Swanson	1802	Innkeeper	Glanton.
Clement Stephenson	1799	Farmer	Whittingham.
John Turnbull	1799	Butcher	Glanton.
Joseph Waterman	—	Innkeeper	Whittingham.
George Renton	1799	——	Shawdon Wood House.
Thomas Allison	1803	——	Powburn.
Robert Crozier	1803	——	Folleans.
William Donkin	1803	——	Lorbittle.
Robert Jobson	1803	——	Glanton.
Peter Stephenson	1803	Butcher	Whittingham.
George Stephenson	1803	——	Little Ryle.
William Waterman	1803	——	Whittingham.
George Mellican	1803	——	Dean House.
Jacob Mills	1803	——	Glanton.

In the Muster Roll of the Coquetdale Rangers Troop of Volunteer Cavalry, dated November, 1806, the following names occur:—

Commander—	Captain Thomas Selby	Alwinton Parish.
Lieutenant—	John Mills	Whittingham Parish.
Sergeant—	John Stevenson	ditto.
	Thomas Anderson	ditto.
	Thomas Allison	ditto.
	Joseph Burns	ditto.
	John Morrison	ditto.
	Robert Moody	ditto.
	John Embleton	Alnham Parish.
	William Lumsdain	ditto.

As several of the above appear in the Muster Roll of the Cheviot Legion for 1803, they had evidently been transferred to the Troop of Coquetdale Rangers between the years 1803 and 1806. Glanton appears to have always been a sort of military centre for the district, where the troops mustered and were inspected.

The following notice is found in the *Newcastle Courant* of April 26th 1806:—"The Coquetdale Rangers, commanded by

Capt. Selby, were inspected at Glanton on the 22nd inst., by Lieut.-Col. Rawdon, who expressed his entire approbation of their discipline and soldier-like appearance. The troop have just received new clothing, &c., and have unanimously determined to continue their services so long as Government may deem them useful to their Country."

The following lines, written about this period by "Tam o' Glanton," clearly shows the prevailing idea of a French invasion :—

"An Acrostic to a Young Recruit.

Allan, my lad, here comes a line ;
Lang look'd for's come at last.
Lang may you i' your armour shine,
An' gie our foes a blast.
Now news is gaun that *Buonaparte's*
Refitting to come over ;
Old England's tars will coup his carts,
Conduct him into *Dover*.
Hae at him, ere he gets in ;
Engage him wi' the *local ;*
Sae nicely they will skelp his skin,
They'll smash him like a cokle.
E'er be steady 'midst these war's alarms ;
Rely on God to aid the *British* arms."[1]

Our account of Glanton would scarcely be complete without some notice of its poet, Thomas Donaldson, a weaver, who, in 1809, published his poetic effusions in a small 8vo. volume of 234 pages, printed by William Davison, Alnwick, and illustrated with several of Bewick's woodcuts. We, therefore, give in full his curious dedicatory lines, and one of his poems :—

Dedication.

I make this dedication,
To all men in the nation,
In ev'ry situation
With greatest veneration
And hope their acceptation
And warmest approbation
Will on deliberation,

[1] The Poetical Works of T. Donaldson, p. 44.

Crown this my publication
And when they know my station,
And useful occupation
Allow my penetration
In Scots versification;
Though I've no education.
So I remain,
'Gain and again:
Your humble servant:
Well-wishes fervent
Shall not be wanting
From Tom of Glanton.

On the Death of a Favourite Hen.

Ye wives lament thro' a' the lan',
Let tears rin like the *Keppin*[1] stran',
O'erpowr'd wi grief I canna stan',
Come haud my head;
Ne'er sic a Hen was seen by man,
But *Muffie's* dead.

My *Muffie* was a Hen o' Hens,
This ev'ry honest neebor kens;
Wi' her ten claws, lang wi' her friens,
She'd seek her bread;
Now I may gang an' get my men's,
Sin' *Muffie's* dead.

She laid an egg, ay ev'ry day.
She never wander'd far away
Like ither hens, that gang astray
Amang the weeds;
Like her, alake! I hae nae mae,
Now *Muffie's* dead.

She bought me *Sugar*, *Tea*, an' *Bread*,
Needles, *Thimbles*, *Twist*, an' *Thread*,
An' mony ither things, indeed,
To mak' me braw;
But now, alake! poor *Muffie's* dead,
'Tis warst o' a'.

I brought her frae *Langhoughton* Town;
I've had her twenty seasons roun'.
My Hen she was a shining Brown,
Wi' *Muffi'd* head;
She was weel kend, ay a' will own,
But now she's dead.

---

[1] Alluding to a well in Glanton.

She hurt an e'e ance in a fight,
Which for a lang time spoilt her sight,
Yet after she gat hale an' tight,
She'd gie them battle;
An' ne'er a Hen o' *Muffie's* weight
Could stan' her brattle.

That donsie[1] laddie, *Billie Brown*,
I wadna' car'd to've crack'd his crown,
Wi' his twa clogs he ran her down—
That idle scholar;
I swear I'd rather gi'en the loun[2]
A Spanish Dollar.

I gar'd the rascal tak' her hame,
Just like a present till his Dame.
A' that I charg'd her for the same
Was but a shilling;
She bang'd poor *Muffie* back again—
She was not willing.

Now sin' they hae return'd her hale,
An' ploted neither head nor tail,
My Hen will mak' a pot fu' kail
I' time o' need;
Sae I conclude this mournfu' tale—
That *Muffie's* dead.

Bill's hae a present o' her claws,
Wi' her twa wings to dust the wa's.
Hang up her head to scar the craws
Frae aff the seed;
An' mak' a whissle o' her jaws—
For *Muffie's* dead.

[1] Unlucky.
[2] A mean fellow.

CHAPTER XV.

CRAWLEY TOWER.—CRAWLEY DENE.—SHAWDON.—BOLTON.—LEARCHILD.—LEARCHILD BURN.

CRAWLEY TOWER.

Strategic Position—British and Roman Occupations—A Border Fortress—The Warlike Herons—Curious Legend—Crawley Dene: Its Bosky Dells and Woodland Scenery—Geology and Flora.

SHAWDON.

Barony of Wark—Robert de Ros—Tower at Shawdon—Its Owners: Lilburn, Proctor, Brandling, Hargrave, Pawson—Shawdon Park: Its Trees, Rookery, and Relics of Antiquity.

BOLTON.

Surrey's Army, 1513—North-Country Chieftains—Scots Herald at Mile—Ancient Road at Mile—"The Guards" at Bolton—Hospital at Bolton.

LEARCHILD.

Low Learchild, once a place of some extent—Old Enclosures—Border Watch—A Member of Beanley Barony—Held by Roger de Merlay, Clavering, Storey, Buston—High and Low Learchild, now part of Shawdon and Eslington Estates.

LEARCHILD BURN.

Its Course—Different Names—Its Flora and its Adders—A-Nutting in Roughlee Wood—The Old Forester—Homeward Bound—Thrunton Tile Works—The Old Farm-house at Thrunton—The Stephensons—Thrunton Fire.

CRAWLEY Tower, an interesting Edwardian structure of the old Border days, occupies an elevated site on the eastern ridge of Crawley Dene, which, "on account of its strategic position and most commanding view northwards, standing at an elevation of 535 feet, looking defiantly towards Scotland, and commanding a most delightful view of the Vale of Whittingham, and nearly the whole length of Breamish, from its source to Horton Pele, where it joins the Till, it has been occupied successively by the Ancient Britons, by the Romans, by the Normans, by the Edwardians, and by the Elizabethans. . . . . . . What remains of the Ancient British and Roman occupation of this fort may be below ground, and a digging into the entrenchment, which is 290 feet long and 160 broad, would doubtless discover many relics. But above the ground there is nothing visible except the modern farm buildings which environ it, and the central feature of the ruined pele, with its lowly farm-house crouching below and within it, mixed up within them."[1] Except in the immense thickness of its walls, and two small lancet headed windows in the upper part of the tower, there is not much to illustrate the original character of the building.

From a very early date Crawley was in the possession of the Herons, a powerful Northumbrian family.[2] In 1343, John Heron obtained a license from Edward III. to crenellate or fortify Crawley, as follows:—"20th Nov., 1343. Ed. III. at Westm. to John Heron for 'mansum suum de Crawelawe.[3]

The list of Border strongholds of 1415 thus records Crawley:—"Turris de Krawlaye . . Johis. Heron, Chlr."[4]

In the Survey of 1541, we read:—"At Crawley there is a lytle toure of thinherytance of the daughter and heyre of S. Wll'm Heron in greatt decaye for lacke of contynuall reparac'ons."[5]

A sixteenth century deed (1576) shews that a William Heron and his son John Heron then resided at Crawley.[6]

---

[1] Proceedings of the Newcastle Society of Antiquaries, Vol. iii., p. 98.

[2] The first notice of the Northumbrian "Hairuns" is found in the Pipe Rolls of 30 Henry II., 1184, and for many subsequent centuries the Herons continued to be one of the most potent families in the north. Several families bearing this old Northumbrian name are yet living in the valleys of the Wansbeck, the Coquet, the Aln, and the Breamish; while, curiously enough, the writer had the pleasure, in 1893, of having tea with a William Heron, living at Crawley in the very tower of his ancestor, Sir William Heron of 1541. We append to this note the names of some of the members of this family who held lands and occupied border fortresses in Northumberland in the year 1415:—Sir John Heron, of Eshott; Sir John Heron, of Twizel; Nicholas Heron, of Meldon; Emerici Heron, of Howick; Sir John Heron, of Crawley; William Heron, of Whittingham; Alexander Heron, of Chipchase; Sir William Heron, of Simonburn; and Sir William Heron, of Ford.

[3] Border Holds. C. J. Bates, Vol. i., p. 9. [4] Ibid., p. 17. [5] Ibid., p. 42.

[6] Proceedings of the Newcastle Society of Antiquaries, Vol. vi., p. 202.

Mr. John Hearon was the proprietor of Crawley in 1663, when its annual value is recorded at £50.

A curious legend connected with Crawley is given in a note to the following lines, which occur in a poem entitled "Widdrington."[1]

> "Harehope now shew'd his heath-clad brow,
> And Eglingham her wild woods shook;
> Grim Beanly smil'd, and Crawley now
> Frown'd from its height, with lordly look."

This Tower was, at one period, the residence of one of the author's (Mr. Hall's) ancestors named Harrogate, of whom many anecdotes are yet extant, and amongst others is the following:—"Mr. Harrogate possessed a remarkably fine *white horse—for he was not behind his neighbours in making excursions north of the Cheviot*—and the then proprietor of the Crawley Estate took so great a fancy to this beautiful *charger* that, after finding that he could not tempt Harrogate to sell *him* for money, he offered him the whole of this fine Estate in exchange for the *horse*; but Mr. H., in the true spirit of a Border rider, made him this bold reply:—'I can *find* lands when I have use for them, but there is no sic a beast i' yon side o' the Cheviot, nor yet o' this, and I wad na' part wi' him if Crawley were made o' gold.' How little did the value of landed property appear in those days of trouble and inquietude, and how much less were the comforts of succeeding generations consulted! The only property of value then to a Borderer was his trusty arms and a fleet and active horse; and these seem to have been the only things appreciated by this old gentleman."

CRAWLEY DENE, whose almost primeval solitude is now broken by the snorting engines on the Alnwick and Cornhill railroad, and its sylvan beauty marred by unsightly embankments—the usual concomitants of the great civilizer—is yet,

---

[1] "Widdrington," a Tale of Hedgeley Moor, in two Cantos, by James Hall (1827), p. 91.

notwithstanding, a charming bit of woodland scenery, its bosky dells and swampy bottoms affording to the botanist and the naturalist a rich field for research and exploration ; while the geologist can read its story in the Tuedian rocks seen in its cliffs and scaurs. Besides those rarer plants and lower pond life, only found by diligent search, a hasty glance during a ramble through the dene one summer's evening revealed to us several plants of interest. Great beds of the Lesser Celandine *(Ranunculus ficaria)* and the Marsh Marigold *(Caltha palustris)* covered the damper spots. There, too, were the Melancholy Plume Thistle *(Cnicus heterophyllus)*, the Broad Leaved Helleborine *(Epipactus latifolia)*, St. John's Wort, Ragged Robin, Great Valerian, the Yellow Pimpernel *(Lysimachia nemorum)*, Prickly Shield Fern, Broad Buckler, Male Fern, Lady Fern, with feathery masses of the graceful Wood Horse-tail *(Equisetum-sylvaticum)*, and many other interesting plants.

The village of Powburn stands at the north end of Crawley Dene, to which a pleasant walk may be had from Glanton, by going down Playwell Lane to Dene House, thence along the highway to the left through the Dene to Powburn, and back by the old coaching road past Greenville to Glanton. That portion of the road was anciently termed "The Bellway." When coals and the produce of the country were carried by pack-horses, tied head to tail, in single file, the leading horse carried a bell, that was heard a long way off when a file of pack-horses ascended and descended the steep bank from the Powburn to Glanton. Lincombe Dene is a continuation of Crawley Dene, and extends on the south towards Shawdon.

SHAWDON Manor in feudal times was a member of the ancient barony of Ros, and belonged for many centuries to the Lilburns. In "Magna Brittannia" (1724) it is described as "SCAUDON, one of those Towns and Lordships which belonged to the Barony of *Werke*, which *Robert de Ros* the younger held of King Henry III. by the Service of two Knights' Fees, as his

Ancestors had done from the Time of King Henry I." (p. 689.) Traces of a strong tower yet exist, probably the remains of the "1415 Castrum de Shawden (of) Thomas Lylburn." Amongst a number of carved stones, evidently brought from old buildings, and now arranged within the grounds, there is one on which are represented the water bougets of the Lilburns,[1] armorial insignia, that originally belonged to their overlords, the Lords de Ros.[2] Shawdon, in 1541, was "thenheritaunce" of Cuthbert Proctour, and the tower was then in good repair. While the "Rentals and Rates," 1663, informs us that Shawdon and Shawdon Woodhouse were the property of Mr. Robert Brandling. The estate eventually passed into the possession of the Hargraves and the Pawsons. Shawdon Park is well wooded, and in it are some grand patriarchal trees—Oaks, Elms, Ashes, Sycamores, and Limes, several of which are known by the following names:—"The Big Elm," "The King of the Forest," and "The Hanging Tree," which still survives, although it has lost a limb. There is also a remarkable double line of hollies, forming an avenue 60 feet long and 14 feet wide. It was the approach to the old mansion, which, unlike other pele towers of the district, was ornamented in its stone work. The largest holly in the avenue measures, at four feet from the ground, 6 feet 10 inches. It is greatly to be regretted that age and storms are fast diminishing this remarkable avenue of hollies. The measurements of some of the best of these trees was communicated by Mr. James Thomson (who for forty-five years has been gardener at Shawdon), and recorded in the History of the Berwickshire Naturalists' Club, Vol. xii., No. ii., p. 177. At one foot from ground—Oak, 19 feet 6 inches; Ash, 15 feet; Beech, 16 feet; Elm, 17 feet 7 inches; Sycamore, 19 feet; Lime, 13 feet

---

[1] The Arms of the Lords de Ros—Gules, three water bougets, argent.
The Arms of the Lilburns—Sable, three water bougets, argent.
The Arms of the Proctors—Argent, three water bougets, gules.

[2] History Berwickshire Naturalists' Club, Vol. xii., No. i., p. 177.

9 inches; Scotch Fir, 10 feet; Silver Fir, 13 feet 3 inches; Alder, 8 feet, in circumference. In Shawdon Hall are preserved a number of curiosities collected from various parts of the estate, viz.:—Fragments of Red Deer antlers found near Shawdon House; an antler of Red Deer, with five tines, found near Titlington; a tripod brass flagon, with a handle and spout, found in a bog at Hoppen; a small caldron of copper plate, found near Bolton Church.

Shawdon is famed for its rookery, and on an autumn evening motley flocks of "Shawdon Craas" may be seen winding their lofty flight homewards down the valley from their distant feeding grounds in the west. The following interesting paragraph anent the Shawdon Crows appeared in "North Country Notes" (*Newcastle Daily Journal*, July 20, 1894). Mr. James Thomson writes:—"A winter rookery has existed here, at Shawdon, time out of mind. There is no bird whose habits are more interesting than the rook. Were I to detail some incidents that have come under my notice in the nesting season, they would scarcely be believed. My purpose is to state that a crow with a white feather in her wing nested in a tree close to the garden here for at least seventeen or eighteen years. She was the only crow with a white feather in her wing amongst the hundreds that resorted to the rookeries here. In the same nesting rookery, a bird with an extremely discordant call note built for many years, otherwise there was nothing to distinguish her from other crows. It is not perhaps generally known that very few summer rookeries are occupied during the winter by the birds which nested in them for breeding, hence the distinction between a summer and a winter rookery."

The Jay once frequented the woods at Titlington, but is now extinct; while the white, the horned, and the hooting owls are still found in the neighbourhood of Shawdon.

About a mile to the east of Shawdon lies the little historic hamlet and church of Bolton, in the parish of Edlingham, with its interesting Norman chancel arch; for, according to tradition, it was in the chancel of this church that the Earl of Surrey, and the illustrious leaders of the 26,000 north-countrymen who here joined the noble Earl on his way to Flodden—amongst whom were Lords Clifford, Conyers, Ogle, Scrope, and Lumley; Sir William Percy, Lionel Percy, Sir George Darcy, Sir William Bulmer, and Richard Tempest—partook of the Holy Communion and pledged themselves to defeat the Scots or die on the field. Here we may remark that while the English army lay encamped on Bolton Moor, Islay (herald), who had been despatched by James IV. with a message to Earl Surrey, was detained at "The Mile," a place about two miles south-west of Glanton, until Surrey and his captains considered the prudence of holding a conference:—

> "At a little village poor
> Ilay did light, and took lodging,
> Constrained for to stay;
> And lodged there in a little village,
> Lest he their order might display:
> Which might turn to the Scots' advantage."
>
> —*Flodden Field* (Weber's Edition, p. 79).

"At a village," says Hall, "called Mylo, twoo myles[1] from the felde, untyll the coming thether of the sayde earle the next morrow." The interview had taken place at or near Mile. "The sixte day of September, early in the mornynge, the earle, accompaynied with the mooste parte of the lordes, knyghtes, and gentlemen of the felde, euery man hauying with hym one man to holde hys horse, and so the sayde heraulde met wyth the earle." Surrey kept Islay prisoner and pledge at Mile till the King of Scotland delivered the English herald, Rouge Cross, whom he detained. This was effected; and "Ilay came home before none, and shewed of his gentell enterteyning, and then Rouge Crosse was deliuered and came to the Englishe Armye." On the 9th

[1] According to modern computation, about four miles.

of September, 1513, two days after the exchange of heralds, Flodden was fought.

Standing at the present day on the ridge near to Mile farm-house, and looking northwards, distinct traces of an ancient trackway can be seen leading from "The Green Lonnin" to the river Breamish, which it crosses at Brandon, and thence northwards on by Roddam and Roseden. This old road was doubtless the route taken by the Scots' herald, which brought him to the outposts of Surrey's army at "Mylo."

Near to Bolton there are the remains of a large camp called "The Guards," sometimes supposed to have been Roman, of which Mr. MacLauchlan in his "Memoir" says:—"It might be reasonably expected that some traces of a Roman place of defence would be found in the neighbourhood of the intersection of Roman Ways, and we visited an entrenched place at Bolton called *The Guards*, fully expecting to find traces of Roman lines, particularly as we had heard that remains having a Roman character had been disinterred on the spot;[1] but though the place is naturally strong, and has been occasionally surrounded by water, and though it bears in addition the marks of ancient enclosure, we could not fix on any outline to indicate Roman occupation. Bolton is about a mile N.E. of the junction. *The Guards* is probably the site of the hospital founded by Robert de Ros in the thirteenth century."

In Mackenzie's History of Northumberland, Vol. ii., p. 37, we read:—"Here (at Bolton) was an hospital, founded by Robert de Ros, Baron of Wark, before the year 1225,[2] for a master and three chaplains, thirteen leprous men, and other lay-brethren, dedicated to St. Thomas the Martyr, or the

---

[1] A bronze Patella, now in the Museum of the Archæological Institute, Edinburgh.

[2] History Berwickshire Naturalists' Club, Vol. xii., No. ii., p. 175.—Report of Meetings by J. Hardy gives an earlier date, 1214.

Holy Trinity; subordinate to the abbey of Ryeval and the priory of Kirkham, in Yorkshire, He gave it the villa, lordship, impropriation, and advowson of Bolton, and a waste of 140 acres; a corn mill and a tenement at Mindrum; lands at Paston and at Kilham. . . . . . . The master, chaplains, and brethren of the hospital, were to keep a good table, dress neatly, and provide themselves with proper necessaries and conveniences out of their annual revenues, and apply the remainder to the relief of the poor, and helpless strangers. At the dissolution, it came, with the manor and villa, into the possession of the Collingwoods of Eslington." Bolton is also famous as having been the place of meeting of King John and William the Lion, in 1209.[1]

LOW LEARCHILD—a small hamlet in the parish of Edlingham, where all the cross roads of the country meet—has evidently been a place of some extent, as many grass-grown foundation mounds yet testify. A vacant green space surrounds it, in which are remains of old earthen enclosures for sheep or cattle, for it was liable to be swept by Border forays, or thievish inroads, even in times of peace. In 1552, there was a nightly watch kept by two men between Newtown and Learchild, while other two perambulated the distance between Learchild and Barton.[2] It was ravaged during a period of truce, in the winter of 1585-6, along with Lemington and all the country besides. Learchild was the "vill beyond the moors" which Gospatrick, out of Beanley barony, conferred as part of the dower of Juliana, his daughter, when married to Roger de Merlay, lord of Morpeth.[3] In the Pipe Rolls of 37 Henry III., 1253, the vill of "Luerescheld" pays to William Heyrun, sheriff of the county, the sum of 12d. *Nova Oblatas—i.e.*, gifts or voluntary fines. Eventually Learchild came into the hands of the Claverings—the Tillmouth and Learchild branch—and,

[1] History Berwickshire Naturalists' Club, Vol. xii., No. ii., p. 176.

[2] See Border Watches.

[3] History Berwickshire Naturalists' Club, Vol. xii., No. ii., p. 168.

in 1663, Mr. Robert Clavering was the owner. From the Northumberland Poll Books we learn that it was the freehold of John Storey, of Alnwick, in 1747 and 1774, and of Thomas Buston in 1825.

The township of Learchild is now divided, and consists of High and Low Learchild. The latter forms part of the Shawdon estate, and High Learchild is the property of the Earl of Ravensworth.

The little burn that flows through the fields of Learchild and Low Field rises far up amongst the rocky wilds of the Coe Crag. There it is the Coe burn, also locally known as the Blackcock burn—a little further down its course, it is called Elliott's burn and Roughlee burn; but ere it reaches the river Aln, of which it is a tributary, it bears the name of Jackey's burn, and is crossed by the Alnwick turnpike at Jackey's bridge, emptying its waters into the Aln, just beyond Jackey's Dyke Nook Field. The course of the stream is skirted with a line of native alders, guelder rose, heckberry, brambles, crab apples, oaks, hazels, and wild gooseberries, while in the shady glens of the adjoining woods may be found an abundance of primroses and wild hyacinths, often called blue bells *(Agraphis nutans)*; true love-knot *(Paris quadrifolia)*; broad-leaved helleborine *(Epipactis latifolia)*; and masses of dog mercury, mingled with the broad green leaves and the pretty white flowers of the wild garlic, or, as it is called by the local name of "ramps," a plant that has an intolerable stench. Although it was esteemed in early times so beneficial to health, that one of our oldest proverbs say:—

> "Eat leeks in Lide, and ramsins in May,
> And all the year after physitians' may play."

For some distance its mossy waters wimple along by the edge of Roughlee wood, which is as famous for its nuts as the banks of the stream is for its adders. On one occasion as two lads were fishing in the burn, they disturbed a large adder lying coiled up, basking in the sun. When the reptile began to shew its disapprobation in a truly vituperative manner—darting here and there, all the while making a peculiar hissing noise. On being attacked by the lads with sticks, the adder glided rapidly towards the stream, and, plunging into a pool, swam across, with its venomous head erect—in the same fashion the sea serpent is usually portrayed in our illustrated papers after one of the periodical visits of the sea monster—taking shelter under a stone on the opposite bank. The plucky lads, determined not to lose their prey, gave pursuit, and, tying a penknife to the butt end of their fishing rod, pinned the reptile through the head just as it was peering forth to reconnoitre its position. When killed it measured over two feet. Seeking nuts in Roughlee wood is one of the pleasant memories of our boyhood, when with other happy romping school companions, we went a-nutting in the bright autumn days, by the special leave of Willie Haning, the woodman, who, for nearly fifty years, held that post under the Swinburns, whose care it was to shew his favoured proteges the hazel glades, where the best laden bushes were; and woe betide the hapless youth found within the precincts of Roughlee without the permission of the old woodman—his hoard of hardly-earned nuts were ruthlessly taken from him, and appropriated by the forester as his lawful spoil, and distributed afterwards amongst his own particular friends. Having baskets, bags, and "pillow slips" filled with nuts, we, on our homeward way, frequently called at the house of George and Bessie Sanderson, who lived at Thrunton tilery. George was a curious character, and a great snuffer. He was for many years manager of Thrunton tile-works, where thousands of draining pipes were annually made during the time the Eslington estate was being thoroughly drained. One of George's men, Hughie Chambers, a Scotchman, was another character. Hughie very often went home—especially on pay nights—three sheets in the wind. Late one Saturday night he entered his house his thirst still unquenched, therefore going, as he expected, to the water mug for a drink of that liquid as a last resource, he fell, and in falling clutched at the jar and brought it down with him. The jar, however, happened to be full of newly-made black currant jam, and there lay the huge form of Hughie on the broad of his back covered with black currant jam, calling loudly on Mary, his wife, for help, all the time imagining that something worse had befallen him, for he was sure "he had brussen." Thrunton also lay on the way home, and it was our own fault if we passed by the farm-house of the Stephenson's, the quaint old rambling farm-house, under whose hospitable roof there was always a Northumbrian welcome from Mr. and Mrs. Stephenson. Then followed a glorious tea, with girdle cakes, thick cream and fresh churned butter—Thrunton butter! Thrunton was notable in those days for its kirn and its fire! Many can yet remember of the disastrous fire which occurred in 1855, when the barn and fodder house were completely gutted—said to have been the work of "Fire Wull." Well do we recollect of the midnight alarm and the exciting run through the fields to Thrunton, carrying with us everyone a "tin can" or a bucket—the bands of willing workers, augmented by a score or two of country lads and lasses from the "merry night" at the "Buston Arms," which had been brought to a sudden close by the alarm that "Thrunton was a-fire," the dancers hastening to the scene, regardless of their white muslin dresses, white stockings, and patent leather slippers, where they carried water from the village pond, ever and anon, during breathing time, having a sly word or two with their rustic swains—their festive apparel, shewing its whiteness in the glare of the flaming onstead, adding a somewhat weird and picturesque effect to the dreadful sight of an incendiary fire.

> "Eslington for bonny lasses,
> Callaly for craws,
> Whittingham for white bread,
> THRUNTON for Faws."
>
> —*Old Rhyme.*

CHAPTER XVI.

FOLK LORE.

Local Place Names—Local Events—Village Games and Rhymes—Old Villagers—"Fire Wull"—Coquetdale Rangers—Eslington Rent—Nicknames—The Old Vicar, R. W. Goodenough—"Low Church" Views—His Love of Jokes—His Parish Clerk—Musical Tastes—Wedding Customs.

UNDER the general term of folk lore shall be given local place names, local associations, and sketches of village characters, which some of our readers may be tempted to call mere trifles; but it is these very trifles, telling of the manners and customs of past generations, that will help the future historian in compiling his history of the people. Therefore, folk lore is now a subject of study and enquiry, a society, known as the Folk Lore Society, having been established in 1868 for that purpose.

"Up afore Piles as far as the Lonnin" is the road to Whittingham Lane in front of the Castle Inn.

"The tree i' the Lyen" is a fine old ash tree standing on the east side of the lane that leads to the Castle Inn. This tree, the survivor of four that once stood in the lane—two on each side—is upwards of eighty feet high.

The "back lonnin" is the Callaly road, which goes up the village, past the "short lonnin end" and up the "Kiln Bank," by the side of "Waterman's Field" to the "White Knowe"—a moorland field on the south side of the road at the Callaly "Mairch Dyke," just at the entrance to Callaly Avenue.

The road from Whittingham Tower to Eslington might be described thus: "Doon the brae an' ower the witter, up past the Chorch an' through the witter at the heed i' the toon, bye Sprittle Dowes, the Two Trees, the New Road End, an' up through the Pairk ;" while the road to Glanton would be—"Across the styen bridge, bye the Hole-i'-the-Waa', on past Hawklemass, the Howbalk Road End, the Lonnin Hoose, the Rothill, the Pound, an' the Camp Hills."

The farm-house next to the Castle Inn was at one time known as the "Ark." Several families lived in it then, and the number of men, women, and children that daily came out and went in over its well-trodden threshold no doubt gave origin to the name. Then there were two cottages connected with the farm, near to the burn side, called the "Havannah ;" and an open ditch, that in our early days ran through the middle of the village on the south side, rejoiced in the extraordinary title of the "Goat"[1]—a name that puzzled many a stranger. This ditch or gutter was said to have derived its name from the circumstance of a goat having once gone up the "cundy" (conduit), when, getting fast by the horns, it could get neither back nor forward, and was suffocated. The "Goat" was the favourite resort of the village children—especially after a heavy rain—whose great delight consisted in cutting sods from off the village green and therewith making a dam across the "Goat," thus forming a nice big pond, which caused the water to run out of the channel over the main road. Frequently was the sport turned into fear and sudden flight when the cry of alarm was raised—"There's Jim Wulson!" James Wilson was the roadman, who lived at High Barton, and many an hour's extra labour poor Jim had in clearing away the sod dykes, and in cleaning out the "cundy," which always got stopped up, the result of the continued dam-building of "them idle scoonderells," as he called the boys.

The river Aln is a quiet, rather sluggish running stream,

---

[1] "GOTE (North Northumberland)—a stream of water approaching the sea through sand or slake." Also "GUT—a narrow stream."—Northumberland Words, R. O. Heslop.

winding its way through level green haughs, where it has cut for itself a deep channel in the rich alluvial soil, its banks fringed with Alders, Willows, the broad flag of the Yellow Iris, the Great Hairy Willow Herb, Bur-reed, and the large Rhubarb-like leaves of the Butter Bur.[1] After heavy rains amongst the hills, the little burn comes down a "red flood," overflowing its banks and covering the haughs with water to a great extent. Formerly it was quite a common custom amongst the rural population of Northumberland to take unusual occurrences—such as "The Drifty Year" (1823), "The Drouthy Year" (1826), "Thunnery Monday," "Windy Monday," and the like—as data by which they could calculate the time when other minor incidents had happened. Even the floods in our own little Aln had their special names. One was referred to for many years as "The Eslington Ball Flood," for on that memorable night there was a magnificent ball given at Eslington Park by the late Lord Ravensworth, to which all the gentry in the district were invited, when, after a day's heavy rain, such a volume of water came down the Aln as to render the fords impassible. Therefore the carriages conveying the guests to and from Eslington had to go, some round by Callaly, others round by Mountain and Howbalk, not being able to get through the Aln at the Whittingham ford. "Albert's Flood" was another notable flood in the annals of Whittingham, which occurred on the wedding day of Mr. Albert Errington, chief forester to the late Lord Ravensworth, on the 25th of September, 1851. This was a day long remembered by the employees on the Eslington estate, with whom the bride and bridegroom were held in high esteem. Neither did the youth of the village soon forget it, or the "scammelling" of the pennies amongst the "glar" on the way from church. For many years after, this flood was spoken of as "Albert's Flood."

[1] Locally known as "Allers," "Wullies," "Segges," "Apple Dumplins," and "Monk's Rhubarb."

During the hot days of summer, dozens of merry school-boys might have been seen disporting themselves like so many porpoises in the Aln at the dinner hour in the various bathing holes "up the Leaside" and down "Ross's Haugh," diving from the "brae edge," or learning to swim on bundles of "segges," utterly regardless in the midst of their enjoyment, of the flight of time, and often, very often, were the said bathers late for school, when, for this most serious breach of discipline, the kind-hearted master, much against his will, would give the whole batch four "pandies," two on each hand. "Dookin'" was only practised by those not brave enough to bathe, or go overhead in the water; but "plodin'" was indulged in by all, and the great feat amongst the school lads and lasses was to plode or wade to the "big stone"—a large boulder lying in deep water in the middle of the burn. Catching "lyars,'" "streamers," and "barnacles," by sticking them with a fork or pocket-knife underneath the stones in shallow streams, or dragging eels from amongst the "eel beds"[1] —many of them eighteen inches and two feet in length, as well as a smaller sort known as "niney eels," which was thought to have nine eyes, and to have originated from horse hair—were amongst the very chiefest summer delights of the old Whittingham lads. The winter games were "Warney," "Dumper," "Moont the Cuddy, one, two, three"—local games difficult to describe—"Hunt the Hare," and "Football." The latter was played on Easter Monday, in the "Charity Grass" or "Pallister's Haugh," at other times in "Pile's Field"; while "Kitty Cat and Buckstick" was played in the "Little Croft."

Amongst the girls' out-door games were the following :—

> "Hisket a hasket,
> Buy a penny basket;
> One a penny, two a penny—
> Turn round the cheeses."

---

[1] Water Crowfoot *(Ranunculus aquatilis.)*

Another :—

" Here's a poor widow from Sandiland,
With all her children in her hand;
The one can bake, the other can brew,
The other can make a lily white dough;
One can sit by the fire and spin,
The other can make a bed for the King.
Please take one of my daughters in."

The old game, "Through the needle eye," was played under the name of :—

" Blankets and sheets !
Blankets and sheets !"

Other favourite games for fine weather were "Hippy beds," "Chucks," and "Keppy baa.'"

"Foxey" was an exciting out-door game very popular with both the girls and boys of Whittingham, in playing which the following rhyme was used :—

" Foxey ! Foxey ! Foomilerie,
How many miles to Boomilerie ?
Eight an' eight, an' other eight.
Will aa' get there by candle light ?
Reply—Oh ! yes, and back again."

"Jenny Lingo" and "My Daughter Jane" were also games at which the girls played : the rhyme of the latter was some-like the following :—

" Here are three knights just out of Spain,
Who come to court your daughter Jane.

My daughter Jane is far too young;
She cannot learn the Spanish tongue.

If she be either young or old,
For her beauty she must be sold.
Then fare thee well my lady gay,
We will call again another day.

Turn back, turn back, ye gallant knights,
And take the fairest one you see.

This is the fairest one I see;
Therefore, come and follow me.

Here comes your daughter, safe and sound,
In every pocket a thousand pounds,
On every finger a guinea gold ring;
Please to take your daughter in."

Whittingham school was built in 1849-50, and it is amongst the first recollections of the writer of standing looking on while Tom Watson, the mason, carved the letters H. T. L., the date, 1850, with a lion rampant (the Ravensworth crest) in the centre, on the tablet inserted in the south gable, about which we had the following rhyme :—

" Henry Thomas Liddell
The lion in the middle.
Eighteen hundred an' fifty."

There was usually a " bubbly jock " in Ross's stackyard, of which, as children, we were much afraid ; yet notwithstanding the remonstrances of old Bella Heslop, we used to venture in, and, going as near to the turkey cock as we dare, vex it by shouting :—

" Bubbly Jock ! sauter ! sauter ! sauter !
Bubbly Jock ! sauter ! sauter !"

" Morry's ganer" was the dread of all the village youngsters, for with a serpent-like hiss, and a run, it could put the bravest to flight. On one occasion he seized and knocked down a little girl, then stood upon her, pecking and flapping his wings in a most triumphant manner, until he was driven off. Another time a boy was flying from his clutches, when the gander caught him by the seat of his trousers, and a most comical " tug of war " took place ; but a bigger lad took the gander by the neck and swung him three or four times round, which completely disconerted the web-footed tyrant. " Whitey ! Whitey ! " and " Philey " were the usual calls for gathering the flocks of geese from off the village green. Mrs. Dickinson, the good-wife of the farmer, was famed for her flocks of geese and her poultry, for which she required extensive accommodation. Many years ago, a curious half-witted old woman, a native of Whittingham, called Nanny Trummell, was seen parading up and down the village, announcing in a loud voice —" Hurrah ! Hurrah ! for Morry Dickison's gettin' a new hen hoose."

Some forty years ago, the favourite places of rendezvous for the lads in the village during the long dark nights of winter, or on a stormy Saturday, were the "Blacksmith's shop" in the days of Robert Clark, then William Rogerson, and now his son, John Rogerson; the shop of Willie Suthren, the joiner, who was succeeded by his son, Joseph Suthren, the present occupier, where there was always something to interest the juvenile mind; the shop of Jim Chambers, the shoemaker—the greatest tease in the village, but withal a friend of the boys—where, by the light of the naphtha lamp, Robert the herd used to read aloud from the weekly newspaper the dreadful details of the Crimean War; and the workshop of Christopher Thompson, the cooper, whom we are glad to record as a resident in Whittingham to this day, and to whom we gratefully acknowledge our indebtedness for much valuable information kindly given respecting the old tower. Pleasant are the recollections we have of many happy hours spent in "Kit the Cooper's" shop, where, sitting by the warm stove on a cold wintry night, we played game after game at "checkers," the cooper, himself a noted player, occasionally giving his advice as to the next best move. The only conditions imposed upon us youngsters by the good-natured tradesman was "not to make a noise, and to keep the fire on," and then we might stay as long as we wished to.

In those happy old times of our forefathers, before this age of worry and high pressure, long accounts were run in the books of the village tradesman, and monetary transactions were conducted in a somewhat primitive and patriarchal fashion, not exactly in keeping with our modern ideas of business; yet the following shows the great confidence there then existed between friends and neighbours:—Two tradesmen in the village, old and fast friends, both of an easy-going disposition, had contra accounts, which now-a-days would have been squared at least once a year; but this settling day with them was constantly put off until a more convenient season, so after many years, by mutual consent, they agreed to settle this long account by amicably shaking hands over the affair, and then make a fresh start, which they accordingly did.

Like all villages, there were many curious squibs and rhymes current amongst the children, which, although not altogether peculiar to Whittingham, we here relate. At that period farm servants were mostly paid in kind, therefore their corn, which they received as wages, had to be ground at the Mill. The local mills then in use were Bolton, Abberwick, Edlingham, and Thrunton, so when the Miller—the "Poker," as he was termed—came through the village with his cart, laden with the "batches" he had ground for his customers, he was often hailed by a chorus of voices shouting—

> "Millery! millery! moonty poke!
> Put in your hand an' steal a loke."[1]

This referred to an old custom, the "mouter,"[2] by which the Miller paid himself for grinding the corn.

On Alnwick fair day, when the west-country people were returning home from the fair at night, when the village green was the playground of the children, their ears were greeted with :—

> "Fair folks! fair folks! gies wor fair,
> Yor pockets is ripe an' wors is bare."

If at any time a few sea gulls were seen flying up the valley—a sign of stormy weather—the shout was quickly raised :—

> "Sea gull! sea gull! sit i' the sand;
> Its never gudweather when yor i' the land."

When a heavy shower of snow fell—especially if the first of the season, and the snowflakes large, it was welcomed by the children with general delight :—

---

[1] A small quantity.

[2] "Multure—the Miller's wages, taken in kind; as a quart for grinding a bushel, or a bushel for grinding a quarter. Two different multures were formerly used: the "gowpenful"—that is, two handsful; and the "handful"—a term which explains itself. In more recent times the *mooter* allowed was more clearly defined, though each mill had its own scale of charges. The miller's portion is also called a *mooterin*."—Northumberland Words, by R. O. Heslop.

"The folk i' the East are plotin' their geese,
An' sendin' their feathers to huz."

"Billy, Billy burstie, whe speaks furstie!"

often said by children when they had something nice to give to their companions.

The following was a very popular old rhyme:—

"Eslington for bonny lasses,
Callaly for craws,
Whittingham for white bread,
Thrunton for faws."

The only ghost Whittingham possesses, or did possess, was the "Hawklemass Ghost," whose reputed haunt was a lonely spot on the Glanton road, near to the Howbalk Lane end, where is also the "Hawklemass Stile" and the "Hawklemass Well." This was a place never passed after nightfall by the youth of the village without feeling an eerie, creepy sensation, and with many a furtive glance on either side. This unearthly visitant, in its gambols and uncanny pranks, was said to rattle the chain by which it was supposed to be bound in a fearsome manner. It was usually seen or heard by persons who, having lingered long at the village inn, could say with "Tam o' Shanter":—

"While we sit bousing at the nappy,
An' gettin' fou and unco happy,
We think na on the lang Scots miles,
The mosses, waters, slaps, and styles
That lie between us and our hame."

One Saturday night many years ago—perhaps fifty—a poor fellow on his way from Whittingham to Glanton fell into the roadside ditch at "Hawklemass," where he was found, quite dead, the next morning by some persons on their way to "Glanton meeting." This sad affair may have given rise to the tradition of the "Hawklemass Ghost."

There lived in Whittingham, during the first half of the present century, a notorious character, whose name was held in as much dread as the "Hawklemass Ghost," and that was

Wull Trummell, who was also known throughout the district as "Fire Wull," a nickname deservedly acquired from the number of stackyards and farm onsteads he was said to have fired.

William Turnbull was born and brought up in Whittingham. When a lad he was of a most sullen and morose temper, and early showed his malicious and revengeful disposition. In a frenzy of passion, he once seized a child by the feet and dashed the poor little thing against a wall, and, but for the interference of some other boys, he would have killed the child outright. Another of his early exploits was that of cutting the ivy which the vicar, the Rev. Edmund Law, had been at some trouble to plant around the old church tower. Wull had heard the vicar give instructions to old Betty Stirling to be sure and water the newly-planted ivy every morning. This was too good a chance for Wull to miss; he owed the vicar a grudge for some fancied affront, and to vex poor old Betty was to him a special delight. Therefore, watching his opportunity, he carefully removed the soil, cut the ivy roots, and again replacing the soil, thus hid all traces of the deed; then with that cunning laugh of his, which those who knew him will well remember, he daily watched the assiduous Betty engaged in the fruitless task of watering the ivy, and heard also the daily scoldings the poor old woman had to endure from the vicar for her seeming neglect. As the ivy gradually faded and withered, so the worthy vicar's anger increased. However, on examining the roots, the cause was soon apparent, and Mr. Law at once knew who had done the malicious trick. The Rev. R. W. Goodenough succeeded the Rev. Edmund Law, upon whom also Wull's grudge fell, and one night the quiet villagers were aroused from their slumbers by a splendid bonfire—

"April 20, 1839.—Two stacks of hay and one of straw, belonging to the Rev. Robert Goodenough, vicar of Whittingham, were destroyed by fire, and there is every reason to believe that it was the act of an incendiary."—*Local Records.*

Shortly after this followed the Priests' Hemmel, and one morning when Dickinson's kilnmen went to their work at Whitton Lea kiln, not a tool could be found! Picks, shovels, planks, and wheelbarrows, all had disappeared. But the mystery was soon cleared up, for the ironwork came out at the kiln eye when drawing the lime. Who had done this? They need not ask! After a lapse of several years a destructive fire at Thrunton showed that Wull was again on the war-path; and in the autumn of 1856, when the stack-garth was well filled, there was a magnificent conflagration at the Rothill, near Whittingham, when no less than twenty-seven stacks and the barns were ablaze at one time. Wull was taken on suspicion of having been the cause of the fire, and brought before the magistrates in "Pile's Big Room," but as nothing could be proved against him, he was acquitted. We well remember, being amongst a batch of other schoolboys, looking eagerly in at the open window of the "big room" whilst Wull was being examined by the magistrates—the late Lord Ravensworth, the Rev. R. W. Goodenough, and Mr. F. J. W. Collingwood. His pocket-book underwent a most scrutinizing search, but the entries therein could not be deciphered; meanwhile, Wull stood looking on with a disdainful leer in his repulsive countenance. Wull Trummell died an inmate of Rothbury Workhouse in January, 1881, in his 75th year.

Two old troopers of the Coquetdale Rangers—a troop of Volunteer Cavalry raised during the great French War of 1793 to 1815—lived in Whittingham. These were George Henderson, tailor, and George Vint, saddler, both of whom lived to an advanced age, respected by all who knew them. It was always great fun for the village lads—the writer being often one of the number—to stand in a row on the village green and be drilled like soldiers by George Vint, the Coquetdale Ranger, who put them through a drill after his own fashion, and very much he enjoyed the display. But the great performance of the old trooper generally took place at the Eslington Rent Dinner, which was held at the Castle Inn, when, for the amusement of the company, he would get astride a chair and, with a stick, go through all the cavalry cuts and guards, now and then in his excitement giving the luckless wight nearest to him a good sound whack over the head, which added to the fun. The only time Trooper Vint drew blood was when he accidentally shot himself in the leg with his own carbine. The poor old man was often annoyed by the village children shouting after him—

"Reed back'd bummeller,
Cock-tail'd tummeller.
Fire-side soldier,
Darna gan te war."

About the same time, there also attended at the Eslington Rent Dinner, a well-known stock farmer from the foot of the Cheviots—Andrew Armstrong, of Blakehope, on Breamish Water. Andrew always sang the same song, without any regard to the musical gamut. We can remember only a fragment of this song:—

"There was a fox in yonder wud,
Upon his hinder legs he stud,
He thought a bit flesh wad de him gud."
. . . .

For many generations there have been Armstrongs at Blakehope. Old George Armstrong (Andrew's father), held it a hundred years ago; and at the present day a great-grandson of Old George's fills the place of his great-grandfather. It was said that old George had such a dread of three things that he never failed to mention them in his prayers, thus:—"Frae the sword, the heuk heft, an' the gallace, may the Lord deliver us!" viz.:—from war, shearing, and the gallows.

A bevy of farmers living in and around Whittingham used to congregate at the Castle Inn, in the days of Adam Pile. These gentlemen were on the most intimate terms with each other, and there existed amongst them that good old-fashioned type of friendship, duly kept warm with friendly visits and social intercourse. These worthies amused themselves by having nicknames for each other, by which they usually addressed and spoke of one another. With all due regard to their memories, for they were gentlemen, very much respected, we venture to give as many as we can remember :—

John Coull, of the Rothill, was "Paddy."
Adam Pile, of the Castle Inn—"Old Roderick."
James Ross, of Whittingham—"Lord Kelburne."
James Rea Nicholson, of Yetlington Lane—"The Colonel."

In the *coterie* were also—

John Stephenson, of Thrunton.
Thomas Swanson, of Thrunton Mill.
Luke Weatheritt, of Whittingham.
William Colville, of Yetlington.
Robert Swan, of Eslington Low Hill.
Dr. Henry Crea, of Glanton.

Many were the practical jokes they played upon each other. James Ross had the greatest horror of vermin and reptiles. On one occasion, Adam Pile and Dr. Henry Crea accompanied James Ross into the harvest field, to see how the "shearing," under the vigilant eye of "Jimmy the Stewart," was progressing. As they followed the shearers on the harvest rig, Dr. Crea espied a frog amongst the stubble; this he picked up unobserved, and, knowing Mr. Ross's failing, he quietly dropped it into his snuff box pocket, knowing that the old Scotchman would presently want a snuff. In a few minutes the "sneesh" was required; and when Mr. Ross dug to the bottom of his deep outside coat pocket for his snuff box, he suddenly gave the most dreadful yell—his fingers having gripped the cold frog instead of his favourite "mull." Mr. Ross being a very stout old gentlemen, made unavailing struggles, amid much strong language, to divest himself of his coat, but only succeeded in getting his arms half out of the sleeves, and there he stuck in the greatest terror and alarm, pinioned as fast as if in the folds of a strait jacket, until Dr. Crea came to the rescue. For long after, Mr. Ross's adventure with the "paddock" was often related as a good joke.

A very curious-tempered old man, named George Sanderson, then had Thrunton tile works. George never failed, as Saturday night came round, to put in an appearance at the Castle Inn, where he frequently remained until a late hour. On his way home he had to go round by Thrunton Crag End—a lonely bit of the old coach road, with a dark fir plantation on one side, a wide stretch of moorland on the other, the reputed haunt of a ghost—withal a dreary spot on a dark night. One Saturday night, before George started on his nocturnal journey homewards, some of the company said: "George, ye'll see the Crag End Ghost the night." "Aa' divvent care if aa' saw the deevil," sulkily replied George, as he sat on the "long settle" in Pile's kitchen, with his glass before him, enjoying the warmth of the blazing fire, trying to screw up the courage to enable him to venture forth on his lonely walk. Meanwhile, an idle village wag, having heard George's boastful reply, slipped out at the inn door, and quietly brought a young donkey along the passage into the kitchen, and stood it close to George's elbow. The fear depicted in poor George's countenance, when he suddenly turned himself round and saw close to him the enormous face and lugs of the cuddy, cannot be described; whilst the strong verbal expressions of fear and anger that issued from his lips are not to be found in any ordinary dictionary. George was fully under the impression that his foolish boast had brought its own reward, and that, in very truth, it was the visage of his Satanic Majesty that he beheld.

One other personage we must notice in this chapter on Village Folk Lore. For forty-five years the Rev. Robert William Goodenough was vicar of Whittingham. When he first came to the parish, in 1835, he was greatly exercised—

being a Yorkshireman by birth—to understand the Northumbrian "burr," and nothing amused him more than to hear the "Whuttinjim" vernacular pure and simple.

On Sunday mornings it was generally his custom to be at church long before service time, greeting his parishioners and asking after their welfare as they entered the church. Every man, woman, and child throughout the length and breadth of the parish were known to the vicar, and he could at any moment tell their names, ages, and occupation. Occasionally, when two or three children came to the church door, he would hold it fast on the inside, keeping them outside in the porch until they shouted through the big keyhole, "Wise uz in."[1] This expression, as well as its counterpart, "Wise uz oot," always afforded him a hearty laugh.

One of the churchwardens—the late John Coull, of the Rothill—and the vicar were great friends. John was a brusque, plain-spoken Northumbrian, and, for the entertainment of his south-country visitors, the vicar frequently took them to see Mr. Coull at his farm, when the old practical farmer was sure to delight him by expatiating, in his mother tongue, on the advantages to be derived from the liberal use of manure. "Aa' put on a lot i' muck," John would say; "there's nowt like muck —plenty i' gud muck, sor."

Mr. Goodenough was what is termed a low churchman, and very much disliked innovations, or "new-fangled notions," as he called them; and although from the very first he went so far as to turn his face to the east when repeating the Creed, he long held out against the practice of preaching in the surplice, which was then (1840 to 1850) considered the mark of a high churchman.

The Hon. and Rev. Robert Liddell, vicar of St. Paul's, Wilton Place, when staying at Eslington Park with his brother, the late Lord Ravensworth, frequently assisted Mr.

[1] Let us in.

Goodenough in the service, and one Sunday morning gave great umbrage to the Evangelical vicar by preaching in his surplice; but, towards the close of his ministry, even the low church vicar laid aside his old black gown and preached in the surplice. He was of an extremely sensitive, irritable temperament, and during divine service could not tolerate the least movement or noise in church. One Sunday evening, whilst he was preaching, some unruly boys sitting in a corner of the gallery disturbed him very much, so, casting a stern look at the culprits, he sat down in the pulpit, with the remark—"I shall sit down until you boys up in the gallery can be quiet." No other reproof was needed, for after that there was good behaviour in the gallery. If he noticed a child rather restless, he would stop in the service, and say, "Sit still, my girl," or "Sit still, my boy;" and he was once heard to tell one of his congregation, who was listening most intently to his sermon, 'Don't stare at me like that." And another time, when out of all patience with the behaviour of a boy, he made a full stop, and exclaimed, "Whinham, put that boy out," waiting until the boy was put out and the person had returned to his pew. He disliked anyone who had a cough to come to church, and once gave great offence to poor George Vint, one of the most regular attendants at Whittingham Church. George enjoyed the singing of the hymns very much. His favourite was the 136th Psalm, which was set on the barrel organ to the tune "Darwell," P.M.; this old George sang with might and main. George once had a very bad cold, and annoyed Mr. Goodenough with his constant coughing, so when the service was ended, the vicar hurried up the middle aisle—Mr. Goodenough always came straight out of the pulpit and up the church to the vestry amongst his congregation—and waiting for George as he came round from the north transept, where he sat, he said to him, "George, you should'nt come to church when you have such a cold; you sat cough, cough, coughing, during the whole sermon." Two or three

Sundays after, the rev. gentleman himself had a cold, and could scarcely preach for coughing, so old George remarked to a neighbour on the way home from church, "how would Mr. Goodenough like it if I had said to him, Mr. Goodenough you should'nt come to church when you have such a cold; you could scarcely preach for cough, cough, coughing;" but the vicar was not a man to play pranks with, therefore George did not venture the remark. Mr. Goodenough was an excellent preacher, and seldom exceeded twenty minutes. Often on warm drowsy summer afternoons, when the service was at three o'clock, he would look at his watch, and say to himself in an audible whisper, "six minutes," and rarely preached longer. He said he felt sorry for the poor people sitting nodding and sleeping in their pews. Occasionally he forgot his sermon, and would thus announce the fact to his congregation:—"My dear friends, I find I have come without my sermon, therefore we won't have one to-day." A frequent expression of his in the pulpit was "depend upon it;" and when he made any startling statement, "what do you think of that?" He had a keen sense of the ludicrous, and was full of humour, yet in some points he was austere, and required from those under him the strictest obedience to his orders. Ned Hudson, the parish clerk, was the only person who could ever outwit him. On one occasion there was a week-day service. Mr. Goodenough was in a hurry, and in reading the Psalms—a duty which the vicar and his clerk performed, by reading verse and verse about—he, without any warning, missed several verses, leaving the clerk to find out for himself which verse he had to read. Ned, who was very sharp, soon found his place, and read his verse in due order, but after the vicar read his next verse, Ned took his turn at "skipping," which caused the vicar to flounder about amongst the verses of the Psalm, until he found where his clerk had gone to. After service, the irate parson said "Edward, what business had you to miss the verses in the Psalm?" "Well, sir," replied the clerk, "I thought I had as much right to miss them as ye had!" "Well! well! Edward," said Mr. Goodenough, "We must'nt do that sort of thing again."

The vicar was highly amused at another trick his parish clerk once played. As we have already remarked, Ned was an excellent musician, and was in great request at merry nights and dances. He was fiddling at a dance one night in the Castle Inn, when he delighted the dancers very much with a new waltzing tune. On being asked what tune that was, he gave a funny laugh, and, playing the waltz very slowly over, it was found to be one of the church hymn tunes, played in quick time.

Whilst some alterations were being made in Whittingham Church, a piscina was discovered in one of the transepts. This interesting relic of pre-Reformation times was cleared out, and left *in situ*. Mr. Goodenough, always fond of a joke, said he would lay a wager with his churchwarden that a certain old gentleman who sat in that part of the church would, as sure as Sunday came round, put his hat in the piscina. Accordingly, on Sunday morning the vicar watched for the entrance of the worthy old man, who went to his seat, and perceiving for the first time the curious opening, he deliberately deposited his "long hat" in the convenient recess, and continued to do so Sunday after Sunday, at which the vicar was in high glee.

In time Mr. Goodenough became very fond of Whittingham and its people. He used to remark, when telling how long he had been vicar, that R. W. Goodenough came in 1835, Adam Pile in 1836, and William Dixon in 1837. As a native of the singing county of Yorkshire, he had an idea that Northumbrians could not open their mouths to sing. He did, however, eventually try them, and used to teach the choir himself. During the intervals at practice he frequently entertained his choir with telling them funny stories, of which he had any amount. Once, when trying over a chant to the

133rd Psalm, he stopped the choir at the end of the second verse, and, much to their amusement, expressed his disgust at the greasy, dirty state Aaron must. have been in with the ointment; whilst his letter of congratulation to a newly-wedded friend, whose name happened to be David, was characteristic of the man—"Lord remember David, and all his trouble." His idea of the harmony of a tune seldom agreed with that of the composer. We possess his organ copy of "Hymns Ancient and Modern" (1861 edition), and there is scarcely a chant or hymn that has not been considerably altered and "improved." It was only certain hymns that he would allow his choir to sing; and if a chant did not please him, he thought nothing of composing a new one straight off to suit his purpose. Some of his pencil note remarks in the old hymn book are so very amusing that we venture to quote them :—

Hymn 23 (Eisenach). "A runaway tune."
,, 84 (Vexilla Regis). "Certainly not."
,, 92 (Caswall). "Very nice."
,, 97 (Passion Chorale). "Oh dear no !"
,, 106 (St. Fulbert). "Tune good; lines bad."
,, 120 (Rogation Litany). "Worse and worse."
,, 123 (Bishop). "Bad tune."
,, 136 (Old Hundreth). "Bad setting of Old 100th."
,, 142 Part i. (St. Alphege). "Popular, but vulgar tune."
,, 142 Part iii. (Ewing). "Super-horrible."
,, 149 (Westminster). "Too high and too low; by my old friend Turle, of Westminster Abbey."
,, 167 (Old 44th). "Worse and worse."
,, 194 (Jam lucis). "Rot."
,, 221 (Dies Iræ). "Horrible."
,, 230 (St. Cecilia). "Super-horrible."
,, 237 (Ein'feste Burg). "This tune is like a wheelbarrow."

Whilst others are endorsed with "yes," "better," "good,' "' too high," "awkward bass," "blasphemous."

Mr. Goodenough died in 1880, when the following obituary notice appeared in the *Newcastle Daily Journal* of October 23rd, 1880 :—

"The deceased gentleman was educated at Westminster and Christ Church, Oxford, was presented to the living of Whittingham in June, 1835, by his uncle, Edmund Goodenough, Dean of Wells and Prebend of Carlisle, and was inducted on July 11th, 1835. He died on Thursday morning, at the Vicarage, Whittingham, the place he loved so well, after having held the living for the long term of forty-five years. During this period many improvements have been effected both in church and vicarage, chiefly through his instrumentality, and under his own supervision and direction. In 1840, the church was restored; in 1871, the chancel was rebuilt by the late Earl of Ravensworth; and within the last few years the whole of the church has been restored. Mr. Goodenough was well known and respected throughout the whole parish by all denominations. He made a point of being personally acquainted with every one in his parish, and could at any time tell the name, age, and circumstances of even the most obscure person in the most outlying hamlet. He was an able scholar and eloquent preacher, his preaching being in a style peculiarly his own. His sermons were original, and full of deep thought, forcible argument, and lucid illustrations. He was a great favourite, and a frequent guest of the county families, where his rich fund of humour and quick repartee made him a most sociable visitor. In his daily walk also he was pleasant and kind, either with his equals or the lowest peasant in his parish, and his death is much regretted by all."

The old wedding customs of Whittingham, which may also be classed under the term folk lore, are amusing, and will form a fitting conclusion to this chapter. Some five-and-twenty or thirty years ago, the custom of jumping a bride over the "petting stone," was observed at Whittingham in the following manner:—As soon as the wedding party were safely inside the church, the doors were closed, and the young men of the village proceeded to erect the "petting stone" within the porch, immediately in front of the church door. This obstacle, despite the incongruity of the articles, consisted of three short stone pillars, which, at one time, had been the supports of an old "trough" tombstone. These were placed Stonehenge fashion—two supports and one crosswise—and two of the most sprightly amongst the young men, very often personal friends of the bride and bridegroom, stood ready to jump the bride over the petting stone. These two gallants waited patiently in the porch, keeping "watch and ward," by "keeking" through the keyhole, until the ceremony was concluded, when so soon as the marriage had been duly entered in the parish register, and the priest was seen coming from the vestry, the church doors were thrown open. Then came the bridal party, when the two guards immediately seized the bride, one on each side, and jumped her over the petting stone. The bridegroom and the rest of the party were next vaulted over in the same vigorous fashion, while each of the ladies were saluted with a hearty kiss from the two knights of the petting stone. If the fair young bride was foolish enough to demur, and with pouting lips and frowning face object to the ordeal, she was said to have taken the pet, and her conduct was the theme of much gossip amongst the villagers, who one and all agreed that her husband would have a sorry life with her. When all the party had got safely over the barrier, it was customary for the bridegroom to give a fee to the two young fellows who had taken so prominent a part in the proceedings. This money was reserved until the evening, when all who had assisted at the out-door ceremonies—the petting stone, the wedding guns, firing the "studdies," and other noisy demonstrations of joy common on such festive occasions, repaired to the village inn, and there, amid music and innocent merriment, the evening and the money both, were spent in drinking to the health and happiness of the newly wedded couple.

The village inn was at that time kept by good old Adam Pile, whose well-known name, we feel sure, must ever awaken pleasing memories within the hearts of those who spent their early boyhood in the village of Whittingham, when Mr. Pile was landlord of the Castle Inn. Recollections of many a pocketful of the sweetest of apples, given us by the kind-hearted old man for going an errand for him, and of the ever ready and cheerfully given penny for working at "Pile's hay," are even yet bright spots in the remembrances of our youthful days.

In some instances whilst the nuptial knot was being tied inside the church, the door was being tied outside the church ;

and it was not until the bridal party had paid a sort of "blackmail" to the "freebooters" in the porch, by passing money through beneath the door, that they were allowed to come forth. The "petting stone" may be a relic of the ancient custom, which would not allow the bride to step over the threshold in entering the bridegroom's house, but was lifted over by her nearest relations.

Throwing of money amongst the village children is one of the most popular customs at a country wedding, and is one yet observed at the majority of weddings in Alndale, thereby earning for the newly married pair a good name with the children.

In certain villages within our ken, woe betide the luckless wedding party if they neglect to comply with this somewhat lavish custom of throwing money. Then are they accompanied, much against their will, from the very door of the church, through the village street by a crowd of youngsters bawling at the utmost pitch of their voices "a fardin' weddin'!" "a fardin' weddin'!!" "a fardin' weddin'!!!" On such an occasion we have known the bridal party beat a hasty retreat, and reach the welcome shelter of the nearest public house, where the bridegroom and the "best man," having obtained a supply of coppers, returned and scrambled them at the inn door, glad to purchase peace at any price from their youthful tormentors, who then at once changed their war-cry to "hurrah for the weddin'."

At Whittingham this custom was generally kept up at the period of which we are speaking. Directly the party had passed through the west gates of the churchyard, the bridegroom and the other gentlemen began to feel in their pockets. Then the youngsters knew there was going to be a "scammell," which they hailed with ringing shouts of applause; and as handful after handful of coppers were thrown out on the road amid dust or "glar," according to the state of the weather, there it was eagerly struggled for by a score or two of school children, resulting in many a damaged nose, torn pinafore, scratched faces, and bruised limbs. The bridal party, to prolong the entertainment, very often reserved some of their coppers until they arrived at the "Stone Bridge," if going east, or the "Eslington Ford," if going west, where they threw another handful or two into the burn, when the fun of seeing ten or a dozen hempy village laddies splashing and diving about in the waters of the Aln for the coppers afforded them much amusement, and in some measure repaid them for their liberality.

In those days there was no government "time-table" hanging on the walls of the village school, and the kindly master — William Ternent — usually allowed the scholars an hour's play whenever there was going to be a wedding. Therefore, what with the shouting of the children and the firing of the guns, the weddingers were certain of a hearty and noisy reception. Every man in the village who possessed a gun, pistol, or blunderbuss assembled at "Sitheren's gate" and "Dunn's corner," where they fired a *feu de joi*, blazing away with their heterogeneous weapons, volley after volley, not only at the risk of blowing out their own brains and those of their nearest neighbour, but scaring the horses and frightening all the women and bairns in the place; while from the "other side i' the witter" boomed the loud cannonade of the blacksmith's "studdies." The firing of the "studdies," or anvils, was a curious and rather a dangerous operation. The several square chisel holes usually found in a blacksmith's anvil were filled up with gunpowder, and a wedge of hardwood driven tightly into the aperture; a hole was then bored with a gimlet through the wooden plug and primed with dry powder. When the holes in the two or three anvils were thus loaded, they were placed in a row in front of the smithy, and fired with a long rod of iron heated red hot at one end.

During the days of the Commonwealth the law regarding the celebration of marriages was exceedingly strict, the ceremony being performed in accordance with the "Directory," the service book then in use, and amongst our Puritan ancestors it is very doubtful if there would be any rejoicing, such as we have described, even at so auspicious an event as a wedding.

The following extract from the "Whittingham Parish Register" shows how carefully the entry was made:—

"John Bell, senior, of Whittingham, and Anna Stot, of the Myle-house, both of this parish (after lawful publication three severall Sabbaths in the Parish Church), were married at Whittingham, by Mr. Hume, Minister of the plase the 17th day of May, 1659."

The publication of marriage banns is of very ancient origin. In Anglo-Saxon times it was customary to publish the banns at the church door as in earlier days it had been done at the "tun or moot," and now-a-days it has again become the fashion to be "called" instead of being married by license. There used to be a north country saying, respecting any one who had had the misfortune to be "called through the church" but never married, that they were "hanging in the bell ropes." Nelly Anderson, a crusty-tempered old woman, formerly lived in Whittingham with her brother, "Aad Jacky Annerson." Nellie's evil temper was always said to be owing to the fact that she was "hanging i' the bell ropes."

The custom of throwing an old shoe after a person is still in many districts believed to propitiate success, as in servants seeking or entering upon situations, or about to be married. But it may be questioned whether the old shoe has been thrown for luck only; and we are rather inclined to agree with Mr. Thrupp, in *Notes and Queries*, No. 182, that in Scripture "the receiving of a shoe was an evidence and symbol of asserting or accepting dominion or ownership: the giving back of a shoe the symbol of rejecting or resigning it." The latter is evidenced in Deut. xxv., where the ceremony of a widow rejecting her husband's brother in marriage is by loosing his shoe from off his foot; and in Ruth we see that "it was the custom in Israel concerning changing, that a man plucked off his shoe, and delivered it to his neighbour." Hence Mr. Thrupp suggests that "the throwing a shoe after a bride was a symbol of renunciation of dominion and authority over her by her father or guardian; and the receipt of the shoe by the bridegroom, even if accidental, was an omen that the authority was transferred to him." In Yorkshire the custom of throwing an old shoe over a wedding party is called *trashing*.

As the publishing of the banns, or being "called" in church, was the first, so the "Appearance" of the newly-married pair at church on the first Sunday after their marriage was, and is yet, in many north country parishes, the concluding public act in the wedding drama. Pleasing allusion is made to this in the following lines:—

> "Lo! where the hamlet's ivy'd Gothic tow'r
> With merry peals salutes the auspicious hour
> With sounds that thro' the cheerful village bear
> The happy union of some wedded pair.
> . . . .
> . . . .
> Now Sunday come, at stated hour of prayer,
> Or rain or shine, the happy couple there;
> Where nymphs and swains, in various colours dight,
> Gave pleasing contrast to the modest *white*."
>
> —"Happy Village."—Rowe.

"F for France and I for Jance,
And N for Nickley Boney,
I for John, the 'prentice boy,
And S for Sammy Coney."

FINIS.

APPENDIX.

ANNALS OF THE VALE:

A RECORD OF LOCAL EVENTS

FROM

1716 TO 1894.

GATHERED FROM THE OLD FILES OF THE "NEWCASTLE COURANT," "NEWCASTLE CHRONICLE," "NEWCASTLE JOURNAL," "ALNWICK MERCURY," "ALNWICK AND COUNTY GAZETTE," "SYKES' LOCAL RECORDS," AND VARIOUS OTHER SOURCES.

APPENDIX.

ANNALS OF THE VALE, 1716 TO 1894.

1716, September.—Michaelmas Sessions.—Foreasmuch as oath hath been made unto me this present day yt Willm. Dixson of Eslington, Miller, did on yesterday being the eight of this instant August, did assault and beat Margaret Collingwood wife of John Collingwood of ye same Town in very desprit manner so yt ye sd Margt Collingwood craves ye peace & good Behaviour against him ye sd Willm. Dixson. These are therefore in his Majsies. name to command you or one of you doe upon sight hereoft bring before me Willm. Dixson, or some other of his Majesties Justices of ye peace of this county with sufft securities for his personall appearance at ye next Quarter Sessions of the peace to be holden att Morpeth & in ye meane time yt he keep the peace and good behaviour towards his Majestie and all his liege people and especially towards ye sd John Collingwood & Margaret his wife which if he shall refuse to do ye then &c &c.

To all high and petty Constables &c &c.

(Signed) THOS. BURRELL.

This John Collingwood.

Dixson was apprehended & entered into a recognizance for his appearance to answer to the charge he being bound in 20£ & two sureties John Nicholson of Great Ryle & James Dinning of the same in 10£ each :—The matter appears to have been settled & the sureties exonerated.—October 3rd, 1716.

1720.—Eslington House, near Whittingham, was erected this year.

1728-9, March 22.—Newcastle-upon-Tyne, March 21.—The magistrates, clergy, and gentry of this town and county, having taken into their consideration the calamities which the poor house-keepers, &c., have been driven to by the length of this sharp winter season, unanimously agreed to collect for their relief, which was accordingly done, and attended by a bountiful benevolence, as appears by the account following:—

		£	s.	d.
Given by the Corporation		30	0	0
By Sir Henry Liddel		50	0	0
Gather'd by the Clergy of	St. Nicholas's	40	18	0
	St. John's	52	0	0
	All Saints'	76	0	0
	St. Andrew's	14	0	0

Private Charity, given by Sir Henry Liddel,		£	s.	d.
To the Parish of	St. Mary, Gateside	20	0	0
	Lamesly	20	0	0
	Wickham	20	0	0
	Eslington	20	0	0
Do. to the Hostmens Company for Keelmen		20	0	0
Total amount of Charity given		362	18	0

1728, May 11.—Stolen from Eslington, in the county of Northumberland, on the 22nd of April last, a light bay gelding, at or about 14 hands high, rising four years old. Natural pace'd, carries his head well, but a little thin-skirted behind. —And wheras a gelding answering all his descriptions was since seen in the possession of one John Miller, near Cockfield, in the neighbourhood of Barnard Castle, in the county of Durham, who, on Saturday, the 4th instant, went away from his said house with the said gelding, has not been since heard of, and there being the strongest suspicion that the said John Miller stole him from Eslington as aforesaid, all persons are desir'd to stop the said man and horse, or either of them, and give notice at Ravensworth Castle, and they shall be well rewarded for their trouble. N.B.—The said John Miller lived some time since at Chatton, near Wooler, in Northumberland, and is a broad set man, about 40 years of age, wears his own hair, which is short and turning grey, and had on when he went away a home-spun grey coat.

1738, October 21.—On Tuesday last died Mrs. Mary, wife of Mr. John Pawson, wine merchant. She was daughter of Mr. Nathaniel Hargrave, attorney-at-law, and sister of James Hargrave, Esq., of Shawdon, present High Sheriff for the County of Northumberland. She was reserved without pride, religious without noise, a prudent wife, and a discreet mother. And as she enjoyed in her life, so she preserved to her death, an even, peaceable, resigned disposition.

1738, November 25.—To be lett, and to enter on at May-day next, with proper encouragement to good tenants, Barton Farm, Thrunton Low Field Farm, Esslington East Farm, and Esslington South Long Bank, near Esslington, in the county of Northumberland. Also two farms at Kibblesworth, near Ravensworth Castle, and a farm at Helme Park, in the county of Durham, with all necessary conveniences. Whoever is desirous to treat for the same, may send their proposals, or apply to Mr. Ellison, Mr. Walton, or Mr. Boag, at Ravensworth Castle, or to Mr. W. Anderson, at Esslington.

1745, August 10.—We are assur'd by a letter from Capt. Collingwood to a gentleman in town, that he (the Captain) receiv'd a wound in his back by a musket ball in the late action near Ghent; that the ball enter'd near his kidneys, and went quite through him. His wound was not dress'd till he arriv'd at Lisle, when it was laid open about eight inches, and he now grows better every day.

1745, November 8.—Lord Kilmarnock, who styles himself colonel of a regiment of horse, had sent a summons upon the 3d inst. to the Provost of Kelso, for furnishing quarters and provisions for 4,000 foot and 1,000 horse of the rebels, requiring him also to send the same orders to the magistrates of Wooler. That on Saturday, the 2d, Gen. Guest had made a sally from the castle of Edinburgh and seized about 2,000 loaves, which had been provided for, and were to be sent after, the rebels, who had with them, as it was said, only four days' provisions when they marched. The two regiments of Dragoons of Hamilton and Ligonier were posted at Wooler, Whittingham, &c., to observe their motions. They are under the command of Col. Ligonier.

1745, November 30.—Northumberland.—Whereas Thomas Collingwood, son of — Collingwood, of Thrunton, in this county, was committed on Wednesday last to the gaol in and for the said county at Morpeth, for high treason, and made his escape from thence in the night between the 27th and 28th of this instant November: These are therefore to give notice, that if any person or persons shall apprehend the said Thomas Collingwood, and deliver him to the keeper of the said gaol, such person or persons shall have paid to him or them, by the Treasurer of this county, a reward of £50. N.B.—The said Thomas Collingwood is a person of middle stature, about twenty-five years of age, has a round face and short nose, and wore when he escaped a light-colour'd wigg, a dark-colour'd coat, and a silk handkerchief about his neck.

1745, November 30.—On Saturday last was brought hither Thomas Collingwood, who was taken the 22d inst. by one of the Cumberland Light Horse, at the Swan, in Thirlwell-gate, about 12 miles off Carlisle. He had about him £114 and a letter to one of the rebels from A——n H——n, Esq., of Tone, near Hexham, in which was a list of those who subscribed towards the above sum.

1751, July.—This month, as Sir Henry Grey, Bart., was shooting near the Cheviot Hills in Northumberland, he shot a very large eagle, which had seized his dog in its talons, and was in the act of carrying it off, when Sir Henry put a stop to its flight. The people in that neighbourhood had suffered great damage from that eagle among the flocks, one person having lost lambs to the value of £6.

1758, November 4.—Monday, died at Unthank, in the 58th year of his age, Alexander Collingwood, Esq., one of his Majesty's Justices of Peace for the county of Northumberland; a gentleman much regretted by his acquaintances. He was buried at Whittingham, and the pall was supported by the Right Honourable Lord Ravensworth, Sir Henry Grey, Bart., Nicholas Brown, Robert Fenwick, Christopher Reed, Collingwood Forster, Bryan Burrell, and Gilbert Park, Esqs.

1761, January.—As some workmen were digging in a plantation, at Shawdon, in Northumberland, they found two Roman urns, containing human bones. They were of a globular form, about eighteen inches in diameter, and were made of a bluish earth. Near the urns were also found a stone chest or coffin ; and on digging further, an entire foundation of a triangular building, with three rows of steps, and also a Roman causeway.

1761, March.—During this month a great deal of disturbance about the balioting for the Militia took place in Northumberland. On Monday, the 2nd of March, a large number of pitmen, waggonmen, husbandmen, and servants assembled at Morpeth, and not meeting with such indulgence as they expected, obliged the deputy-lieutenants and justices to quit their duty for their own safety, no military force being at hand. The rioters then seized all the lists and books relative to the militia from the constables, and tore or burnt them before their eyes. The next day, Tuesday, March 3rd, they went to Whittingham, and acted in much the same manner. Flushed with such success, and reinforced to near five thousand, they made a similar attempt at Hexham, but had not the like success.

1763, January 15.—On the 5th inst. died at Carlisle the Rev. Erasmus Head, A.M., Prebendary of that Cathedral, and in the Commission of the Peace for Cumberland, Vicar of Whittingham and Newburn, in Northumberland. He was remarkable for a disposition truly humane and charitable, exceeded by few in a sincere concern for religion, and a zealous attachment to his King and country.

1763, October 29.—The Rev. Mr. Charles Ward, of Morpeth, is presented to the Vicarage of Whittingham, in the county of Northumberland, by the Right Rev. the Bishop of Carlisle, vacant by the death of the Rev. Mr. Eramus Head.

1764, February 4.—To be sold, together or in parcels, a neat Freehold Estate, situate at Glanton, in the parish of Whittingham, in the county of Northumberland, and within six miles of Alnwick, consisting of about 100 acres of rich arable, meadow, and pasture ground, well hedged, and in good condition; with a newly built stone house, fit for a gentleman's family, stables, barns, byres, outhouses, and other suitable conveniences, and late in the possession of Mr. John Hopper. The said estate, in part, adjoins the Great Western Road from Newcastle to Edinburgh, is pleasantly and conveniently situated on the north side of a large improved vale (through which the river Aln runs), and commands an extensive prospect along the same. For further particulars, enquire of Thomas Ilderton, of Hawkhill, Esq.; or of Mr. Coll. Forster, or Mr. Thomas Adams, attorneys-at-law, in Alnwick aforesaid.

1764, June 30.—That the following Sub-Divison Militia Meeting:—Coquetdale Ward, at Mr. Thomas Scott's, innkeeper, at Whittingham, on Thursday, the 5th.

1764, August 4.—We hear from Brandon, in Northumberland, that last week a field of barley, containing 10 acres, belonging to Mr. Robert Curry, was cut down, and afforded a plentiful crop; and what is more remarkable, it was sown this week with turnips.

1764, August 25.—Last week was married at Paris, Ralph Clavering, of Callaly, near Alnwick, in Northumberland, Esq., to Miss Lynch, daughter of Mr. Lynch, merchant, of Bordeaux.

1764, September 8.—That day (Sunday, Sept. 2) her Grace the Duchess of Grafton passed through here (Newcastle) for Eslington, in Northumberland, the seat of Lord Ravensworth.

1764, December 29.—To be let, and entered upon immediately, or on the 12th of May next, Titlington North Farm, in the parish of Eglingham, containing

1,081 acres of good arable, meadow, and pasture lands, well watered and fenced; also, Titlington South Farm, containing 1,085 acres of good arable, meadow, and pasture ground, well watered and fenced. If the said farms are not immediately let, the winter eatage and several good fogs, with a field of turnips, are to be disposed of. Enquire of Mr. Forster, of Alnwick, or Mr. Alder, of Mounton, who are empowered to let the same. Edward Potts, of Titlington, aforesaid, will shew the premises.

1765, March 5.—A storm of snow, &c., came on in the evening with such violence, and continued all night, that not only many flocks of sheep were drifted, but sundry persons lost their lives by being exposed to the excessive cold and the severity of the weather. One remarkable instance happened near Alnham, in Northumberland, where two sons of a farmer, being at school, a servant lad, about 14 years of age, was despatched with a horse to bring them safely home, but on their return (being confounded by the raging of the tempest) they lost their way and wandered about until their dismal situation so terrified them that they deserted the horse, and the youngest of the boys laid himself quietly down in the snow; but his eldest brother being in great distraction, ran backward and forward till, being quite spent, and his strength exhausted, he sank down and expired. His brother and the servant continued still alive, but in a torpid and benumbed state, till they were found the next day, the servant leading the horse and the youngest boy (between six and seven years old) on horseback, holding the dead body of his brother before him.

1765, May 15.—On the 8th inst. died, after a short illness, the Lady of Ralph Clavering, of Callalee, in the county of Northumberland, Esq. Her amiable disposition endeared her to every one, and the poor lament the loss of her great benevolence.

1765, November 16.—Monday (11th) was married, at Morpeth, Captain William Dickson, of the Navy, to Miss Jenny Collingwood, daughter of the late Alexander Collingwood of Unthank, in Northumberland, Esq.

1765, November 30.—County of Northumberland.—Whereas a bridge is intended to be built in the said county, over the water called Breamish Water, in the most convenient place, having communication with the road leading from Glanton Bank to Piercy's Cross, all persons, therefore, aminded to undertake the building of the said bridge are desired to deliver in plans for building the same, and estimates of the expence, to the Justices of the Peace, at the next General Quarter Sessions of the Peace, to be held at Morpeth, in and for the said county, so that the same may be then had under consideration.—By order, Geo. Cuthbertson, Clerk of the Peace.

1767, January 31.—We hear from Callaley, in Northumberland, that Ralph Clavering, Esq., from his great humanity and charitable disposition, has provided for all the poor under him this last year, and proposes to continue to do the same on the following plan:—He allows them flour, meal, and bread corn at a price which is looked upon by the poor themselves to be very reasonable. A sufficient quantity, in proportion to each of their families, is weekly distributed on a certain day, when a servant attends, and receives ready money for what he delivers. Thus the poor is quite easy, and insensible of the dearness of the markets. It is much wished others would follow some method like this; then the poor would have no reason to complain. When money, or other provisions, are given at large, the poor live well for a short time; after which are starving, and in as much distress as ever.

1767, June 27.—That day (Sat. 20th) was married Ralph Clavering, of Calliley Castle, in Northumberland, Esq., to Miss Mary Walsh, eldest daughter of Edward Walsh, Esq.

1767, August 22.—Saturday (15th) was married, at Whittingham, Mr. John Whitham, of Rothill, aged 60, to Miss Lenney, aged 21; an agreeable young lady with a handsome fortune.

1768, December 20.—To be let, and entered upon at Whitsuntide next, all that farm of land called Karslaw Moor, in the parish of Whittingham, in the county of Northumberland, consisting of 200 acres, or thereabouts, with a draw kiln and limestone quarry upon the premises.—For further particulars enquire of Alexander Collingwood, of Unthanke, Esq.

1770, May 19.—Last week was married, at Ingram, in Northumberland, by the Rev. Mr. Brown, Alexander Brown, of Doxford, Esq., to Miss Babby Brown, daughter of Alexander Brown, of Branton, Esq., a most agreeable and accomplished young lady.

1770, May 19.—Monday (14th) was married, in London, Gifford Collingwood, of Great Ormond Street, Esq., brother to Alexander Collingwood, of Unthank, in Northumberland, Esq., to Miss Pye, of Morpeth.

1770, July 28.—We can with pleasure assure the public that the account in the London and other papers, of the death of Thomas Liddel, Esq., brother to the Right Hon. Lord Ravensworth, is false, that gentleman having arrived at his seat at Newton, near Durham, the beginning of this week, from Harrogate, in perfect health, it being Henry Liddel, Esq., a relation to his Lordship.

1772, April 11.—We learn from the neighbourhood of Eslington, in Northumberland, that, to the west and north of that place, there has been, for thirteen weeks past, a very deep storm of snow, and for want of hay many of the farmers have suffered considerably in their stocks of sheep and cattle; and had it not been for the charitable and timely assistance of the Right Hon. Lord Ravensworth, who generously ordered his agents to distribute a stack of hay to the poor of that parish, and to sell a large quantity at 40s. per ton to every person in distress, when hay was selling at £6 10s. per ton, many families must have been ruined. A truly meritorious act, and from a just spirit of benevolence.

1772, October 3.—We hear from Whittingham, in Northumberland, that, on Thursday se'nnight, Breamish river was so much swelled by a heavy rain, that it carried away two arches of the new bridge over that river, near Branton. And from Alnwick we learn that the Abbey Mills, re-built since the November flood, were also swept away.

1772, October 31.—Yesterday se'nnight, William Atkinson, a herd, belonging to Mr. Bartholomew Hare, of North Middleton, near Wooler-haugh-head, was robbed at Glanton, near Whittingham, of £5 10s., by two highwaymen. A description of their persons, and a reward of £40 for apprehending one or both of the offenders, which will be paid upon conviction.

1772, December 19.—Yesterday se'nnight, a woman going to Greenock was stopped, near Weldon Mill, in Northumberland, by a man and woman, and robbed of some money, after which they crammed her mouth with a handkerchief, tied it over with another, and her hands behind her back, then threw her into the ditch, where she was found almost suffocated by the landlord at Weldon Mill. The woman in company with the man had on a black beaver hat, with a blue ribbon round it.

1773, January 23.—Sunday (17th) night last, as Mr. Laidler, the driver of the Edinburgh fly between this town (Newcastle) and Morpeth, was coming between Glanton and Morpeth (having been upon some business at his master's at Glanton), he was attacked nigh Weldon Mill by three foot-pads, armed with pistols, who knocked him off his horse, rifled his pockets, and took from him five shillings and twopence. They afterwards very generously returned him the brass, that he might not be stopped, as they said, at the turnpike gate.

1773, January 30.—Last Friday, the body of one Alexander Moffat, a mason, was found murdered at Lilburn Alders, in a most shocking manner. The Coroner's inquest brought in their verdict wilful murder by persons unknown.

Murder.—Whereas one Alexander Moffat, a mason, who had been missing from his lodgings, at Roseden, in the parish of Ilderton, in the county of Northumberland, about thirty days, and on searching for him, his body was found on the 23rd of January instant, concealed under a sand bank, on the south side of a burn, about 40 yards west of the common highway leading through the Lilburn Alders, in the said parish of Ilderton, towards Wooler, with a large wound above the left eye which penetrated through the brain, the left eye struck out, and a large contusion upon the right temple bone; it is supposed he had about ten pounds in his pocket, he was stripped of a pair of buck-skin breeches; his coat, waistcoat, stockings, and shoes were left upon him, they being of little value. The jury, on the Coroner's inquest, have brought in their verdict wilful murder by persons unknown; therefore in order to discover the person or persons who have been guilty of the said murder, a reward of Twenty Pounds is hereby offered to any person who will give information against the person or persons who have committed the same. The said reward to be paid on conviction.

1773, February 6.—"General Hue and Cry."—Highway Robbery. —On Tuesday, the 2nd day of February, 1773, about four o'clock in the afternoon, one John Snyder, a gardener, was stopped by two men on foot on the high road between Wooler-haugh-head and Whittingham, in Northumberland, and robbed of three guineas and a half in gold and six shillings and sixpence in silver, a light coloured rough surtout coat with buttons of the same colour, a silver watch with a china dial plate (the maker's name, Donkin, Edinburgh), with a steel chain and a common seal set in brass; on one side of the seal was a Turk's head, on the other a lion; also a pair of black worsted breeches, a pair of white cotton stockings, and a man's shirt marked J. S., tied up in a blue and white striped handkerchief. One of the men was about six feet high, with short black hair, and had on a blue half-wide coat, and had a pistol with him which he presented to the same John Snyder's breast; the other had a cutlass, and was about five feet eight or nine inches high, had on a whitish coat, with his hair tied behind; both of them had their hats over their faces. Whoever apprehends the above two persons, or either of them, will be entitled to a reward of Forty Pounds, on conviction. By order, J. French, Deputy Clerk of the Peace.

1773, February 20.—Extract of a letter from Capt. Geo. Burne, late of the Edinburgh packet of this place (Newcastle), dated Wooler-haugh-head, February 10, on his passage overland from hence to Leith:—"On my passage from Whittingham to Wooler-haugh-head, this evening, I met with four sail of pirates, one of which attacked me on the starboard bow and took the command of my helm, another seized me on the larboard bow and bid me deliver. I reply'd, gentlemen, you'll allow me to be commander of my own vessel. But he that deprived me of my steerage presented a pistol to my breast, which I parried, and the ball went over the vessel's head; the other on the larboard bow then presented a pistol, which I likewise parried, and then jumping overboard, bore round under my vessel's stern, where I knocked one of them down, the other being almost dead by my jumping against him when I came from on board my vessel. I was then attacked by a third, whom I knocked down likewise; but there being a fourth which I did not then see, he knocked me down, but not to deprive me of my senses. I lay still till he came to take my watch and money, at which time I seized him by the collar and strangled him, and so subdued the whole, after which I found my vessel had forged ahead about 100 yards under the lee of a weather shore, where I found her brought up for shelter. I then got on board again, and am now arrived at Wooler-haugh-head. The pirates seemed to be in sailors dress, but did not return one sea term as such. I supposed them to be in disguise. I find myself much bruised and one guinea out of pocket, which I suppose I have lost in struggling with my adversaries."

1772, July 31.—The Rev. Mr. Law is presented to the living of Whittingham, in Northumberland, by the Dean and Chapter of Carlisle, vacant by the death of the Rev. Mr. Charles Ward.

1773, August 14.—Sunday, as a person was bathing in the pond at Callalee, in Northumberland, he was unfortunately drowned.

1773, September 18.—A correspondent informs us that the Right Hon. Lord Ravensworth had generously, and with a true spirit of benevolence, ordered his steward at the late rent day to receive in payment from his tenants their light gold at the original value.

1773, September 25.—The Rev. Mr. John Law, son of the Dean of Carlisle, was last week inducted into the living of Whittingham, in Northumberland.

1773, December 11.—Tuesday (7th) evening as Mr. Thomas Cassell, of High Barton, near Eslington, was crossing a burn near his house on his return from Whittingham, he unfortunately fell from his horse and was drowned. He was one of the greatest dealers of sheep in this country, a most affectionate relation, and whose house was ever open to his friends, and his probity in his dealings makes his death much regretted. Dying a bachelor, he has left a considerable fortune amongst his relations.

1775, June 17.—On Wednesday (14th) se'nnight the Rectory House at Ingram was entirely consumed by a chimney taking fire and communicating to the roof, which was thatched. Most of the household furniture, which belonged to Rev. Mr. Dixon, was saved by the uncommon spirit and activity of the neighbours, than, from the suddenness and violence of the flames, they had reason to hope for. The whole misfortune is said to have arisen from the nest of a jackdaw, which first took fire in the chimney.

1775, September 9.—Monday (September 4) at Whittingham, there was a great show of black cattle, and a number of buyers from the south, which occasioned a brisk market in the morning, but towards noon, from the numbers, the prices rather dropped.

1775, December 16.—Thursday (14th) se'nnight, the pocket-book which Mr. George Ditchburn lost at Whittingham fair, on the 4th of September last, was found by Mrs. Scott's servant amongst some nettles near Howe's cottage, but much defaced, and without any of the bank notes it contained when lost.

1776, September 7.—Wednesday (4th) being Whittingham fair, there was a very great show of black cattle, which sold in general at good prices.

1777, January 11.—Friday (10th), in an advanced age at her house in Morpeth, Mrs. Collingwood, relict of Alexander Collingwood of Unthank, Esq., and sister to Sir Francis Blake of Twizell, in Northumberland, Bart. She was deservedly esteemed for her amiable disposition, benevolence, and piety.

1777, January 11th.—Friday (10th), the Hon. Mrs. Collingwood, in the 94th year of her age, at Longbirch, near Wolverhampton, widow of George Collingwood, Esq., of Northumberland, and sister of the late Lord Viscount Montague.

1777, February 15.—"Hue and Cry."—County of Northumberland.—February 6. Stolen on or about the nineteenth of July last, out of a barn at Bolton, in the parish of Edlingham, a quantity of wool; and whereas there is reason to believe that Andrew Crea, late of Low Barton, in the parish of Whittingham (who hath lately absconded), was concerned in stealing the same; he is about five feet nine inches high, about thirty years of age, wears light short hair, light eyebrows, round faced, short sighted, and a large mole betwixt his mouth and chin.

1777, April 5.—Mr. Robinson, keeper of Boulton Park, killed on the 15th inst. a woodcock, the wings entirely white and almost the whole body of the same colour. It appeared when on flight like a tame pigeon.

1781, October 20.—Yesterday (19th) se'nnight, a fire broke out at Rothbury about one o'clock, which, in three hours time, consumed 16 houses, but happily no lives were lost.

1781, November 3.—To the printer of the *Courant.*—The people of Rothbury, in general, are of opinion that the following most remarkable act of benevolence and compassion ought not to be concealed but displayed in the most public manner, as a most laudable example for imitation; therefore they humbly beg that you would be pleased to give it a place in your paper this week. Lord Ravensworth has, out of an exuberant goodness peculiar to himself given, with marked kindness, a benefaction of Twenty Guineas towards the relief of the poor persons in Rothbury who suffered by the fire that happened on the 19th October last, which charity has been most judiciously and satisfactorily distributed amongst the poor sufferers by Thomas Storer, Esq. His lordship, as soon as he heard of the sad catastrophe, glowing with sociable grief, despatched a particular messenger to make a careful and exact enquiry what loss each individual had sustained. The opportune, secret, and speedy manner by which his lordship transmitted his charity, which was on the next day after the distress of the poor sufferers was made known to his lordship, may with the utmost propriety be called additional charity, *bis enim dat, qui dat cito.* But what adds to the lustre of that humane and benevolent character, is his having no property in that neighbourhood; it chiefly belongs to His Grace the Duke of Northumberland.

1783, November 8.—On Sunday the 19th day of October, a person was committed to Morpeth gaol for robbing one Patrick Wallace on the highroad, on Rimside Moor, who says his name is Sylvanus Broadwater, of Bampton, in Oxfordshire; he is about five feet seven inches high, squints with both eyes, of a fresh coloured countenance, had on a blue surtout coat with a red collar, an olive green coat, a Manchester velvet waistcoast, and corduroy breeches. The said highwayman says he had been at sea and served on board the "Dolphin" and "Dromedary," and that he left the service in April last; he had with him a grey or rather white mare galloway, very lean; all along the ridge of its back the hair is worn bare, it had a switch tail with a piece of the hair cut off. A small enamelled snuff box with a looking glass on its inside; also three pieces of old silver three penny and four penny coins; also a brace of pistols (maker's name Ward, London) were in his possession when taken.

1784, January 17.—We, the subscribers of the Association Club, at Whittingham, for the prosecution of all felonies committed upon any of its members, at a joint expence, according to the property we sign for, do give this public notice to all the neighbourhood of Whittingham aforesaid, that they may be admitted into the said association, by applying to Mr. Brown, of Whittingham, steward, at or before the 20th of February next.

1784, March 20.—The debtors, in Newgate, return sincere thanks to Sir Henry Geo. Liddell, Bart., for his kind present of five guineas.

1784, June 12.—To be let, for the term of 9 or 15 years, and entered upon at Whitsunday, 1785, Unthank West Farm, in the parish of Alnham, containing about 300 acres (more or less) of good arable, meadow, and pasture ground, with a suitable house, and other offices for the accommodation of a tenant, now in possession of Mr. Thomas Jobson. Mr. Thomas Pattison, at Unthank, will show the premises.

1784, July 3.—The creditors of John Wealens, late of Lorbottle, in the county of Northumberland, farmer, are desired to meet at the house of Mr. Anthony Bell, the sign of the Half Moon, in Rothbury, on Monday the 19th day of July instant, at ten o'clock in the forenoon, when and where a state of the affairs of the said John Wealens will be laid before them for their information.

1785, March 26.—Stolen, from Thrunton, in the parish of Whittingham, and county of Northumberland, on Monday night the 21st inst., or early on Tuesday morning following:—Two mares, one the property of Robert Witham; she is a bright bay mare, about fifteen hands high, a remarkable long head, wide eared, a bald face, both fore legs and far hind foot white, a switch tail, and with foal. The other a black mare belonging to James Gibson, about fourteen hands and a half high, a bald face and far hind foot white, a thin switch tail, a stroke upon the far fore shoulder not yet haired, and a remarkable swirle of hair upon her far hind hip. Two suspicious persons were observed to saunter and loiter about Whittingham that evening, were in a public house till after ten o'clock at night, they decamped without notice; one of them was about five feet nine inches high, of a thin, dark complexion, and long necked, had on a claret coloured greatcoat, the strait coat blue, and three waistcoats, the upper one red. The other about five feet six inches high, a full face with a roman nose, had on a claret coloured great coat, with a pair of corduroy breeches. Whoever can give any account of the said offender or offenders, so as he or they may be brought to justice, upon conviction for the said offence, shall receive Ten Guineas reward from the Clerk of the Association at Whittingham, who are determined to prosecute with the utmost severity all thefts whatsoever, when committed upon any of its members.—Joseph Brown, Clerk.

1785, July 2.—"General Hue and Cry."—Whittingham, June 24th, 1785. Whereas a threatening letter has been brought by the post from Neweastle to Mr. Robert Whitham, of Thrunton, on Monday last, an exact copy I here send you to insert in your useful *Courant*. Five Guineas reward is hereby offered by the Association of Whittingham to any person or persons who shall give information of the author, and npon conviction of the said offence, shall be paid the reward by the Clerk of the Association.—Joseph Brown, Clerk.

1785, June 13th.—Sir, this comes to you and to let you now that this mare which this mane is aprehended upone suspecion of taken your mayore and he payed me nine guines fore the blacke mayore and I wold you be carefull in parsecuting of inesent man for if you do it is in my pouer to redus you and your nyubour Gibson to begg your Bread and taket in Consthereation and mind what I seay and it will come upon you like a clape of thunder so this all at present from me till you heare furder account.—G. G.

1786, May 24.—Sir Henry George Liddell, Bart., of Ravensworth Castle, in the county of Durham, in company with Mr. Bowes and Mr. Consett, embarked at Shields on board the "Gottenburgh Merchant," Captain Fothergill, on a tour through Sweden, Swedish Lapland, Finland, and Denmark, which was performed in about three months. It is said that this tour was undertaken in consequence of a wager made by Sir H. G. Liddell of going to Lapland, returning thence in a certain time, and bringing home two females of that country and two reindeer. Whatever truth there may be in this report, it is certain that Sir Henry brought two Lapland women and two reindeer to England. The women, whose names were Sigree and Anea, were kept for a time at Ravensworth Castle, where they were considered as great curiosities. Many presents were made to them, and they were sent back to their native country at the expense of Sir Henry with about £50 in money, which they looked upon as great riches. An account of this tour, with plates by Bewicke, was published by Mr. Consett.

1787, May 12.—The reindeer brought from Lapland by Sir Henry Geo. Liddell, Bart., has lately fawned at his seat at Eslington.

1787, May 26.—Married, Monday se'nnight (21st), at St. George's, Hanover Square, London, Charles Mitchell, Esq., of Forcett, Yorkshire, Captain in the 49th regiment, to the eldest daughter of Alexander Collingwood, Esq., of Ryal, Northumberland.

1787, September 22.—Northumberland—Game Duty.—A list of certificates issued in the county aforesaid, with respect to the said duty, for the year 1787, pursuant to an Act of Parliament, granting a duty on such certificate.

	£	s.	d.
Bell, Mr. John, of Eslington ...	2	2	0
Boag, J., of Lemington-hill-head ...	2	2	0
Collingwood, Gilfred, of Unthank, Esq. ...	2	2	0
Clennell, Percival, of Harbottle Castle, Esq. ...	2	2	0
Donkin, Samuel, of Great Tosson ...	2	2	0
Farquhar, Colonel Robert, of Rothbury ...	2	2	0
Hickson, Robert, of Biddlestone, Gamekeeper for the Manor of Biddlestone ...	0	10	6
Hand, Mr. John, of Eslington ...	2	2	0
Liddell, Sir Henry George, Eslington, Bart. ...	2	2	0
Mills, Jos., of West Glanton, Gent. ...	2	2	0
Pattison, Thomas, of Unthank, Gamekeeper for Manors or Lands of Unthank, Great and Little Ryal, Caraby, and Cropden ...	0	10	6
Storer, Robert, of Rothbury ...	2	2	0
Wilson, William, Gamekeeper for the Manors of Ravensworth and Eslington ...	0	10	6
Whitfield, George, of Shawdon, Gamekeeper for the Manor of Shawdon ...	0	10	6

1788, February 16.—"General Hue and Cry."—County of Northumberland.—Stolen from Eslington Hill, on Wednesday night last, the 30th of January, a large Ewe Sheep, the head, skin, entrails, and two lambs she was with, left; the four quarters and suet carried off.—Whoever can give such information as may be the means of convicting the offender or offenders of the said offence, shall receive Five Guineas from me.—Thomas Vardy, Ryal Hill, February 1st, 1788.

1788, June 14.—Alnwick Races.—N.B. During the races a Long Main will be fought at Mr. George Wilson's new pit, between Sir Henry George Liddell, Bart. (Small, feeder), and Charles Gray, Esq. (Lumley, feeder).

1788, September 27.—Northumberland—Game Duty.—A list of certificates issued in the county aforesaid, with respect to the said duty, between the 1st July and the 25th September, 1788, pursuant to an Act of the 25th of Geo. 3d., for granting a duty on such certificates :—

Clavering, John, of Callaly, Esq.
Collingwood, Gilfred, of Unthank, Esq.
Devisone, James, of Whitton Tower, Esq.
Farquhar, Col. Robert, of Rothbury.
Farquhar, George, of Hollystone, Esq.
Hand, the Rev. Mr., of Eslington.
Hadkin, Mr. Robert, of Glanton.
Liddell, Sir Hen. Geo., of Eslington, Bt.
Mills, Joseph, of Glanton Westfield, Esq.
Pearson, Jacob, of Titlington, Esq.
Storer, Robert, of Rothbury, Gent.
Wilson, Wm., of West Hepple, Gent.

Gamekeepers.

Pattison, Thomas, of Unthank: Unthank, Great and Little Ryle, Carsley, Cobden, Long Craig, and Coatlands.

Wilson, Wm., of Ravensworth Castle: Eslington, &c.

1790, October 30.—Married, Tuesday (26th), at Alnham, by the Rev. Mr. Smith, John Tarleton, Esq., of Liverpool, to Miss Collingwood, daughter of Alexander Collingwood, Esq., of Unthank, in the county of Northumberland.

1791, January 15.—On the 6th inst., at night, one Andrew Allan, of Framlington, an old offender, was detected stealing a large quantity of iron from a smith's shop, in Whittingham-lane, but contrived to escape before an opportunity was found to convey him before a magistrate.

1791, July 2.—Last week a child, 15 months old, going along the bridge at Whittingham, in Northumberland, fell into the river Aln, where it laid several minutes. On being taken out it appeared to be lifeless, but fortunately Mr. Crea, surgeon, in that village being near, he inflated its lungs with his breath, when signs of life appeared. By persisting in the methods prescribed by the Humane Society, the child gradually recovered, and is now in perfect health.

1808, June 25.—Married, at Whittingham, on the 31st May, 1808, Mr. Joshua Crea, surgeon, to Miss Frances Richardson.

1808, November 12.—Collections were made in Whittingham parish for prisoners of war in France.

1810, January 10.—Died, at Alnham, in Northumberland, John Rutherford, aged 100 years. He had formerly been a shepherd.

Circa, 1820.—During the winter of 1820, or sometime thereabouts, Mr. Clement Stephenson, farmer, of Whittingham, and one of his men, were returning from Morpeth market where they had been with a drove of cattle. The day being stormy, they called for some refreshment at the beer shop, then kept by Jenny Knox, at Rough-castles. On coming out snow was falling very heavily, and on resuming their homeward journey the two travellers came to where the road divided. Owing to the severity of the snowstorm, it was difficult to tell which was the right path. The man, thinking he was right, took one, and although he did his utmost to persuade his master to accompany him, Mr. Stephenson, in the firm belief he was right, took the other, which unfortunately led into the midst of the wild moors of the Coe Crag and the Blackcock. Next day the body of Mr. Stephenson was found in the snow, not far from Jamie Macfarlane's hut on Thrunton Moor.

1828, October 16.—A most splendid entertainment was given by the Hon. H. T. Liddell, M.P., and Mrs. Liddell, at their seat at Eslington House, Northumberland, to celebrate the baptism of their youngest daughter. At half-past five o'clock p.m. the ceremony was performed by the Rev. H. G. Liddell, in the presence of a select party of relatives and friends. Her Grace the Duchess of Northumberland, Miss Seymour, and the Hon. Mrs. Dawson, were the sponsors. A beautiful china font was presented for the occasion by Her Grace, and the lovely infant was named Florentia, from Her Grace's second name. After the ceremony the distinguished party sat down to a sumptuous dinner at six o'clock. At half-past nine o'clock the ball company began to arrive, and the elegant ball-room was thrown open to the admiring assemblage. The ball was opened by the Hon. Mr. Liddell and Her Grace the Duchess of Northumberland, and the dancing was kept up with great spirit till one o'clock, when the company retired to a splendid and elegant supper. The health of the Lord-Lieutenant of the county and of Her Grace was proposed in a neat and appropriate manner by the Hon. Mr. Liddell, and was drunk with long and loud applause; after which the healths of the honourable host and hostess were proposed in a most gratifying manner by His Grace, and loud cheers accompanied this toast. The healths of the distinguished sponsors were then proposed by Mr. Liddell, and received with great applause. The healths of Lord and Lady Ravensworth and family were given, and drunk with great enthusiasm. The company then returned to the ball-room, and a varied succession of waltzes, quadrilles, and other dances were continued until the dawn of the morning warned the happy party of the necessity of quitting the scene of festivity. The ball-room was most tastefully decorated with wreaths of flowers and evergreens, beautifully arranged in various devices; and the name bestowed by Her Grace the Duchess of Northumberland upon the young Christian was distinctly seen at the head of the room in large gold letters, intermixed with moss and flowers; and on the side of the room were seen the initials of the Duke and Duchess, with their respective coronets, most skilfully executed by Mr. Athey, of Alnwick. There were about 160 persons present upon this occasion, comprising several of the most distinguished families in the country.

1829, January.—This month, one of those rare and beautiful gold coins—a rose-noble of Edward I.—was found on the estate of William Pawson, Esq., of Shawdon, in Northumberland. On the impress is a figure of the monarch seated in an ancient ship, bearing on his shoulder a shield containing the arms of England, France, and Ireland, with the legend, "Sic ib at per undas."

1829.

LEMMINGTON BRANCH ROAD.

At a meeting of the landholders, occupiers of lands, and persons interested in the intended improvements on the Lemmington branch road, held at the house of Mr. Daniel Ross, Castle Inn, in Whittingham, on Monday, the 7th day of December, 1829, the following resolutions were unanimously agreed to:—

The Honorable H. T. LIDDELL, M.P., in the chair.

1. That the improvement of the branch road of the Alnwick and Rothbury turnpike, between Alnwick Moor and Jockey's Dike Bridge, is much to be desired; and when accomplished, will be a great and general benefit to all classes resident in the vale of Whittingham and neighbourhood.

2. That this meeting pledges itself to contribute its best assistance towards carrying into effect the improvements contemplated in the reducton of Garment-Edge and Lemmington Banks.

3. That a subscription be entered into for that purpose.

4. That the chairman be requested, on the part of the meeting, to write letters to all persons of property interested in the matter, soliciting their co-operation and subscription.

5. That a committee be appointed, whose duty shall be to ascertain the amount of subscriptions in money and the promised assistance towards the work in labour; who may likewise engage the assistance of a surveyor or other competent person to determine the best mode of effecting the proposed improvements, and may receive offers for executing the same by contract.

6. That this committee do consist of

Sanderson Ilderton, Esq.
William Burrell, Esq.
William Pawson, Esq.
Adam Atkinson, jun., Esq.
William Lynn Smart, Esq.
John Allen Wilkie, Esq.
John Tewart, Esq.

John Collingwood Tarleton, Esq.
Walter Selby, Esq.
John Frankland, Esq.
The Honorable H. T. Liddell.
John Hopper, Esq.

with power to add to their number, and three to be a quorum.

That Mr. Russell be Secretary to the Committee.

Signed, H. T. LIDDELL, Chairman.

The thanks of the meeting were unanimously voted to the Honorable Mr. Liddell for his conduct in the chair.

SUBSCRIPTIONS TOWARDS IMPROVEMENTS ON THE LEMMINGTON BRANCH ROAD.

	£	s.	d.
The Honorable H. T. Liddell, M.P., Eslington House ...	25	0	0
William Pawson, Esq., Titlington House	30	0	0
William Lynn Smart, Esq., Trewit House	10	0	0
Adam Atkinson, Esq., Lorbottle House	10	0	0
Adam Atkinson, jun., Esq., do.	10	0	0
John Lambert, Esq., Alnwick	10	10	0
John Tewart, Esq., Glanton	10	10	0
John Hopper, Esq., do.	3	3	0
Joseph Hughes, Esq., do.	3	3	0
Sanderson Ilderton, Esq., Lemmington House	10	10	0
Robert Thorp, Esq., Alnwick	5	5	0
William Burrell, Esq., Broomepark	25	0	0
John Allen Wilkie, Esq., Glen Allen House	20	0	0
Messrs. Taylor (Lessees of Shilbottle Colliery)	20	0	0
Mr. D. Ross, Whittingham	2	2	0
Mr. John Stephenson, Thrunton	2	2	0
Mr. George Weatheritt, Mount Healey	1	1	0
Mr. George Thompson, Reaveley	1	0	0
Mr. John Pattinson, West Unthank	1	0	0
	£200	6	0

9th December, 1829. THOMAS ADAMS RUSSELL, Secretary.

1833, September 3.—A most diabolical attempt was made on the night of this day, by setting fire to a house belonging to Lord Ravensworth, on Thrunton Moor, not only to destroy the property, but to sacrifice the lives of the inmates. A reward of twenty pounds was offered for the discovery of the perpetrators.

1833.

WHITTINGHAM VALE ASSOCIATION FOR THE PROSECUTION OF FELONS.

N.B.—Every member is requested to keep a copy of these Rules by him.

We, the undersigned members of the above Association, do hereby mutually agree to and with each other to prosecute at our joint expense all and every person and persons who shall, from the day of the date hereof, commit or attempt to commit any robbery, burglary, felony, theft, or misdemeanor whatsoever, whereby the person or property of any member or members of this Association shall or may be injured or affected; and also to detect and prosecute to the utmost rigour of the law all and every person and persons who shall be found breaking down the hedges or fences, injuring the trees and plantations, or making footpaths over or otherwise trespassing upon any of our farms, lands, or grounds; or entering (unauthorized) any of our gardens, houses, outhouses, or other buildings; robbing our gardens or orchards, or pulling or destroying turnips, potatoes, or other produce growing upon our said farms, or who shall wilfully injure, furiously drive, or otherwise ill-use any of our horses, cattle, or other stock.

That the limits of this Association shall be confined to the parishes of Whittingham, Edlingham, Alnham, and Ingram, and the several townships of Eglingham, Hedgley, Ditchburn, Beanley, Crawley, Titlington, Branton, and Brandon, in the parish of Eglingham.

Right Hon. Lord Ravensworth, Woods and Plantations at Eslington.
Hon. H. T. Liddell, Eslington.
Sir J. E. Swinburne, Bart., Edlingham Castle and Woods.
William Pawson, Esq., Shawdon and Titlington Halls, and Plantations at Lemmington and Bolton.
William Burrell, Esq., Broome Park, Woods and Plantations.
Edward Clavering, Esq., Callaly Castle and Plantations.
Robert Ogle, Esq., Eglingham House and Plantations.
A. Atkinson, Esq., Larbottle House and Plantations.
A. Atkinson, Esq., Jun., Larbottle West Farm.
Rev. E. Law, Whittingham Vicarage.
John Tewart, Esq., Glanton, Woods and Plantations.
J. A. Wilkie, Esq., Glen Allen and Broomwood House Farm.
Mr. W. Smith, Lemmington Hill and Overthwarts.
Mr. J. Pattison, Crosshill Lodge and Mount-Pleasant.
Mr. R. Barker, Shawdon Hill.
Mr. A. Marshall, Alnham.
Mr. R. Storey, Beanley, Hesselton Ridge, Hebburn Moor, Sandyfords, Haydon, and Bewick Folly.
Miss Heslop, Low Broome Park.
Mr. A. Thompson, Whittingham.

Mr. G. Thompson, Reavely.
Mr. Robert Jobson, Branton and Mile End.
Mr. J. Stephenson, Thrunton and Yetlington Lane.
Mr. John Thompson, Titlington.
Mr. J. Pallister, Howbalk, Eslington Lane, and Eslington Hill.
Mr. John Hopper, Glanton.
Mr. Geo. Weir, Battle Bridge and Crawley.
Mr. John Turnbull, Glanton.
Miss Mills, Glanton.
Mr. W. Taylor, Follyons.
Mrs. Storey, Powburn Cottage.
Mr. W. Purvis, Abberwick Mill.
Mr. Christopher Avery, Yetlington.
Mr. Geo. Bolam, Titlington Mount and West Alwinton.
Mr. John Bolam, Fawdon and Clinch.
Mr. Crea, Whittingham.
Mr. T. Allison, Powburn and Crawley.
Mr. I. Mathewson, Glanton.
Mr. M. Moffitt, Glanton.
Mr. R. Carnaby, Shawdon Woodhouse and Shepherd's Law.
Mr. J. Scott, Mountain and Mile.
Mr. George Dippie, Glanton.
Mr. G. Landers, Glanton Pike.
Mr. J. Wealleans, Thrunton Low Field.
Mr. John Pallister, jun., Moor Laws.
Mr. W. Bennett, High Learchild.
Mr. D. Ross, Whittingham Inn and Farm.
Mr. J. Mills, Edlingham.
Mr. Geo. Weatheritt, Mounthooly.
Mr. F. Turnbull, Lemmington Mill.
Mr. J. Davidson, White House and Featherwood.
Mr. F. T. Strother, Rothill and High Barton.
Mr. J. S. Rea Nicholson, Branton.
Mr. J. Barnavelt Maidment, Bolton.
Messrs. T. & J. Tindle, Edlingham and Whollop.
Mr. C. Coulson, Newtown and Rufcastle.
Messrs. Bell, Edlingham Castle Farm.
Mr. James Young, Edlingham Castle Farm.
Mr. John Wardle, Moor House and Wandy Steed.

WILLIAM SMITH, Secretary and Treasurer.

Whittingham, December 2, 1833.

1837, July 12 to 16.—The counties of Northumberland and Durham were visited with dreadful thunderstorms. These visitations were exceedingly capricious in violence and duration, but the most awful storms appear to have occurred in the districts remote from Newcastle. On the 14th, at Shawdon Woodhouse, near Glanton, Northumberland, Miss Donkin, niece of Mr. Carnaby of that place, was struck dead by the electric fluid. It appears that Miss Donkin had gone into the kitchen and unfortunately sat down below a bell, when just at that moment the electric fluid entered the house, ran along the bell wire, and struck the young lady down with great violence, killing two dogs that lay near.

1839, April 20.—Two stacks of hay and one of straw belonging to the Rev. Robert William Goodenough, vicar of Whittingham, were destroyed by fire, and there is every reason to believe that it was the act of an incendiary.

1839, July 30.—During the Chartist riots in Newcastle, 600 persons were sworn in as special constables. Notwithstanding the repeated cautions which were issued by the authorities, a number of men from the country marched to the Forth on the 30th, and expressed their determination to hold a meeting. As soon as this was known the Mayor and Dr. Headlam left the Manors on horseback. On reaching Collingwood Street they came into collision with a body of Chartists, when the Mayor seized hold of a banner and a banner bearer, commanding an instant surrender, but he refusing a sharp struggle ensued, in which a tailor from Whittingham received a wound in the body, and was instantly conveyed to the infirmary.

1840, November 7.—The proceeds of the bazaar held at Alnwick last week in aid of the fund for enlarging and repairing the parish church of Whittingham amounted to upwards of £300.

1845, August 20.—In consequence of the rain which fell on this and the two days preceding, the river Aln rose to a greater height than at any former period within memory, and vast quantities of hay and corn on the banks of the stream were carried away. Several sheep and goats were also lost, and at Bolton a farm steward and his son, named Cook, were drowned whilst endeavouring to save some sheep. The Till was also very much swollen, and serious damage was done in many parts.

1846, February 3.—A boy named Foggon, little more than two years old, wandered from his home at Lorbottle. The following morning the neighbours having dragged the mill ponds and searched the burns, afterwards repaired to the adjoining hills, where a shepherd lad belonging to Mr. Drysdale was attracted by his cries, and found him lying on his breast at a place called the Long Crag, a distance of nearly four miles from his home, and after having endured the exposure more than twenty-five hours. His preservation is the more remarkable from his having passed several old coal workings during the night.

1848, December 4.—The estate of Collingwood House, in the parishes of Whittingham and Alnham, Northumberland, were sold by auction in London to the Hon. H. T. Liddell for £60,000. The estate comprised 1,965 acres, and the yearly rent amounted to £2,045.

1849, May 27.—A fire of a most terrific nature occurred at Shawdon Hall, near Alnwick, the seat of William Pawson, Esq. The hall itself was preserved, but all the outbuildings were entirely destroyed. The damage was estimated at upwards of £3,000. The intensity of the heat may be calculated by the fact that the lead poured down from the roof like water, and the bell of the turret clock, which had been brought from the monastery at Alnmouth in the reign of Henry VIII., was melted in the conflagration.

1855, September 1.—The beautiful gardens of Lord Ravensworth at Eslington Park, near Alnwick, have recently undergone great improvements under the presiding taste of the noble proprietor. Terraced walks leading from the river have been tastefully laid out, and a superb flower vase in stone, from the chisel of Mr. McMillan, of Alnwick, designed in the Grecian style and adorned with the ram's head, and encircled with the vine branch, has just been mounted on its pedestal, which, with those already erected or about to be raised, will greatly add to the classic beauty of the floral shades of Eslington.

1855, October 1.—Lieut. Goodenough, one of the wounded of the 8th ult., is a son of the Rev. R. W. Goodenough, vicar of Whittingham.

1856, January 16.—A public dinner was held at the Bridge of Aln Inn, Whittingham, in honour of Captain J. R. Carr, son of Ralph Carr, Esq., of Hedgeley, Northumberland, to congratulate the gallant captain on his safe return from the Crimea, and also to present him with a sword as a token of their respect and esteem, for which 150 guineas had been subscribed by his friends and neighbours. Captain Carr landed in the Crimea with the first expedition, and was present at the different engagements with his regiment.

1856, August 1.—At Eslington Hill, 12th ult., aged 59, deeply regretted by a large circle of friends, Mr. Joseph Pringle. For about thirty-five years he was an elder in the Presbyterian Church at Branton, and was distinguished by unblemished integrity and unfeigned piety.

1856, September 1.—Monument to a Crimean Hero.—Mr. Craggs, of Percy Street, Newcastle, has just finished an elegant monument to the memory of Lieutenant Goodenough, son of the Rev. R. W. Goodenough, of Whittingham, and one of the sufferers during the siege of Sebastopol. The base of the monument is dove-coloured marble, the tablet and devices being in white, and the pilasters in sienna marble. Over the inscription there is an appropriate and effective grouping of military insignia, the arms of the family being incorporated, and the family motto, "Ad sanguinem," being also inscribed. Beneath is a chaplet formed of the laurel and oak leaf. All the sculpture is executed in high relief, the work proceeding from the chisel of Mr. Joseph Craggs. The following is a copy of the inscription:—"To the memory of Reginald Cyril Goodenough, aged 18, Lieutenant of the 97th Regiment of Foot, first-born son of the Rev. Robert Goodenough, M.A., Vicar of Whittingham. He fell mortally wounded within the great Redan Battery, Sebastopol, on the 8th of September, 1855, having led on his soldiers to the assault in the first storming party. This monument is erected by his sorrowing friends, inhabitants of this his native parish and the immediate neighbourhood, who witnessed his early promise and mourn his untimely death. 'I know that my Redeemer liveth.'" The monument will shortly be placed on the walls of Whittingham Church.

1856, October 1.—The Whittingham Vale Floral and Horticultural Society.—The Whittingham Vale Floral and Horticultural Society held their thirteenth annual exhibition on Thursday, the 4th ult., at Whittingham, in a spacious pavilion erected on the green in front of the Castle Inn. Owing to the late season, the centre table was not so well filled as on previous occasions, but the quality of the flowers was good; and the society felt deeply indebted to Mr. Oliver, gardener to the Right Honourable Lord Ravensworth, for his assistance in supplying a quantity of very excellent greenhouse plants, &c., for the decorative part of the show. The vegetables, however, were nothing inferior to those of previous years, the potatoes especially attracting general attention. There were some very good devices exhibited by Messrs. Blackey, Edlingham (a model of Durham Cathedral); R. Clark and C. Thompson, Whittingham. There were also some very pretty bouquets. An excellent dinner was provided by Mr. Pile, Mr. Errington in the chair. The healths of the noble president, the Right Hon. Lord Ravensworth, and the vice-president, the Rev. R. W. Goodenough, the vicar, were drunk with enthusiasm.

1856, November 1.—Supposed incendiarism.—Twenty-nine corn stacks destroyed by fire.—On Monday last, between the hours of eleven and twelve o'clock at night, Mr. Elliott, rural policeman, Whittingham, when going his rounds, observed from what appeared to him at a distance some of the stacks in the garth of Mr. Coull, Rothill, near Whittingham, to be on fire. He proceeded thither with all possible haste, and found such to be the case and immediately raised an alarm, when a number of persons assembled to render assistance, the fire engine was despatched from Alnwick, and all available means put in force to stop the raging and destructive element, but the flames spread so rapidly from one stack to another that it was impossible to subdue them until the whole of the corn stacks, twenty-nine in number, and the barn and fodder house were entirely consumed. After the most strenuous exertions a portion of a large hay stack and other parts of the premises were saved. Mr. Coull is insured. It is not known how the fire originated, but from the stacks being on fire at various parts of the garth at one time, it is supposed to be the act of a malicious incendiary. Mr. Coull was from home when the unfortunate circumstance occurred.

1857, October 1.—Mrs. Goodenough gave her annual tea party, on the 27th ult., to the children of the Whittingham Sunday school, to the number of 100. The children assembled in the schoolroom at 3 p.m., and proceeded to the vicarage where they were regaled with tea and buns in abundance, after which they proceeded to a field adjoining where races were run and prizes awarded, then they returned to their homes highly pleased with their entertainment.

1857, October 1.—The Rev. L. S. Orde, incumbent of Alnwick, preached an effective sermon in behalf of the funds of the Alnwick dispensary and infirmary, in Whittingham church on Sunday, 20th ult., when the sum of £3 8s. 6d. was collected.

1859, February 1.—A pig was slaughtered by Mr. J. R. Nicholson, of Whittingham, on the 4th ult., under fourteen months old, weighing 36½ stones, from which were taken the extraordinary quantity of 4 stones 8 pounds of lard.

1860, February 15.—On Friday last, Mr. J. Taylor, teacher, Glanton, was presented with a handsome rosewood writing desk, bearing a suitably inscribed silver plate, by the pupils of the Tonic Sol-Fa singing class, established a few months ago under Mr. Taylor's able superintendence. The desk was presented in the name of the class by the Rev. D. Fotheringham, who made some appropriate remarks, and the proceedings of the evening were varied by the singing of some pieces of music.

1865.—This year a supply of water was brought to the village of Whittingham from the "Niney Wells," a series of nine springs on the margin of Whittingham wood, about a mile west from the village. The cost was defrayed by public subscription; and the late Lord Ravensworth caused a pant to be erected on the south side of the village, opposite to the Police Station, which bears this inscription:—

ERECTED BY
THE RT. HON. HENRY THOMAS
BARON RAVENSWORTH,
A.D. 1865.

May this pure fount perpetual streams supply
To every thirsty soul that passeth by,
And may its chrystal waters ever run,
Unchanged by Winter's frost or Summer's sun.—"R."

1870, April 21.—Married, at Brinkburn Priory Church, in the presence of a large circle of friends and relatives, Alexander Henry Browne, Esq., eldest son of Alexander Browne, Esq., of Lesbury House, to Mary Isabel, eldest daughter of C. H. Cadogan, Esq., of Alnmouth. The bridegroom's wedding gift was a dressing case in gold and crystal. Major Browne's presents to the bride were a set of diamonds set in gold and blue enamel, and a tea and coffee service in silver. The other wedding gifts included a great number of beautiful and costly articles from relatives and friends, and also a claret jug and biscuit box by the villagers of Lesbury. There was a grand ball in the evening in honour of the occasion, and tea was provided the following day for the villagers.

1871, April 3.—One of the most venerable of our Northumbrian patriarchs, the bearer of a familiar and respected name, died this morning, among his native hills, in the 96th year of his age. Born on Sunday, 9th July, 1775, Robert Donkin, of Ingram on the Breamish, was a native of Great Tosson, near Rothbury, within ten or a dozen miles of the farm which he had occupied for three score years and five. He was the last remaining member of the family of Samuel Donkin, of Great Tosson, who died in St. John's Lane, Newcastle, in 1794, in the 64th year of his age, having gone to that town to undergo a surgical operation. Samuel Donkin was one of the most intelligent, active, and successful men of his age, farming extensively under the Duke of Portland, at that time owner of the barony of Hepple. An ardent sportsman, he kept for many years the famous Tosson foxhounds. He was the namesake of his father, who died at Great Tosson in 1791, his age being 102. After the sale of the Hepple barony by the Duke of Portland, Robert Donkin, then farming Ryehill and other lands, entered upon the extensive farm of Ingram, and settled there for life. He married in 1798, some years prior to his removal, his half cousin Susan, daughter of William Donkin, of Lorbottle, who died in her 88th year on the 5th January, 1867, after a happy union of sixty-nine years.

1874.—A pant was erected this year in the village of Whittingham by the parishioners in memory of Mrs. Goodenough, wife of the vicar, Robert Wm. Goodenough. This pant, which is an elegant structure, stands on the north side of the village near to the church, and contains a tablet with the following inscription:—

THIS FOUNTAIN
WAS ERECTED
IN LOVING MEMORY OF
ELIZABETH ANNE,
THE LAMENTED WIFE OF
THE REV. R. W. GOODENOUGH,
VICAR OF THIS PARISH,
BY THE
INHABITANTS OF WHITTINGHAM
AND NEIGHBOURHOOD
AS A TOKEN OF RESPECT
AND AFFECTION.
1874.

LOVING FRIENDS,
POOR AND RICH,
PLACED THIS STONE
IN MEMORY OF
ELIZ. ANNE GOODENOUGH,
WIFE OF THE VICAR OF
THIS PARISH.
1874.

R. W. GOODENOUGH,
VICAR OF THIS PARISH,
FROM 1836 TO 1880.
BORN SEPT. 2, 1809,
DIED OCT. 21, 1880.

1876, December 22.—A sad incident has occurred near Whittingham. Robert Young, the postman between that village and Alnham, was returning from the latter place on Wednesday night. It was late when he left Eslington, and though a strong and stalwart man, he appears to have been exhausted by his tempestuous journey, which he had to perform on foot. After leaving Eslington he had been bewildered by the storm and darkness. Loosing his way he wandered into the fields near Low Barton, and there he perished when not far from home. His body was found next morning.

1879, January. — The Whittingham church choir had their annual treat on Thursday last, when about thirty, including the churchwardens, Messrs. Drysdale, Ternent, Dixon, and Weatheritt, sat down to an excellent dinner prepared for them by Miss Dunn of the Castle Inn, in her usual and most satisfactory manner. After the toasts of "the Bishop and Clergy," coupled with the esteemed vicar of the parish, &c., &c., were given, the company adjourned to the schoolroom, where they met several of their friends who had been invited to join them in the dance and amusements of the evening, and a very enjoyable night was spent by all. The music was supplied by Mr. Hudson, Whittingham, with his wonted ability.

1879.—On the 22nd of January, at Isandula, Africa, killed in action, Charles John Atkinson, of Lorbottle, in the county of Northumberland, Esquire, a lieutenant in the 1st battalion of Her Majesty's 24th Regiment.

1879, October 9.—Glanton.—Since the purchase of the Callaly estate by Mr. A. H. Browne, the Roman Catholics in the district have been at a loss for a place of worship, but now, through the liberality of the Earl of Ravensworth, who has granted a site on the Eslington estate midway between Whittingham and Glanton, this difficulty has been overcome. A commencement has been made this week with the erection of a church and presbytery, to be called "St. Mary Immaculate." The contract for the building has been let to the firm of Messrs. Dryden & Sons, Glanton.

1881, January.—There died in the Rothbury Workhouse, on Tuesday last, in his 75th year, a well-known Northumbrian character, named William Turnbull, formerly of Whittingham. The deceased was better known as "Wull Trummell," or "Fire Wull."

1885, September.—We have to record the death (on September 6th) of Mr. George Henderson, merchant tailor, the oldest inhabitant of the village of Whittingham, in his 100th year. Although reaching this advanced age, he retained all his faculties to the end. Only a few weeks ago he was able to read his daily paper and take an interest in the current topics of the day. He was remarkable for his bodily strength and vigour, and when over eighty he was able to lead on the farm of his nephew at the hay-leading or in the harvest field. He was much and deservedly respected in the village and neighbourhood, having been all his life in Whittingham, and enjoyed the confidence of the Ravensworth, the Pawson, and the other leading families in the district. He retired from active business life many years ago, and was succeeded by his son, Mr. Luke Henderson. In his youthful days old George was a trooper in the Coquetdale Rangers Volunteer Cavalry.

1888, January 23.—On Monday evening, the committee of the Whittingham Floral and Horticultural Society met at the Castle Inn, Whittingham, to present to Mr. William Dixon, the secretary and treasurer of the society, a valuable and handsome timepiece, on the occasion of his marriage. The company sat down to a very excellent supper, at which several members and supporters of the society were present, including—Mr. Wolfe, Whittingham Grange; Mr. Tait, Eslington Hill; Mr. Oliver, bailiff, Eslington Park; Mr. Douglass, Cheshire; and Mr. Stephenson, Hillhead, together with most of the committee. Mr. J. Thomson, of Shawdon, occupied the chair, with Mr. Rogerson in the vice-chair. After the usual loyal toasts, on rising to make the presentation, the Chairman said that the subscribers were glad of an opportunity to do something in recognition of Mr. Dixon's valuable services on behalf of the society, and he had much pleasure in asking him, on their behalf, to accept a very handsome timepiece—"Presented to Mr. William Dixon by the committee, members, and friends of the Whittingham Vale Floral and Horticultural Society, on the occasion of his marriage." He trusted that it would measure out many years of happy wedded life to Mr. Dixon and the object of his choice. Few young men in the district were more esteemed or had a better reputation for integrity in business. He was a worthy successor to his late respected father, who had held the same office for the society, and took a deep interest in its success. Mr. Dixon said he rose to thank the kind friends who had so unexpectedly presented him with such a valuable gift; but he felt that words were wanting to express what he intended to say. He had always taken an interest in the society, never expecting such a recognition of the service he had rendered. The timepiece would be cherished by him as a precious heirloom. Other toasts were proposed and responded to, and a most harmonious and enjoyable evening was spent. Several humorous songs sung by Mr. Scott added greatly to the pleasure of the evening. The Chairman proposed a vote of thanks to Mr. and Mrs. Brown for the very excellent supper served to the company. After singing "Auld Lang Syne," the company left for their respective homes, delighted with their night's entertainment.

1888, April 2.—Presentation to Mr. W. Ternent, Whittingham.—Interesting proceedings.—The presentation of an address and a purse of gold to Mr. W. Ternent, who is retiring from the post of master of Whittingham parish school, after upwards of 40 years of useful and faithful work, took place yesterday in a large marquee (lent by Major A. H. Browne, Callaly Castle) erected in front of the Castle Hotel, Whittingham. When Mr. Ternent intimated his intention to resign the post which he has filled with signal success for so long, some of his many friends at once suggested that the occasion would be a fitting one on which to give him something tangible to mark their high sense of his worth, and to afford some indication of the respect and esteem he has won from those amongst whom he has laboured so long. The suggestion was warmly taken up by the people of the neighbourhood and by present and former pupils. His former pupils are scattered all over the country, and the manner in which many of them are making their way in their various walks of life speak volumes of the excellence of the instruction he has imparted. Amongst his former pupils are numbered the Earl of Ravensworth, the Hon. Atholl Liddell, Major A. H. Browne (Callaly Castle), Mr. Tait (H.M.'s Customs, London), and others in positions of distinction. A committee was formed, with Mr. G. M. Tait as chairman and Mr. Wm. Dixon as secretary, and in a very short time the suggestion assumed practical shape. On all hands the response was prompt and hearty, and in due course it was decided that the form of the recognition should be that of the presentation of an address and a purse of gold. Upwards of a hundred guineas were soon in hand, and after allowance had been made for the unavoidable expenses it was found that there was exactly one hundred guineas to put into the purse. The address reads as follows:—"Presented to Mr. William Ternent, of Whittingham, together with a purse of gold, by his numerous friends in this district, as well as by the past and present scholars of Whittingham parish school, in commemoration of forty years' faithful and highly esteemed services as master of the school.—Easter Monday, 1888." The address was signed by the chairman (Mr. G. M. Tait) and the vice-chairman (Mr. W. Cowley), the secretary (Mr. W. Dixon) and twenty members of the committee. The presentation was made on behalf of the subscribers by Mr. G. M. Tait, the chairman.

1888, October 11.—Presentation at Whittingham.—On Thursday evening last, the committee of the Whittingham Games and other friends assembled together, at the Castle Inn, to do justice to an excellent supper, served in faultless style by the host and hostess, Mr. and Mrs. F. Brown. After supper, the treasurer, Mr. John Mills, was the recipient of a handsome testimonial, which consisted of a beautiful mahogany writing table of the latest design, from the establishment of Mr. D. Thompson, Alnwick, to whom much credit is due for the excellency of the workmanship. The inscription read as follows:—"Presented to Mr. John Mills by the committee of the Whittingham Games, in recognition of his long and valuable services as treasurer. Oct. 11, 1888." The chairman (Mr. T. Weatheritt) made the presentation, and in doing so said they had met to honour one to whom honour was due, and referred especially to the marked energy and ability which had at all times been displayed by their guest in connection with the games. Mr. Mills feelingly returned thanks, and said that he had great pleasure in receiving so handsome a gift. It was quite unexpected and quite uncalled for, but he would cherish it as long as he lived, and would always think of the great kindness of them all. Mr. J. Rogerson proposed the health of the secretary, to which Mr. W. H. Brown responded. Mr. J. G. Liddell proposed "The town and trade of Whittingham." Mr. W. Dixon replied, and moved a hearty vote of thanks to the chairman. Several other toasts and songs were rendered, after which a most pleasant evening was brought to a close.

1889, April 27.—Death of a Centenarian.—In our obituary column this week, we record, at the remarkably long age of 101, the death of Mary Biggs, relict of the late John Biggs, of Whittingham, who for many years was a steam thrashing machine proprietor. The deceased woman was able to walk about and do a good deal of house work up to a recent period, when she fell and lamed herself, from which accident she never quite recovered. She retained her mental faculties to the very last, and talked with the greatest accuracy of events that occurred 80 and 90 years ago. Mrs. Biggs was a native of Whittingham, and until she was 75 years of age she walked to Alnwick nearly every Saturday. Her father, William Carr, was master tailor for the 61st Regiment of Foot, and died in India. Deceased had six children, twelve grandchildren, and several great grandchildren, and had she lived until the 18th of June next, would have attained 102 years of age.

1893.—During the latter part of the month of May and the beginning of June, the inhabitants of the Vale of Whittingham were much charmed by the dulcet notes of a strange bird which every evening took up its position in a certain tree in Whittingham wood and there for hours, night after night, poured forth its lovely song. A large audience assembled nightly to hear the nocturnal songster, amongst whom were several local ornithologists, and many thought it to be one of the warbler tribe. However, this feathered visitor to our northern clime proved to be a nightingale, and the following paragraphs appeared in the *Newcastle Daily Journal* at the time:—

A sweet singer in bird life is at present delighting the inhabitants of Whittingham Vale, who turn out in hundreds at night to listen. Opinions about the bird appear to differ, some maintaining that it is a nightingale, others say it is a warbler. Whatever it is, nothing like it has been heard thus far north.—June 9, 1893.

Mr. George Bolam, Berwick, a well-known naturalist, writes:—In reference to the numerous letters on the subject of nightingales in Northumberland, which are appearing in the *Journal*. It may be of interest to your readers to know that the bird which has (to use the words of your correspondent) "been delighting the people of Whittingham Vale for some days past with its song," is without doubt a nightingale. Being in that neighbourhood on Sunday, I walked over to Whittingham wood in the evening and enjoyed listening to the song for some time, and, strange though it may seem that the bird should appear so far to the north of its usual haunts, I have not the slightest doubt in pronouncing it to be a genuine nightingale.—June 13, 1893.

1894, October 16.—The late Mr. John Gibson, Callaly.—A correspondent writes:—By the death of Mr. John Gibson, gardener, of Callaly Castle, one of the oldest and most respected residents of the district has been removed. His services under the late proprietor and Major Browne, the present owner of Callaly Castle, had extended over half a century. Although in a humble position, deceased was characterised by many qualities that made him an excellent and energetic gardener, able to keep abreast of the many changes that have taken place—especially in the culture of flowers—since he first entered upon his duties at Callaly. It speaks well for the penetration of Major Browne that when he took possession of Callaly he discovered the excellent qualities of the old gardener and retained him in his service, and treated him with a respect and kindness that has cheered the declining years of his life. By his death we believe the oldest gardener in North Northumberland has been removed.

ADDITIONAL NOTES.

Note to line 9, p. 114.

BIRD LIFE AT ESLINGTON.—Mr. Joseph Oliver, writing from Eslington Park, says:—"I have counted no less than fifty varieties of birds within a radius of one hundred yards from my own house, while beyond that radius I have noted other twenty varieties—not including colonists."

Note to line 13, p. 115.

TREES IN ESLINGTON PARK.—Earl Ravensworth's woodman, Mr. John Mills, of Whittingham, has kindly forwarded the following measurements of the "King of Trees" in Eslington Park, a magnificent Silver Fir, which was blown down in the gale of Saturday, December 29th, 1894:—Height, 122 feet; circumference at bottom, 27 feet; circumference at 25 feet from bottom, 12 feet 1 inch; circumference at 50 feet from bottom, 9 feet.

Note to p. 157.

POPULAR BELIEF IN FAIRIES.—In "Horsley's Northumberland," p. 9 (1729-30), we still find traces of that belief:—"The stories of fairies seem now to be much worn, both out of date and out of credit. Adam Crisp, who lived at Crawley Dean, is said to have had frequent encounters with an apparition there. They talk also of his going to London and coming back in 48 hours. Mr. Punshon told me that Crisp had sent to him about the apparition."

Note to line 7, p. 205.

CHANTRY OF ST. PETER, WHITTINGHAM CHURCH.—Mr. James Hardy, LL.D., Old Cambus, Cockburnspath, N.B., in a note about the founding of this chantry, states:—"I have not the paper at hand, but have recently been thinking that the chantry at Whittingham may have been founded by Lord de Ros, the owner of Titlington and half of Glanton, Shawdon, &c., which all belonged to Werk barony. It must have been the owner of the lands furnishing the endowment who founded the chantry."

INDEX.